DATE DUE

OCT 2 7 2016	

THE
DEATH
OF
PUNISHMENT

THE
DEATH
OF
PUNISHMENT

SEARCHING FOR JUSTICE
AMONG THE
WORST OF THE WORST

ROBERT BLECKER

palgrave
macmillan

THE DEATH OF PUNISHMENT
Copyright © Robert Blecker, 2013.
All rights reserved.

First published in 2013 by PALGRAVE MACMILLAN® in the United
States—a division of St. Martin's Press LLC, 175 Fifth Avenue, New York, NY
10010.

Where this book is distributed in English in the UK, Europe and the rest of
the world, this is by Palgrave Macmillan, a division of Macmillan Publishers
Limited, registered in England, company number 785998, of Houndmills,
Basingstoke, Hampshire RG21 6XS.

Palgrave Macmillan is the global academic imprint of the above companies and
has companies and representatives throughout the world.

Palgrave® and Macmillan® are registered trademarks in the United States, the
United Kingdom, Europe and other countries.

ISBN 978-1-137-27856-2

Library of Congress Cataloging-in-Publication Data

Blecker, Robert.
   The death of punishment / by Robert Blecker.
      pages   cm
   Includes bibliographical references and index.
   1. Punishment. 2. Criminal justice, Administration of. I. Title.
K5101.B54   2013
364.6—dc23

                                                              2013014703

A catalogue record of the book is available from the British Library.

Design by Letra Libre, Inc.

First edition: November 2013

10 9 8 7 6 5 4 3 2 1

CONTENTS

PART I

MAN THE MEASURE

1

KILLING THE
WRONG PEOPLE

It is easy to get angry—anyone can do that ...
but to feel or act towards the right person to the right extent at the right time
for the right reason in the right way—that is not easy

—Aristotle, *Ethics*

AS A SMALL CHILD, I KNEW THAT NAZIS WERE EVIL AND
Adolf Hitler deserved to die. My mother staunchly opposed capital punishment, but she made an exception for Hitler. I was five when controversy flared in our house as the United States executed Julius and Ethel Rosenberg, accused Soviet spies. My ultraliberal mother believed the Rosenbergs innocent and insisted they were killed because they were Jews. My father, always sober and rational, taught me that any citizen who gave or even tried to give Joseph Stalin the atom bomb deserved to die.

In elementary school, kids would pull legs off spiders and laugh as the creatures struggled. I once pulled two limbs from a daddy longlegs. Then I thought about it from the spider's point of view. I felt sick and tried to make it up to this creature I'd crippled by leaving dead bugs for him to eat.

But Leech Rock was different.

At summer camp, we'd come in after swimming in the lake, bleeding, slimy leeches still clinging to us. You couldn't rip them off without losing your skin too. So we flicked them off with a lit match. The animals fell, helpless at our feet. Now what to do? We certainly wouldn't throw them back to attack us again. So we burned them in a ritual at Leech Rock. After all, unprovoked, they had shed our blood. It never occurred to us they were just being leeches. But then, too, maybe by killing them, we were just being human.

During the Cold War of the 1950s, the Soviets killed political dissenters and prepared to destroy the United States. I learned in school that tyrants have always killed dissenters. But never here. I loved the United States, and in fourth grade I wrote patriotic poetry.

As I grew up, freedom became a big issue for me. I refused to keep my parakeet Tippy locked in a cage; he had a right to fly around the room whenever he wanted. My mother threatened to abandon my room to filth. I took her dare. Amanda, our black housekeeper, hated the dirt and scolded me for letting the bird make a mess. But when I explained why, Amanda snuck into my room to clean droppings from my shelves. My parents detested racism and racists. In Mississippi in 1955, the Klan murdered Emmett Till, a 14-year-old black boy, for flirting with a white woman.[1] I wasn't focused on the details, but I remember how upset they were when an all-white jury in Mississippi acquitted young Emmett's killers.

My parents also told me the story of Leo Frank. How in 1913, someone murdered young Mary Phagan in the basement of an Atlanta pencil factory. An ambitious prosecutor pressured witnesses and convinced a jury to convict Frank, the prominent Jewish factory superintendent. The real killer—a janitor there—"cooperated" with the prosecution. Frank's lawyers desperately fought to postpone his execution date while the judge who sentenced Frank to die admitted serious doubts about his guilt. Even the real killer's lawyer urged the governor to spare Frank's life. On his last day in office, the Georgia governor commuted Frank's death sentence, then fled the state with his family.[2] Vicious anti-Semitic attacks in the press stirred up public passions, and a Klan-led mob stormed the prison. They drove Leo Frank back to Mary Phagan's childhood home. While Frank protested his innocence and begged the mob to return his wedding ring to his wife, they lynched him.[3] No one prosecuted Leo Frank's killers[4]; his prosecutor, Hugh Dorsey, went on to become governor.

So I knew early on that prejudice stained the system; trials did not guarantee justice. The guilty might walk free while innocents were wrongly accused, falsely condemned, and killed. Those in power would make it murder or make it all right with a wink. And yet I still felt certain that Hitler and the racists who killed Emmett Till deserved to die.

Then came that day in eighth grade when I discovered Abraham Lincoln did not free the slaves. I idolized Lincoln and carried around Carl Sandberg's multivolume biography.[5] My social studies teacher, determined to strip me of idolatry, demanded I actually read the Emancipation Proclamation and report to the class exactly which slaves Lincoln in fact freed. Of course it turns out that the Great "Emancipator" freed exactly no one he could. Slaves living in the Confederacy were now "free" to rebel and die in the attempt. But everywhere the Union Army controlled—in Maryland, for example—the commander in chief left all slaves in bondage.

Lincoln fell, and then came God. Reading the Old Testament in Bible study class revealed a divine support for genocide[6]—a God who would command the death penalty for homosexuality,[7] failing to keep the Sabbath,[8] or mouthing off to your parents.[9] A God who let the Holocaust happen. And when I challenged my Sunday school teachers, they could only insist, "No man can comprehend His ways," while they had no problem preaching against the death penalty, although the Bible clearly called for it.

First slavery, now segregation, tore America apart. I grew up looking down on the South. How could segregation be the *law?* I hated Southern sheriffs with attack dogs tearing up freedom fighters. Civil rights crusaders became my new heroes. The Soviets might be ahead of us in the space race, but Martin Luther King Jr. stirred me, while John and Bobby Kennedy glamorously and gloriously forced racial integration.

November 22, 1963, eleventh-grade social studies, seventh period. Studying the American Civil War again, only this time I knew that Lincoln hadn't freed the slaves. So no big surprises. The principal's metallic voice crackled on the intercom: President Kennedy had just been assassinated. Then Jack Ruby assassinated Kennedy's assassin, Lee Harvey Oswald, on TV![10] What was happening?

Off I went at 17 to Tufts University, loving my country, still grieving Kennedy, and believing in the death penalty. In 1965, we college freshmen fought to keep our door nearly closed with a woman in our dormitory room, while the women fought for the right to wear pants on campus. By our senior year in 1969, we had occupied buildings in protest and shut down the school. In addition to sex, drugs, and the Beatles, the war in Vietnam consumed us. And not only because we might be drafted to fight and die. Our political science professors taught us that Ho Chi Minh strove for a more just society. An admirer of the United States, although a Communist, Ho had modeled Vietnam's Constitution on ours. Only he wanted Vietnam—and not American big business—to control his country's natural resources. So President Eisenhower canceled promised elections because, as he explained, "If free elections had been held, Ho Chi Minh would have won 80 percent of the vote."[11]

In 1966, I marched against the war. We protesters formed a thin, ragged line down the middle of Manhattan's Fifth Avenue, while large, hostile

crowds lined the sidewalks. That summer in Chicago, Richard Speck murdered eight student nurses in their dorm. As he took them off to a bedroom,
one by one, to strangle or stab each one to death, Speck lost count. Curazon
Amurao, his would-be ninth victim, numb with terror, witnessed the scene
from under a bed. She lived to identify Speck by his tattoo: "Born to Raise
Hell."[12] Richard Speck, a monster by any measure, awaited society's verdict.
Most of America cheered the jury that sentenced Speck to die. I wanted him
killed, badly.

I was no law junkie, but the US Supreme Court made it exciting: *Miranda v. Arizona*[13] led an avalanche of opinions applying the Bill of Rights
to the states, while court orders restrained local prosecutors and police from
violating defendants' rights. Back on campus, along with the war, guilt at
our nation's racist legal past tore at the breasts of moderate whites. We the
People had screwed the Indians and then the blacks. And now, at last, our
Supreme Court took seriously constitutional commands of equal protection
and due process. The most radical among my fellow antiwar activists hated
the United States and sneered at the justices' token gestures, laying their
liberal guilt trip on the nation. They denounced the court as just another
part of the system and characterized me and my fellow patriotic protesters
as only "halfway."

The death penalty, though, really got me ostracized from the antiwar
movement. Capital punishment provoked volatile arguments among us
19-year-olds. An unofficial national moratorium covered the United States,
as judges and governors stayed all executions while a hundred different constitutional challenges from abolitionist lawyers made their way through the
courts. For several months, no state had executed a condemned killer. But to
me, that made the Vietnam War all the more perverse: In Asia we napalmed
and killed thousands of innocent women and children, while in Chicago
corrections officers served condemned killer Richard Speck his breakfast
each morning.

Hugo Adam Bedau, this nation's leading academic opponent of capital
punishment, chaired the philosophy department at Tufts. In 1968, students
and faculty organized to abolish the death penalty in Massachusetts by popular referendum. The department could not be my home. When the people
of Massachusetts voted decisively to keep capital punishment, campus abolitionists bitterly reacted in defeat, attacking my "absurd inconsistency."[14]
How could anybody be antiwar yet pro–death penalty? (You hear echoes of
that even today—how can a person oppose abortion, be "pro-life," and also
be pro–death penalty?)

To me it was simple: We were killing the wrong people.

My protests against authority became my own. In college, I refused to major and almost did not graduate. But a tolerant administration bent the rules. After school, while my friends camped out at Woodstock and the United States fixated on the moon walk, I wandered around Europe on a playwriting fellowship and taught American culture at Vincennes, a left-wing French university. In the library there, I discovered the Great Books of the Western World.

For the next several months, I tried to soak up the wisdom of the classics—those highest lights of abandoned skies. Different worlds reached out to connect me to the Great Scene. Much of it is a blur now, but from the start, Plato's struggle with the Sophists struck home. The Sophists insisted that everything was relative, subjective, and arbitrary, including justice.

"Man is the measure of all things," proclaimed Protagoras.[15] Whatever a person could be made to believe became the truth—for him.

But Plato clung to real, objective, absolute truth and justice. And I clung to Plato. Of course the Sophists might have a point: Smoking pot, resisting the draft, and gay sex could get you punished. But only because those in power outlawed it. Killing eight student nurses in their townhouse or 6 million Jews in gas chambers made a man deserve to die. Not because I wanted it, not because most of us wanted it—but because objectively, in fact, he deserved to die.

Aristotle's concept of "equity" grabbed me: The strictest justice—legal justice, by the book, according to the rules—can sometimes be the greatest injustice.[16] We need equity—fuller justice, particular-to-the-situation justice. Did equity include mercy, I wondered? And how did it relate to poetic justice?

I was soaking up this stuff in Paris when Charles Manson hit the *International Herald Tribune*. Fiend *du jour*, this counterculture perversion had commanded his crazed followers to butcher the pregnant actress Sharon Tate and other innocent victims, smearing "PIG" and "HELTER SKELTER" on the walls in the victims' blood.

"The voice of your brother's blood cries to me from the ground," God said to Cain in Genesis. "Blood pollutes the land, and no expiation can be made for the blood that is shed in it except by the blood of him who shed it," the Bible later declares. "Blood pollution" may sound archaic, but it still captured my feelings of anger and disgust. Manson and Speck deserved to die regardless of whether anybody else would be deterred by their deaths—regardless of whether they continued to threaten us. As long as they lived, I felt polluted.

I moved on in the Great Books to John Stuart Mill, which led me to his mentor, Jeremy Bentham. According to these great utilitarians, people seek pleasure and avoid pain. Because a crime brings a criminal immediate pleasure, in order to restrain these rational, calculating pleasure-seekers from satisfying their harmful desires, society must make its threatened punishments more certain, swift, and severe.[17] Bentham's utilitarian calculus appealed to me—so orderly and crisp, with costs offsetting benefits. But in the end, Bentham's worldview, although rational and logical, *felt* wrong and unreal.

Bentham would have executed only those traitors whose lives posed a continuing threat of massive violence and social disruption. (Contrary to popular opinion, the Catholic Church, even today, tolerates the death penalty in this very unusual circumstance.[18]) But who counted as a "traitor"? War supporters labeled Americans who refused to fight as "traitors," although many of us loved our country. The British Crown in 1775 ordered Samuel Adams and John Hancock to hang for treason.[19]

History had taught us: Might makes right. Nobody described it better than the ancient historian Thucydides. In their great war, Athens controlled the seas and Sparta the land. The little country of Melos only wanted to be left alone. But the Athenians would not allow this tiny island nation to remain neutral. So they gave the Melian representatives an ultimatum: Pay tribute to Athens or die. When the Melians tried to protest this injustice, the Athenian representatives cut them off: "Justice depends upon the equality of power to compel. The strong do what they can; the weak accept what they must."[20] Perhaps there was no truth, no justice. Perhaps everything was relative, arbitrary, subjective. Maybe, as the Sophists insisted, justice *was* nothing but the interest of the stronger.

For an extended moment I doubted my commitment to moral truth. Then I remembered Charles Manson and Richard Speck. I felt certain that whatever the future costs and benefits, they should die—for the sake of the past. Plato had it right. Evil was real. When it came to justify punishing it, however, Plato disappointed me:

> In punishing wrongdoers, no one concentrates on the fact that a man has done wrong in the past or punishes him on that account, unless taking blind vengeance like a beast. No, punishment is not inflicted by a rational man for the sake of the crime that has been committed—after all one cannot undo what is past—but for the sake of the future, to prevent either the same man or, by the spectacle of his punishment, someone else, from doing wrong again.[21]

According to Plato, we may only kill those criminals we cannot correct, incorrigibles whose souls were beyond repair.[22] I needed a great mind to tell me that Hitler, Speck, and Manson must die, regardless of whether they could someday be converted into amiable golfing companions. The suffering of their tortured victims simply demanded it.

My flirtation with Plato and Bentham's pragmatic justification for punishment ended. Back in the Great Books I found Bentham's arch-opponent, Immanuel Kant: "A human being can never be manipulated merely as a means to the purposes of someone else. He must first be found deserving of punishment before we give any consideration to the utility of this punishment for himself or for his fellow citizens. Only the law of retribution can determine exactly the kind and degree of punishment."[23] At last a kindred spirit? "If he has committed a murder, he must die," Kant insisted. "There is no sameness of kind between death and remaining alive even under the most miserable conditions."[24] I carefully copied these passages into my notebook: "But the death of the criminal must be kept entirely free of any maltreatment that would make an abomination of the humanity residing in the person suffering it."[25]

Kant came closer to how I felt. But Kant, too, ultimately disappointed me, simplistically lumping all murderers together. Hitler, Speck, and Manson deserved a fate much worse than that reserved for common killers. Besides, Kant seemed too detached and devoid of anger. I understood our abstract duty to kill these monsters: They had committed capital crimes. But unlike Kant, I hated Charles Manson, Richard Speck, and other vicious predators like them. I wanted them to feel their victims' pain before they died. I searched further in the Great Books but could not find my voice.

2

PLAYING THE GAME

WHEN I RETURNED FROM PARIS IN 1970, AMERICA HAD lost its taste for the war. Revelations that American soldiers had raped and murdered Vietnamese women and children at My Lai became America's national shame. Ohio national guardsmen killing protesting students at Kent State soon became our national tragedy. Even police assigned to antiwar protests now seemed sympathetic to our cause.

On March 29, 1971, after seven months of trial and nine days of deliberation, the jury that convicted Charles Manson of capital murder now decided his fate. "In determining which punishment shall be inflicted," the trial judge instructed them, "you are entirely free to act according to your own judgment, conscience, and absolute discretion. The law itself provides no standard for your guidance."[1] Each juror for herself, each situation on its own merits. Ideally, like Plato's Statesman, unconstrained by rules but with a full view of the particular set of circumstances, the jury would decide the best response. Each juror would search for Aristotle's equity—particular justice, greater justice than rule-bound justice.[2] With no rules to bind them, no written standards to guide them except their own outrage, Charles Manson's jury fixed the penalty as death. Three weeks later, the judge confirmed the jury's choice, pronouncing the death penalty "almost compelled by the circumstances."[3]

It was one thing to sentence sadistic predators to die—but another actually to kill them. In the real world, translating choice into action introduces uncertainty and indeterminacy. An athlete might *choose* the right shot, pass, or kick but can rarely perfectly *execute* it. In a game, we automatically play the exact move we choose. A sport, however, requires skill to execute it. An architect draws up plans, but the construction crew must deal with the facts on the ground. The composer selects the sequence of notes, but an orchestra must still perform it, never exactly as the composer imagined.

The jury and judge had announced Manson's death as their officially chosen move. But nobody moved to kill him. Public officials had put all executions on hold until the US Supreme Court spoke definitively.

Three weeks after Charles Manson's judge pronounced sentence, the US Supreme Court decided *McGautha v. California*. McGautha's jury had received the same instruction as Manson's: life or death according to their absolute discretion. Unlike Charles Manson, however, Dennis McGautha committed felony murder. A robbery gone bad had produced a dead victim. Although legally he had committed first-degree murder, McGautha hardly qualified as the worst of the worst. Appealing for his life, McGautha's lawyers challenged the jury's unguided discretion as "fundamentally lawless" and unconstitutional.[4]

England had already gone through this. For centuries all murders (and most other felonies) carried an automatic death penalty. But no one actually executed the majority of these officially commanded death sentences. A merciful king would spare the condemned and commute the sentence. Or savvy juries knowing better than to trust in executive clemency rebelled against mandatory death penalties, resisting the written law and ignoring the facts in order to acquit. It got so bad that bankers lobbied Parliament to eliminate the theoretical possibility of capital punishment for fraud.[5] Only then would jurors actually convict, thieves would fear real but lesser punishment, and the law would better safeguard property. Parliament eventually rejected the death penalty for most lesser crimes, reserving mandatory death for murder.

Pennsylvania took the next step, in 1794, declaring that "several offenses labeled as murder differ so greatly from each other in the degree of their atrociousness that it is unjust to involve them in the same punishment."[6] Thus, Pennsylvania made a great moral leap and became the first state to restrict its mandatory death sentence only to "Murder of the first degree," which it defined as "premeditated murder" and also "any kind of killing committed in the perpetration or attempt to perpetrate any arson, rape, robbery, or burglary."[7] Other states soon adopted this radical reform. But Pennsylvania's new First Degree Murder proved too broad. Distraught, unmarried mothers killing their newborns, survivors in failed suicide pacts, battered women killing their abusers as they slept—all these unlawful intentional homicides could be labeled "deliberate and premeditated murder." And yet surely these killers lived in a different moral universe than Manson or Speck. They hardly deserved to die.

American juries continued to disregard the law and acquit the guilty in order to spare their lives. Finally states surrendered and moved to the opposite extreme. Thus, California instructed McGautha's and Manson's juries that they had "absolute" and "unfettered discretion" to decide life or death.[8]

Unrestrained juries can act arbitrarily or methodically discriminate because of race or ethnicity, thus violating basic constitutional guarantees of equal protection under law. By treating like cases differently, unfettered discretion easily leads to moral anarchy. However, mandatory capital punishment statutes, which treated all cases of first-degree murder alike, easily led to manifest injustice: People who did not deserve to die would be executed.

In the end, although admitting the surface appeal of McGautha's argument, the Supreme Court majority insisted on the uniqueness of each killer and each killing and held it "beyond present human ability" to channel a jury's discretion.[9] Confirming the wisdom of the ancient Greek philosopher Heraclitus, that "you cannot step in the same river twice for fresh waters flow on," the Court held that unlimited discretion did not violate due process.[10]

So that summer of 1971, the Supreme Court seemingly signaled the states it would not interfere with their death penalty schemes. Under basic principles of federalism, each state defines, detects, prosecutes, and punishes crime as it sees fit. Would judges and governors once again sign death warrants? Would the move chosen be executed as chosen? Would they finally kill Manson and Speck?

My wife's Harvard Law School professor, Philip B. Heymann, whose course I was unofficially auditing, alerted us to the Court's holding in *McGautha*. Professor Heymann also taught us how lobster poachers had lobbied the Florida legislature to enforce antipoaching laws because the catch was getting too thin for them to poach efficiently. It struck me watching football how sometimes a team could be better off getting "punished"— penalized five yards for delay of game. Moving away from the goal only improved the kicking angle, actually making it easier to score. "Taking the penalty" could apply perversely or paradoxically in a number of places. Should day-to-day prison routine become better than hardscrabble life on the street, it might be best to take the "penalty" of a warm bed and hot breakfast. Professor Heymann welcomed my perspective and urged me to come to law school. I hoped instead to develop my game/sport philosophy into a doctoral thesis at Tufts. But when my would-be adviser dismissed a first draft as crap, still believing in game and sport as metaphor worth mining, I listened to the law professor and applied.

Before starting Harvard Law School, I got a summer job as a researcher at *Newsweek*. My duties included cutting and distributing the Associated

Press wire reports. "Blind men climb Mt. Fujiyama. . . . The annual meeting of the International Anarchists Convention breaks up in disarray!" I don't recall whether it made the magazine that week, but I was outraged when the AP reported that the US Supreme Court had reversed Richard Speck's death sentence and remanded the case back to Illinois because Speck's jury had been tainted by excluding death penalty opponents.[11] How could any fair-minded jury deny that this sadistic mass murderer deserved to die? But then why put the state to the expense of a retrial when no one was being executed? The Illinois Supreme Court just added Speck's case to its growing "hold" pile.

That summer, *Newsweek* executives accepted my cover story suggestion: Bobby Fischer, an American hero in the making, demolishing the Soviet elite on his way to the world chess championship.[12] I loved chess and couldn't play it worth a damn. But I did get to spend a couple of days alone with Bobby Fischer. Other players, Fischer explained, would make moves they knew to be unsound, relying on an inferior opponent to miss the flaw. But not Fischer. If he saw a move's defect, Bobby insisted, he simply would not make it. He would search for a move he, himself, couldn't figure out how to defeat. He would search, if necessary, until his time ran out. Better to lose, trying to find the answer, than to rely on your opponent's stupidity and make a knowingly unsound move, even if it won.

So I imagined the United States and the Soviet Union squaring off, vital interests in conflict all over the globe. At the brink of all-out nuclear war and with no obvious way to resolve the crisis, in one final desperate moment, the US president and Soviet premier agree that instead of annihilating each other, one side would prove their superiority by a single game of computer chess.

One game for the fate of the free world.

For six months, missiles at the ready, each side developed and programmed its best chess machine, but, by mutual agreement enforced by inspection, neither side could try it out in advance. On the day of the Great Contest, with liberty hanging in the balance, the USSR got the white pieces and thus the first move, a standard king pawn forwarded two spaces.

The American computer instantly resigned.

It turns out the United States had in fact solved the "game" of chess. We discovered and our program proved it: With perfect play on both sides, moving second was fatal. With best play, white wins from the first move. By solving the game of chess, the Americans had reduced it to a puzzle, like tic-tac-toe. The Soviets hadn't discovered this. But while we sought and found the answer and solved chess, nobody on the American side programmed the machine to fight, to take advantage of its own tactical superiority—even if it found itself (initially or ever) in a theoretically losing position. Never resign. Fight on. Norman Mailer found this story most original and urged me to publish it. The lesson from this tale, however, came from Fischer's clock running out while he searched for the perfect move. Some death penalty opponents remind me of Fischer: Demanding perfect justice, they will reject the best we can do at the moment.

I admired the theoretical purity of this weird genius whose chess philosophy struck me as a profound, though dangerous, metaphor. The best can be the enemy of the good. A search for perfection could disable effectively good but imperfect choices. As we sat in a dive of a Chinese restaurant Fischer had chosen, flies happily hitching a ride on the slowly turning fan blade, I asked the grandmaster if he thought computers would solve chess and thereby destroy the game. Fischer believed that no machine could be programmed with the intuition necessary to actually solve the game. But computers would someday defeat the best of men. "Just because a racing car can circle the track in seconds doesn't mean people won't go watch Olympic athletes run the mile."

Regardless of whether computers ever solved chess, I found it comforting that justice could never be mastered by machine. Transcending the strict application of rules, equity could never be reduced to an algorithm or written into a single, simple formula. Centuries of experience made it established wisdom: No legislature could perfectly guide juries in advance to morally consistent decisions as to who should live and who should die. The *McGautha* Supreme Court majority had declared it "beyond present human ability" to "identify before the fact those criminal homicides and their perpetrators which call for the death penalty."[13] And because no legislature could do it perfectly, no state needed to try.

During that first semester at law school, dozens of challenges moved up through the courts as the death penalty moratorium continued to hold. Abolitionists fought each execution tenaciously, sometimes getting commutations for condemned killers. While isolated attacks on capital punishment might succeed, this committed band of scholars and activists must have been pessimistic, post *McGautha*. The US Supreme Court had just rejected due process challenges to standardless discretion. The Court could hardly be expected to outlaw those same systems as "cruel and unusual" under the Eighth Amendment.

That year, I was cast out as a racist but only by the whites. In his first semester teaching, Duncan Kennedy, later a founder of the left-wing Critical Legal Studies movement, assigned us the case of an unmarried black woman on welfare, summarily expelled from public housing after taking drug dealers as lovers who used kids in the building as runners. These were times of great liberal guilt and self-consciousness at giving offense, at being thought insensitive, let alone racist as the civil rights movement picked up steam. Her summary and discriminatory expulsion from public housing angered our class. The air in the classroom felt stifling, polite, and politically correct. So I raised my hand. "It's a shame there's not enough good housing to go around," I declared. "But if somebody has to live in crud, let crud live in crud."

Stunned silence. Then the hiss rose like a steam radiator. My section publicly shamed me. Afterward, classmates turned away and avoided me—except for a couple of black students who approached. "We have no problem with what you said," one assured me. "And we understand where you come from. The ones that hissed you are either lying or they don't know where they're at." I appreciated their kindness and company, but I never quite got what was so terrible about believing that crud should live in crud.

In those days, publicly expressing retributive sentiments was a little like farting in class. A single incident, the talk of the moment, might soon blow away. But in criminal law class, when only a handful of us openly supported capital punishment, again I publicly declared the unacceptable: "Some people deserve to die. We have an obligation to kill them." I wasn't ashamed but I did feel the power of ostracism—"denunciation," I would later learn the sociologist Emile Durkheim called it.[14] Years later, killers on death row would tell me how it hurt to hear the jury formally declare they should be cast out to die.

After *McGautha* allowed states to give juries unbounded discretion, individual challenges continued. Hundreds of condemned killers on death rows, including Charles Manson, waited. Millions of Americans, impatient for them to be killed, also waited. No one I knew could have predicted that within months, the Supreme Court would lurch capital punishment to a grinding halt, and then, in response, capital jurisprudence would explode into the modern era.

The local preshock struck in the land of *McGautha*. In February 1972, California's Supreme Court struck down that state's death penalty across the board! Capital punishment, the Court held, "cruel[ly] degrade[d] and dehumanize[d] all who participate[d] in its process." Death as punishment was "unnecessary to any legitimate goal of the state" and "incompatible with the dignity of man."[15]

The US Supreme Court might allow "vengeance or retribution" as legitimate under the Eighth Amendment. But in California, the state high court ruled, "We do not sanction punishment solely for retribution."[16] Of course, as the court acknowledged, many condemned prisoners "have committed crimes of the utmost cruelty and depravity." And "such persons are not entitled to the slightest sympathy from society. . . . Nevertheless, it is incompatible with the dignity of an enlightened society to attempt to justify the taking of life for purposes of vengeance."[17]

This from the same court that a few years earlier had upheld McGautha's completely standardless death penalty. Now suddenly the "dignity of an enlightened society" outlawed all capital punishment. Based as it was on the California Constitution, not even the US Supreme Court could reverse that decision.

So six California judges suddenly rendered meaningless dozens of unanimous jury condemnations stretching over decades. By their single opinion, they denied the people of California—and the rest of us around the country—the cleansing that would come from knowing that Charles Manson had, at last, been put to death.

A few months later, the jurisprudential earthquake struck. In June 1972, the US Supreme Court, 5–4 in *Furman v. Georgia*, launched the modern era by striking down the death penalty as administered across the United States.[18] Hundreds of essays have analyzed and dissected the nine separate opinions that comprise this landmark case. Although no justice of the five who made up the majority joined in anybody else's opinion, that group essentially split into two camps.

Justices Brennan and Marshall, absolutists like the California Supreme Court, found the idea of death as punishment an unconstitutional violation of human dignity. The other three, however—Douglas, Stewart, and White—struck down the death penalty *as currently administered,* either because it allowed for racial discrimination or was unconstitutionally arbitrary—like "being struck by lightning." The four dissenters joined together to declare that each state had the right to decide for itself. But no Justice—not one—expressed the slightest support for death as punishment. And although there were nine separate opinions, all nine Justices denounced retribution as a bad reason to punish.

It was a great day for the worst of the worst. As a result of *Furman,* death rows across the United States emptied. Illinois took Richard Speck off the "hold" pile and transferred him to general population to serve a life sentence. Florida emptied its death row of dozens of condemned killers, including one Bennie Demps.

How could I imagine then that 30 years later I would witness his execution?

After *Furman*, leading experts on both sides confidently declared the death penalty dead in America. But they greatly underestimated the retributive instincts of the American people. Life in prison simply could not substitute. Immediately after *Furman*, 35 states scrambled to enact new death penalty statutes. If they could no longer constitutionally leave it to the jury's absolute discretion to decide life or death, 16 states tried to get the Supreme Court off their backs by going to the opposite extreme: Simply remove all discretion from the jury and make the death sentence mandatory once again—automatic for everyone convicted of first-degree murder. Other states tried to eliminate "arbitrariness" by specifying in greater detail who did and did not deserve to die—preserving jury discretion but now guiding it by listing aggravating and suggesting mitigating circumstances. These new legislative fixes would take years to test in the courts. For now, across the United States, the death penalty lay frozen.

3

TWO SIDES TO *EVERY* QUESTION?

LAW SCHOOL WENT BY QUICKLY. LAW, ITSELF, SEEMED A repository of so much practical wisdom. We took pride in our professors making a difference in public affairs, while in class they seemed capable of artfully turning any argument on its head. Of course the legal profession has always trumpeted "professionalism," emphasizing that there are two sides to every question. Any wonder the public has long despised lawyers, even as they sent their own children to get trained in law? This ambivalence goes back to those ancient Sophists who wandered from city to city, paid handsomely to teach the art of rhetoric to the sons of the rich and rising middle class. Success depended on convincing at the law courts and entertaining at the legislative assemblies. Eager to collect their fees without local interference, the Sophists soothed those in power anywhere they found work, supporting each city's values as right for it. Truth was relative; every question had two sides.

The story goes that Protagoras, the greatest Sophist, agreed to train Euathlus on condition that he get half his fee up front and half when Euathlus won his first case in court. But after completing his training, Euathlus did not want to appear in court. Protagoras's competitors spread the word: Euathlus feared to show up in court because Protagoras had trained him poorly. So Protagoras sued Euathlus, arguing to the jury, "Of course Euathlus owes me the rest of my fee. Either you will find for me and by your verdict he owes me my fee. Or you find against me, and by our contract, he will have won his first case in court. Either way, he owes me my fee." The logic seemed airtight.

But Protagoras had trained Euathlus well to argue both sides and make the weaker argument appear the stronger. Because as soon as Protagoras finished, Euathlus countered to the jury, "Of course I *don't* owe him his fee because either you will find in my favor, or if you do find against me, by the terms of our contract, I have not yet won my first case in court."[1]

Someone once defined "tradition" as the forgetting of origins. The first bar association began as an extortion racket.[2] Sophists would threaten to prosecute and derail the careers of the rich and rising unless they got paid off. But why should the victim pay hush money when someone else could then step forward and prosecute? These extortionists needed an association to enforce the agreement. Things haven't changed that much in 2,500 years. Thus, the story goes—have you any doubt that it's true?—that a lawyer and the Pope died the same day and found themselves sharing a ride with Saint Peter who escorted them to their heavenly abode. The Pope happily settled into his one-bedroom garden apartment with a study. Then the lawyer grimaced as St. Peter drove him to the slums of heaven. But they continued to a better part of town, still better, and finally stopped at a palatial oceanfront mansion. "Well," said St. Peter, "this is yours. For eternity." The lawyer stood mute, then found his voice. "Please, I'm overwhelmed. But I must ask. The Pope gets a one-bedroom, and me, this?" St. Peter smiled. "We got plenty of popes up here, but you're the first lawyer."

So here we were in law school, imbibing ancient sophistic traditions. "There are two sides to every question," our professors taught us. That didn't make sense to me. If there were two sides to *every* question, then the question of whether there were two sides to every question *itself* has two sides. And one side flatly denied there were two sides. Thus, its truth would imply its own contradiction. It didn't make sense logically. Worse, it made no sense morally. But our teachers trained us to argue both sides of every question, insisting, "A professional should be willing to zealously represent either side."[3] I never believed that. Most Americans don't either.

The school, however, drove it home as gospel. David Shapiro, a famous ACLU lawyer, gave a talk, "Defending Unpopular Clients." When authorities arrested George Lincoln Rockwell, the leader of the American Nazi Party, for passing out vile hate literature, a friend called Shapiro: No one locally would defend Rockwell; would Shapiro get him a lawyer? Shapiro cast about, but no one wanted to defend the Nazi. "How about you?" his friend asked. "Me? I'm a Jew," protested Shapiro. "So? I thought everybody's entitled to a good defense." Shapiro talked it over with his wife and agreed.

On the opening day of the trial as they climbed the courthouse steps, Rockwell, the Nazi leader, turned to his Jewish lawyer. "Shapiro, however this turns out—win or lose—one day they'll take you to the ovens and I'll be laughing the whole way there." This sunk in during a stunned silence. "I only wish I could have defended Rockwell's assassin," Shapiro added wryly.

Judging from the thunderous applause, most of my fellow law students considered Shapiro a hero. Defending those who would destroy him displayed consummate professionalism and commitment to the adversary system. To me he was a fool. Why choose to serve evil? You only live once.

A few years later, it would be my turn on stage before a packed house of attentive law students. In 1973, accused murderer Robert F. Garrow's court-appointed defense lawyers, Frank Armani and Francis Belge, assured their client he could talk to them in confidence. Had he killed that college student camping in the Adirondacks? "Oh, yeah," Garrow admitted. He had also killed three others including two young women he'd kidnapped and raped in separate incidents. The lawyers were skeptical, but Garrow offered to show them where he'd hidden the bodies. The lawyers found Alicia Hauck's corpse in the underbrush of a local cemetery. The other victim, 20-year-old Susan Petz, he had stuffed down an abandoned mineshaft. Garrow drew a map from which his lawyers found and photographed Petz's body.[4]

Alicia Hauck's parents assumed their 16-year-old daughter had run away. But Susan Petz's family could only hope against hope. She had gone camping with Donald Porter, her boyfriend. Porter's body was found stabbed to death and tied to a tree. Reading that two lawyers now defended a man accused of killing a camper in the Adirondacks, Earl Petz, Susan's father, flew from Illinois and showed the lawyers a photograph of his daughter, begging them for information. Armani and Belge knew "what hell these parents were going through," Armani later admitted. Armani's own brother was lost during an Air Force reconnaissance mission. "I know what torment my mother went through in never having my brother's body returned." They also knew for certain they had photographed Susan Petz's body. But they turned her father away, declaring they had no information to share. "We just couldn't figure any other way."[5]

Armani and Belge contacted the local prosecutor's office, offering to solve two unsolved murders in return for a not-guilty-by-reason-of-insanity plea for their client, suggesting that Garrow should be treated, not punished. The prosecutor refused and took the case to trial. Garrow took the stand at his murder trial, and on cross-examination, he admitted his guilt. "Yeah, I did it. I did two others; I told my lawyers."[6]

So the community turned against the lawyers. How could they value the confidence of a mass murderer over the torment of the victim's family? Garrow's lawyers must be indicted, but for what? A grand jury indicted Belge (not represented by counsel)—but not Armani—for violating the health law in failing to report the location of an unburied body!

The story has two postscripts. Sentenced to life in prison, Garrow appealed on the ground that his lawyers had been incompetent! Motivated by their own sense of guilt, he argued, they had him take the stand, not to demonstrate his insanity, but to admit to the two other murders, thus releasing them from their vow of silence.[7] His appeal failed, but paralyzed in prison and permanently confined to a wheelchair, Garrow got himself transferred to a less secure facility. Only it turned out he had faked the whole thing. One day he climbed a 15-foot fence and escaped. Fortunately the police shot him dead a couple of days later.[8]

Years passed and out of the blue, the bar association's ethics committee formally declared that lawyers in this situation must do what they had done—except they shouldn't have moved the victim's head back to her torso before photographing it. Had they revealed the fate of the daughter to the parents, the lawyers would have been subject to discipline.

In the defense bar's eyes, Garrow's lawyers were heroes; in my eyes, they were cads. "I would have violated the Code of Professional Responsibility and taken what came behind it," I insisted in a public debate before a crowd of law students. "Death is difficult enough to accept," Armani declared. "But worrying and wondering, it'll drive you insane."

How *could* ethics require us to protect the confidences of a mass murdering rapist rather than inform his victim's family and save their sanity? US Supreme Court Justice Louis Brandeis got it right when he called on future attorneys sometimes to look beyond their clients and become "lawyers for the situation."[9] Shapiro should never have defended Rockwell; Garrow's lawyers should have ended the family's torment, allowing them to bury their child and begin the grieving process. But American lawyers, like the priests they imagine themselves, hold lawyer-client confidentiality as sacred. Well, there *was* one emergency exception at that time. A lawyer could break that sacred vow—when necessary to collect a fee![10]

"On every question there are two sides," the Sophists claimed and still do. I knew better. I had always known better. Justice wasn't simply a matter of opinion. Whatever "progressives" might proclaim, Adolph Hitler, Charles Manson, and Richard Speck were evil and deserved to die. That was moral fact.

Graduating law school in 1974, I turned down Wall Street money to join the recently formed special prosecutor's office and attacked corruption in New York City's criminal justice system. Before going out into the real world, I approached Professor Richard Neustadt, a former influential adviser to President Kennedy who taught us future lawyers how to operate within a bureaucracy. What advice did he wish he had received before starting a career of public service? Neustadt paused and leaned back in his chair, contemplating the question. "Sometimes, in order to do good, you have to do bad. If you use public power well, you will still hurt innocent people." At the time that struck me as trite. How wrong I was.

My brief stint as a special prosecutor taught me some lasting lessons. Punishment can be arbitrary. For example, police sergeants in the 114th precinct in Queens who made the rounds soliciting Christmas "gifts" but never actively shook down merchants or took payoffs from gamblers or drug dealers, we called "grass eaters." At our recommendation, the NYPD would fine these cops, but they would keep their pensions. "Meat eaters" typically lost their pensions and faced criminal prosecution. The prosecutor in the office next to mine, however, investigating the neighboring "Sergeants Club" in the 103rd, believed that any cop who took a nickel should lose his pension. So a defendant's punishment depended on geography more than culpability—whether a particular prosecutor assigned to the case sought the ultimate punishment. According to factors never formally articulated, we, the Executive, would exercise a prosecutor's prerogative and decide who deserves what. A defendant's fate depended on the luck of the draw.

Investigating the Sergeants Club exposed me to another problem that would reappear with the death penalty: In an attempt to do justice, should we count the effects of punishment on the family of the punished? Either one of two officers could give us a key piece of information. The more corrupt cop had a wife and seven children relying on his pension. The less corrupt had no dependents. Who gets the break? Someone's life must be ruined. Do I count the effects on the family of the more corrupt cop as part of justice? Or am I bound by my professional self, confined by our official mandate to fight and punish public corruption? Richard Neustadt's voice echoed from law school.

After three days of discomfort, I decided to protect the children and give the worse cop a better deal. Until I reached for the phone. I called the less corrupt cop, who had no dependents, and offered him immunity from prosecution for his cooperation.

Forty years later, we death penalty advocates confront abolitionists who condemn the death penalty because it takes an unfair toll on the families of the condemned. But Neustadt was right; nobody can perfectly exercise official power. Sometimes innocent persons must get hurt for the public good. Sometimes we must reluctantly risk innocent lives for the sake of justice.

This insight has ancient roots. "Will you destroy the innocent with the guilty?"[11] Abraham protested when God prepared to destroy Sodom. In the Old Testament story, God agrees to spare Sodom if 50 righteous persons dwelled within. Suppose there are 40, 30, 20, the defense counsel demands? "For the sake of ten I shall not destroy it," God assures Abraham. Abraham had the guts to lead God down the slippery slope, but he stopped at ten. He did not suggest that God spare all the wicked for the sake of a single righteous soul. The lesson here: We should greatly favor sparing the guilty lest we execute the innocent. But there are limits.

My time as a special prosecutor also taught me to respect the presumption of innocence, another core value with ancient roots. As our investigation progressed, every sergeant in the 114th precinct eagerly offered to cooperate and keep his pension. Except Kurt. He insisted he never took a nickel. Other sergeants scoffed at this: Everybody belonged to the Christmas club. Nobody ever refused. I warned Kurt—no deal unless he came clean. He told me to shove my deal where the sun don't shine and stormed out of my office. I would teach him a lesson, I vowed. Throw the book at him. Then the actual Christmas list surfaced. Kurt's name alone had no check mark next to it. "It wasn't worth the risk of getting dragged into some prosecutor's office," Kurt explained to me with an ironic chuckle after I'd called him to my office several weeks later, this time to apologize. I had been so ready and eager to prosecute an innocent man. Since this incident, I try to take the presumption of innocence seriously. It's a struggle, even now.

My time as a special assistant state attorney general confirmed another painful lesson. In prosecuting corrupt cops, everybody supported us. But when our investigation started getting close to lawyers and especially judges, the system closed to protect itself. I saw double standards: one system for the rich and powerful, another for the rest of us.

One bad blunder made me seriously consider resigning. We were investigating drug dealing and gun running involving a member of Congress, a state senator, and a judge. We hoped to expose them through one of their associates. But I discovered as I reviewed court-ordered wiretaps that our immediate target, Harry, a small businessman and devoted single parent, desperately sought to prevent his two teenage daughters from succumbing to the street life. I convinced myself that confronted with overwhelming evidence of small-time drug dealing, Harry would act rationally. In order to avoid prison, he would surely cooperate, receive immunity, and keep his family intact. So I brought Harry to my office and told him truthfully he was not our ultimate target. I laid all the evidence against him right on the table, literally. I played tapes where he admitted selling coke out of his grocery store. He even counted the money on tape. I offered him full immunity for information about the congressman and state senator. Harry demanded his lawyer. But his lawyer was also the congressman's lawyer. Once that lawyer knew, the congressman would know. I pleaded with Harry not to destroy his value to us. "His people" would sacrifice him in a heartbeat. But Harry wanted this lawyer; he wouldn't budge. I couldn't hate him for refusing to snitch—I could only despise myself for failing to consider it. The investigation busted. We were left with a drug case against a devoted parent, which my informant had set up at my request. Of course I would never personally prosecute Harry. If necessary, I vowed, I would be a character witness in his defense.

About that time a letter appeared at the office with a check in it, making resigning all the easier. Harvard Law School had established the Oberman Prize for the best essay on a contemporary theme. Under the sponsorship of Professor Laurence Tribe, my Game and Sport perspective had won. Essentially the same thesis that my adviser at Tufts had dismissed, Harvard had judged it the best of my graduating year. Sweet vindication! But then it struck me. Maybe the Sophists were right: There was no truth. My perspective was crap, or brilliant, depending on whoever thought so. Anyway, as a result of that award, I accepted an unsolicited offer to become a law professor at New York Law School to help integrate law and humanities.

4

RICHER THAN THE
RULES OF LAW

PREPARING TO TEACH CRIMINAL LAW PUT ME IN TOUCH with perspectives that seemed to transcend time, place, and culture. Amazing how Aristotle had suggested the current New York law of homicide 2,400 years ago! Basic distinctions between culpable mental states—intentional killing, reckless killing, and accidents—go back 25 centuries at least to Solon, the ancient Greek lawgiver.[1] They may be embedded in nature itself. As Chief Justice Oliver Wendell Holmes Jr. famously declared, "Even a dog knows the difference between being kicked and stumbled over."[2] So once again the Sophists were wrong. Not everything was conventional, arbitrary, relative. Some harms were intended, others recklessly produced. Some were simply unfortunate accidents. All other things equal, an intentional killing, worse than a negligent one, deserved to be punished more severely. And not because we say so. We say so because it does.

During that summer of 1976, the United States celebrated the bicentennial of its Declaration of Independence, which declared self-evident truths and inalienable natural rights. Two hundred years from the day the Continental Congress actually voted for independence, on July 2, 1976, four years after it struck down the death penalty in *Furman,* the US Supreme Court upheld new capital statutes in Georgia, Florida, and Texas.[3] These new laws guided juries by specifying aggravating circumstances in advance and established a separate "penalty phase," in which the jury that convicted the defendant of first-degree murder would now decide life or death. "The instinct for retribution is part of the nature of man," declared Justice Potter Stewart for the plurality in *Gregg v. Georgia.*[4] These recently enacted statutes reflected "the community's belief that certain crimes are themselves so griev-ous an affront to humanity that the only adequate response may be the pen-alty of death."⁵ The court's new watchwords became "guided discretion."⁶

Death as punishment once again became a realistic possibility. Of course nothing could be done about Charles Manson or Richard Speck, except to hope that some prisoner gave them the painful deaths they richly deserved.

Meanwhile, I pinched myself when my paychecks came. The law school paid me to study free will versus determinism—did we choose or were we caused to act? Murder versus manslaughter—did heat of passion mitigate murder, and if so, which passions? The limits of self-defense—suppose you killed, realistically anticipating that someday, some way, the victim would kill you? Insanity—if you didn't know what you were doing was wrong, or couldn't control yourself? Duress—if others pressured or threatened you? Entrapment—what if the government put the squeeze but made it too tempting? Each of these doctrines attacks a defendant's full culpability, chal-lenging whether he deserves punishment.

Substantive criminal law—really the "game" of criminal law—which I taught, assumes that the crime as defined will be automatically detected, prosecuted, and punished exactly as the legislature provides. The "sport"—criminal process—introduces all sorts of real-time indeterminacy: Did the search or interrogation that unearthed evidence of guilt suffer from con-stitutional defect? Did the prosecutor offer or accept a plea bargain? Did the lawyers adequately prescreen the jury for prejudice? Did the prosecutor exceed constitutional bounds in closing argument? To teach the rules of the game, I needed better grounding in psychology, history, and philosophy. I could not continue to ignore my own ignorance. So after my first year teach-ing at New York Law School, with the dean's blessing, I returned to Harvard as a graduate fellow in Law and Humanities.

How to compress that magical year into a few paragraphs? Harvard gave the 12 fellows our own house with an office, administrative assistant, paycheck, and free run of the university. I took pieces of courses and found the philosophy department roiled in the same turmoil that consumed Plato and the Sophists: What is real? What is true?

Contemporary sophistic philosophers of science, art, and even math-ematics saw truth and reality as relative, within whatever framework of the moment or culture. "We make by classifying," Nelson Goodman insisted in his graduate seminar, "Styles and Standards: Ways of Worldmaking."⁷ Only within a theory could a statement be true. Need and prejudice regulate what a person sees. As psychologists were fond of saying, "There is more to vision than meets the eye."

What constitutes "realism" of representation, Goodman challenged rhetorically? Deception. A picture is "realistic" only when it becomes a successful illusion. Realism is relative, he insisted, determined by a given culture or person at a given time. We obscure this relativity and label it "natural," failing to specify a frame of reference when it is our own. There was no innocent eye. Nature is a product of art.

These great Sophists dazzled and seduced us, but I knew they were wrong.

"There may be no truth except in a framework," Professor Hillary Putnam wryly acknowledged to W. V. O. Quine and Goodman in an amiable public debate. "Except that while you both claim that, you trust your life to a very specific framework as you cross a bridge." Putnam, a philosopher of mathematics, also believed in moral facts: "Torturing small children to cripples just for the fun of it is wrong," he proclaimed. "I am as certain of this as I am that my hand has five fingers." If a society takes pleasure in its weekly ritual of randomly selecting a child and plucking out his eyes while breaking his bones, not because citizens believe it will help their crops grow but simply because it gives them pleasure, then we can say of that society that although the practice works for them, they're wrong. They're not wrong because we say so; we say so because they're wrong. After class, I had the hubris to tangle one-on-one with Quine—probably the world's leading logician—attempting to demonstrate to this genial giant that even in logic and mathematics, no less than in ethics or aesthetics, some distinctions of truth, goodness, and beauty remain less arbitrary than others.

Underlying this clash of Titans, Kurt Gödel's incompleteness theorem still dominated the scene. Gödel had shattered twentieth-century logic by famously proving that some true statements can never be proved.[8] If this truth hasn't jarred you, if you've never before absorbed this, stop for a moment. It's worth it.

In any consistent logical system, some true statements can never be proved.

Gödel actually proved that. We need a richer language than a system offers to prove all the truths within that system. Gödel's proof instantly ruined careers and changed worldviews. We can never get a system that spells out all the meaning within it. Truth for language was more complicated than anything expressible by that language.[9] After Gödel's proof, we feel the need for a richer meta-language. Plato and Aristotle sensed this: Justice is richer than a rule of law.

Gödel's proof suggested a profound metaphor: In any legal system, justice could not be entirely derived from the consistent application of the rules of law. Within any consistent formal system of rules, some truths could not be produced by applying those rules. We need a transcendent, richer language than the written law to achieve the justice that law strives to produce. Locke called it prerogative: the right to go outside the rules for the good of the whole.[10] Aristotle called it equity.[11] The rules themselves can call for their own transcendence. Consider the "choice of evils" provision in the New York Penal Law: 35.05(2): "According to ordinary standards of intelligence and morality," whenever you would avoid a greater harm by violating the rules, your acts are justifiable, and you commit no crime.

Those who worship consistency but seek justice need a transcendent perspective that tells them when to abandon the logic and classifications within which they claim to operate. We need to test for the justice *of* the rules, John Rawls preached in a course I audited that year, not merely justice *under* the rules. A perfectly law-abiding society could meet its goal of strict obedience and consistent application of rules and yet be thoroughly unjust. A twentieth-century giant of jurisprudence, Rawls famously insisted we impose a veil of ignorance. We could never claim a criminal justice system as fair unless we designed it not knowing what role we'd personally play in it: defendant, victim, prosecutor, juror?[12]

So I came to understand that year that justice was incommensurably richer than the rules of law. We needed a richer language than the Code of Professional Responsibility for defense lawyers to tell innocent parents their daughter was dead. I felt certain that real death penalty justice transcends the strictly rational to include the emotional. Although we might meet *Furman*'s demand for its more regular administration, a death penalty meted out consistently and without racial discrimination might still be unjust. If justice means getting what you deserve, the rules, regularly administered, could still fail to separate the worst of the worst. We need to test for the justice of the categories, not merely justice under them.[13] The language necessary to express the just outcome of a capital trial far outstrips in complexity what the law could state in advance. A jury's decision to kill a murderer who deserves to die requires an informed observer, sharing certain cultural values, bound by categories, but committed to determine the worst of the worst individually. It requires all the richness, including emotion, of a humane judgment as to who should live or die.

That year our program's liaison, Roger Fisher, author of the best-selling *Getting to Yes,* impressed me with a practical distinction between pressure and pain. Palestinians, otherwise no match for the Israelis, could, with carefully targeted bombing, pressure Israel to modify policies, he insisted. But if the Israelis ever began to look at these terrorist attacks as unavoidable, random tragedies, like fatal car crashes or getting struck by lightning, then the Israelis would continue to feel pain—but not the pressure. Anyone who tries to change another person's behavior, Fisher argued to us, should seek the maximum pressure with minimum pain. Applied to criminal law, general deterrence—pressuring other would-be criminals to play it straight—becomes the goal of punishment. Classical utilitarians such as Bentham and Cesare Beccaria have long since claimed that a rational society should design punishment to appear harsher to the public than it feels to the criminal[14] Maximize the pressure, keep the pain to a minimum.

We retributivists view punishment differently. We don't punish to prevent crime or remake criminals. We inflict pain—suffering, discomfort—to the degree they deserve to feel it. Knowing of my interest—he said "obsession"—with philosophies of punishment, one of my fellows turned me on to Adam Smith's *Theory of Moral Sentiments,* published in 1759, 17 years before his classic capitalist manifesto, *The Wealth of Nations.* "Resentment prompts us to punish," Smith declared, in this great work of retributive psychology. "Our heart, as it adopts and beats time to the [victim's] grief," becomes "animated" to "drive away or destroy the cause of it." We feel an "imaginary resentment" on behalf of the dead victim. "We feel that resentment which we imagine he ought to feel and which he would feel, if in his cold and lifeless body there remained any consciousness of what passes upon earth. His blood, we think, calls aloud for vengeance. The very ashes of the dead seem to be disturbed at the thought that his injuries are to pass unrevenged."[15]

The killer must not only die to "fully gratify" our resentment, he must also be "made to grieve for the particular wrong we have suffered from him." We should resent the murderer but not too much. For Adam Smith, "revenge, the excess of resentment" was "the most detestable of all the passions." And yet too little resentment also was despicable. How can we know the proper punishment? What measure to use? Adam Smith too had joined the chorus for a language richer than rationality: God had given humankind not only reason but also intuition. We must, Adam Smith insisted, "oppose to the emotions of compassion which we feel for a particular person, a more enlarged compassion which we feel for mankind."[16]

At last I had found my guide.

As my fellowship year ended, an ongoing international controversy flared up again, and the drumbeat intensified: "Free Rudolf Hess!" Hitler's first deputy führer, Hess had bailed out over Scotland early in the war on a bizarre self-appointed mission to convince the British to dump Churchill and make peace with Hitler. At Nuremberg, the war crimes tribunal sentenced Hess to life in prison at Spandau along with six other high-ranking

Nazis the tribunal did not condemn to hang. Years passed. The others died or were released, and in the end, Hess remained the sole prisoner in Spandau. The British, French, and Americans wanted to ease the harsh conditions of his prison life. The Soviets, however, vetoed compassion for the man who declared at the end of his trial that he had been "privileged" to work under Hitler, "the greatest son" his nation had brought forth. Announcing himself a "loyal follower of my Führer," Hess assured his captives at Nuremberg and thereafter that "I regret nothing."[17]

In February 1977, Hess attempted suicide by slashing his wrists. Soviet guards prevented serious injury, but as a result, the speaker of West Germany's parliament asked the occupation powers to free Hess or at least move him to a hospital. The Russians refused. Then his former warden, Eugene Bird, appealed to President Jimmy Carter as a Christian to convince the Soviets to release "this broken old man." The four powers should end this "wasteful custody" that "cost the West Germans $300,000 a year for one feeble prisoner," the *New York Times* editorially chimed in, calling Hess's continued incarceration "sheer cruelty" and "bureaucratic lunacy," while hinting that Britain, France, and the United States consider violating their postwar agreement to maintain the prison and thereby "end the charade."[18]

The allies called for cost savings through compassionate release, but again the Russians balked. "We remember everything about the past," they replied two months later. "Is it necessary to be merciful to one of those who wanted to drown humanity in blood?" The Soviets refused to relent and release Hess. I don't ever remember agreeing with the USSR in a dispute with the United States. But here they were right.

Life in prison suddenly became "a bit less bleak" for Rudolf Hess: The allies had given him color TV, doubled his visits, and allowed him free access to the prison gardens. I imagined the concentration camps, the ovens, and seethed. Whether Hess ever felt remorse, we retributivists knew that the deputy führer must not, absolutely *must not* die free. We made a covenant with the Holocaust victims. We should respect it, keep our word. The past counts. How many times I would shout that, if only they'd let me, and you'd listen. The past counts! Not rationally, but really. The past counts.

As I was catching up on current criminal law cases in June 1977, preparing to return to teaching, the US Supreme Court jolted me back to more contemporary evil and injustice by reversing Ehrlich Anthony Coker's death sentence. In 1971, Coker had raped and then stabbed to death a young woman. A few months later, he kidnapped and raped a 16-year-old girl, severely beat her with a club, dragged her into the woods, and left her for dead. While serving three life sentences for murder, rape, and kidnapping, Coker escaped from prison, entered the Carvers' house at night, tied up Mr. Carver, ransacked the house, and raped Mrs. Carver at knifepoint. A Georgia jury sentenced Coker to die.

Assuring the public that they did not "discount the seriousness of rape as a crime," and that "short of homicide, rape was the ultimate violation of self," the Supreme Court majority nevertheless insisted that "in terms of moral depravity and injury," rape "does not compare with murder." For the rape victim, "life may not be nearly so happy as it was, but it is not over and normally is not beyond repair. We have the abiding conviction that the death penalty is an excessive penalty for the rapist who, as such, does not take human life."[19]

Ignoring Coker's earlier murder and rapes, the majority found death morally disproportionate for this crime. I was enraged. The jury hadn't sentenced the crime of rape; it had condemned a rapist-murderer to die. And rightly so. Death fit this vicious criminal and not merely his crime. But Coker would get no extra punishment beyond his original three life sentences. In the words of Adam Smith, he was not "made to grieve" for the "injuries we have suffered from him."[20]

But ultimately I parted company with Adam Smith: "Though dislike and hatred harden us against all sympathy, and sometimes dispose us even to rejoice at the distress of another, yet if neither we nor our friends have received any great personal provocation, these passions would not naturally lead us to wish to . . . bring . . . it about."[21] I lost no family or friends in the Holocaust. I did not know the victims of Hitler, Manson, and Speck. Yet I needed these monsters punished, and I felt the need to help bring it about. The great ancient Greek lawgiver Solon said it best: "In a well governed state, citizens like members of the same body, should feel and resent each other's injuries."[22]

Those were my children, my wife that Coker raped and murdered, my sister Speck killed.

PART II
VOICES FROM THE INSIDE

5

ONE RAGGEDY LAWYER

AFTER THE FELLOWSHIP YEAR, I RETURNED TO NEW YORK Law School, feeling better grounded in philosophy. My criminal law course focused on the different types of murder. Felony murder makes us retributivists squirm. Deeply embedded in the American psyche, the "felony murder" doctrine dictates that any death—intentional, reckless, or even accidental—in the course of a felony makes all co-felons guilty of murder. The intent to commit the felony, by a ridiculous fiction, "transfers" into the intent to kill.

Although *Furman* commanded the states to specify in advance who deserves to die, the US Supreme Court respected basic principles of federalism and largely left it to each state to decide who got classified as the worst of the worst. Felony murder, however, provoked the court to step in and stop an execution.

Earl Enmund, a getaway driver, waited while his co-felons robbed and killed their victims. The prosecution couldn't show that Enmund anticipated his cohort would use deadly force. Nevertheless, Florida sentenced this felony murderer to die. In 1982, the US Supreme Court split 5–4 over whether Florida could execute Enmund. The majority characterized the death penalty as "purposeless and needless . . . pain and suffering" unless it "measurably contributed" to retribution or deterrence. The threat of death would not deter a person "who does not kill and has no intention or purpose that life will be taken," the majority insisted.[1]

Furthermore, a felony murderer might not deserve to die. "American criminal law has long considered a defendant's intention and therefore his moral guilt to be critical to the degree of criminal culpability." Enmund's punishment, the majority insisted, "must be tailored to his personal guilt." Putting Enmund to death to avenge two killings that "he did not commit and had no intention of committing or causing does not measurably contribute to the retributive end of ensuring that the criminal gets his just deserts." Thus, in the absence of proof that "Enmund intended or contemplated that life would be taken," a sharply divided Supreme Court prohibited Florida from putting this felony murderer to death.[2]

At last—retribution had returned, this time to limit punishment. We retributivists want killers to get what they deserve. No more, no less. Seemingly, a simple getaway car driver should not be condemned to die.

These years teaching criminal law left me comfortable that I could expose students to long-standing theoretical controversies, along with perspectives and vocabularies to resolve them. But I couldn't really evaluate Enmund's "personal responsibility" or "moral guilt."[3] I didn't know how robbers and killers thought and felt. We should understand what we condemn. How else could I test and critique legislatures' lists of aggravating circumstances that define capital murder?

"Before we can adopt the resentment of the sufferer, we must disapprove of the motives of the agent," Adam Smith insisted.[4] We're enraged—not only at the vile killing but even more at the killer. When we condemn him to die for his conduct, we really condemn his character. "A man's character is his fate," Heraclitus declared 2,600 years ago.[5] But how can we retributivists thoroughly condemn his character without really knowing his motives? Before we can attach our meanings to their murders, we must appreciate what the killings meant to the killers. In order to study and teach murder and other serious felonies, I needed to know murderers and other serious felons.

The tenure committee let me know I had a serious problem. I hadn't published any essays on criminal law; I didn't feel I had anything new to say. Once again fate intervened in the form of Philip Heymann, my wife's former law professor who had urged me to go to law school in the first place. Phil offered to send me on a journey into the minds and lives of criminals living in Lorton Central Prison, just 25 miles south of the streets of Washington, DC.

"They got to think that's fair," explained John Allen, #129375, about his fellow prisoners ganging up and stabbing a guy in the back. "They got to think like that to do like that." Johnny had confirmed it. How he thinks, what he feels as he kills, why he kills—a criminal's attitudes and values determine his behavior. Beyond the intent to cause death or an extreme recklessness that makes him guilty of murder, the killer's thoughts and feelings, his motives for the killing dictate the punishment he deserves. Motive— what moves him to act—differs from intent. He may kill intentionally from a variety of motives: fear, anger, jealousy, greed, pity, or even love. A killer's motive stems from his character, that cluster of attitudes that mostly persists through time and defines each of us as a unique individual. Is he selfish, cruel, cold, cowardly?

So the argument for capital punishment revolves around attitude, his and ours: the killer's attitude as he kills, and society's attitude in killing him. What are we thinking, how are we feeling, when, in our name, legislatures define, prosecutors prosecute, juries condemn, judges affirm, and prison officials execute murderers who deserve to die? What moved him to kill now moves us to kill him. And both of us, as Johnny declared to me the first time I met him inside Lorton Central Prison, "got to think like that to do like that."

Johnny saw me as his only chance to pay back a huge debt to Phil Heymann. As court-appointed defense counsel, Heymann had once gotten Johnny off a stickup charge. Then Professor Heymann fashioned Johnny's life story from his own words, got it published as *Assault with a Deadly Weapon: The Autobiography of a Street Criminal*, and gave Johnny all royalties from the book.[6]

Permanently paralyzed from the waist down and confined to a wheelchair, Johnny bought some bad dope to resell at a profit. "Get out of my face, Wheelchair," snarled the drug dealer, displaying a 9 mm when Johnny demanded his money back. You don't call John Allen "Wheelchair." So Johnny pulled out a sawed-off shotgun from the blanket that wrapped his lifeless legs and robbed the dealer of all his drugs and money. And held him for ransom until his older brother paid another $25,000.

In prison they respected that: robbing and kidnapping a drug dealer from a wheelchair. Anyway, Johnny landed back in prison with a huge debt unpaid to Phil, his lawyer who'd gotten him off an earlier robbery charge, then written his life story, and now kept sending him money in prison. Phil Heymann was God. And I was Phil's younger emissary.

From day one, Johnny, aka "Big Al," vouched for me, "Slim Rob," as "alright." He assured his older friends and wild young prison associates that they could trust me. That was 90 percent of it. The last 10 percent also came from Phil. Formerly the Justice Department's Criminal Division chief under President Carter, Phil called his buddy, Norm Carlson, the well-respected director of federal prisons, who contacted Walter Ridley, the director of the DC Department of Corrections, who issued a memo to the wardens inside Lorton Central: Let this criminal law professor meet who he wants, when he wants. And the key: I could bring a tape recorder, candy, and cigarettes into the prison.

Kick back with a young killer for hours, no guards present, the tape recorder under joint control and in plain view, melting out of sight. Let him know that you value his point of view, that his way of looking at it is all that counts. Engage him in a common search for why he kills and what it means to him; challenge him with your own restrained but undisguised mixture of sympathy and anger, trusting he will not kill you. Show concern for his unique life story as he sees it. Tone down your rage and revulsion that he could spray-shoot a crowd on a street corner. Settle into comfortable chairs and let these conversations go where they go while they let you take them where you want. And they will reveal their character in an honest, some-times angry, often mellow light.

Thus, for 12 years and thousands of hours, I wandered freely inside Lorton Central, flagship of the nation's only all-black prison system, engag-ing the older and younger generations of street criminals confined there. Long, intense conversations sometimes ended with a question: "Why have you opened up like this?" Typically the same reply: "I got nothing to lose by being truthful with you." Looking at the yellow highlighter stain seeping through my leather briefcase and shaking his head at my beaten-up shoes, one prisoner confessed pity as his motive: "Man, you're one raggedy lawyer. So I figure I'll take a chance."

No statute of limitations protects murderers against prosecution and punishment for their unsolved killings. We dwelt on "situations," scrupu-lously avoiding names, dates, and details that could turn them into self-accusers or snitches and me, on reflection, into a witness against them.

Curious for something new, applying the same casual indifference they displayed on the street, whether from sheer exhibitionism, bravado, or a psychological need to unburden, they opened up. They said it felt good to be truthful without getting hurt. So they took stock of themselves while a lawyer-professor took them seriously as subjects and expert street guides in a common search for right and wrong along with the meaning of the lives they lived and took.

6

BETWEEN RIGHT
AND WRONG

IT ALL STARTED WITH JOHNNY ON A MISSION TO PAY OFF his debt to Phil by giving it to me straight. "In my day, for me to pull a perfect stickup, get the money, make a smooth getaway, and not have to shoot nobody or hurt nobody—that was a groove. That's what got me off. Now things are sloppy," Johnny complained in our first meeting, as he described the current young street crop. "Firing on people for no reason—the least little move, killing them. It's messed up the whole stickup game. If it came off smooth, that proved something to me. Now if they hurt somebody, it proves something to them."

On the streets and inside the prisons in the late 1980s and early 1990s, things were out of control. Phil Heymann sent me inside, partly to investigate how this new drug called crack deformed a generation into more vicious young criminals. Johnny introduced me to his prison buddies, older street criminals who decried the younger generation even as they sought to understand them. "When we were young," explained Leo Simms in our first group conversation, "certain things was showed us that we kept in our heads. Certain values were just there. The generation now, never been exposed to that. Most of their mamas and daddies are on the same time they are."

"Youngsters today don't have no moral inputs; they don't have no moral values," Henry Daniel agreed. "These young people have no sense of fair play," Pete Arnold chimed in. "No sense of 'OK, this guy's not bucking [resisting], so we can leave him alive. At worst he'll tell on us and we'll end up in jail for this.' Instead it's, 'You not going to get a chance to tell because we going to snuff you out.'"

"If you're never taught that your own life means something, then his life means nothing," Leo agreed. "Somebody got to make it register to you that *your* life is valuable. That the next man's life is as valuable as yours. You get it at home and off the street. When I come up, I was taught a man's life, that's all he got. And I value mine, so I can understand you valuing yours. But if I don't value mine, then how can I understand you valuing yours?"

"They *don't* value their lives," Henry Daniel agreed.

"They'll spray a street with kids there," Leo continued. "You can't tell me—black, white, I don't care what color you are—that if you have had value put on life, you would be able to do that. To these guys, these days, your life is no more than that candy bar. Nothing more than whatever material value I am about, feed on, live for. A Mercedes? Your life ain't shit towards a Mercedes. Or Adidas? Any time you take a man's life for a pair of tennis shoes can you tell me that you have any value about your life or his life? Or life in general? None at all."

The elders sang the chorus of the ages: Kids today have no values. Were they right? Inside Lorton Central, older prisoners won't probe younger ones about the meaning of their lives and killings. It can be dangerous to press a wild youngster about these things. However, "Slim Rob," the "raggedy" white professor-lawyer, didn't know better and came with a different attitude. So the elders brought me the young killers, and together we provoked them to reveal themselves. For days and nights, scattered over years, we leaned back and listened as young inner-city street criminals examined closely how and why they killed, what they thought and felt as they killed, and what it meant to them—then, and now.

"The shooting I got locked up for," explained Marshall G., 24,[1] "was this dude, his baby's mother and his baby. We were at a light. He opened up the window. 'Hey Marshall. You don't know me, but I'm going to kill your bitch ass. You killed my cousin.' Words going back and forth. We didn't try to fire her up. We just tried to fire him up. His baby was there too. I didn't hit her, but they gave me attempted murder on her. And murder on him."

"Did you see the baby before you started shooting?" I asked.

"Yeah. I didn't care. It was destroy or be destroyed."

"So you are that drive-by shooter we read about?"

"No," Marshall protested. "Some people you hear about just kill at random. I was trying to kill somebody who said they were going to kill *me*."

Almost nobody likes to think of himself as the most morally despicable. Even vicious street criminals like Marshall will point to others worse than themselves. "My intentions were not to shoot his baby's mother or his baby. My intentions were just to do him."

"But you're willing to risk it," I pressed. "If he's standing on the corner and there's a crowd around him, would you take out the gun and shoot, and anybody that's around him, if they go, they go?"

Marshall laughed nervously. "Yeah. I've done that before. Some dudes I was beefing with all in a crowd. So we just rolled past and shot the whole crowd. Whoever got killed, I don't know nothing about that. I just shot. And that was it."

"The other people on the corner never did anything to you. They're just standing there."

"All the other dudes that's around him, I can't say whether they with him or not. They might have been just innocent bystanders. And if they standing next to him, yeah, they may be in trouble. I don't go over there to shoot innocent people."

"But if an innocent person happens to be standing next to the guy?"

"There's nothing you can do about that," said Marshall indignantly. "If you beefing with somebody, the issue is not who's beside him. The issue is to get your man, kill him and get him out of the way."

"And looking back on that, you don't think that's wrong?"

"For shooting innocent people? Yeah it's wrong. Nobody supposed to shoot anybody that just happened to be standing at the wrong place at the wrong time. But if they get hit, I mean, they S.O.L.—that's the bottom line—they Shit Outta Luck. They shouldn't have been there. That's the way I look at it."

"What chiefly enrages us," Adam Smith explained in 1759, "is the unreasonable preference which he gives to himself above us, and that absurd self-love, by which he seems to imagine that other people may be sacrificed at any time, to his conveniency or his humour."[2]

"All I wanted to do was make money and be happy," continued Marshall. "I didn't care about who got hurt in the process."

Of course, mostly we love ourselves and those closest to us. But there are limits to self-love the rest of us will tolerate. Marshall's callousness seemed extreme, but he had lots of company, I soon discovered.

"The whole crowd got to go," explained Jerry G., aka "Big Foot."

"Why don't he wait?" pressed Pete Arnold.

"The game has changed. You have to get your man when you can get him. If you let him go, he might walk up to your door the next morning, or drive up behind you and boom! So you got to work your man when you see him."

"But what about the innocent people?" I growled.

"You don't think about that. The fact is you."

"Though it may be true that every individual in his own breast naturally prefers himself to all mankind," Adam Smith conceded, "yet he dares not look mankind in the face, and avow that he acts according to this principle."[3]

"The fact is you," Big Foot had countered matter-of-factly.

Society hates the spray shooter, as Adam Smith understood, from "a compounded sentiment made up of two distinct emotions; a direct antipathy to the sentiments of the agent, and an indirect sympathy with the resentment of the sufferer."[4] Thus, we condemn their absolute selfishness and cowardice coupled with their extreme indifference to other human life.

These spray shooters who callously killed innocent bystanders deserved to die, yet they may not have intentionally killed their victims. Once again, the criminal law employs another fiction of "transferred intent"—the intent to kill one person transfers to the unintended victim. And the felony murder rule further transfers responsibility for the killing to all co-felons. But we never need to base the death penalty on legal fictions.

For centuries we've recognized that a *depraved recklessness* can be every bit as bad or worse than an intent to kill. The Old Testament's homicide law mostly reserved the death penalty for intentional murder. But it did make it a capital offense to let loose a goring ox that the owner knew was vicious.[5] More recently, Thorsten Sellin, a leading twentieth-century death penalty opponent, in his official commentary to the Model Penal Code, flatly rejected traditional felony murder death penalty statutes as "too broad": They included low-risk "unintentional homicides," which might be "truly accidental."[6] And yet, although a fervent abolitionist, Sellin admitted that a death penalty statute, if states insisted on one, must include a "recklessness so great as to manifest extreme or callous indifference to the value of human life."[7]

Whichever side you take on capital punishment, depraved callousness really deserves to be punished most severely. "Shouldn't have gotten in the way of my bullet," another spray shooter sneered, curling his lip while referring to an innocent victim he'd permanently paralyzed.

In *Enmund,* when the court stopped Florida from executing the getaway car driver who neither killed nor intended that anybody die, four Supreme Court dissenters, per Justice Sandra Day O'Connor, refused to second-guess Florida's punishment. Enmund's death penalty was not "grossly disproportionate" to the two deaths he helped produce, however unintentionally. But the majority emphasized that because Enmund did not intend to kill, he could not deserve to die. Using retribution to *limit* punishment, they ignored depraved recklessness, seemingly making intent a constitutional prerequisite for death as punishment.[8] Until *Tison.*

The Tison brothers somehow smuggled a chest full of guns into a prison and sprung their father along with another convicted murderer. When the escape party's car broke down, passing good Samaritans stopped to offer assistance. The brothers helped rob the victims, then stood by as their father and the other convict they had sprung killed the family. Apparently the brothers never intended these victims' deaths—they both claimed to be surprised by the shooting.[9]

A jury and judge sentenced them to die anyway. Under *Enmund*, it seemed, there must be proof of intent to kill before a felony murderer could be executed. Attacking felony murder itself as a "living fossil" while citing *Enmund*, four dissenting justices in *Tison v. Arizona* would forbid capitally punishing reckless killings "if we are to retain the . . . moral culpability on which criminal justice depends."[10] These dissenters obviously missed a moral fact.

A majority, 5–4, affirmed the Tison brothers' death sentence. *Enmund* had dealt with two extreme situations, Justice O'Connor, a dissenter in *Enmund*, explained for a new majority. A state could not execute "a minor actor in an armed robbery, not on the scene," who did not intend to kill. "*Enmund* also clearly dealt with the other polar case: The felony murderer who actually intended to kill." States could definitely execute these criminals. The Tison brothers fell into neither category. "Some non-intentional murderers may be among the most dangerous and inhumane of all—the person who tortures another not caring whether the victim lives or dies, or the robber who shoots someone in the course of the robbery, utterly indifferent" to the victim's fate. "This reckless indifference to the value of human life may be every bit as shocking to the moral sense as an intent to kill." Thus, *Tison* held that "major participation in the felony combined with reckless indifference to human life" can be as blameworthy as intent.[11]

The Tisons did deserve to die, but Enmund, the getaway driver, did not. What of Enmund's co-felons, Sampson and Jeanette Armstrong, who robbed and did intentionally kill their victims? The Armstrongs had gone to the Kerseys' back door, requesting water for their overheated car. When Mr. Kersey came out of the house, Sampson Armstrong grabbed him, pointed a gun at him, and told Jeannette Armstrong to take his money. Mr. Kersey cried for help, and his wife ran outside with a shotgun, shooting and wounding Jeannette. Sampson Armstrong then shot and killed the Kerseys, dragged them into their kitchen, took their money, and fled. The victims had resisted and paid with their lives.[12]

"I don't look to hurt you, but I would if I have to," Johnny Allen explained about his reputation on the street as a "thorough" stickup man. "If

I went into a joint, and I see a guy pull a pistol, then it's me or him. But coming into a joint and we got all the money and then just shoot someone, it's wrong, and it's stupid."

"Why is it wrong?"

"If someone's cooperating with you, why should you hurt him? They didn't do anything to you other than what you say. Another thing about stickup. Most times, someone's going to see you. Shooting him only make the police search harder for you."

Johnny had moved smoothly from "wrong" back to "stupid" to kill a guy who doesn't buck a stickup. Street criminals get very slippery. What seems at first like morality or principle quickly dissolves into practical expediency. Why restrict it to street criminals? Probe most people's business or personal ethics and at some level, what's "right" works, what's "wrong" doesn't. Philosophers and anthropologists have long located the origins of morality itself in efficacy.

I pressed Johnny. What made it morally worse to kill an unresisting victim? "You're wrong because there's got to be a reason. If you taking money and he buck, saying, 'It's mine; I'm not letting you take it'—man this is work time! You doing your profession—so that's why that ain't wrong. You're a lawyer. If you defending a case, you know it's your duty to win the case. Well when I do stickup, it's my obligation to get paid. I *got* to take this. I don't want to have to kill this guy, but if it comes to it, I will. I'm hoping he will say, 'OK, I'll make some more later.' If he's smart he won't fuck with a pistol. Then he's being the fool. I got a shotgun and you telling me, 'No'? If you come at *me* with a gun, I'm going to give it up. I might catch you tomorrow, but I'm going to give it up right then. It's foolish, it's foolish to buck a guy with a gun."

Ironically, states that limit the capital felony murder doctrine still consider it an *aggravating* circumstance that the robber intentionally killed to overcome a victim's resistance. But the old-timers confirmed Johnny's point: It was much worse to kill an *unresisting* victim than one who "bucked" a stickup.

"You stick up a guy. He hands over his wallet, and the robber still shoots him right in the face?" I asked.

"If it's cut and dried like that—pull the switch on him," declared David "Itchy" Brooks. "Give him his juice."

"Suppose he's got a shotgun under the counter you didn't know about, and he pulls it?"

"He's foolish." Itchy shook his head.

"He doesn't deserve to die," I countered.

"No, but I don't deserve to die, neither. Not for a robbery."

"But for killing him?"

"It's still on the level of robbery. When *he* pulls the shotgun, he's elevated it from money to life. Once he's made that choice, it's out of my hands."

Was Itchy claiming self-defense?

"Not according to the law, but to me it would be self-defense. And I didn't really want to do that. I had no problem with killing somebody I thought was a threat to me: I just didn't want it to be about their money. I didn't want to be wrong in doing it."

"Wrong?"

"I definitely knew the difference between right and wrong," Itchy insisted. "At least I made that distinction. Some people deserved to die and some people didn't. And a guy didn't deserve to die trying to protect what was his. And that's why I drifted into bank robbery. Because it was safe for everybody. All the employees instructed to give up that money: 'Don't create a situation where somebody gets hurt, and then we get sued out of more than they took in the bank anyway.' So when you know that—I mean if it's money you want, where do *you* go? Where it is. So if they're *instructed* to give it up if you get the drop—that was the ideal situation for me. To present the pistol to them, get the money and go on about my business."

7

THE LIVING LEGEND

THE FIRST TIME I SAW ITCHY BROOKS, HE SINGLE-handedly kept in check a mob of prisoners. Johnny had gleefully broken off our interviews to see the prison fights. The captain assigned two unhappy lieutenants to escort me into the gym by a side door. These "white shirts" stood on either side of me, right near the door, about 20 feet from the ring, our backs pressed against the gym wall. My eyes swept the gym, packed to the rafters and pulsing with energy—ivory walls and a cheering ebony mass. I noticed prisoners dressed in sweatshirts up in the balcony of this stifling hot gym. Johnny had taught me: If you're on a mission to kill, a sweatshirt covers your weapon; if you fear you're a target, that sweatshirt covers a stab vest made of magazines. The officers next to me fidgeted.

On the floor level, 50 feet away, a flimsy, eight-foot-high, unanchored picket fence separated us from hundreds of prisoners pressing toward Lorton's makeshift boxing ring, a padded canvas square stretched with ropes. One man alone restrained the surging mob behind the fence's widely spaced wooden slats and wire. A prisoner dashed around the fence and bolted toward the ring. Itchy, his muscular frame pushing back against the mob, roughly grabbed the guy and threw him behind the fence back into the crowd. As skirmishes broke out, I watched that fence, inch by inch, scraping along the floor toward us. The officers on either side of me obviously didn't like what they saw. I wished the captain had allowed Johnny to be here with me, to vouch for his professor friend. Everywhere I looked in the yellow light, eyes stared at me.

A swath slowly snaked through the ground-level crush. Itchy allowed the fence to curl back. Johnny Allen wheeled his chair just on our side of the fence. I tried to catch his eye. The crowd roared at a knockdown, and the fence spurted a few inches toward us. Itchy fought a losing battle to hold back the tide. When the guards on either side of me became openly agitated, I instinctively bolted to Johnny's side, barely five feet from the mass of prisoners. I knelt beside Johnny in the wheelchair, and we watched the bout end when the timekeeper struck a "gong"—a piece of iron—with a large screwdriver. Johnny laughed as he noticed who fought next. "That guy got the worst heroin habit in this joint. He's not going to even raise his arms the last round, if it get that far." Sure enough, after a strong first round, and a back-and-forth second, the guy got beaten to a pulp in the third, while Johnny belly-slapped the chair. We laughed and watched the fights together, next to the fence, which reached us and stopped.

"You know, Rob, you done a smart thing coming to me like that," Johnny told me the next morning before our first interview. "The guys all seen it." That day Johnny introduced me to Itchy: David Leon Brooks, the "living legend."

A thick scar snaked Itchy's neck. Years before, three prisoners armed with a knife, an ice pick, and a razor had attacked Itchy, unarmed and naked in the shower. Within a minute, two of his attackers lay dead or dying while the third fled. Itchy, all slashed up, his head hanging by a thread, nearly bled to death on the shower floor.

Since then, no one inside tested Itchy. Those scars and the legendary story behind them made it unnecessary for him to prove himself again.

As Lorton's boxing coach, David Itchy Brooks controlled the gym. He also controlled the law library. A rare combination of toughness and smarts, Itchy demanded that every youngster on the boxing team learn enough law to be involved with his own case. And anybody who got into a brawl, Itchy immediately suspended from the team. "Boxing's not fighting," he insisted. "I'm teaching you how to box, not how to fight." The thick scar testified that Itchy Brooks knew the difference.

I asked Itchy, the jailhouse lawyer, about *Enmund.* "You never know when robbery's going to turn to murder," he explained. "Felony murder carried an automatic death penalty back then. Most guys knew that, but it never made any difference 'cause nobody never saw themselves in that position."

While robbers routinely fail to anticipate that a stickup might turn into murder, the felony murder rule also ensnared guys who never anticipated the robbery itself. "I'll give it to you straight," said Willie M., 47, who had already served 19 years of his 20-to-life. "I took my brother to a store. I didn't know he was going to rob. I wasn't part of it, but when my brother got into my car, *then* I became a part of it. He shot the victim and got away from the scene. It was my car, so the police came looking for me for felony murder. I didn't do anything to be charged with murder. I'm naïve about the law at this time."

"Did you know he was armed?"

"No. We traveled in different circles. He was more with the dope fiends; I dealt with a different crowd. I didn't know he was carrying [a gun]."

"Weren't you pissed at your brother?"

"I was more than pissed. I had no knowledge he was going to rob anybody. I can deal with that part. But for him to shoot somebody and they end up dying, and then I'm implicated in a murder. Yeah, I'm highly pissed with my brother. My mother told me the police came to the house looking for me. So I turned myself in. If I didn't kill anybody, then I didn't need to worry about it. We got separate court-appointed lawyers. So I told my lawyer what happened. They don't believe you. To them it's a formality. So I got charged with felony murder."

"Was your brother trying to cut you off the beef? [release you from the charge]"

"No. He said he wasn't there! When you thinking about yourself, it's hard to think about somebody else."

"Did you offer to take a lie detector test?"

"I took a paraffin test to show I ain't fire no gun. They don't care. With felony murder you can get everybody in the car. All of them guilty, whether they killed or not. They ain't worried about whether or not I shot him—that's irrelevant. They going to try to put me with the robbery. And if I'm guilty to the robbery, then I got the murder charge automatically. They severed our trials. Once he got 10-to–30 for second-degree murder, they offered me to cop [plead guilty] to second-degree murder. But I wasn't copping to something I didn't do. I expected to be convicted as an accessory-after-the-fact. So I go to trial. They found me guilty of felony murder. I got 20-to-life. I never killed no one. But somehow I'm guilty of murder in the first degree.

"They were using felony murder to get as many black guys as they could off the street," Willie continued. "Whether you participated or not, the fact that you were there prior to the killing allowed them to give you the murder. The more the merrier. Come on, I mean, I ain't no lawyer. But I ain't crazy either. It defies logic. But that's how it is. I'm mad, but I can't let it eat me away in the inside. And there's no point in being bitter."

I found that difficult to believe. "What did you say to your brother?"

"He was in the feds when I come down here. And I told my mother, 'If he come in here, I'm going to kill him.' Then older guys like Itchy talked to me. 'Man, your brother was scared.' They made sense. If I do something to him, is that going to change my sentence? I come out better trying to research the law and find out where they made some mistakes."

Willie told his story with more resignation than bitterness. I think he told me the truth. What had he to gain by lying? He knew I would do nothing on his behalf. That was the deal with everyone: "Be honest with me. Whatever you tell me, I won't hurt you. But I won't help you. Even if you're innocent." Looking back on it, I wish I had told Willie I believed in his innocence. He probably would not have cared, but it would have made me feel better.

"Young at the time," explained Anthony P. "Three of us in a car. Two guys went there to buy marijuana. They robbed him, killed him. That's how we all got murder first degree."

"When did you know they had killed the guy?"

"I heard gunshots ring out. Then they come back to the car. I didn't know at the time the guy had died."

"Did you know they were armed when you went with them?"

"No. When I left my home my intentions was to buy marijuana. I didn't even know they were going to rob him."

"Did it cross your mind they might rob?"

"No. I was very upset. At the time I was in the DC National Guard, just back from basic training."

"Had you been hustling before then?"

"As a kid. Shoplifting or possession of marijuana. No hard-core crime."

"So just one day you were out with a bunch of friends—"

"I only knew one of them; the other guy was a friend of his."

Facing a first-degree murder charge with the shooter ready to falsely implicate him to lighten his own sentence, although he was innocent, Anthony pled guilty to second-degree murder, another victim of the felony murder rule.

I heard a dozen variations on this same tale. "We were coming from a party at a Go-Go, and we had been drinking, riding around about four o'clock in the morning," explained Lenny E. about his felony murder. "They say he went to rob, and the gun went off. I was in the car, and I stepped out to see what was going on. I asked him, 'What you shoot the man for?' He said, 'Come on man, let's go.'"

"Had you done stickup?"

"Never. Never. This wasn't a planned thing. It's just something that happened. So I went to trial and got found guilty. Because if you commit a capital offense and I'm with you, but I'm not with the killing, I get what you get. I think that's wrong. I'm going to get the death penalty with you. I went to trial first. My attorney wanted me to take a cop and testify against him, but I wasn't going to do that. You don't tell."

The felony murder rule ensnared a shocking number of innocents, especially in the inner city. These guys did not come close to qualifying as the worst of the worst. Yet because of the legal fiction and the code of "no snitching," in the eyes of the law, they had committed first-degree murder. My time inside Lorton quickly confirmed it: We must abolish capital felony murder if we have any hope of reserving the punishment of death for those who deserve to die.

Stickup guys intentionally killing their unresisting victims to eliminate them as witnesses should still qualify for the death penalty. Roughly half the death penalty jurisdictions in the United States today do make a person death eligible for killing a witness. "They almost have to," Itchy said pragmatically, "to keep other witnesses testifying. But then the death penalty might be what makes people kill witnesses. So they're putting the cart in front of the horse. Because he's thinking, 'If I kill somebody here and you witnessed it, and I already got a possibility of getting the death penalty, why not kill you too?' The death penalty will do that. Life without parole will do that. Because if you getting the death penalty, and you already killed a person, what's the difference between killing one and two? Society is setting witnesses up, for real," Itchy concluded, pointing out the irony inherent in this death penalty aggravator designed to keep witnesses alive.

Carefully picking his spots at night, Joe W., a convicted murderer in his late 30s, went to great lengths to make certain there would be no witnesses. But, he conceded, you could never be certain.

"A guy who happens to be wandering down the street. He's just an innocent bystander and a victim of circumstance. Does he go too?" I asked.

"Of course. Why you going to leave him alive knowing he can be damaging to you? In all honesty, if I kill a person and this person done witnessed it, he's going."

"In spite of the fact he did nothing to you?"

"He's not doing anything to me *then*, but later on he's going to do something real damaging that cause me to spend life in the penitentiary. If I let him go, he's going to hurt me down the road, and I'm not going to take that chance."

Joe's attitude typified the younger, savvy street criminal. Although Itchy too displayed a selfish, rational, calculating attitude, emphasizing caution with careful planning, he emphatically condemned robbers who killed innocent people who *might* testify. "You're supposed to go in there in such a way that a witness doesn't know who to tell on," Itchy insisted. "Some places we robbed you could not come in with a mask on, so I would do a makeup job in the parking lot. Melt a chocolate bar and put it on my face like it's a scar. It's still damp and flexible enough so if I change my expression it's not going to break off. I'd take the foil inside candy or cigarettes and make a gold tooth. Make sure the person sees that. Rub the chocolate on my bottom teeth—make it look like they're decayed. Then I would put on glasses. A person may remember the scar on my face, the gold tooth in my mouth, they may remember the decayed teeth—but that will be all they remember because from the time I pull the gun, their focus is on the gun. Believe me, they don't take their eyes off that gun for any reason.

"When you hustle you take gambles. And when you get caught you take what comes behind it." No disguise, however, protects the robber against a special kind of witness: Your co-felon could always cut a deal and give you up. For Itchy there was nothing worse than a snitch.

"A long time ago, in the Atlanta Penitentiary, I had to stab a guy," Itchy recalled. "I hit him in the bathroom, then I went back out and stood by the police with a book in my hand. They brought the guy out on the stretcher right by me. Bubbles of blood coming out of his nose, so I knew his lung was punctured. He looked up and saw me. Spat blood on me. No one really knew why he did that.

"So he got to the hospital. And the doctor told him, 'There's nothing we can do for you; all you can do now is let us know who did it.' You know what the guy told the doctor? 'Your mammy did it.' He knew he was going to die but that was that. You just don't tell. Under no circumstances. If a guy stabs me, if I'm on my dying bed, I'm not going to tell on him. I'm going to hope that I live so I get him back. Even if he did me dirty. It doesn't make any difference. He's off it."

"Do you want to pass this Code on to your children?"

"Definitely not. Because I don't want them to have this lifestyle." Itchy paused and then made the crucial moral distinction that Joseph W. denied: "I don't blame you if *you* take the stand on somebody. Because you don't have these same principles—these nonserving principles that I've adopted as my own. You haven't committed yourself to this. Whatever you have chosen to be about, once you make your choice, I think you should stick by the Code."

"But if the innocent victim of a robbery happens to look out his window—"

"You expect him to tell," said Itchy. "It's their job; they got to do that. I'm supposed to go in there in such a way that he doesn't know who to tell on if it comes to telling. Like I said, I don't blame you for taking the stand. Because you haven't adopted my principles. So I wouldn't be thinking about killing you. The only people you expect to honor the Code are people who make an agreement that 'this is what I'm going to do. This is my lifestyle. And I'm going to do all the things that go with it.' I don't believe in betrayal. I mean betrayal of any kind."

Where did this value system come from?

"I was raised that way," said "Ducky" J., smiling, as he recalled it. "When I was seven, we were over at my uncle's house. The next day we all going to a picnic. And one of my uncles stuck his hand in one of them sweet potato pies.

"'Who put their hand in this pie?' my grandfather asked. He come to each; I was the youngest. 'Who put their hand in that pie?' 'I don't know. I don't know. Not me.' 'Who put their hand in that pie?!' When my grandfather got to my cousin next older than me, my cousin pointed to my uncle.

"'If you don't tell, I don't know who done it,' my grandfather said. 'I can't give nobody the beef. But now you already told who done it. So for doing that, *you* going to get the punishment.' Everybody else was clear. So it gave me that 'Don't never tell, regardless whatever the situation is. Don't never tell.'"

But most of the younger street criminals seemed entirely unrestrained by any morality except selfishness. They killed unresisting victims to eliminate them as potential witnesses, and once caught, they snitched to save themselves. "They tell all in the police car. Don't even wait till they get you to the station," Itchy lamented. Itchy himself lived his commitment to the Code. "I'm here for something I didn't do," he said almost matter-of-factly about his conviction for murdering a man he never met in a place he never was. "I knew who did it. And I could have told. It's too late now." He sighed and continued. "I don't regret that, but I feel like a fool."

"Why?"

"I know he wouldn't have done that for me, if our positions had been reversed."

"I thought it doesn't matter whether he would do it for you. You're doing it to honor the Code." Of course, ultimately all moral codes do confer advantage, at least to the communities within which they operate.

"Right. But every now and then you reevaluate your principles to see if they're serving you. But I still come to that conclusion in spite of everything. I'm never testifying against anybody. Never. If it costs my life, then that's it. It's a foregone conclusion." And then, too, the moral corollary that goes along with no snitching: Someone who snitches has to go.

"Is it OK to snitch on somebody who's dead?"

"Yeah," Itchy explained. "A dead man takes all the weight. If you're in a robbery, and a guy gets killed, he did everything. Everything is supposed to be about saving the living and let the dead be dead."

In the street, it made it easier to kill an "innocent" witness, when you see him as no different than a snitch. "You keep calling them 'innocent witnesses,'" Ricky B. complained. "But they don't become 'innocent' after they see it—and decide to tell. They become hostile to whoever committed the crime. If I knew—not now, but back then when I was young and silly—if I knew that I can get the death penalty, and I knew that this person saw me, you think I would leave that person alive to testify?"

Those like Itchy, however, who know that it is wrong to kill people over their own property, also believed it doubly wrong to kill an unresisting robbery victim or any other innocent witness. Mask down or makeup and take your chances.

A robber, of course, can minimize the odds of victims later testifying against him by sticking up those who settle it themselves. "Robbing a drug dealer, I didn't have to worry about anybody telling on me; the only problem I'd have is dealing with him," Leon R. explained.

Drug dealers have little patience for those who rob them. "Guys that do stickup are the lazy dudes that don't feel like going out and hustle to get money," complained Carlos H. "So they go stick up a dude after he hustle all day. Nobody like no stickup boys."

Least of all, Ronald D. Johnny Allen respected "Young Ron": brave, bold, and "about something," rare these days for a young drug lieutenant on the strip. "If anyone take dope or money from my runners, if I don't straighten it right away, other people going to do the same thing," Ron explained. "If I just say, 'I'm not going to kill nobody, I'm just going to sell dope,' I wouldn't last two days. Every time my dope get on the strip they would take it. Simple as that. They would just outright take it from whoever had it, or if I had it, they would take it from me.

"So if somebody robbed me, they ain't got a chance of going to jail. I'm going to settle that one myself. Once I established myself, that's the way I had to carry it. There was no backing back. The money was not the issue. It was the principle about them taking something from me, knowing that I wouldn't take from them. And the guys that are doing the taking, they know the consequences. They know it's kill or be killed when you come after them about taking your stuff. That's understood."

Ironic. Most states allow the victim to kill a robber to stop the robbery or prevent his escape. That's fully justifiable and legal. Yet some of those same states classify a "drug-related" killing *in retaliation* or to prevent other future robberies as capital murder—the worst of all possible crimes.

8

UNDER THE INFLUENCE

AS CRACK COCAINE FLOODED THE INNER CITIES IN THE
1980s, homicide rates soared. Some death penalty states adopted three new
aggravators, often interrelated—drive-by, gang, and drug-related murder—
to make these killers death eligible. When rival drug gangs compete for turf,
lives and livelihoods are at stake. Killing competitors becomes the norm.
Guys in the life on both sides of the gun accept and expect it as part of the
game. Everyone involved knows, as Joe W. explained, "drugs breed bodies."
Surely, then, although some states make these "drug-related murders" death
eligible, killing those who choose to play this deadly game should not by
itself count as the worst of the worst.

Drugs do take their toll. In a series of post-*Furman* decisions, the US
Supreme Court has insisted that juries consider all relevant mitigating cir-
cumstances that might lead them to spare a convicted murderer facing death.
If he killed when he was high, did that killing qualify as "drug-related"?
Should being "under the influence" matter?

We retributivists ultimately punish the killer's attitude. As Kant said,
"the only purely evil thing is an evil will."[1] Many of us insist that a killer high
on drugs still knows what he's doing and can control himself. "I say kill him,"
declared Leo Simms, a hopelessly hooked heroin addict and hard-liner on
the death penalty. "I've been shooting drugs all my life and I ain't never
killed. I mean even though it's a must behind me trying to get the drugs, I'm
aware of what I'm doing. I'm not so fogged up that I can use that as a reason
for taking your life. That don't excuse me from the death penalty." Others
insist that being high could conceivably mitigate (where it does not eliminate) a killer's intent to kill. In capital punishment states that accept *Tison*'s invitation and include extreme recklessness, does a killer's intoxication

diminish his callous or "depraved indifference" to human life? What does a killer know, how does he feel when he kills "under the influence"?

I asked them.

"You know what you are doing under heroin," Reginald B. agreed, explaining its effects on him as a terrified young soldier facing combat in Vietnam. "Heroin detached me from that fear. I knew danger was there, but I was totally numb to it. I could function, but I was detached from what I was doing."

Heroin also numbs combat veterans of the inner-city streets to their day-to-day life, detaching them from fear but leaving them knowing and choosing what they do. Crack, however, was "something else."

"'Rock'—crack cocaine—opened it up, changed the whole game," explained Jerry G., aka Big Foot. "That craving is so bad. People do anything to get that drug. Set you up; rob. Anything. A girl let young guys piss on her for crack."

"Just to get a piece of rock to put in that pipe," Charlie W. agreed with disgust and pity. "Women suck dogs' dicks. That's what they call 'a show.' A broad you been after and could never get to. All of a sudden you got a rock and she want it: 'Alright, Bitch, there's Spot. . . .'"

"I smoked cocaine," explained Itchy, who did not touch drugs until his early 40s. "The paranoia that the drug produced made me a time bomb for real. It made me think everybody was trying to do something to me. Nobody could say or do nothing without me interpreting it as some kind of plot. And then being exposed to a lot of people who *were* trying to do something, it was just a bad result."

Crack: a vicious drug that caused bad behavior, all agreed. But "boat"—marijuana soaked in PCP—a hallucinatory drug of choice on the streets and inside Lorton Central, produced even worse consequences. Under PCP, users report feeling paranoid *and* omnipotent: Everybody is out to get you while nobody can stop you.

"You don't know what you going to do next," explained Robert S. "In my mind, I thought what I was doing was right; I was conscious of what I was doing, but if I wasn't high, I wouldn't have did that."

"They're responsible," Ricky B. agreed. "You know you going to do something crazy. Exactly what? You don't know. But that's why you want to smoke it: 'Man, let me smoke this PCP and see what it going to make me do.' I did crazy things. Things I wouldn't do if I wouldn't smoke boat. I knew I was doing it. But I didn't fear the police coming, or anybody. I didn't care. It don't have you caring about nothing."

"But you *were* aware of what you were doing?"

"Yeah, I was aware. But another time, me and my girl smoked some boat. I took all my money, thinking everybody around me was poor and I'm the only one who got money. So I just started throwing it up in the air."

Some users disagree. "I've smoked PCP. From the moment that I smoked it to the moment that I came back," Silvester K. declared, "a lot of things that happened I wasn't conscious [of]. I was with my best friend and he wouldn't lie to me. 'Man you were real hostile.' And I don't remember any of this stuff. And that scared me to the point where I said, 'Hell, that ain't for me.' I never went back to it. But some people don't really know that they be out of control."

"When somebody kills under the influence of crack or PCP, should that save his life?" I asked.

"If he's responsible for taking the drug, then he's responsible for what comes as a result of that," Itchy insisted. Then he hesitated. "I don't know, maybe in some cases. But how would you know which ones were which? Because if a person's been high before, and he knows that this makes him like that, he's responsible for everything he does under the influence of it." Itchy paused, then reflected aloud. "But suppose it's the first time that he had this experience under it?"

As Itchy reconsidered it, the biblical responsibility for a goring ox, but only if the owner knows it has gored before, popped into my head. I broke a long silence. "The law puts the burden of persuasion on the defendant for mitigating circumstances. If he can show that he had no prior experience with this drug or its effects on him, would you allow it to mitigate capital murder?"

"Yeah, I would," said Itchy. "But the burden should definitely be on him. And it would be almost impossible for him to prove."

Drug-using street criminals by and large agreed: Except for crack and boat, drugs don't make a different person. They loosen inhibitions, amplify a personality, make character more manifest and clear. Or as one addict explained, "It takes you where you want to go, only more so." In most cases, the killer knows what he's doing when he kills or at least knows he may do anything as he gets high. Sometimes, though, PCP and crack do destroy your perception or control. Retributively, the mitigation of killing "under the influence" should only exempt from death those killings unreflective of the killer's true personality. He must show the drug-induced killing was out of character and also that he did not suspect the drug's likely effects. If he did suspect what he might do, then by taking the drug, he displays his depraved indifference to the consequences of his own behavior.

The "under the influence" mitigation, then, should mostly fail. But not always. With shame and self-contempt, Mickey R. recalled his own unforgivable and near-tragic behavior while high on PCP: "My sister was carrying her firstborn. I tried to kick the baby out of her stomach. She was hollering at me about something. And I just started beating her. Kicking her and just beating her and beating her. When you out on drugs, you don't want nobody to talk to you; you don't listen to nobody or nothing. You don't try to understand people's situations or circumstances. I always try to make up for what I did then. Our mother and father is dead. She's my mother now, and I'm her father. So we the best of friends. But if something had happened to that little boy. . . ."

Walter G. somberly recalled his "voluntary" manslaughter. "I had gone to my friend's apartment. I was under PCP and using cocaine. We sitting watching the football game together. At the half he went in to take a shower. After he gone, I walk in the kitchen, see a butcher knife sitting in the sink. And I grab it. It was dark. When I come back in the living room, I sit back down, and put the knife on the table next to me. He come out in a bathrobe and the next thing I know he's on the floor, balled up, saying, 'Why you do this to me?' 'Why I do what?' I gave him the phone. He dialed 911 and said, 'I've been stabbed.' Then he started vomiting blood out his mouth. So I'm prancing around his house. It's like I went into a blackout with myself. He told me to leave. I got in my car and went home. When I got to my house, I paused, looked up to the sky, wondering, 'What have I done?'

"The next morning, I got my head together. So I call his house. He wasn't there. I start calling the hospitals. George Washington University Hospital said this man has been discharged. I'm thinking he home. I call his house again. The phone kept ringing. So then I called the DC morgue. And there he was. I was afraid of myself. Why had I killed someone that hadn't done wrong to me? I never had no brother. He was like a brother to me."

Paranoia-inducing drugs such as PCP and crack diminish self-control, distort perception, and can move people to kill "for no reason." One remorseful soul who demanded to remain nameless destroyed the relationship with the woman he loved when he smoked PCP and then put her young child in the oven to cook like a turkey.

"Progressives" or "libertarians" who insist we legalize drugs across the board strike me as dangerously naïve. I'm all for decriminalizing pot. But we should continue to ban and severely punish the manufacture and sale of PCP and crack, which regularly turn users into paranoid, vicious predators. Besides, robbers and burglars who switched to dealing drugs for bigger rewards give the lie to those who claim that taking the profit from narcotics will automatically reduce violent crime. Make their product legal, these drug dealers assured me, and they will switch back to stickup. But, assuming it went down as Mickey and Walter described—and they had no reason to lie about it—sometimes killing under the influence is just that: killing under the influence.

9

PLATE SIN WITH GOLD

WHEN THEY ENACT CAPITAL ROBBERY-MURDER STAT-
utes, legislatures wrongly assume that all armed robbers with loaded guns
come prepared to kill. And if death results in the course of that robbery, the
felony murderer therefore killed from a "pecuniary motive."

Most street crime does stem from a pecuniary motive. Criminals themselves readily acknowledge this, but they claim this motive as universal.
"Hustling is all about preying on somebody," Itchy insisted with characteristic cynicism. "But so is a lot of other things they call 'legitimate.' We're in
a world that's centered around power related to violence. And violence gets
you what you want. So that's what we use. In the straight world it's still a
system of preying. It's just using your mind instead of your muscle. The
lawyer, the doctor, it's a con game; it's no different."

I couldn't let that pass. "What's the doctor's con?"

"The money he gets from the insurance. He sees your gall bladder as
a new car; your tonsils as a suit. You ain't got to have tonsil problems; he'll
take them out cause that's a ring his wife wanted. It might seem warped to a
person who's never looked at it from that angle, but that's what's happening.
People preying on people. Doing the same thing we're doing. They just got
different methods.

"I don't think they should be mad at me for playing my con," Itchy continued, "if I'm not mad at them for playing theirs. I try to get off as cheap
as I can in dealing with their con. And when they deal with mine, they got
to try to get off as cheap as they can. I know I'm at a disadvantage when
I'm playing by their rules. And they've got to understand that they're at a
disadvantage when they're playing by mine. I'm hustling you; you hustling
me. Only difference is, the law doesn't frown on your kind of hustling—it
just frowns on mine."

On the streets and inside prisons—everywhere—prisoners see confirmation of universal selfishness and indifference. As Itchy said, "Everybody's looking for an edge." Morality boils down to prudence: doing it well, getting away with it; right and wrong labeled by whoever is in power.

A "thief snatches a loaf from the baker's counter," declared George Bernard Shaw, and "they promptly run [him] into jail. Another man snatches bread from the tables of hundreds of widows and orphans," and they run him into Parliament.[1] This moral relativism takes us back to the Sophists.

Were these convicted thieves inside Lorton any worse than Enron executives who secretly cashed out their own stock options while counseling lower-ranking employees to keep pouring their life savings into the failing company's stock? Over and over, prisoners evaded all moral responsibility for their crimes by insisting, "I'm no worse than you: Everybody's doing the same thing—you just give it a different name." And most of the time it annoyed me to hear it, although I know all too well how the system favors powerful people who commit electronic thefts and swindles, or "lobby"—of course that's not bribery—with heavy "campaign contributions" and take their cut for using their clout.

I taught 12 prisoners, mostly convicted murderers, about the social contract that brings us all from a state of nature—that "war of all against all" as Hobbes's *Leviathan* famously described the inner-city streets 350 years ago, where life is "solitary, poor, nasty, brutish, and short."[2] Standard political theory has us driven into a state of society to gain protection and justice in exchange for obedience. One student raised his hand respectfully, although we had agreed to chime in at will. "You say we all promise to obey the law if society protect us?"

I nodded. "That's the social contract."

"Well coming up, society never protected me or mine. My little sister got shot up walking home from school. My mom can't go on the street at night. Everybody knew we was subject to getting beaten or robbed or shot at any time. In the house or on the street. Cops ain't do shit about none of it. So according to that, we don't have no obligation from the start to obey the law. Unless I misunderstand."

Recalling my time investigating corruption, forgetting where I was this moment, I began to concede their attack on double standards and hypocrisy. "When I was a special prosecutor—"

"You were what?" Silence. Itchy, Leo, and Johnny knew my background. But the younger guys thought of me as "Johnny's lawyer." Now it struck them full in the face. I was the enemy.

"A prosecutor," one convict snarled. Then he grinned: "You're the Man." A hostile silence filled the room. Here they were, 12 black street criminals, mostly murderers, serving life sentences, alone with a white prosecutor. Two of them glared at me. Then everybody looked around, sizing up the situation. Without a word spoken, they were choosing sides, calculating costs and benefits. Was it worth killing me?

Itchy's jaw tightened. His face wore a cold, detached look I had never seen before. Itchy shifted slightly toward me and shrugged. His eyes said, *Do what you gotta do but if you kill him, you gotta kill me too.* Leo always backed Itchy. Johnny had been released from prison so he wasn't there. Pete Arnold puffed up, putting up a good front, still grateful I had surprised him by showing up to watch him deliver a graduation speech as valedictorian at the University of District of Columbia, Lorton. That made it at least 9–3. A couple of other guys I hoped might side with us or walk away from it. But I was scared as my jury looked around at each other, deciding whether to kill me.

"You were a prosecutor?" another guy demanded, his voice dripping with hatred and contempt. "Yes." I gulped. "A special prosecutor. We prosecuted corrupt cops, judges, and lawyers." "Oh yeah? You *prosecuted* judges, and lawyers? And *police?* That's something else, man," he said and high fived me. The tension broke. I'll never be sure whether this gave them the face-saving excuse to avoid confronting Itchy. I do know I gave thanks that moment for "foolishly" declining the offer from the Manhattan district attorney's office, instead choosing to become a special prosecutor.

Itchy and I got closer over the years, as we peeled back layers of his extraordinary life, worthy of a screenplay. How could I hate a man who now spent his days inside Lorton striving to keep young prisoners and other at-risk inner-city kids from repeating his mistakes? And yet when he was 19 years old, decades before I met him, Itchy, David Leon Brooks by his own account, shot 57 people in the street. How many had he killed? "I didn't stay long enough to find out." The past counts. Sometimes I had to repeat it to myself to fully believe it. Especially after Itchy saved my life inside the classroom that night.

That moment passed, and we continued to explore the social contract. They loved John Locke's famous line: "Great Robbers punish little ones but the great ones are rewarded with laurels and triumphs."[3] And they ate up Shakespeare's passage from *King Lear:*

A man with no eyes may see how this world goes
See how justice rails upon a simple thief,

Change places, and which is the justice,
Which is the thief?
Plate sin with gold
And the strongest lance of justice breaks;
Arm it in rags, a pygmy's straw will pierce it.
None does offend, none, I say, none.[4]

Little as I wanted to hear it from them in this prison setting, earlier that day, I had made their exact point to my own criminal law class: With relatively few exceptions, the system not only protects its great thieves, it shelters some of its most depraved killers.

Barry Kibbe saw a guy in a bar, obviously drunk, flashing hundred-dollar bills. Kibbe offered the victim a ride, stripped him of his money, and left him on the side of a snowy winding road, a quarter of a mile from a lit gas station. George Stafford, the victim, crawled out into the middle of the road where a speeding truck ran over him. Convicted of depraved indifference murder—he could just as easily have been convicted of felony murder—Kibbe appealed, claiming that Stafford himself, or the truck that ran him over, had caused the victim's death. Affirming Kibbe's murder conviction, however, New York's highest court declared Kibbe criminally liable for murder as long as "the ultimate harm should have been foreseen as being reasonably related to the acts of the accused."[5] The ultimate harm, Stafford's death, was foreseeably related to leaving him drunk on the side of a snowy road at night.

A few years later, ranking corporate executives of Warner Lambert Inc. knew that explosive levels of magnesium stearate dust endangered their employees' lives. The vice president of operations and the director of plant safety deliberately ignored insurance company warnings and allowed several machines to continue to operate dangerously, instructing employees to wear masks when the dust cloud got too thick.[6] TV viewers may remember Freshen-Up chewing gum for that liquid center that went "ping" in the ads. But the employees inside the Warner Lambert plant found themselves trapped in a fiery inferno when a machine issued a spark that caused an explosion, killing six and burning more than 40 others.

The New York Court of Appeals had denounced Kibbe, the robber, for his depravity and supported punishing him as a murderer even though he did not intend to kill because the "ultimate harm"—the victim's death, whether by freezing or truck—"was foreseeably related" to his leaving the helpless victim on the side of the road. The Warner Lambert executives consciously risked scores of lives and killed six helpless employees. But when a grand jury indicted these callous executives on six counts of manslaughter, this same New York high court stepped in and *dismissed the indictment*, refusing to allow it to go to trial! Although the Court of Appeals had held that Kibbe caused *his* victim's death as long as the ultimate harm was foreseeably related to the acts of the accused, with a straight face, that same court now held that even if the defendants had acted with criminally reckless minds, no jury could possibly find these executives had *caused* their employees deaths!

Years before that, Ford Motor Company executives had refused to modify the Pinto's exploding gas tank, preferring to absorb the costs of defending and delaying lawsuits than to prevent hundreds of drivers and passengers from being incinerated by rear-end collisions.[7] What did society do to these multiple killers, who truly acted with a depraved wantonness? Nothing. Across the United States, these "red collar killers," as I call them, go unpunished. They, too, have exposed innocent victims to grave risks of death but from the purest of motives: the profit motive.

Like the hit man, they too make a calculated business decision to kill people for money. Most citizens, certainly most legislators, would scoff at equating hired killers and those who hire them with business executives who profit from killing innocent people indiscriminately. Entirely irrelevant, legislators insist that corporate but not street killers pay taxes, contribute heavily to political campaigns, and travel in the best social circles.

The guys inside Lorton knew better. But *Kibbe* and *Warner Lambert* did not bother them. They expected society's double standard. "In a capitalist society, it's very hard not to commit crimes, even when you don't come to jail," rasped Alvin H. "Once they are taxable, they are no longer crimes. As long as the government gets its cut. Alcohol and cigarettes kill many more people than marijuana and heroin together. These people commit crimes; they also put into the Treasury. And that's what it's all about in a capitalist society. It's all about money."

Straight society refuses to condemn its business killers, so street society refuses to condemn its killers. I denounced their equation. Paid assassins kill intentionally, whereas Warner Lambert execs recklessly exposed their employees to a risk but never intended for anyone to die. But the criminal law has long recognized that as the victim's death approaches near certainty, "knowingly" becomes morally indistinguishable from "intentionally." Anyway, now we're contrasting mental states—intent versus recklessness—and no longer motives. The values and attitudes of the depraved reckless spray shooter, the cold indifference of the hit man, and the wanton money-driven callousness of the corporate killer all share a core character. In corporate memos and on a golf course, they may express themselves with greater refinement, but in essence, these red collar killers saw their innocent victims, too, as just S.O.L.—shit out of luck.

Some of us retributivists see them for who they are. And we would punish them for what they do. Even as I write this, part of me emphatically rejects morally equating assassins with callous executives. Yes, when it comes to commercial exploitation and theft, concede the convicts their claim of society's double-dealing. Concede that when callous schemers bilk the elderly out of their life savings, society generally treats them more leniently than simple gunpoint robbers. Concede the prisoners inside Lorton their claim that we tax some forms of drug dealing (alcohol and nicotine) while prosecuting others: Some drug dealers spend their lives on corporate boards as pillars of society, while others serve lives in prison as its hated dregs.

From the beginning, America embraced double standards, irregularly defining and punishing theft and exploitation. I conceded all this to the prisoners. We "law-abiding" citizens still cheat on taxes, inflate insurance claims, and fraudulently obscure defects in items we sell. And sometimes, after a few days inside the prison, returning to New York by train, reflecting on sympathetic stories and mishaps, injustices and abused childhoods, moral relativism and hypocrisy, my own included, I began to doubt the reality of the very capital categories I sought. How dare we attempt to identify objectively the worst of the worst, those who deserved to die?

Then I remembered Hitler, Manson, and Speck. And I heard Paul W. describe his favorite pastime. To hear him tell it was to hate him for it: "Burglarizing—that was my thing. Go over to somebody's house, catch him coming home at night, or early in the morning, going to work. Just run up on the man and his wife. Take them back up in their house. I always grab the little kids first. 'Cause that's my security. Everybody's going to cooperate once you get the kids. Then you just tie 'em up, and ransack the house. Knowing me, I'm on pussy hotter than a motherfucker. I'm going to fuck the wife. I always fuck their wife. The husband right here, he looking at me—I know he got so much anger in him. What can he do though? I got a 9 mm pointing to his wife's head, fucking her."

"What did you shoot them for?" Johnny cut him off with obvious contempt.

"Some of them, they resist. Someone you just have a hate feeling for. Or you fucking and get to coming, you can't control your emotion and your strength. With the pistol to her head, one little squeeze, boom!"

This burglar-robber-rapist-murderer—a "real shithead," Johnny called him—clearly deserves to die. We do not need the broad, undifferentiated felony murder aggravator to execute him. He tortured his victims and murdered them "especially heinously, atrociously, and cruelly."[8] Aristotle was right. We do find pure evil at the extremes: those who kill for the thrill and, at the other extreme, those cold, callous killers who feel nothing.

Surely among these most depraved we find the professional hit man. "We should definitely execute the hired killer," I insisted. Who more clearly kills from a pecuniary motive?

"Then you execute everybody in the army," Itchy snapped back.

"That's in defense of society."

"He's a hired killer," Itchy insisted. "What difference does it make who he kills for? The government got the law to stop me. But when *they* have a beef with somebody, they send the army there to kill everybody they can. So what are they telling you about getting a pistol and killing somebody to solve your problems? How much respect can you have for the law, when they telling you not to kill so they can do all the killing?"

Although the hired mercenary—the soldier of fortune—and the assassin might seem retributively comparable, equating hit men with citizen soldiers who fight terrorism and tyranny perverts heroic sacrifices made for constitutional democracy and human dignity.

"The guy who hires himself out to kill anybody," I pressed.

"I think he is crazy and needs to be dead," Itchy admitted, dropping his sophistry in a different mood. "Somebody once tried to hire me to kill," he recalled. "People think because you'll do one thing, you'll do *any*thing. But I can't do that kind of work because I'm concerned about whether or not the person deserves to die. I happened to know the guy I was approached to kill. His woman was messing with another guy, and she could see getting money from insurance. I went to him and told him. This really was a violation of the Code, but I knew he wasn't going to the police. 'Man, she would never do that,' he insisted. A lot of people went to their graves thinking like that. So he confronted her, told her I had told him, which put *me* in jeopardy. Because she could decide she wanted me *and* him killed, if she really was that cold. I went back to the guy: 'It's my problem now. So if you want me to get rid of her. . . .' Basically, I believed she deserved to die. Because even though I used deception on strangers with con games, it was different when you do it with a person who breathes in your face while you sleep, and cracks your eggs in the morning. When you have that relationship, and you plot and connive for gain, you deserve to die.

"Anyway, he told me he was giving her another chance. And he gave me six thousand dollars, which I thought was pretty good. If I had killed her, it might have opened up a Pandora's box: Obviously he loved this woman, and if I killed her, I might have felt threatened by him then. It was something though. She tries to pay me to kill him, and he ends up paying me not to kill her."

"The hit man? He should get all of it," Marcus T., aka Tweet, insisted. "Not only is that premeditated, he's doing it for money. He takes lives. For a living. This motherfucker is just a straight motherfucking menace." It turned out that Tweet was the rare exception. Society largely measures and bases respect on money. Not only do we pay great teachers, nurses, and poets less than mediocre lawyers, bankers, and baseball players because we value them less—we value them less because we pay them less. The unpaid amateur rarely measures up in social standing to the well-compensated professional. In any field, including killing.

"You know guys who kill for a living?"

"Yeah," said Joseph W. "They're very intelligent. Society stigmatizes these people, but the guys I know personally, they're not sick at all. This is what they do for a living. This is their job. They are professionals. It's just the occupation they chose to get into."

"What about a hired killer?" I asked Ron D., the young drug lieutenant who would neither rob nor tolerate those who do. "A guy who will take out anybody? Does he deserve to die?" I hoped "Young Ron," the principled killer, would separate himself from the hit man, just as I hope, in vain, legislatures will separate themselves from corporate killers who contribute to their campaigns. "He's hustling," said Ron. "Hit men get paid for what they do. They don't kill for fun. It's a job with them. It's wrong, but I would respect the person that killed for money more than I would respect the person that's outright killing."

Frustrated that Ron D. would neither condemn hired killers nor support society's right to execute them, I switched to his own pragmatic cost-benefit language. "Why should taxpayers pay money to keep the hit man alive when he's already been paid to kill?" This economic twist hit home. "It's hard to say," admitted Ron, turning the question over in his mind.

At this moment, Johnny Allen, who hour after hour kept silent vigil in his wheelchair, uncharacteristically interrupted, turning to me: "I don't want to break your train, but I need to ask you a question bad as shit. Could anything happen to you personally or to your family that make you want to hire somebody to do the person that did it to your family?"

Johnny stared at me. For three years, together we had been probing the consciousness and consciences of inner-city street criminals with one simple ground rule: Tell the truth as you see it. Johnny had never before turned the tables with anyone else present. But now he put me on the spot. I couldn't lie to him.

"If somebody raped and killed my wife, my daughter. . . . And if it took hiring someone else to kill him. . . . But other than that, no, because they dissed me or for business reasons, absolutely not," I insisted, clearly separating myself from them. "Suppose I write this book someday, and someone viciously attacks me in print. Destroys my reputation and standing—"

"I wouldn't kill him," Ron countered. "I'll use the same tools he used to get where he at to bring him back down. The only difference is, we use different tools. See, on the streets I can't *write* a person down."

"Everything ain't a killing offense," Johnny agreed. He looked at me. "Man, we the same, and we think the same; it's just we do it different."

"No!" I protested. "You refuse to condemn the hired killer who will take out anybody, regardless."

"That's his job," said Ron.

"That his hustle," Johnny agreed.

"He is the worst," I insisted. "He should be executed!"

"What about the person that paid him to do it?" asked Ron.

"We should take him out too," I snapped back.

"But you said if somebody do something to your family, that's the same man you will go to for help." My moral gyroscope wobbled. Walt Kelly's cartoon character Pogo swirled in my head: "We have met the enemy, and they are us."[9]

Johnny and Young Ron gave me a moment to reply. Hearing none, they burst out laughing at the obvious distress of this tongue-tied criminal law professor. Johnny, looking to ease my discomfort, only made it worse: "Don't worry; all you got to do is make a phone call and it wouldn't even cost you nothing."

"If somebody raped and killed my wife, my daughter"—the most horrible nightmare I could conceive. I never imagined then that a survivor in that situation would someday ask me to help him have his wife and daughter's rapist-murderers killed, legally. And that mission would, for a while, consume me.

I'm no saint, but I would never kill for hire. I will not *do* that because I *am* not that. Retributivists need to sort out what it really means to "kill from a pecuniary motive." We must face our own hypocrisy. But killing over money and killing for pay—both hiring and firing—do aggravate murder.

We regularly and rightly condemn adult children and spouses who kill, or hire others to kill, in order to inherit or collect on a life insurance policy. But we must eliminate the class bias that infects killing "from a pecuniary motive." We who would condemn hired killers and those who pay them—most deserving of death because they put monetary profit above human life—must also condemn corporate killers who intentionally or recklessly, with a depraved and callous indifference, take innocent life for pay. Let one particularly cruel and heartless red collar killer be executed or imprisoned for life for giving his unsuspecting employees mercury baths. Let the pharmacist be condemned who dilutes chemotherapy and rips off the government while unsuspecting cancer victims suffer. Let us kill just one such depraved, lethal monster, and deadly corporate behavior will radically change overnight. How many innocent lives will be saved! But deterrence only adds a benefit; it hardly supplies the justification to execute the most callous and depraved among us. Until we equally condemn and punish unjustified hired killers across the social spectrum, their utter lack of sympathy combines with our elemental hypocrisy to make a mess of the Golden Rule.

10

THEIR CRIME/
OUR PUNISHMENT

DURING 12 YEARS INSIDE LORTON, I HAD COME TO KNOW dozens of lifers. Many states make it capital murder when a lifer (or sometimes any prisoner) kills again. Unless you threaten him with death, conventional wisdom holds, a lifer has nothing else to lose: No other threat can deter him. This simplistic assumption ignores the reality of life inside. In fact, generally lifers have the most to lose. They expect to live out their lives in prison and thus they cherish their privileges. The threat to revoke these privileges and transfer a lifer to an unfamiliar setting thus acts as a most effective deterrent.

Retributively, the theory goes, a person serving life for murder who kills again has proven himself incorrigible. He has not merely killed, he *is* a killer. I saw this lifer-who-kills-again aggravator fail miserably during one visit to Lorton. Two prisoners revealed off tape how a prison killing had gone down that the FBI investigated but could not solve. A prisoner working in the kitchen tried to smuggle a cocaine-laced peanut butter sandwich to his buddy on lock-down. The guy delivering the food tray, a lifer, had no idea he was being used as the conduit. A third prisoner who worked in the kitchen witnessed it and snitched. Officers busted the unsuspecting lifer while he delivered the contraband. As a result, this generally well-behaved lifer lost all privileges he'd worked for years to accumulate. He now faced disciplinary segregation and eventual transfer to a remote prison where his family could no longer visit. Inside, anybody who puts an unsuspecting prisoner in this position commits a killing offense. Soon after, the lifer, now himself locked down, ordered the hit on the guy who slipped coke into the sandwich. That murder, while death eligible, hardly qualifies as the worst of the worst.

After thousands of stories from more than a hundred criminals, my sense of appropriate aggravating circumstances crystallized. However difficult it might prove, legislatures could draft statutes that made morally relevant distinctions in advance (see Appendix B). States could obey *Furman* and guide juries' discretion in separating the worst of the worst. While some appropriate statutory aggravators remain murky, clearly states must eliminate capital robbery felony murder.

Rapist-murderers, of course, remain death eligible. Rapists should expect their victims to resist. Therefore, a rapist who kills his resisting victim, even while defending his own life, deserves to die. But we don't need the felony murder doctrine. Rape is torture. Torture remains a clear case of the core aggravator: a killing especially heinous, atrocious, and cruel. The heart of evil remains selfish cruelty.

As convicted criminals taught me about life on the streets, I came to know much better what made bad street killings worse. But their day-to-day lives inside prison still made no sense. In theory, prison incapacitates criminals from committing more crimes. Inside Lorton, however, nearly everyone had a hustle of some sort. All the prisoners but none of the officers had weapons. Drugs and other contraband flowed freely. In theory, prison should act as a general deterrent, pressuring other would-be criminals to resist temptation. But too many inner-city kids lived in the "for now"— assuming they'd never reach their twenty-first birthday. And while some criminals could not be deterred because they did not calculate, others remained undeterrable because they did. Lorton seemed to them a rite of passage— expected, accepted, awaited.

In theory, prison should specifically deter the criminal himself once released, who remembers the unpleasant experience inside and stays straight on the outside. The rate of recidivism gives the lie to that theory. Supposedly, we incarcerate to rehabilitate the criminal, to give him a new set of skills and values to convert him from a criminal into a law-abiding citizen upon release. Inside Lorton, rehabilitation rarely mattered. Except for lessons on how more skillfully to commit crimes upon release, prison taught mostly useless skills such as making barbecue pits. Those whose values had changed found it nearly impossible to go straight upon release.

Few released convicts could find a legitimate job. Only hustling street buddies would offer him a fresh start. Hard-pressed to stay legitimate in the streets, his memories of Lorton quickly fade. "In 25 days you forget the experience of 25 years," Itchy explained. The immediate dangers, the uncertainty, and the insecurity in the "free world" could seem worse than life in Lorton Central with its three hots and a cot.

Johnny Allen himself suffered the fate so often described to us by others who couldn't make it on the outside. Transferred to a halfway house whose staff could not find a job for a paraplegic ex-convict, Johnny was released to the streets, jobless but determined to go straight. With no money for rent, he applied to shelters, but none had space for a wheelchair-bound ex-convict.

A cocaine dealer offered his old buddy Johnny an apartment unit, rent free. "You don't have to hustle. You don't have to move any packages, but you got to accept what's going on around you," Johnny explained. Johnny knew himself. In that environment, "You hold, you bag, you count up." So he refused the lodging, joining the ranks of the homeless. "All they can arrest me for now is vagrancy."

Still hoping for admission to a shelter, Johnny slept on a filthy mattress in a cold, abandoned building, with Sterno for heat, until the fire department and arson squad forced him out. For a while he wheeled around the streets of DC, sleeping in his wheelchair in a hallway of an apartment building where a friend of a friend had persuaded the janitor to look the other way. Unable to lie down or bathe, hungry and hating life, Johnny desperately clung to his self-respect and his freedom, determined to keep the promise he made to himself and me never to return to Lorton. "I don't want to add on to what I've done," he wrote me with no return address. "I want to make up for it. I don't want to sell the goddamn poison to our children. So here I am, one patriotic nigger, chasing the American dream. I'm cold and I'm hungry but I'm free. And it's killing me."

John Allen eventually died, a paralyzed, homeless heroin addict, wasting away and clinging to a barely functioning radiator in the basement of a semi-abandoned building.

As his release date from prison approached, Johnny had made me promise to speak at his funeral. "He made us feel safe," his brother, a minister, declared in the first eulogy—a truth I experienced myself more than once inside Lorton. When my turn came publicly to say goodbye, I kept my promise to Johnny and delivered the message he demanded. "John Allen was no hero; he lived a wasted life," I insisted, looking at his nephews and grandchildren who had looked up to him. His family scowled, but Johnny hoped this message would inspire the next generation to reject his path.

We do so little for those we release, and yet we wonder at the rate of recidivism and prison's failure to rehabilitate.

"You can institutionalize a person," Leo explained, returning from one of his many short stays outside. "I know what to expect here. It's a lesser threat. We have a closeness here that you don't have in the street. When you're sick here, everyone want to know how you are."

Worst of all, perhaps, Lorton failed as retribution. Do we inflict pain and suffering on a criminal because, and to the extent, he deserves it? Day to day inside Lorton Central, officers intentionally ignored these men's crimes. "What a man is in here for is not our concern," explained Captain Frank Townshend, a long-time, well-respected, tough-but-fair officer. By severing the crime committed outside from the quality of time spent inside, the guards, the prisoners, and the administration destroyed retribution. Often, short-term, first-time offenders suffered most, while the most hardened lifers who had committed the worst crimes and deserved the harshest punishment—those with the best contacts, the best hustles, and the best jobs inside—suffered the least. Inside Lorton Central, day to day, the past did not count.

In 1998, the feds took back control of DC's prison system, shutting down Lorton Central. During my years inside this wild world, I had learned plenty about crime and witnessed the perversity of punishment. Searching for the worst of the worst, I had found some. Oddly, almost no one in print had tested the theoretical justifications for punishment by the prisoners' actual experience. My book-length *Stanford Law Review* article, "Haven or Hell?," revealed how all traditional justifications failed miserably inside one prison system.[1] The essay got me tenure. It also attracted attention. "Among Killers: Searching for the Worst of the Worst" landed on the front page of the Sunday *Washington Post* Outlook section.[2] The media anointed me an authority on life-and-death as punishment. I knew life inside the crazy world of Lorton Central, but I hardly expected the nation's only all-black prison system would be replicated anywhere else. Besides, Washington, DC had no death penalty and thus no death row. Since states executed only a tiny fraction of convicted murderers they had already condemned to die, with appellate delays stretching sometimes for decades, I needed to understand *life* on death row.

And of course I needed to witness an execution.

PART III
WITNESS AT AN EXECUTION

11

BEHIND THE GLASS

"ANYTHING YOU NEED?" RICK MATASAR, OUR NEW DEAN, asked the first time we met.

"I need to witness an execution," I replied, bemused at Matasar's startled and disapproving look. But the ex-dean of University of Florida's Law School called in a favor on my behalf. Next up on Florida's gurney: Bennie Demps.

Obviously, I wouldn't watch the ritual killing of a helpless man without knowing why he died. A quick check revealed bad news. Florida condemned Bennie Demps for helping to kill Alfred Sturgis, a prison snitch serving a life sentence for murder. (There's a victim to grieve.) Worse, the evidence cast shadows on Demps's guilt. Sturgis's death scene came right out of a grade B movie: "He was chalky looking. His eyes was rolling back and forth in his head," correctional officer A. V. Rhoden testified to the jury. "Mr. Rhoden, you got to help me. I don't believe I'm going to make it," Alfred Sturgis cried out, in his dying declaration. "Mungin and Demps. They held me and Toothless Jackson stabbed me. You have to get them for me."[1]

Dying declarations have their special status in law and life generally. Courts allow these statements into evidence, which would otherwise be inadmissible hearsay. When we gather after funerals, we want to know the final moments of the dearly departed. Murder victims' families often hunger for their loved one's last words. Historically, the dying victim's final words of forgiveness alone might spare the killer. Even dying declarations of the condemned have special status, as if we all speak more profound truth as we die. Early American execution rituals emphasized the final speech at the gallows as the ultimate call for reconciliation with the State and God. Today, published books collect the dying declarations of the condemned.

But whatever deep emotional status we confer on those declarations, a prison snitch on his deathbed can hardly be counted on as conclusive proof of guilt. Sturgis could have retaliated for other quarrels by accusing Demps. The only other evidence came from Larry Hathaway, a fellow prisoner desperate for a transfer, who testified that while walking past Mungin's cell, he saw Sturgis struggling inside the cell. Mungin kept watch, the witness claimed, while Demps held Sturgis down on the bed and Jackson thrust the knife into him 30 times. But no physical evidence, such as the victim's blood spatter, connected Demps to the murder. Demps's two co-felons, Mungin and Jackson, got life. Demps, alone, got death—the only death sentence Florida ever gave a prisoner for killing another prisoner. It didn't make sense. Why would Florida kill this man? I would rather protest than witness *that* execution.

Demps's death sentence had been scheduled and stayed, rescheduled and restayed many times. But the warden, James Crosby, took very seriously this new death date. As a favor to the state's attorney, Rod Smith, the warden would help me better understand the process by allowing me to watch the walk-through, a behind-the-scenes dress rehearsal for the execution of Bennie Demps. A week later I would return to witness his killing.

I watched as the rehearsal for Demps's execution proceeded almost mechanically. No jokes, no banter. Everyone did what they'd be doing execution night, except of course the officer lying on the gurney. Corrections had removed Demps from his cell on some administrative pretext to spare him watching the dress rehearsal for his own death. The team had practiced forcibly extracting a condemned killer who might decline to go quietly into that gentle night. Number one priority: a smooth execution without incident.

A prisoner's final hours—surrounded by loved ones, spiritual advisers, and other tranquilizers at the ready—should prepare the condemned to meet God without fanfare or fuss, the warden explained. I had always assumed that final scene where the prisoner embraces loved ones represented our humility and humanity before launching the condemned into eternity. I assumed we sought to assuage our doubt or guilt or to show compassion. (Of course some might counter that the victims never spent their last moments enjoying favorite foods and embracing loved ones.) Now I began to see it more from corrections' point of view. Keep it calm, quiet, and running smoothly: the perfect bureaucratic killing. The warden could make the last moments more comfortable by loosening the leather straps that restrain the prisoner's hands and legs. But he would exercise this compassionate prerogative only if he felt confident the condemned would not resist. Privileges to the end.

The officers went through the drill. The guy playing Demps hardly resisted, and of course no one actually put a catheter in him or located a backup vein. They wheeled the gurney into the room. I looked around at the microphone, the telephones, and the clock, like we've seen in the movies but drained of any drama. They discussed boring details about telephone lines and other technical stuff. I got antsy—nothing much happening here. The warden had invited me to look around as long as I didn't get in anyone's way. What was behind this small door, I wondered, open a crack?

Like Toto in the *Wizard of Oz*, I pushed my nose inside and suddenly found myself in a tiny room next to a tall man at the controls. He watched the rehearsal through a one-way mirror, two rows of giant plungers before his large hands. I don't know who was more surprised to see the other, but I know the executioner showed it less. Only one man should ever see his face. That officer picks him up at a remote location, then escorts him to the prison to a room off the side of the chamber. Once all other officers are in place and out of sight, the executioner, unseen, slips into the death chamber. Afterward he slips out, again unseen.

Executioner looked at me with a slight scowl, then back to the large window just beyond the plungers at the rehearsal playing out on the gurney on the other side of that one-way mirror. Standing next to him, squished into a corner in this cramped chamber built for one, I shuddered. Those eyes behind glasses—those cold, dead eyes. Did I see him as I wanted to?

Why "the contempt and indignation with which everyone looks on the executioner," Cesare Beccaria demanded in 1766? Why the near universal repulsion at this "innocent executor of the public will; a good citizen, who contributes to the advantage of society; the instrument of the general security within, as good as soldiers are without"? What can we "read" from "this contradiction"? Beccaria's brief and brilliant essay *On Crimes and Punishments* profoundly shaped the views of America's founding generation. In this first and most influential abolitionist attack, Beccaria mocked the "absurdity" that "laws, which detest and punish homicide, should, in order to prevent murder, publicly commit murder themselves."[2] Abolitionists still attack the "hypocrisy" of the death penalty: "Why kill to show that killing is wrong?" reads one common bumper sticker. We debase life by taking it, they still argue in public debate.

When we imprison kidnappers, do we debase liberty? When we impose fines on thieves, do we debase property? Punishment, here, acts as a like-kind response, inflicting pain on a person who inflicted pain on another. Of course, celebration and reward also act as a like-kind response, returning pleasure for pleasure. The basic retributive measure, like for like—"as he has done, so shall it be done to him," "giving a person a taste of her own medicine," "fighting fire with fire"—satisfies a primal urge. Reciprocity, not hypocrisy, constitutes the core of capital punishment. So that classic but now well-worn argument, if it proves anything, proves too much. But Beccaria's abolitionist attack on the executioner still stands unrebutted.

Why *do* we despise the executioner? (Would you want your daughter to marry one, even if it carried job security?) He does society's bidding, ridding us of our worst predators. He will kill anybody the state commands—for a fee. Perhaps that's why: The executioner does not care who he kills. He does his job. In Florida he's a civilian volunteer who supplements his income as a part-time executioner. A legal hit man, a hired killer.

I could execute Manson or Speck. Oh yes, I could. I might even pay for that privilege. But I would never be paid to do it. Did this man standing next to me with those cold eyes know or care why Florida condemned Bennie Demps, the man he would kill next week?

After the walk-through, I hoped the warden would answer questions and show me around the prison. Crosby had other pressing business but, nodding to me, instructed the deputy warden to "show him what he wants to see." I wanted to see daily life on death row. I wanted to see Danny Rolling. Danny Rolling never quite achieved the infamy of Manson, Speck, or Ted Bundy. But Florida, especially the college town of Gainesville, will never forget him.[3]

August 24, 1990. Sonja Larson, talented and beautiful, slept peacefully, not yet fully unpacked in her off-campus apartment, her freshman year at the University of Florida about to begin, her whole adult life ahead of her. All 60 seconds of it. Sonja awoke to duct tape stretched across her mouth and a blade plunging into her chest. She desperately tried to scream and kick her attacker, but the black-gloved hand furiously stabbed her to death.

Sonja, 18, fared better than her apartment mate, Christina Powell, 17, asleep on the couch downstairs. Right after Rolling stabbed Sonja to death, Christina awoke to a hand over her mouth and a snarl: "Don't fight me! If you do, you're dead." Danny Rolling played with Christina Powell, threatening her if she resisted. He fondled her, tore off her clothes, forced her to give him oral sex, raped her in different positions, screaming out in pleasure as he ejaculated inside her. Then he dragged her to the kitchen, duct taped her mouth, rolled her onto her stomach, and stabbed her five times in the back until she died. As a parting gesture, the monster cut off her nipples before he left the apartment, taking care to rip away the duct tape and take it with him, along with her nipples in a baggie.

At this point, Danny Rolling was less than halfway through his savage rampage.

The day after he killed Sonja Larson and Christina Powell, the Gainesville killer struck again. Rolling broke into Christa Hoyt's apartment and waited. Garbed in his usual black ninja outfit, wearing gloves and mask, and armed with handcuffs, duct tape, and the same Ka-Bar marine attack knife, designed to allow easy penetration and release, Rolling waited in an alcove for Christa to return from her racquetball game. She entered and sensed someone's presence, but he leaped on her from behind. "You've got one chance! Do you hear me? One chance! Behave and live—or fight me and I'll kill you!" he warned, waving the blade before the terrified girl. He duct-taped Christa Hoyt's mouth and stripped her naked. She was menstruating, but Rolling ripped out her tampon and raped her anyway. Finished with her sexually after 15 minutes of torture, he turned her on her stomach and stabbed her to death. Then he flipped her over and gutted her, placing her nipples on her innards. The butcher fled, but feared he'd left his wallet in the apartment, so he returned. As an afterthought, he cut off Christa's head, propped it on a mantel, and posed her corpse to resemble "The Thinker"— only headless and with her legs spread open.

The next day, Rolling broke into the apartment of Tracy Paules and Manuel Taboada. Earlier that evening, Rolling had peeped through Tracy's window and overheard her chatting with a girlfriend on the phone: "I wish Manuel was here. I'm worried about these murders." Manny was tending bar at Bennigan's, and when he returned at 2:45 a.m., Tracy felt safe.

Rolling returned, masked down, armed with duct tape and his marine attack knife. After breaking into their apartment, he found Manny in his own room, lying on his back, deep asleep. Rolling plunged the knife into Taboada's chest. A football player, Manny struggled desperately, punching his attacker, who slashed him to death by stabbing him 30 times. Tracy Paules heard the commotion and confronted the killer dripping in blood. Terrified, she retreated into her bedroom, but Rolling smashed the door from its frame. "You're him, aren't you?" Tracy whimpered. Rolling subdued and raped her. "Take the pain, bitch!" he yelled when she protested.[4] Then this calculating monster stabbed her to death, washed and posed her body, and left the area free of fingerprints. But although he douched her with a cleanser, Danny Rolling had left his DNA inside his victim.

In 48 hours, the killer had massacred five students in their prime and left Gainesville a town paralyzed in terror. Fifteen months and 130,000[5] person-hours later, after the biggest manhunt in Florida history, law enforcement knew Danny Rolling beyond doubt as the Gainesville killer. Probably hoping to save his own life, Rolling pled guilty at the eve of trial. But the jury recommended death, and the judge followed suit. So this vicious beast joined others like him, there, on Florida's death row.

Now, nearly a decade after his rampage, the summer of 2000, Danny Rolling still sat on Florida's death row awaiting execution while abolitionists and much of the media coordinated an attack on capital punishment, crying out to end the death penalty as inhumane. "At least adopt a moratorium," these critics urged. How could any fair-minded person not agree to suspend executions until we fix this broken system? Nothing would be lost and much could be gained, they assured us—except, of course, that during this moratorium, these poor wretches on death row would be forced to endure their living hell.

After the jury recommended death for Danny Rolling, the newspapers reflected overwhelming public sentiment that Rolling should die. But Brad Gray, a crime reporter, was not so certain. "I have often wondered," Mr. Gray mused, reflecting many abolitionists today, "which is the more severe punishment? To execute a convicted murderer is to put him out of his mental and physical misery. However, to keep him alive in solitary Death Row confinement for the rest of his natural life, hoping he will live many years and awaken every morning to the memory of why he is where he is—is that not a greater punishment?"

Giving voice to that uninformed public who honestly oppose the death penalty as too good for these killers, Gray continued: "Were I a family member of a victim in a similar case, I believe I would hope the murderer would live to be a very old man on Death Row so that he could count each and every morning as a living hell for a very long time."[6]

After watching the walk-through, I saw Danny Rolling in his cell on death row, relaxing, reading a book, a pillow tucked behind his head, reading glasses comfortably perched on his nose, oblivious to the visitor seething with hatred who stared at him. I thought of Sonja Larson, future teacher; Christina Powell and Manuel Taboada, would-be architects; Christa Hoyt, who planned a career in forensics; and Tracy Paules, who hoped to be lawyer. I thought of their agonizing deaths and the lives they never got to live. As Rolling turned the page, I silently cursed him, and something from the core of my being growled, "Why aren't you dead?" But he wasn't. In fact, the officers told me, Rolling played a mean game of volleyball there on the Row. And loved nothing more than a spirited game of chess with Paul Hill, his next-door neighbor and closest friend. They each had a board and called out the moves. "They laugh and joke all the time," one officer informed me.

"When I first arrived in the prison, I looked out and saw these guys exercising," recalled a ranking officer. "And one of them was shirtless, so he was getting a tan. He was playing basketball in sneakers and shorts and seemed to be having a fine time with a friend of his. It was Danny Rolling with his closest friend. I was taken aback."

Danny Rolling's fiancée, Sondra London, first made his acquaintance on death row and visited him regularly for many years. Together they wrote his autobiography, revealing the details of his killing spree. "Why should he be able to visit the woman every weekend and the four young women whose lives he took don't have their loved ones to visit them any weekends?" an officer demanded indignantly, recalling Rolling's face lighting up in a smile as he declared, "I thank God to be able to visit this woman every weekend."

The Florida Department of Corrections ran into a firestorm when it announced its plan to eliminate contact visits for death row inmates. Opponents denounced the proposal as cruel and unnecessary. The department justified the change in the name of security: Contact visits pose potential threat of smuggling contraband or taking hostages. "If there is one point I can make to you, *we are not doing this to punish anyone*," said C. J. Drake, the Department of Corrections spokesperson.[7]

Why not?

The next day in the basement of a local courthouse, I viewed Rolling's crime scene photos, too hideous and lurid to describe. They still crop up sometimes in a recurring nightmare. The devastation, the mutilation. I thought of the victims' families, their lives ruined, every day drenched in pain.

Jim Larson, the brother of Rolling's first Gainesville victim, only got through his sister's brutal killing with the help of his wife, Carla. Then, as some people seem cursed, seven years later, while Rolling and Sondra London fought for the royalties from Rolling's life story, Larson's wife was abducted from a Publix supermarket parking lot and strangled.[8] By a twisted irony, her murderer had now joined Rolling on death row. Perhaps over a volleyball game or a cold root beer they compared notes about the sisters-in-law.

12

ONE STEP REMOVED

NOBODY INSIDE FLORIDA STATE PRISON SEEMED TO know or care why they were scheduled to put Bennie Demps to death that next week. But it really bothered me. How could Florida let Danny Rolling live after what he'd done and yet execute Bennie Demps for assisting in killing a convicted murderer and prison snitch? Was Demps even arguably the worst of the worst? We must reserve the very worst punishment only for the very worst crime. We shouldn't leave it to the vagaries of the legal process or the calendar. Scour our death rows and investigate the stories behind the murders that led to the sentence. Do not execute a robber for a killing he committed from nervousness at the convenience store. Not while we let Danny Rolling live. Let us reduce randomness and arbitrariness in carrying out executions. My new sound byte for media interviews: "Worst First."

On my return from the prison, my research assistant, Megan McMullin, greeted me with different news: Many years earlier, Celia and Nicholas Puhlick, a good, loving, hardworking Connecticut couple, had saved and scraped, looking forward to retiring together to Florida. Celia cleaned houses while Nicholas renovated them to supplement his salary as a defense plant worker. Together they struggled to put their kids through college. Known locally as the "flower lady" for her green thumb, Celia dreamed of someday living in an orange grove. One day, her cousin, R. N. Brinkworth, a Florida real estate agent, called them, all excited. He'd found their perfect retirement house, a handyman's special in an untended orange grove. The Puhlicks immediately drove from Connecticut and, with Brinkworth, reached the long dirt road that led to their dream house. As luck would have it, Bennie Demps and an underage accomplice, Jackie Hardie, had just robbed a house nearby. They couldn't crack open the safe there, so they took it with them to this abandoned orange grove. Demps had worked as a fruit picker in an orange grove. He and Hardy were attempting to crack the safe when the Puhlicks' car came down that road.

Demps pulled a gun and announced a stickup. Celia Puhlick fumbled nervously for her wallet inside her pocketbook and dropped her lipstick. As she instinctively bent to pick it up, Bennie Demps shot her in the stomach. The robbers then forced Nicholas to remove the spare tire from their car and then climb back in. Next, Brinkworth. Finally, they forced Celia Puhlick, bleeding badly, into the trunk. Demps slammed the car trunk shut. And before he left that orange grove, hearing the desperate cries of the three locked inside, Bennie Demps and Jackie Hardie, his 16-year-old sidekick, riddled the trunk with gunfire, killing Brinkworth and Celia Puhlick, who absorbed bullets meant for her husband. Trapped inside that trunk for hours with his dying wife, Nicholas Puhlick lived to corroborate what forensic evidence proved beyond a shadow of a doubt: Bennie Demps cold-bloodedly murdered his wife and her cousin. A Florida jury recommended that Demps die, and the judge agreed. But then in 1972, when the US Supreme Court in *Furman* struck down the death penalty across the United States, the states released into general population all their condemned killers. Florida's 95 newly minted lifers now included Bennie Demps.[1] Four years later in *Proffitt*, the Supreme Court upheld Florida's new death penalty statute.[2] Two months after that, Demps allegedly helped kill Sturgis.

I know progressives resist any suggestion that one person's life can be more valuable than another's or more worthy of concern and respect. But Demps's judge and jury must have rejected this "equality of human dignity" argument and ignored their own doubts when they legally condemned him for killing Sturgis, the convicted murderer and prison snitch. They really sentenced Demps to die again for that earlier rampage in the orange grove. Demps had displayed there, a rare combination of intent to kill and depraved indifference to his victims' suffering when he riddled that car trunk with bullets that killed R. N. Brinkworth and Celia Puhlick—and left her husband in the trunk to bleed and then grieve, with the guilt that his wife had absorbed bullets before they could strike him. Their fate made Bennie Demps deserve to die. That's why, after considering his prior record in the penalty phase, a jury and judge spared his accomplices but once again condemned Bennie Demps. That's why, with a clear conscience, I prepared to witness the People of Florida kill him.

Many appeals, many stays littered the legal path to Demps's execution chamber. In 1982, the governor signed a death warrant, but Demps still had moves to make. He petitioned a federal appeals court for a new trial, claiming that the trial judge had excluded four types of mitigating evidence that might have moved the jury to spare him: His "honorable military combat service; drug abuse; problem-free adjustment to prison life; and his two co-felons got life while he alone got death."[3]

Demps did enlist in the Marines but was dishonorably discharged after being court-martialed for five assaults, among other things. He never saw combat while stationed at Camp LeJeune, North Carolina. Demps's drug abuse might have made a difference, except he killed Sturgis in prison with no evidence that he was under the influence at the time. Convicted murderers must be allowed to introduce *all relevant* mitigating circumstances. What would good behavior in prison suggest? That the incarcerated killer will not pose a further danger? Perhaps. So what? We are punishing him for who he was and what he did, not rewarding him for being a good boy afterward. Contrary to the Supreme Court, we retributivists insist that good behavior in prison should not count. The fiercest and most vicious predators who show their cowardice by preying on children and other vulnerable victims, once captured and confronted with overwhelming state power, often become obedient and subservient pussycats inside. Does that make them less deserving of their punishment? Anyway, Demps's prison records showed continuing disciplinary problems during his seven years as a lifer prior to the stabbing.

So Demps lied in his first three claims. His last—that his two co-felons got life sentences—the Florida Supreme Court had already recognized as mitigating fact. However, "only Demps had the loathsome distinction of having been previously convicted of the first-degree murder of two persons and attempted murder of another, escaping the gallows only through the intervention of *Furman,*" declared that same Florida Supreme Court, affirming his sentence.[4]

Because Demps so obviously deserved the ultimate punishment from his earlier killing, the federal appeals court brushed aside his objections, finding it "harmless error" "beyond a reasonable doubt" to have excluded this evidence in his favor. "The proposed mitigating evidence regarding Demps's character would not have influenced the jury to recommend life."

More than 20 years had passed since Bennie Demps riddled that car trunk with bullets. Had the condemned changed? Bennie Demps, through his lawyers, declined to meet with me. Still trying to understand the event from many different points of view, I did track down the family of Demps's latest victim, Sturgis, the murdering prison snitch. "My brother was no good. He left the family a long time ago. We have no interest in any of this," a voice said and hung up. Then I attempted to contact the survivors of his real victims.

"My father died a somber man," Nicholas Puhlick's son informed me, "resolute that no mercy be shown his attackers." Demps's younger accomplice, 16-year-old Jackie Hardie, had died in prison in 1999. Although Demps viciously killed Puhlick's mother, officially Demps would die for a different murder. Thus, corrections had not even notified the Puhlicks of her murderer's execution, much less invited them to witness it. Officially, they no longer qualified as a victim's family.

Victims' families have long counted specially in capital prosecutions. And they should. In ancient times, the family caught and killed the murderer if they could. Or the family might accept a "blood price" as a settlement, buying the killer peace and the victim's survivors some measure of satisfaction. All pre-biblical Near Eastern cultures allowed the victim's family to settle up and be compensated for their loss.[5] Seemingly the killer's moral guilt did not matter. The victim's family might find the slayer worth more alive, perhaps as a slave. For utilitarians, the death penalty has always been about costs and benefits. And still today. The blood price worked: No one complained, and anyway, why cry over spilt blood? Just put it behind you and move on.

But then came a great advance, when the ancient Greeks and, at about the same time, independently, the ancient Hebrews treated murder as a community concern. "In the best governed State," declared Solon, the great Athenian lawgiver, "those who are not personally wronged are no less diligent in prosecuting wrongdoers than those who have personally suffered."[6] Nor did the Bible allow murderers to live who deserved to die: "You shall accept no ransom for the life of a murderer who is guilty. But he shall be put to death."[7] Recognizing that money can never truly compensate for murder, that no value given could ever equal the value of the innocent life taken— that justice shall not be bought, nor the victim's family be bought off— Western civilization abolished the blood price for murder, seemingly forever.

Today, 2,500 years later, victims' families still occupy a special place. Prosecutors routinely consult them before deciding whether to go for death. During the penalty phase, they often supply "victim impact statements," giving the jury a portrait of their lost loved one and the effect the murder has had on the family. Initially, in 1987, in *Booth v. Maryland,* a bare majority of the US Supreme Court outlawed these statements in assessing the defendant's moral guilt. Victim impact statements, the court held, introduced morally "irrelevant" information "wholly unrelated to the blameworthiness of a particular defendant." This impact evidence unfairly disadvantaged defendants whose victim's families "were willing and able to express its grief." Furthermore, the majority found itself "troubled by the implication that

defendants whose victims were assets to their community are more deserving of punishment" than those defendants who killed victims "perceived
to be less worthy. Of course our system of justice does not tolerate such
distinctions."[8]

But four years later, in *Payne v. Tennessee*, the Court reversed itself. "Just
as the murderer should be considered as an individual, so too, the victim is
an individual whose death represents a unique loss," the new majority declared. Victim impact statements could better help a jury assess the killer's
"moral culpability and blameworthiness." Victim impact statements could
"help keep the balance true." The surviving family, however, should never
express an opinion about the appropriate sentence.[9] But as Kevin Doyle, for
many years New York's Capital Defender, insisted in class, jurors can read
between the lines.

I firmly believe that juries should consider what the *victims* themselves
would have wanted. For years now, abolitionists have circulated and signed a
"Declaration of Life": "Should I die as a result of violent crime, I request [my
killers] not be subject to the death penalty under any circumstances, no matter how heinous their crime or how much I have suffered." Death penalty
advocates wrongly scoff at this. No court has ever allowed these declarations
in evidence. Had the British hanged Ghandi's assassin, they would have
betrayed Ghandi himself. The past counts. We make and keep covenants
with the dead. Where we can, we should give the victims themselves a voice,
if not a veto. Of course, should a victim sign a statement that "If I am murdered, I want my killer executed," assuming the murder otherwise qualifies
for death, that too should count.

The closest survivors sometimes call themselves "the victims of homicides." But they are not the dead. The victim's family has survived the murder and are in fact "one step removed," I insisted as a speaker at Skidmore
College's conference for the families of murdered victims. I felt uncomfortable telling surviving families that they were not the victims. But "one step
removed, we all are, from the murdered victim," I began my talk. "I am
sorry for your loss. Of course your healing takes priority: And compared to
your agony—those nagging memories, lost loving moments, stabs of painful
longing, taunting might-have-beens—*our* righteous indignation, *our* rage at
the callous or sadistic murderer is mere commentary.

"But know this, We, the *political* family of the victim, in our righteous
indignation, in our need for justice, we—strangers but fellow citizens, fellow survivors, equally vulnerable to viciousness and terror, feel—yes *feel* immediately and continually connected to the slain." I looked at them, each a
survivor of a loved one murdered, some devoting their lives to abolishing

the death penalty, ready to forgive and move on. Others, raw and wounded, still searched for consolation. I didn't want to compound their pain, and yet some things needed to be said. And those who still hated their loved ones' murderers deserved their advocate. "We remain continually connected to the slain," I assured them. "Because for us retributivists there is no deeper truth than this: The Past Counts. The earth does not belong only to the living. So *we* will not forget or forgive. We remember the victim. 'As we put ourselves in his situation,' declared Adam Smith, 'we feel that resentment which . . . he would feel.'[10]

"The victim's family was never a fully reliable moral barometer. Their anger needed to be kept in check—to spare less evil killers a death they did not deserve." I linked them to history, reminding them how the Old Testament commanded cities of refuge where manslaughterers not deserving death could flee.[11] "Although homicide became a community concern, the victim's family still played a key role. In ancient Athens, a killer convicted of unpremeditated homicide was banished until he received a pardon from the victim's family. But the family had to be unanimous. One lone holdout's simmering anger, a desire to continue punishing overrode the collective will to end it reasonably."[12] I hoped this history would give strength or at least validate the status of a spouse or child who wouldn't or couldn't forgive. But I also hoped it would validate those who split with their siblings and decided to move on. "Sometimes we must ignore the wishes of the victim's families." That statement trod on sensitive ground with those victims' families who badly wanted the killer executed, bitterly disappointed that prosecutors refused to seek death, or the jury did not give it.

"Some of you could come to terms with your loss, but for this nagging feeling that if you ever put your anger behind you, you will have let down your loved one. You fear that only by keeping the wound fresh can you keep their memory alive. Do you feel guilty in giving up the hate; allowing your anger to diminish; getting on with your life? As if to look forward turns your back on your beloved and lets him die a second time." I looked at the audience, trying to read their expressions. I had prepared carefully to walk a fine edge—to volunteer in a weird way to take my turn at the watch, to sit in for the family.

"Would you find it easier to forgive, knowing that we will not? We accept our responsibility directly to the victim we never knew, to keep the fire burning, sustain the anger, never to forgive or forget—until justice at last is done. The voice of your brother's blood, your parent's blood, our children's blood, the blood of your beloved cries out to us from the ground. We pledge to you—we will not let our anger cool, our memory decay. We will not allow anguished deliberation to diminish our felt need for justice—to execute as quickly as possible those who most deserve to die. I am sorry for your loss."

And I sat down.

Afterward, a few family members thanked me feverishly. A couple came up to me and said I had no right to say what I said. But I know we do need to represent the victims, as well as the survivors. So there I was, and would be, sitting in for Celia Puhlick and R. N. Brinkworth as I prepared to watch Bennie Demps die.

13

CURTAIN TIME

JUNE 7, 2000. THE TAXI PICKED ME UP AT 4:45 A.M. POURING rain all night. I left my wife, Marcia, and her very ill father awaiting his own fate at the hands of the Sloan Kettering surgeons. LaGuardia to Orlando, then that two-and-a-half-hour drive. As I drove a rental car through small-town speed traps, west from Starke, past flat parched fields and grazing cows, toward housing strips in the distance—Florida State Prison—I began to wonder how I'd feel. I had prepared emotionally and jurisprudentially to witness this execution. I wanted Demps to die, but to actually watch him be put to death? I had a dull headache. Perfect atmospherics.

A few days earlier, Demps had issued a statement: "Quite simply I am innocent of this crime." Prosecutors and prison officials, Demps insisted, "perceived me as having 'escaped' the death penalty when the US Supreme Court struck it down, commuting my sentence to life."[1] I believed Demps told the truth; I hoped he told the truth. That somehow the People of Florida had found a way to overcome the morally indiscriminate effects of *Furman*.

Against the advice of his attorneys, Demps held a press conference the day before his scheduled execution, once again accusing the state of using the Sturgis case to make up for his earlier commuted sentence.[2] Joy Purdy, a local reporter, asked Demps whether he regretted his earlier murders in the orange grove. "That's a stupid question. That's not why I'm on death row." Maybe not. But that's why he deserved to die. And that's why Florida prepared to kill him. Bennie Demps proclaimed his innocence to the end, largely through the tireless efforts of his devoted Canadian email-order bride, Tracy, who married him on death row.

Death row groupies mystify me. These women spend their lives visiting the condemned religiously, writing them daily, falling in love with them, and marrying them if they can. For some women, perhaps, condemned killers have that special aura or sex appeal. Apparently it gratifies their sense of romance or martyrdom. The Canadian Coalition Against the Death Penalty maintains a free web site for every death row inhabitant in the United States. It can get so taxing to have to keep up with all those eager to make your acquaintance that Ohio condemned killer Robert VanHook posted a notice, alerting the adoring public that "he is no longer able to accept new pen pals at this time." Anyway, Bennie and Tracy declared his innocence in public releases and at the press conference.

Potential innocence, these days, provides the abolitionists their strongest point of attack. The thought of executing an innocent person on the basis of lies, frame-ups, and misidentifications horrifies retributivist proponents as much as anyone. But there's innocence and there's innocence, however politically incorrect to suggest this. Bennie Demps may have been innocent of killing Sturgis, but he still deserved to die. Poetic justice, if not legal justice that Florida execute him. They had a saying inside Lorton: "It's not for what you've done that you do time all the time, but all the time you do, it's for what you've done." So in the end, I did not worry too much about the "innocence" of Bennie Demps.

Demps had spent blocks of time with Tracy. They hugged and kissed. He ate a last meal of barbecue chicken and beef, French fries, salad, Spanish rice, rolls, cherry vanilla and butter pecan ice cream, a mango, banana pudding, and Pepsi, a corrections spokesperson informed the media. But alas, he only ate half his meal. Demps was laughing this morning." He had talked to his spiritual adviser and was "polite, upbeat, and friendly."[3]

After driving through the rain, I arrived early. Three uniformed officers checked my ID to make certain I belonged at this event. As I waited to be scanned, another witness kept setting off the metal detector. She took off her shoes; it went off again. Removed a hair clasp; her locks came tumbling down. Eventually they waived her through.

An officer directed us to a large conference room set aside for witnesses to this execution. A table set with large platters of cookies, Ritz crackers, vegetables and dip. And coffee urns. Not a lavish spread but a thoughtful touch. Had the other witnesses done their homework? What did they know about Demps? Why had they volunteered to view this, I wondered? I wanted to ask, but it felt wrong to interview witnesses here. No reporters in this room—presumably they had their own waiting space. Only citizen witnesses belonged here, and me, this one special observer. Would an abolitionist among them attack Demps's conviction as a trumped up charge? I'd counter by telling them of the Puhlicks and Brinkworth.

People drifted in and stood around, but no one talked. Finally, I picked up some dialogue: "Should I stick a new toothpick in each piece of cheese?" one witness asked another. Nobody talked about the condemned or what he did. Demps was due to die at 6 p.m. Suddenly at 5:55, officers ushered us into the witness observation room: relatively small, four rows of seven chairs each. Citizen witnesses sat front and center, reporters filled in around the edges and behind. Before us, a large brown curtain, shards of white light poking through. Two cheap speakers mounted at the corners, an air conditioner in the wall, humming. Silence.

Let the show begin. Suspense built, waiting for the curtain to rise. 5:58, 6:00, 6:03. . . . Still waiting. It was clearly past curtain time. What was happening? The dress and tech rehearsal had gone smoothly, usually a bad sign for opening night. But the producers designed this play to open and close the same night.

Only the air purring through the vent and pencils scribbling on reporters' pads broke a chalky stillness. 6:05. Three times Bennie Demps had death warrants. Three times last-minute stays stopped his execution. Would he cheat death once again? My stomach churned. 6:07. Did he fight extraction? Were they wrestling him into place on the gurney at this moment? Did the Supreme Court issue a last second stay? 6:15, 6:20. An eerie silence. Reporters have run out of things to write. It feels odd—supposedly on the inside of this event, separated from the death chamber only by a window and curtain, yet knowing less than the outside world. 6:27. Everyone's exchanging glances, solemnity oozing away, replaced by uncertainty. Witnesses show their wrist watches to each other. Reporters fidget. 6:32. Suddenly, movement behind the curtain. Something's happening in that room bathed in white light. Vaguely, probably because I've seen the rehearsal, I can make out Bennie Demps being wheeled in.

The play begins. The curtain parts. On the other side of the window directly in front of us, bathed in light, the Warden stands at his place on the telephone. Bennie Demps lies on the gurney, his eyes open and shut. He's blinking. The microphone switches on. Demps begins his final statement. "Mr. Shaeffer, you did everything you could," he assures his lawyer. Then he addressed the world: "They cut me in the groin, cut me in the leg. They butchered me. I was bleeding profusely. I'm in a lot of pain. This calls for an investigation." (Two witnesses at the autopsy later told me there was so little blood, the coroner had to search for the needle's entrance point.) "This is not an execution; this is murder. I am an innocent man." I hoped he believed that.

Demps finished condemning this legal "lynching." The executioner no one could see stood at the controls in his tiny room behind that one-way mirror. He pushed the plungers and poisons flowed through the IV tube, which nobody could see, that led to the gurney and under the white sheets. The fatal fluid coursed into Demps's veins.

As his eyes fluttered, I closed mine, concentrating on the Puhlicks and Brinkworth trapped in the trunk of that car, crying out, struggling, bleeding, dying. I did my best to reconnect the crime with the punishment, to keep a covenant with the past.

Outside the prison, I wanted to engage protesters at the vigil, but I had one pressing phone call to make. "Your mother's killer is dead," I told Celia Puhlick's son. "He died, convinced this execution was Florida's response to her murder."

"At last," he said. "It's over. Thank you. I'll tell my sister. We'll move on." We never spoke again.

So Bennie Demps had died on a gurney, wrapped in white sheets with an IV in his veins, surrounded by his closest kin, monitored by sophisticated medical devices. Demps's execution appeared and seemed so medical. Witnessing the execution, I shuddered. It felt too much like a hospital or hospice where I watched my father-in-law die mercifully. *How we kill those we condemn should in no way resemble how we kill those we love.* We have reached the point of obliterating a clear line between treating the sick and punishing the heinous. From that moment on, I joined abolitionists such as Professor Deborah Denno in especially condemning lethal injection, not because it possibly causes pain, but because it certainly causes confusion, wantonly merging punishment and treatment, arbitrarily severing crime from punishment, pain from justice.

14

THE PRIVILEGED AND
THE DAMNED

BY 2001, THE MOVEMENT FOR A DEATH PENALTY MORA-
torium had grown. The Philadelphia City Council and other municipali-
ties passed resolutions.[1] Maryland joined Illinois and halted all executions,
pending further study and reform.[2] It felt like the late 1960s again, in the
years before *Furman,* as doubts spread about whether those who were being
executed deserved it. Then the United States executed Timothy McVeigh,
the Oklahoma City bomber, with the support of more than 80 percent
of the American people[3]—including many who generally opposed capital
punishment but made an exception for this domestic terrorist who killed
168 victims, callously characterizing 19 dead children in day care as "col-
lateral damage."[4] Waiting for the public outrage to fade with the next prob-
lematic execution, abolitionists now employed a new moral benchmark
against which other condemned killers would be measured: "Not as bad as
McVeigh."

Then 9/11.

New York Law School sits a mere half-mile north of Ground Zero. One
of my students, a court officer on a coffee break, had run to the World Trade
Center with two fellow officers to help out. He lacked ID so police barred
him from the Twin Towers; his buddies died inside. He did his best right
outside to help those fleeing. As the building came down, he fled for cover,
huddled under nearby scaffolding. Falling debris killed strangers on either
side of him. He survived without a scratch. How arbitrary, life and death.
How determined we proponents of death for those terrorists and others who
deserve to die to help counterbalance that arbitrariness.

Some of us found it strange as the United States fought the war against Al Qaeda—religiously fanatic mass murderers targeting not only our civilians but our civilization—that the instant we captured those who would incinerate us by chemical weapons, or waste this nation by pandemic, "progressives" seemed more concerned with their civil liberties than our own survival. Post-9/11 terrorists seemed to make a mockery of the Model Penal Code's suggested mitigating circumstance: The killer believed the killing to be morally justified.[5] Most Americans reject any claim that a zealot's pleasure in going to heaven for destroying the West mitigated his responsibility for mass murder.

Post 9/11, evil seemed more real, clear, and present. Abolitionists abandoned their attempt to convince the public that no crime was so heinous, no perpetrator so wicked as to ever deserve the punishment of death. Instead, they shifted their focus to the expense, racial discrimination, and real, if remote, possibility of executing a factually innocent person. Committed abolitionists continued to champion the standard "state-sponsored murder" hyperbole. Aided by leading media outlets such as *The New York Times,* which downplayed contrary voices, selectively reported, relentlessly slanted, and shamelessly spun death penalty news, the abolitionist bench and organized bar continued their relentless attack.

After 9/11, public support for the death penalty did not spike appreciably. In this new "normal" state of heightened anxiety and resolve, states and the federal government continued to administer their flawed death penalty schemes. Meanwhile, abolitionists pressed on at all levels, more and more effectively. Only the popular sentiment of solid majorities in most states slowed them down. Steadily they chipped away at that mass of public support.

After *USA Today*'s cover story, "Death Penalty Gains Unlikely Defenders," heavily featured my retributive perspective,[6] increasingly I found myself invited to national and international conferences dominated by abolitionists. Although we fundamentally disagreed on the ultimate issue, both sides seemed to agree that the death penalty should be reserved, if at all, for the worst of the worst. Thus, later that year, James Liebman, a leading abolitionist, and I jointly published an op-ed in the *Houston Chronicle,* "Common Ground," calling for an end to the rhetoric.[7] We should stop trying to best each other in debate and instead cooperate in narrowing the penalty only to the worst of the worst.

Abolitionists, however, continued to proclaim death row as "living hell." Before I visited Florida's death row, I too imagined it as terribly bleak and forbidding, something out of a James Cagney movie. Itchy had described the somber isolation of his brief stint there: "A black cloud hung over death row. Everything there was dead serious. You seldom heard anybody talking there. I'll never forget this blind guy there. He came in the house—his wife and another man had been drinking and they were sleeping. This guy went to his bedroom and felt four legs in the bed. So he just got an old flat iron that was holding the door open, the kind that you heat on the top of the stove. And he crushed both their skulls. Somebody that can't even see ends up killing two people!

"I used to joke with that guy, 'Man, they going to dim the lights for you, when they hit that switch. They going to make toast out of you.' He laughed when I said that. 'Don't you understand? I ain't got no reason to live. I killed what I live for. It's you got to worry. They going to put you through misery here. My troubles going to be over soon when they pull that switch.'" It could be a relief to die, especially if life on the Row were the "living hell" so often described—and deserved, perhaps—by those who inhabit it.

And then I saw it for myself.

Florida State Prison (FSP) housed the worst of the worst: Corrections transferred the worst disciplinary problems from other prisons to FSP, including those who attacked staff. And it also housed savage killers condemned to die. A prisoner transferred to FSP for disciplinary segregation could, with good behavior, advance to less confining levels, with less restrictions and more privileges. On average a well-behaved prisoner took six years to work his way out of FSP to a better prison. Except of course those on death row. Unless the courts overturned or the governor commuted their sentences, the condemned would wait a decade or more to escape their living hell and reach the next and better world.

First the officers took me to the confinement wing, the harshest setting reserved for the misbehaving. Solid cells had solid metal doors, a food slot, and a smudged Plexiglas window with dot holes to yell through, their only contact to the outside world. Isolated from each other, these prisoners sat within stifling hot cages in virtual solitary confinement. The officer escorting me suddenly stepped on a pedal in the hall, nodding at a prisoner inside a cell. "I just flushed his toilet; he can't flush it." Thick metal doors and narrow slatted windows provided little ventilation. So the prisoner lived with his own stench until an officer chose to flush. If newly arrived "disciplinary problems" deserved this close confinement, what must death row be like, I wondered?

Surprise! Death row cells had the best ventilation in FSP, with widely spaced bars. Death row inmates could talk to each other. One convicted mass murderer might yell to the whole group, "Hey, catch what's on *Jenny Jones!*"

Almost in lockstep, the condemned would flick on their TVs to check out and whistle at the big-breasted woman on the screen. Yes, death row prisoners had their own individual televisions, in their cells! (Nobody else in that prison did.) The worst convicted and condemned killers could watch *whatever they wanted*—basketball games, news shows, movies—*whenever they wanted.* Only rarely did death row generate complaints or disputes at FSP. But one officer did describe a recent bitter complaint issued by a condemned killer: "It's not fair; his TV reception is better than mine!"

"They have the best deal in the building," another officer explained, mostly suppressing his bitterness. Death row inmates got much more liberal commissary privileges than the other prisoners in FSP. They could get cold sodas and hot sandwiches. The entire FSP was a No Smoking facility. Nobody—neither officers nor prisoners—may smoke *anywhere* inside—except, you guessed it, death row inmates were allowed to smoke in their cells! "You know these things will kill ya," one officer warned a chain-smoking condemned killer. They both had a good laugh.

Most prisoners locked up in FSP got to rec once a week for two hours. They exercised alone, one prisoner to a dog run, a narrow concrete strip, approximately 15 feet long, 3 feet wide, fenced in on all sides, wire mesh barely above their heads. When I asked to see where the condemned rec, the officer blanched. Their yard was just on the other side of a thick metal door at the end of the tier. But the door that opened from the Row to the outside had no keyhole. Thus, if death row convicts ever escaped from their cells, overpowered the officers, and seized their keys, they still could not get off the Row. To get to the rec yard on the other side of that thick door, we'd have to leave the Row, walk down a long corridor, and go outside and around the entire perimeter of the prison. The officer looked at me as if to ask, "Is this really worth it?"

It was.

Traditionally, "hard time" has included hard labor—perhaps psychologically hardest of all, useless labor such as digging holes and filling them or moving rock piles. In FSP, the condemned also toiled at nonfunctional labor, but no solitary exercise in a dog run for them. I stared, dumbfounded. There they were, playing basketball! Together, ten at a time, for three hours on an open court. Next to the basketball court was a volleyball net. So Danny Rolling really was a helluva volleyball player. But it wasn't all basketball and volleyball. Sometimes softball, with prison mitts provided. And of course, that refreshing shower right after a hard game, along with a change of clothing. In fact, death row inmates got three sets of new clothing each week. And a weekly change of linens.

Other inmates at FSP brushed their teeth with security toothbrushes, their handles cut off. Prisoners must grab the bristles between the tips of their fingers. Death row inmates got full-sized comfortable toothbrushes. "They have it better than everybody else in the prison," an officer told me. "And so do we." As perverse as that seems, all the officers agreed, death row was the "the easiest place to work. Death row inmates give you less problems than anybody else. They are quiet, abide by the rules, respectful." Death row officers tended to be older, laid-back, less angry, and less resentful. "Over here, you slow it down," one officer observed, explaining how the tension level drops as you enter the Row.

The medical staff confirmed this. The nurses compete to take care of the condemned: "If they say they don't feel well, they really don't." Death row guys don't trump up medical complaints. Abolitionists do decry this "living death." And yet, as old-time medical staffers pointed out, the condemned rarely attempted or faked suicide. Other prisoners regularly took Paxil and Zoloft. But these "tortured souls" on the Row, consigned to a fate worse than death, rarely used tranquilizers. Of course the condemned would get "somber" around the time of an execution. "They do ask for Tylenol but that's about it. But they don't constantly want attention," explained one experienced medical staffer. "They get plenty of attention in other ways."

And so they did.

"When religious volunteers come to minister to the needy, everybody wants to visit the condemned. They get all the concern," the chaplain complained. "The other prisoners sit there alone; their prayers just hit the ceiling of their cell, left alone and forgotten." The courts mostly ignored complaints from the general population, but "they jump when a death row inmate files." And then, once the governor signs a death warrant, the dream team of abolitionist lawyers tirelessly struggles to save him. "A prisoner's handwriting really shows his agitation, but the death row inmates, their handwriting shows they're at ease," the chaplain explained.

Only death row inmates got contact visits. "I'd be better off killing an officer," a lifer complained. "Get much better privileges if they moved me to the Row." Yes indeed. Taking the penalty sometimes pays off.

At first I was stunned. Then, when I saw Danny Rolling lying in bed, reading his book, this retributivist perversion made me furious. Was I alone? Weren't the officers appalled? "If you start feeling, you're finished as an officer," one told me. And the others all agreed. How Florida executed Bennie Demps bothered me. That execution scene mocked retribution surely. But when it came to the worst of the worst, the problem went way beyond how they died. What bothered me most: *How they lived until they died.*

If the officers didn't care, the public must. When I returned home from FSP, I immediately wrote an essay, "The Privileged and the Damned," describing what I'd seen. Every magazine rejected it, mostly with form letters. One preprinted postcard had a handwritten note: "Good stuff! They'll never publish it here." Perhaps they thought I exaggerated. Maybe they refused to believe it—no officer at FSP would allow me to quote him by name. So I vowed to rebut the abolitionist rhetoric and expose the truth: Inside FSP, the Privileged were the Damned.

Because a picture is worth a thousand words, I would visually document life on the Row. But how to get permission? I closed my keynote talk, titled "Countering the Abolitionists," at the Association of Government Attorneys in Capital Litigation (AGACL) yearly conference, asking for help in exploding abolitionist portraits of death row as a living hell and life in prison as worse than death. One prosecutor passed along a copy of a 200-page autobiography that a condemned killer had written, typed, and copyrighted while on death row. He now claimed he couldn't be legally executed because he suffered from mental retardation.

After the US Supreme Court struck down Arizona's capital sentencing regime because a judge and not a jury found the aggravating circumstances, approximately 30 death row inmates knew they would be resentenced.[8] "Most of them came from Maricopa County, the largest in Arizona," Paul McMurdie, an Arizona capital prosecutor, informed me immediately after the talk. "Every single condemned killer except one specifically requested that they remain on death row until they actually had to go up for resentencing. Their defense attorneys stated it in their motions: That they would rather be on death row than go back to the county jail."

An Ohio prosecutor passed along a most remarkable artifact: stat sheets from the Ohio death row's basketball league. Yes, you read it right. Ohio had a death row basketball league! They carefully kept statistics on each individual player's scoring, field goal percentage, free throws, and offensive and defensive rebounds. It seems that one condemned killer, convinced that he'd been unjustly left off the all-star team, sued the Department of Corrections. The stat sheets surfaced during that lawsuit. Perhaps he had hoped to replace Coleman, a relatively marginal player who barely made that all-star team. Coleman led both sides in violations in the West's 96–78 victory over the East. But off the court, Coleman held his own record of sorts, as the only person in the United States separately condemned to die in three states at the same time.

Best of all, capital prosecutors in Tennessee and Oklahoma persuaded corrections to grant me access. I would visually explode the myth of death row as living hell and life inside as worse than death. I would make a documentary that showed the world the truth. The truth about how they died— the truth about how they lived until they died.

PART IV

FOR WHOM THE CANDLES BURNED

15

FLIP A SWITCH

DAVID KEEN GAVE ME THE CREEPS WHILE HE GAVE ME A tour of his "home" on death row inside Riverbend Maximum Security Institution, just outside Nashville, Tennessee. After showing off his craft—popsicle stick houses he'd constructed to sell—Keen proudly displayed his just-completed masterpiece: a large painting of puppies with angels he painted to console his girlfriend, whose dog had just died. "When my woman comes, we talk about everything," Keen told me. "She used to work at a law firm that's representing me on my appeals." But to avoid a conflict of interest, she transferred to a different law firm. "She doesn't look at why I'm here; she knows, but she met me after that." Officers, too, meet the condemned only afterward, I thought. "We could get married, but there's no type of intimacy here—brief hug, brief kiss, sit down and visit. At the end of the visit, brief hug, brief kiss, she goes her way, you go yours."

I looked around David Keen's cell at his extensive collection of art supplies. "This doesn't look like living hell to me," I insisted. Keen agreed. Death row was nothing like he'd imagined. "My vision was that I was going to be locked in my cell until they execute me."

"When did you realize that wasn't going to happen?"

"When it didn't happen," Keen laughed heartily.

I asked him about his routine. "I work outside Monday to Friday doing laundry. I was done with my work, so I came out to do my own laundry. My day? Do my arts and crafts or go to the yard, play cards, spades and rummy. Cards gives us something to do to break up the monotony," Keen continued. "If we win, we win. Just going out to have fun. Some people play Scrabble, pinochle, Monopoly, handball, basketball. Some lift weights. I do pushups and sit-ups in my house. We joke around, tease the officers; the officers tease us."

"Sounds pretty relaxed," I said, trying to hide my disgust.

"Yeah. It's pretty laid-back for the most part. Everything's based on one's behavior in here. So you dictate what happens to you. We don't care what another guy did. We're all here for one reason—the death penalty. If you misbehave and get locked down, that has nothing to do with your crime. That has to do with how you behave here."

"There's a fair amount of kidding around and teasing."

"You got to be able to laugh, and joke, and kid around," said Keen.

Laugh it off, David Keen, you who raped little Ashley Reed, then strangled the eight-year-old child with a shoelace, dumping her, still living, into the Wolf River. Laugh and sing.

"What about those who say, 'The child is gone, the victim is dead, and he can construct wooden houses, can live in his home, can play spades. Where is the justice?'"

"The justice is I'm off the streets. I'm not a threat to society. You've got people out in general population with the same charge I'm on. Nobody's worrying about why he's got his freedom," Keen complained. "Why do you look at the death row inmates and say 'Hey, they have it too good?'"

"You're playing spades."

"My guard is always up. Because there are guys here who don't like my charge. Sometimes they'll say it to your face, they'll call you 'baby raper.' They got all kinds of names. You don't give them a reason to attack you just for your charge."

In the old days, the convicts wouldn't put up with the likes of David Keen. They would have attacked him. And taken their extra punishment. Then things changed.

"The baby-rapist-murderer, should he be playing basketball?" I asked Michael Bane, a death row inmate sentenced to die for strangling, then drowning, his robbery victim.

"You're putting me in a spot," Bane squirmed, trying to avoid the question. Six months after he first arrived, Michael Bane smuggled five guns onto death row and nearly pulled off an escape. Now, years later, as the office manager, Bane had access to all sorts of weapons, handing me a stapler from the drawer.

"A guy who smuggled five guns onto death row and now they let you—"

Bane laughed. "It's unreal, ain't it?" But with this level of comfort, he explained, the administration had nothing to fear. Bane had too much to lose. "It's too big a price." Did child killers deserve his laid-back lifestyle? I pushed Bane. "No. They're the worst of the worst."

"So what's up with Tennessee," I demanded, "letting baby murderers—"

"I don't know. I seen you talking to one yesterday. He murdered a baby. And they let him out here with us because he's not going to hurt nobody. Ain't going to bust a grape."

Today, convicts might ostracize child molesters, but they rarely attack them. "I may not like him, I may not deal with him," one convict explained, "but I'm not going to kill him. If the state lets him live like this in here, why should I do their job for them?" Live and let live. Not my job to punish, declare the prisoners—and their guards.

Sergeant Hugh Rushton, straight arrow, no-nonsense Vietnam vet in charge of security, commanded everyone's respect on Unit 2, Tennessee's death row. After 17 years at Riverbend and soon to retire, the sergeant, a man of few words, surprised me by agreeing to talk.

"Our death row inmates take pride in the unit. They live here and they like it. Inmates refer to their cell as their house—the only house they got. But they call all of Unit 2 'home.'"

"What's your goal here?" I asked Rushton.

"To keep the inmates safe, staff safe, and the people safe."

"They can walk around. Four hours a day lifting weights, playing handball, basketball, cards. And these guys raped and murdered children—is that justice?"

"I wouldn't call it justice to justify what we do to get them to cooperate. It puts our staff safer," the sergeant explained patiently.

"I recognize *why* you do it. But doesn't society have a right to expect punishment?"

"Death row is only a housing unit. This is not a punishment unit."

The sergeant had history on his side. Prisons initially housed inmates awaiting their punishment. Think of Socrates in prison, surrounded by disciples, awaiting the hemlock that would carry out his death sentence. In its infant years, however, America invented the penitentiary. The new republic, conceived in liberty and priding itself on rationality, largely rejected bodily punishment, substituting the loss of liberty calibrated in units of time to correspond to the seriousness of the crime. Most citizens today assume that punishment must be expressed and measured as years behind bars. But death row was different, the sergeant suggested—not a place *for* punishment but a place to be housed *until* punished with death.

"The appellate process takes at least a dozen years," I protested. "So if you're not punishing them for the first 12 years they're here, when *will* they experience their punishment? Tennessee has executed one person in 40 years—"

"Blame that on the court system. My job is safety, security."

"Do you know what these guys did?"

"I know what they've done—what they can do. I don't trust them, but I can depend on them without having to supervise them."

Sergeant Rushton had agreed to talk to this New York Law School professor, he confessed to me later, expecting to rebut the usual accusations, veiled or pointed, about corrections' brutality. But this probe came from a totally unexpected angle.

"You know better than anybody what life is like here. As a citizen, would you feel that justice is being done?"

Citizen Rushton would not lie. "No, sir."

"Would you be angry?"

"I sure would. As Citizen Rushton, he's supposed to suffer. If I were on the street, I'd demand he suffer. But I'm here to protect them. I'm a professional. As Citizen Rushton, it's not justice at all—it's not fair to the families of the victims."

The victims' families should feel unfairly treated by the killer's day-to-day life on the Row. But the voices of the dead cry out loudest: "How can you let those who murdered us live like this?"

"Lawyers pump up these inmates with hope," the sergeant continued, shifting responsibility. Hope does surface, even on the Row. Psychologists have documented the various "coping mechanisms" that make life for the condemned bearable: They feel themselves martyred, find religion, focus on self-improvement, or most commonly immerse themselves in their appeals, living with hope of a new trial or commutation.[1]

"If the professional part of you is at war with the citizen, why do it?"

"I watched my friends die in Vietnam. The government treated us like dirt when we came back. If I let that interfere, I'd be a cold-blooded killer myself. I was trained to be a professional." Rushton steadfastly refused to side with those demanding punishment on death row, insisting on safety as his only mission. "I haven't had an officer hurt, except one got cut. I've dealt with hundreds of them. On an individual basis—not on the basis of the past but moment to moment."

"So the past doesn't count," I said.

"It counts, but you can't let it interfere with what you're doing."

"It sounds like, 'the past counts, but you can't count it.'"

"If I did, I wouldn't be a professional." I tried but just couldn't puncture the sergeant's carefully constructed professional persona. "They've got to know they'll never be executed," I pushed. "A guy on death row at Level A has a life experience at least as good as the average lifer."

"Better."

"Ping pong tables on death row?"

"Ping pong tables makes it more convenient—" Rushton stopped. He'd had enough. His tone changed. "I agree with you, what can I tell you?" The dam broke. "Officers are like waiters. We feed them, wait on them, take out the trash. They're being waited on hand and foot, that's what it boils down to. You can call it a correction officer if you want."

"If you had the authority to administer death row?"

"They'd be locked on their cell 23 hours a day. I'd let them see the sky, but I wouldn't let them have contact with an inmate or staff."

"Why would you let them see the sky?"

"To let them know what they're missing. In Vietnam, you see a plane fly over, if you can see the sky. . . ." The sergeant winced. "When you get in a closed environment, the outside world doesn't exist because you don't see it. But when you have a window, you see what you're missing. What they deserve to be missing—but if you lock them away, they don't miss nothing. Level A and B wouldn't exist," the sergeant continued. "It would be full restraints, everywhere he goes. The meals here are better than what I used to get."

"Our soldiers eat worse than our condemned killers?" I asked, emphasizing this perversion.

"While they await ultimate punishment, their daily life should be miserable," the sergeant continued, his indignation pouring out. "I have to treat them better than we treat our senior citizens—we make sure our incarcerated inmates get that shunt put in their hearts. It's not fair, what more can I tell you? Our level system works for the Department of Corrections—they like it."

"If the people knew what was being done in their name?"

"You'd have some angry citizens—there'd be hearings. I'm doing what the Department of Corrections asked me to do."

"So corrections is the last place we should be looking to find solutions," I declared—a truth becoming increasingly plain to me. Originally I had dismissed corrections' anti-punishment attitude inside Lorton Central as confined to the most lax prison administration in the United States. Brief conversations with Florida's officers made me wonder. But Oklahoma and Tennessee really cemented it.

"The World's Largest Prison Rodeo," the giant colorful sign greeted visitors at the entrance to Oklahoma State Penitentiary (OSP). Cameron Harvanik, OSP's good-natured deputy warden, caught in jeans and a baseball cap on a Sunday, a video camera thrust unexpectedly upon him, summed up his overall mission including supervising H-wing, which housed punitive segregation for guys doing "disciplinary time" and also death row. "Our job is not to punish or do anything other than provide them what constitutionally they have coming to them—I hate to use those words, 'have coming to them,'" Harvanik said. "What the Constitution says they have to have."

"If he killed children—you're not angry?"

"Well, I mean, there's some things, you think, my God, why doesn't somebody just put a bullet in their head and be done with it? But as an employee, when I come to work every day, I flip a switch that says, 'I'm at work. These people are human beings; it don't matter what their crime is, they deserve fair treatment.'"

"Do they deserve to laugh and play ball?"

"When those guys are out there playing softball, mentally, they're not inmates for that 45 minutes or an hour—the convict rules are set aside. If I slide into second base and knock inmate Jones down, that's softball. So those activities are a good release for them and take pressure off them and off the staff as well."

Harvanik had participated in 50 executions. "People think anybody involved in the process dwells on that stuff, just eats it up. That I'd be involved with the file, and remember it, but I don't. It's part of my job. We don't talk about what they did. And once it's done it's over. We go about our everyday lives and wait for the next one."

None of the executions stayed with him?

"The first one I guess. Because that was my first."

"What were you feeling?"

"I hate to sound cold hearted, but neither satisfaction or regret. Neither way. I don't stay up at night before executions; I don't discuss it with my family. My wife and three kids know if they're going to order pizza, they better order it early or late because the gate's closed on execution nights, and the pizza truck can't come in." The genial deputy warden laughed. "Some people ask, 'How can you work there?' I tell people, 'Here I know who I'm dealing with every day. When I'm in line at Walmart, I don't know who's standing behind me or what they've done.'"

Lee Mann, the warden's assistant, succinctly explained and defended the laid-back life-style of prison administration, including death row: "We want to make the time as easy for them as we can because it makes it easy for us if it's easy for them."

16

BUT GOD SPARED CAIN

"I NEED WATER."

"Nothing else, just some water?"[1] the detective asked the man who had walked into the Shelbyville, Tennessee, police department on November 30, 1997, at 9:44 p.m., and told dispatcher Bonnie Hill he wanted to report a "homicide times four."[2]

Alone at the station, Hill radioed for assistance, just as a police sergeant drove into the parking lot. When the sergeant asked the man how he had learned of these homicides, he said he had killed his four children. Then he spontaneously stood up and placed his hands behind his back to allow the sergeant to handcuff him. Daryl Holton—a model prisoner from the start.

"I guess you know we need to talk to you a little bit about this thing," said the detective. "This thing" they call mass murder. "I know you're hurting inside," the police interrogator continued, commiserating with Daryl Holton, a man with blood and bits of his children's flesh still clinging to his clothes.[3]

Before getting Daryl Holton's confession, the detectives had to chant their ritual warning. "I'm required by law to read you your rights. It seems silly, but you know, we've got to do it." Ah, *Miranda*.[4] How silly to the public, how annoying to the police and prosecutors when the US Supreme Court revolutionized police interrogation, giving TV writers their new mantra. Daryl's determination to confess to the police that night did make Detective Collins's warning that he had the right to remain silent seem silly. But as tempting as it may be to have a guilty defendant confess, we protect him from himself. So from the start, the criminal justice system whispered its invitation to Daryl Holton: "Don't tell us the truth. Get a lawyer."

Of course, nine times out of ten, legally but not morally, the defendant fares much better keeping silent. Under a "truth in interrogation act," perhaps the police would actually impress upon the suspect advantages of calling a lawyer and refusing to talk.

"I'm going to ask you questions. Don't take them personal," the detective soothed the suspect. "You've been drinking today?"

"No," said Daryl.

"Have you had any kind of narcotics?"

"If marijuana is a narcotic. I tried to smoke a joint about 9:15."

"That's about an hour and a half ago. Your mind is clear *now?*"

"Right."

Pause on that. A person declares, "My mind is clear." Psychotics broken from reality into splitting personalities or minds ravaged with any kind of madness often insist they, alone, remain perfectly clear headed. And of course those high on drugs, including alcohol, often believe in their own profound clarity. Anyway, before he confessed, Daryl signed their paper: "I know what I am doing. . . . No pressure or coercion of any kind has been used against me." Now there's a rock-solid reliable statement. How many ignorant people insist they know what they're doing? And obviously anyone who can coerce you to confess can also coerce you to deny you were coerced.

Paradoxical preliminaries completed, the real questioning of Daryl Holton began.

"You mind just telling us what happened?"

"And why?" Daryl pleaded. He was here to tell his story.

"Yeah, why."

"The kids had been taken away from me and given back to me, taken away from me and given back to me. Enough." Enough for whom? Him or them? Me, me, me, me—four times in this one sentence.

As prearranged, Daryl Holton picked up the children from their mother, Crystal, his ex-wife, at three o'clock in the afternoon at Walmart in Murfreesboro. "The children were waiting inside in the little game area. They all came up and hugged me. Kayla grabbed me, and she just wouldn't let go."

"She really loved you."

"It was a mutual feeling. We stood there forever, it seemed like. Her mother went in to buy Eric some batteries for his hearing aid. We bought gum balls out of the machine, stood around, got reacquainted. Crystal came back out. She had two two-liter things of Coke and the hearing aid batteries. I remember thinking, 'Well, she's started drinking again.'"

"Could you smell the alcohol on her?"

"No. I had no proof other than the sight of the two two-liter Coke bottles. She was dressed nicely. She was wearing makeup. She said she was happy. And that did not make me happy. She has an order of protection against me. I was not supposed to be anywhere near her. I told her I did not want to pick the kids up at the police station because I wanted to see my kids, not go to jail," Daryl recalled without acknowledging the irony. "So she agreed to meet at Walmart. She thought we were going to McDonald's and to Shelbyville to meet my dog. I had a Staffordshire Terrier. His name is Barney. And all the kids wanted to see him."

When he picked up his children at Walmart from his wife—

"My ex-wife," Daryl corrected the interrogator.

"Was everything alright then?"

"No, because I knew what I was going to do."

Daryl unambiguously admitted it: He planned it and knew it was wrong. His killings were intentional. Worse: In Tennessee's eyes, they were premeditated.

Involving more than the mere intention to kill, premeditation has long separated the worst of the worst. "Whoever strikes a man so that he dies shall be put to death," declares Exodus.[5] "But if he did not lie in wait for him," the passage continues, "then I will appoint for you a place to which he may flee" and "save his life; lest the avenger of blood [a member of the victim's family] pursue and overtake this *unpremeditated* killer."[6] The Bible commands well-maintained roads to allow an unpremeditated killer to reach "cities of refuge" because "the man did not deserve to die."[7] Of course today, instead of keeping the roads in good repair, we keep the airwaves clear, with secure telephone lines to the death chamber, for the governor and courts to issue last-moment stays.

The great nineteenth-century British criminal judge and historian Fitzjames Stephen, my patron saint, rejected any emphasis on premeditation, pointing out that an abused wife who kills her husband after a long internal struggle less deserves to die than does a callous passerby who suddenly and spontaneously pushes a child fishing from a bridge into a rushing river, just for sport.[8]

Reserving the death penalty for "planned and cold-blooded murders appear at first sight to accord with natural feelings," conceded Britain's Royal Commission (1948–1953), which studied the death penalty more deeply than any other commission before or since. "A little reflection," however, would show that "premeditation or deliberation" failed to separate the worst of the worst.[9] And yet, although Tennessee became the first state to abolish mandatory death penalties in 1838, it retained premeditation as the essence of first-degree murder.[10]

"So how long have you been thinking about doing it?" pressed the Lieutenant Szaroleta, eager to have Daryl admit his premeditation.

"There was a domestic assault at the end of September," Daryl replied, locating the seeds of this night more than two months earlier. "That was in the projects."

"That's a rough place," Detective Mathis commiserated.

"I was not happy that my children lived there," said Daryl. "She got an order of protection against me. I would not be able to see my children. I would drive by the apartment, wanting her to call. And then all of a sudden, everything was gone. No lights, no clothes on the line. Nothing. They were gone."

Daryl suffered for weeks, anguished and angry at this sudden emptiness. Then Crystal called him at the garage where he worked and slept. "And I knew I was going to do it then."

"The Friday after Thanksgiving," Detective Mathis added. "You'd made up your mind you were going to—"

"Yes," Daryl confirmed.

"All four children?" Lieutenant Szaroleta asked.

"Yes."

If scheming makes a killing capital, Daryl Holton clearly qualified. So did Cain, who played upon trust and affection to lure his brother to a remote location where he delivered the lethal blow.[11] "Am I my brother's keeper?" Cain, after the first homicide of record, demanded of his Prosecutor, Judge, and Jury, attempting to obstruct justice and evade responsibility.[12] Daryl Holton, in contrast, actively sought the authorities to confess. Tennessee condemned Daryl. But God spared Cain. Abolitionists embrace this biblical story: Just as God declined the death penalty even for this intentional premeditated killing, so too humankind, made in the image of God, should show mercy and spare even premeditated killers, they claim. A leading international abolitionist organization even calls itself "Hands off Cain," apparently embracing the moral of the story. But when Cain begged for mercy after God sentenced him to an insecure life as a fugitive, God further mitigated the punishment, declaring, "If anyone slays Cain, vengeance shall be taken on him sevenfold."[13] And the Bible tells us, "the Lord put a mark on Cain, lest any who came upon him should kill him."[14] Cain's relief at this shows that he, as well as God, believed that the threat of death, and sometimes only the threat of a ferocious kind of death—"vengeance sevenfold"—could deter murder.[15] Ironically then, Cain, the first homicide of record, heard the death penalty pronounced not as punishment for but as protection from the consequences of his own conduct.

Perhaps after brooding and stewing on it, Cain's feelings had exploded in him as he killed his brother in a fit of jealousy that God had accepted

Abel's sacrifice while rejecting his. Traditionally, a sudden heat of passion mitigates an intentional killing from murder to manslaughter, but only if *adequately provoked*. A defendant who horribly overreacts to a minor slight, intentionally killing in the heat of passion *inadequately* provoked, still commits murder—but generally not capital murder.

Cain had clearly planned it; his killing wasn't a momentary outburst. Scripture tells us, however, that Cain was very angry as he slew Abel.[16] Dispatcher Bonnie Hill, in contrast, told the jury at Daryl's trial that when he walked into the police station to report a "homicide times four," Daryl Holton appeared calm and displayed no emotion. Of course appearances may deceive. Every mental health professional who examined Daryl concluded that he suffered from depression. Suppose Daryl did kill in passion but hid his inner turmoil? Can passion and premeditation coexist in the mind of a killer? Could Cain or Daryl have killed in the throes of passion although he carefully planned it? Tennessee said no. "The mental state of the accused at the time he decided to kill must be carefully considered," the Tennessee Supreme Court declared while deciding Daryl's appeal, "in order to determine whether he was sufficiently *free from excitement and passion* as to be capable of premeditation."[17]

Obviously emotion can distort the ability to reflect and exercise judgment, which premeditation requires. Does depression? Witnesses reported a flat, emotionless affect in the man who had just killed his children.

"Is all four of these children yours?" the detective continued.

"Biologically three of them are," Daryl answered, precisely but matter-of-factly. And I raised the little girl from an infant."

"How old were your children, Daryl?"

"Thirteen, ten, six, and four."

"And the little girl is the youngest?"

"Yes."

"How did you plan on doing it?" The detective knew to keep the focus on premeditation.

"The original plan was to do just what I did and then. . . ."

Killing the children was only the beginning. Daryl's other plans, by his own account "a bit more challenging to follow," involved killing Crystal, his ex-wife, along with Morris Rhodes, her "new found love." Then Daryl planned to go to the projects and find little Kiki, Rhodes's daughter, now living separately with her mother.

"I was pressed for time. I wanted to firebomb Crystal's residence and then make it to Murfreesboro," where the other child lived. "I wanted to go through the front two windows. I wanted to shoot the child. I wanted to basically shoot my ex-wife's boyfriend's daughter." Then Daryl planned to kill himself.

"I planned a lot of different scenarios," Holton explained to the police, making his premeditation absolutely clear. "And chose the one that time permitted. I was constantly subtracting—going over my options."

"When did you manufacture the Molotov cocktails?" asked the detective.

"Saturday. I located as many oil filters as we had. I got a gallon of gas, a box of Saran wrap, rubber bands that I had been saving from the daily newspaper. In each I put a teaspoon of black powder and then a pinch more gasoline. I filled it up as much as I could, took a red shop rag and cut it in strips, inserted it down into the main hole in the oil filter, drifting it down where it would touch the edge.

"I put the bullets in first, then put shotgun shells in the hole. I tried to thread it in as much as possible where it would remain intact. So it would make it through the window. I was going to light it and throw it. And hopefully, the flame would ignite the shotgun shell, the gun powder, and anything else that was in the oil filter."

"Is there a bomb in the building?" the detective asked anxiously.

"No," said Daryl. "Those were crude attempts at firebombs. They're in a green filing cabinet right next to where the weapon was sitting."

"Have you got any pressure bombs in there?"

"No."

"Or mouse trap bomb?"

"No, no. There are no other bombs." Daryl no longer posed a danger.

"You made a decision obviously to come in and turn yourself in. At what point did you decide to do that?"

"I decided not to go in and kill anyone or firebomb anybody's house when I got to the projects in Murfreesboro. I turned around and came back. I decided not to kill myself. I decided to turn myself in."

For the next ten years, Daryl would struggle with his decision to turn himself into a prisoner of law rather than liberate himself by taking his own life.

"Any reason why you changed your mind?"

"People would come up with their own conclusions if I had killed myself. This is gruesome. Awful. But if you're going to understand this, you have to talk to somebody that was involved. And I'm the only one that's still living. I'm going to tell you the truth. I may be inaccurate sometimes, but I'm not going to lie to you."

Daryl Holton lived, he claimed, in order to reveal the truth. First he took the children to McDonald's, then back to Shelbyville to his uncle's garage where Daryl worked during the day and slept at night. "We just told each other we missed each other. And I left the two younger ones up at the front of the shop" to play with an electric drill and a hammer, Daryl explained. "Called the two older boys back. Put the shorter one behind the taller one. Shot them point blank from the back of the younger one."

"Did—when you—when this—when you brought both the boys back," the lieutenant stammered, almost choking, "did they know at all what was happening?"

"No. They had no idea."

"They never looked you in the eyes or anything like that?," the detective asked. There was no audible response. "What did you tell them you were doing?"

"I told them I had something for them."

"Anything else said to them?"

"Don't peek."

Daryl shot them point blank. Then he covered the bleeding bodies of the two boys with a tarpaulin. "When you brought the other two back," the lieutenant pressed, "did they ask where their two brothers—when they heard the big loud bang, obviously—"

"They had no idea," Daryl explained. "They didn't even hear the bang. My younger son is hearing impaired—was hearing impaired," said Daryl, reminding himself that the child he killed was no longer. "They did not ask about the noise. They just asked where their brothers were. I didn't say anything."

"You just told them to—"

"Stand in a certain way and 'Close your eyes.'"

"Were all four children killed immediately?"

"Yes, but not at the same time." How could Holton have the presence of mind this moment to distinguish how quickly they died from how quickly he shot them?

"I mean, you done it in such a way that they didn't—"

"They didn't suffer, no," said Daryl.

"It was an immediate thing," said the interrogator, soothingly.

"There was no enjoyment of it at all," Daryl assured them, again self-centeredly shifting the focus from the pain the children did not feel at dying to the pleasure he did not feel in killing them.

Daryl Holton obviously *needed* to tell his story the night he killed his children and turned himself in. But did he need to tell it again? *Could* he tell it again five days later, when Detective Mathis and Lieutenant Szaroleta visited him in the Bedford County jail? Daryl signed a statement declaring,

"I do not want a lawyer at this time." That would become the grossest understatement for the next decade.

Now that a few days had passed, Daryl Holton must have felt the raw agony at what he had done. It should be excruciating to talk about it. Yet when the police produced a diagram of the garage, Daryl readily fleshed it out. "I pulled the mattress over right there. I hid the weapon right there. I asked them to stand one behind the other, the shorter behind the taller, not to peek," Daryl continued matter-of-factly, retelling his story. "I took the weapon from underneath the mattress, kneeled, and shot them."[18]

"Do you remember how they fell?"

"Steven fell to my left. Brent fell to my right."

"When you shot Steven, did you notice what type of injuries he had?"

"I noticed there was a large amount of blood coming from his mouth. Or in his mouth area, around his mouth," Daryl clarified with clinical precision. How could he, how could any parent recount this without choking on the memory?

"When you initially shot Brent, was the weapon barrel touching his back?"

"Yes. I intended to pierce both hearts. That's why I had the shorter stand behind the taller."

"Did they say anything to you just before this happened?"

"No. They were cooperative. I told them I had something for them. I told them to close their eyes. And I told them, 'Don't peek.'"

Detective Mathis took over. "After you were sure that both of them were dead, what did you do then?"

"I dragged the bodies further over and attempted to cover them up with a tarpaulin so the younger children would not see the bodies or the blood." Even in the throes of his killing spree, this man could make and carry out plans efficiently. As the younger children stood pressed against each other, Daryl "placed their hands over their eyes," knelt behind them, with his gun barrel angled up "60 to 75 degrees," and killed them. "Then I picked up the bodies one by one. I picked Eric up first and placed him on top of his brothers. And I picked her up. I placed her at their feet. I still had plans to firebomb my ex-wife and her boyfriend's home. And I knew that with the wrecker service, someone might come in late in the evening and discover it before I was able to complete what I planned to do. I laid [Kayla] down and covered them all as best I could. Made sure the lights were out."

"Were you at any time, Daryl, going to remove the bodies from the garage?"

"No. I had no intent of concealing my actions."

"What were you going to do with the bodies?"

"Nothing," Daryl said flatly. "I pulled out, drove to Murfreesboro." No time left to firebomb Crystal and Morris. "I was going to the apartment, hoping to find the ex-girlfriend and her daughter." And then he changed his mind. "I decided to come on back. I got back. It was 9:15. I listened on the scanner for anything out of the ordinary, and I heard nothing. I attempted to smoke a joint of marijuana and hit it twice, and I couldn't. I just couldn't. I threw it away in the trash can."

Back at the killing scene, if Daryl began returning to his senses, overwhelming sadness would start seeping into the core of his soul. And alone with his children's freshly killed bodies, we'd expect that he'd begin to weep. "Their eyes were open. Gunpowder was heavy in the air. I felt no remorse. I felt no regret, but I could not look at the bodies. And I've worked in operating rooms, and I've seen large amounts of blood."

"Because it was your own children, you were having trouble looking at the bodies?"

"That may be hard for people to believe, but yeah. It's going to be real hard to convince anybody that I love my children. I still do."

17

THE MAN NEEDS TO DIE

"DO YOU KNOW WHAT HE DID?," A CORRECTIONS OFFICER whispered to me.

"I can't even imagine it." I brushed him off, preparing to interview Daryl Holton, the last on my list of condemned killers who volunteered to meet with me during this trip to Riverbend. Really, I only had a one-paragraph description. I knew nothing yet of his confession.

"Holton will be punished for it someday," the officer insisted, leaving it unclear who would do it. In my nearly 20 years inside prisons, corrections officials had almost never expressed support for punishment. It took hours for Sergeant Rushton to come clean, but, as this officer insisted, Daryl Holton was different.

A thin figure in loose-fitting standard prison issue shuffled in, his arms and legs in chains, a guard at each elbow. I looked at this gaunt man in his 40s, red hair, pale, slight stubble, now sitting before me. "You are in restraints by choice," I repeated what the officers had told me.

"I am level C by choice," Holton corrected me. Year after year, Daryl Holton, model death row inmate, obedient, nonviolent, extremely polite, alone among condemned killers in Tennessee, declined to move from the most restrictive level C to B, then A, rejecting the extra privileges. Why stay at level C?

"I'm taking responsibility," Holton explained. How refreshing, how unusual.

"I'm told you are a 'volunteer,' waiving appeals."

"Foregoing them," Holton corrected me again. "And I was told you were a law professor from New York. Are you familiar with Professor Liebman?"

"We jointly published an op-ed piece. But we disagree on the death penalty. I'm in favor of it."

Telling strangers at social events that I favor the death penalty often leads quickly to unpleasantness. First their face reflects surprise, then chagrin, and finally disdain or disgust. Of course informing a condemned killer you favor capital punishment can create its own special reaction. But Daryl Holton didn't care one bit about that, or me. I not only knew but had *published* something with James Liebman, the Revered. "I read his two-volume *habeas* practice text," Holton said proudly. "I'm no expert, but I read all the footnotes. So I can blame some of my ignorance on him."

"Can we talk about what happened and why?" I asked, looking down at the thumbnail sketch of Holton's horrendous crime.

"We can skirt around the issue of why. But recounting the immediate events that brought me here—" Holton shook his head no. "You can't go wrong if you rely on the first statement I gave to the police," he assured me. "Right now I'm in three courts with defense attorneys attempting to involve me in adversarial proceedings against my wishes. When you see an issue on appeal," Holton complained, "generally it's a lawyer using it as a vehicle for his own personal agenda."

"To oppose the death penalty," I suggested.

"For the most part. Or to gain notoriety. Getting a death penalty case overturned looks good on a resume. An attorney should explain what the client is up against and allow him to espouse his own position." And what was Daryl's position? "In some cases, the death penalty is appropriate. For some crimes."

"In your case?"

"I've been convicted of four counts of murder. I'm not saying anything about myself. The death penalty is proportionate to the crime for which I was convicted."

"And the crime you *committed.*"

"These are two different things," Holton insisted.

"Yes they are," I agreed. "So *was* death proportionate in your case?" I asked.

"Everyone's entitled to their own personal view," Daryl said matter-of-factly, either to block further inquiry, make a deeper statement about the subjectivity of proportionality, or simply to be flip.

"Did you agree with the jury's decision?"

"I expected it."

"I'm not surprised you expected it. Did you *agree* with it?" I refused to let him escape into sophistry and moral relativism of "everybody's entitled to their own opinion."

"The death penalty is proportionate to the crime for which I was convicted."

"You haven't answered my question."

"With pending appeals, I'm going to have to decline to answer," Holton explained, sort of pleading the fifth—but strangely on the grounds that his answer might tend to *exonerate* him.

Inside Lorton Central, I once heard a variation of this ironic twist. I asked a convicted murderer, "Do you know of anybody who serves a life sentence for a murder he had nothing to do with?" He signaled me to shut off the tape recorder, something that only happened twice in 11 years. The prisoner watched and waited until I switched it off. Then he made me swear again I would never connect him to what he was about to tell me: "I do know somebody convicted of a murder he didn't have nothing to do with." He paused and looked up. "Me." When he first saw a photo of the real killer, he could swear he was looking at himself. Yeah sure, I thought. Convicts routinely protest their innocence. But I was curious. Why did we have to go off tape? "Because," replied this Washington, DC lifer claiming his innocence, "I got two backup murder charges in Virginia. Those beefs *were* mine. And if this sentence goes away, I don't want to be experiencing what they got waiting for me there."

Years inside Lorton persuades me it's shockingly common for prisoners to serve time for crimes they did not actually commit. Probably the lowest percentage of those falsely accused inhabits death row. We have not yet conclusively proved that any state executed an innocent person during the modern era, although I believe tragically we have. After I made this statement in a talk to Washington, DC criminal court judges, one thoughtful audience member came up to me and gave me his business card, suggesting we continue our dialogue privately. We never did. I hope it's not too late. His card bore the name "Eric Holder." He later became Attorney General of the United States.

Daryl Holton had confessed. The crime scene exactly matched his description; the forensic evidence confirmed his confession. Yet Holton's multiple killings did not settle the question of his guilt. Did he believe he was sane as he squeezed the trigger? "Right now I have attorneys arguing for a new sentencing hearing. Any statement I make about my mental condition could be used in a way I wouldn't want." For the second time, a convicted murderer refused to assert his innocence on tape.

"I still don't get it," I confessed. "If you were trying to take responsibility, why take it to trial?"

Holton bristled. "When I say 'accept responsibility,' I'll take no more nor less than what's mine. I'm not seeing a flicker of understanding there. I don't mind paying my dues if I have any dues to pay."

"Do you have dues to pay?"

"Apparently I have business with the state of Tennessee," Daryl said dryly. He explained his responsibility, legally: "In my case the aggravators were mass murder—the number of victims—and on counts two, three, and four, the age of the victims. The ages of the victims were gravy to the prosecution. The mass murder would have been enough."

But then came a swarm of appellate attorneys, forced upon him, making legal arguments in his name that Holton found ridiculous, claiming that he was denied a fair trial because he had not introduced mitigating evidence during the penalty phase. "It has me complaining about my own actions at trial!" Daryl protested. "Before I knew anything about the law, when I'd hear about an appeal, I'd say, 'Here they go again, bringing up some bunk.' But now I know it's not always the inmate. It's appellate attorneys."

Holton could calmly characterize the ages of his dead children as prosecution "gravy." The deaths of his four children did not arouse him, and his own death sentence left him calm. But defense lawyers arguing specious claims in his name? "It galls me, it really does. 'Holton says, Holton says. . . .' And I never argued this. It pisses me off.

"Personally I think it's pretty hard to mitigate a capital crime," Daryl continued. "And I certainly wouldn't want to mitigate the sentence for the deaths of four children. It's not being noble; I just don't see how you can do it." Daryl looked despondent. I felt frustrated. Why had he artfully diverted us from his own personal responsibility? "I was explaining why I was being evasive," Daryl shot back with irony. "With an insanity defense, you can't say I didn't put on mitigating evidence."

At trial Daryl had tried to persuade the jury he was not guilty due to insanity. The greater excuse, insanity, implicitly included a lesser claim that a diminished capacity not rising to the level of insanity made the crime murder or manslaughter but not aggravated murder in the first degree. Once the jury rejected those claims and found Holton guilty of four counts of first-degree murder, in Daryl's eyes, the jury's verdict—*guilty*—made him guilty. The jury's penalty—*death*—made him a rightfully condemned killer. Legally he should die. And that was the end of it.

True, Holton had personally declined to show the jury he did have some redeeming qualities. But, as he emphasized, citing court decisions, "In Tennessee in a capital case, a defendant does not have to put on mitigating evidence if he doesn't want to during the penalty phase." Daryl had refused the prosecutor's offer to plead guilty to get a life sentence. Later at trial, Daryl again refused to plead, this time with the jury, to spare him. He refused to inform them that his father had abandoned the family when Daryl was a child. And he declined to plead with the jury to credit his ten years honorably spent in the army in Germany, administering a dental clinic.

"Nothing really could ever adequately mitigate killing four children," Daryl insisted. Were there *inadequate* mitigating circumstances? I asked. He saw through this instantly. "Again I have to be evasive. I don't tiptoe very well. I'd never be able to dance ballet."

Our conversation shifted to daily life on the Row. Was this place the living hell that rendered Holton incompetent to make a rational decision to waive appeals? "I'm hanging around a lot of people I wouldn't hang out with by choice," he quipped. "I don't have a lot in common with most inmates here. I stay to myself and stay quiet. Listen to the radio—a lot of conservative talk radio. The biggest danger I have is becoming institutionalized."

Over the years, in many prison settings, convicts vividly described to me their struggles against becoming "institutionalized." Unless you resist, prison transforms your character. An institutionalized inmate thrives on prison's rigid routine, depends on it, becomes incapable of making decisions or living freely on his own. Prison becomes his refuge.

"This is no gulag," Holton explained. "Primarily it's managing your diet, avoiding bad habits. You're going to use caffeine, or nicotine, or eat a lot of sugar in a monotonous environment." Yet he chose this most monotonous environment by staying at level C. "I'm not interested in a group hug," Daryl quipped. "I'm here for one reason—and not to make friends and influence people. I don't want to become part of some mass movement to overturn Tennessee's capital sentencing scheme. I don't have a problem with it. I don't."

But why stay on level C? Why not be freer to play basketball or cards? "My views are not that popular. If I think you deserve the death penalty and your claims of innocence are a lie, I'll tell you. And that would be disruptive to security."

"It would disrupt security to look a guy in the eyes and say, 'You deserve to die, and you're full of shit'?" I asked. Daryl smiled.

"I wouldn't put it that way unless he got under my skin. But he'd get the message. Officers in uniform, I respect them. They have a dangerous job. They keep dangerous people on this side of the fence from hurting people I care about. So if I can make their day-to-day jobs easier, that's what I'll do. If I'm going to expect them to be professionals, I have to allow them to be professionals, which means not causing them problems. And remaining on level C does that."

Who would forego precious privileges and relative freedom for the sake of the staff? "I'm doing it for myself, to stay focused," Daryl explained.

"Stay focused not on fighting your conviction but fighting your lawyers," I mused aloud. "I shouldn't put words in your mouth."

"You're getting it right. I realize that other people will be viewing this," said Daryl, looking at my video camera resting on a Cheerios box next to me, pointing up at him. "But you don't have to be delicate, just spit it out."

"Do you deserve to die?"

"You make it sound like punishment rather than a reward," said Daryl, slipping from my grasp again. "It's proportionate."

"You're retreating to the legal, when I'm asking you a *moral* question."

"I'm in three courts," Daryl snapped back. But then he indirectly answered my question without jeopardizing his legal position. "Yates no, Smith yes."

Andrea Yates notoriously drowned her four children in a bathtub to save them from the devil that already possessed her.[1] She killed the children, she explained, to spare them her own eternal damnation. Yates's madness, her delusional selflessness, arguably excused her from punishment for her killings. In that case, we mourn what she did, but we pity and do not despise her. Susan Smith, in contrast, drowned her children by driving her car off a boat ramp into a lake and jumping out at the last moment with her children seat-belted inside the car.[2] "Yates was stressed out and probably suffering from depression," Daryl explained. "With Smith it had something to do with the relationship with her boyfriend, and the kids were in the way."

Agreeing with Daryl's moral distinction that Andrea Yates should have been spared (as she eventually was) while Susan Smith deserved to be executed, although she got life, I wondered whom Daryl Holton more nearly resembled in his own eyes. By citing parents who killed their own children, he had at last connected morality to motive. I was about to pursue this idea when an officer suddenly interrupted: Sergeant Rushton said to wrap it up. Had we stayed with it, Daryl might have revealed the excruciating burden his children had become to him. He might have clarified his own motives. Or once again, he may have slipped through and dodged my questions. Why waste time trying to figure out this smart but weird man who murdered four children and obviously deserved to die?

"Guys on level A playing handball, having contact visits, playing basketball," I said, unable to hide my indignation at what I had already witnessed on Tennessee's death row.

"There's no reason to be mean to them. They're not here to be punished. They're here to be killed." Daryl had no problem with the death sentences, his own included, but he seemed to reject a punishment of life. "I don't want to hear 'life sentences.' I want to hear treatment plans."

"You don't believe in *punishment?*" I challenged.

"They call it the Department of Corrections. They could change the name to the Department of Retributory Justice," said Daryl, mocking me. "I thought about this question earlier today—it's sort of like bankruptcy court: when a guy is so much in debt and has no hope of paying his bills—so you take away what he has."

"Do you expect to be executed?" I asked, suddenly switching subjects and racing the clock.

"Eventually, but I'm starting to have my doubts."

We had only a couple of minutes left, I guessed, before the sergeant shut us down. "I can't marginalize the value of my children's lives," Daryl explained seriously. "And by arguing that the death penalty is not appropriate to me, I'd be marginalizing their lives." How powerful, this simple explanation for "volunteering" to die. Challenging his death sentence, Daryl would be trivializing the value of the children's lives. But how could he have valued their lives any less than by killing them?

"Your children's memory—" I began, but he cut me off.

"I'd really like to tell you," said Daryl, sensing the end to our interview and drawing a breath as if to sum it all up. "My biggest problem is people involving themselves on my children's behalf because they 'care so much' about them. People think children are a public resource. The public library is a public resource. Amtrak is a public resource. But children are a family resource."

What did he mean by that? How could any sane person who loved his children deliberately kill them? And yet I couldn't just dismiss him as a crazy killer. An intelligent man with a sense of humor who murdered his four children in cold blood and seemed all right with it—it didn't make sense. Although I wanted Daryl Holton to get what he deserved as soon as possible, right then, as time ran out, I wanted to get to the bottom of it, and him.

"I feel like we haven't finished," I said.

"I feel the same way," said Holton.

"Are you free to continue tomorrow?"

"I do not need to check my calendar," he assured me with a twinkle in his eye. We agreed to meet again early the next day, my last at Riverbend, which I intended to spend documenting other parts of the prison, especially the notorious Unit 6. I would compress those plans in order to follow up with Daryl, but only if he really opened up to me.

"I'll try, I'll try."

When Daryl Holton left, I stretched my legs, packed up, and left the interview room, not yet able to digest what I had experienced. "I really appreciated our earlier conversation, sergeant," I told Rushton sincerely, although he had just ended my interview with Daryl. As tomorrow was my last day at Riverbend and the sergeant worked the night shift, I'd not see him again.

"Do many guys turn down appeals?" I asked, trying to make sense of Daryl Holton.

"We have all these bleeding hearts convince them to pick up their appeals. Steve West turned down his appeals. He wanted to be executed by electric chair. Power on, he's calling for his attorney. The other inmates called him 'no nuts.' When he came back, he checked himself into protective custody."

"Tell me about David Keen," I asked, thinking about the child Keen raped and murdered.

"Young, impressionable inmate. Psychological problems. Attempted suicide. I'd take sharp objects away from him. He's grown up a lot. Turned out to be a pretty good inmate."

A pretty good inmate? "Do you know what he did?"

"I try not to let it bother me. You got to treat them all the same," Rushton continued, with that standard claim of the detached bureaucrat.

Reacting to my obvious disgust when he characterized Keen as "a pretty good inmate," Rushton told me a story: "I had to go down to Memphis and testify for Ronald Rickman and Billy Grossclose. Billy Grossclose was a navy recruiter, hired Ronald Rickman to kill his wife for the insurance money so he could pay off his gambling debts. Rickman kidnapped her, raped her, stuffed her in the trunk of the car, and rode around for a couple of days before the poor woman died. They both got the death sentence. But they were good inmates. I didn't have no problem out of either one of them. And that was the only thing I could testify to." Rushton grimaced but continued. "In court, the victim's sister was really throwing daggers at me. I felt bad about it because here I am testifying about how good these inmates are, but they're there to try to get out of the death penalty for killing her sister. And they did. They was given a life sentence."

"And you wanted them executed?"

"Sure did. Still do. But I'm not going to get up in a courtroom and lie. I'm not going to lie for them. I'm not going to lie against them. They were model inmates."

The US Supreme Court brought us this story by holding in *Skipper v. South Carolina* that a convicted first-degree murderer has the constitutional right to present evidence of his good behavior in prison to a jury choosing life or death.[3] When you read the case in a book, perhaps you nod in agreement. But hearing Rushton tell it and picturing Grossclose and Rickman with that poor woman suffering and suffocating in the trunk, you know that good "adjustment" to prison life should not count in deciding whether these murderers deserve to die.

"Tell me about Daryl Holton."

"A unique individual. He knows he shouldn't have killed those kids. He did it to punish her. Now he's punishing himself."

"You think he will be executed?" I asked the sergeant, packing up to leave.

"I hope they will. A man wants to die, let him die. If I were a betting man, I'd bet against it. But I hope they do it. The man needs to die."

18

THE NICEST THING

"I MUST WARN YOU. I HAVEN'T SWEPT," DARYL HOLTON called out to me the next morning from inside his cell.

"That's alright, you ought to see my place," I called back through his food slot, thinking of my own disheveled office. I had caught Daryl neatly folding his shirts, like any good housekeeper self-consciously surprised by an unannounced visitor.

Before I could enter his cell, Daryl had to be shackled. Of course he politely submitted, hands behind him through the slot, carefully chained, and tightly locked together. Then his legs, double chained and also locked. "The brown paper bag labeled 'contraband'—don't let that bother you," Daryl joked as I quickly videotaped his sparse but immaculate cell, foodstuffs and clothing exactly in their place, a newspaper neatly covering the exposed toilet.

I trailed Daryl as he moved slowly in chains through the fluorescent tier, down the stairs across the pod, past the Ping-Pong table, to our interview room. You know the scene—"dead man walking"—all other movement frozen on the Row. Only with Daryl, this security precaution felt like foolish bureaucratic pomp and ritual. Daryl Holton no more needed officers at his elbow or the chains that bound him than I did.

"I paced awhile last night, trying to come up with answers suitable to your questions." Daryl hesitated. Was he waiting for me? I jumped right in.

"The past counts. The memory of your children—that's why you should die."

"I wouldn't take it that far," said Daryl, taken aback by my blunt, aggressive opening, but immediately regaining his balance. "That may be a personal view I may or may not hold. Gee, I'm starting to sound like an attorney," he mused. "As far as the memories of my children, they're private. The *convictions* are sufficient for the death penalty."

The conviction—that public, legal event; the jury's *official* declaration legally justified Daryl's death sentence. Daryl had once again absorbed and then deflected my moral question: What did he feel he deserved, and why? Daryl claimed these feelings as private, personal, and irrelevant. This conversation, I resolved, must not merely repeat our last.

"You said that if a stranger murdered your children, society would be right to condemn him. Couldn't it be *worse* for a parent to kill his children?"

"Yates and Smith were similar but different cases," Daryl reminded me.

"Yates no, Smith yes," I recalled. "You have a subtle nuanced view, distinguishing between two mothers who killed their children."

"I have a more informed perspective," said Daryl ironically.

"I want to return to the past crying out."

"I don't do eloquence."

"Oh yes you do," I shot back and waited for once, allowing him to gather his thoughts and consider his reply.

"You could call it a warped application of the Golden Rule," he finally said. "If the Pope commits a crime, I don't want to hear he's the Pope. I want to hear about the crime. The fact that he's the Pope and knitted blankets for the homeless has nothing to do with the crime." I smiled. "The law has to be even-handed," he continued. "If I ask for special treatment, then I'm not entitled to equal protection. If you're going to have a concept of justice, it has to be even-handed—otherwise it's false advertising, and the law won't command the respect that it should."

"But as you know," I countered, "not only do we demand *equal* protection, but also that we treat each person as an *individual*. Like cases must be treated alike, but each person is unique. That's the great tension."

And so it has been in the modern era. After the US Supreme Court made front-page headlines in *Furman*, striking down the death penalty across the United States as too randomly and haphazardly administered, some states attempted to ensure consistency by defining in advance all aggravated murders that *must* automatically bring a death penalty. The US Supreme Court struck down those death statutes because they focused only on the crime and not the individual criminal. Mandatory death sentences might achieve consistency but at the cost of fairness.

To manage these conflicting demands, states require the prosecution to prove at least one listed aggravating circumstance at trial. Then in the second, separate penalty phase, the defendant may show any relevant mitigating circumstances as a reason to spare his life. Daryl had refused to argue any mitigating circumstances because, he insisted, like the Pope's blankets, they were irrelevant to his guilt or punishment.

Near the end of his career, US Supreme Court Justice Harry Blackmun concluded that we must, but cannot achieve fairness and consistency at the same time. Thus, he famously announced he would "no longer tinker with the machinery of death" and joined the Court's abolitionist camp.[1] Justice Antonin Scalia, Daryl's favorite, also found it impossible to reconcile fairness with consistency, but he denied that the Constitution required both. Scalia, like Daryl, would jettison individual fairness in favor of the law's equal protection.[2]

Thus far in the modern era, however, the bulk of the Court clings to the constitutional hope that a system can reconcile both fairness *and* consistency, where the legislature defines death-eligible murder carefully in advance, yet leaves it open for a convicted first-degree murderer during the penalty phase to convince the jury to spare him. "Individualized, not arbitrary," said Daryl, succinctly restating the twin constitutional goals of capital punishment.

"And you're saying there could be no mitigating circumstances, given the weight of the aggravators?" I was really asking the moral question—whether intentionally killing four children, so horrible in itself, simply cut off explanation or mercy. Daryl again took my question legally.

"In Tennessee, you *can* argue any mitigation. The fact that I was a Cub Scout might be considered mitigating, but I can't make it relevant."

"What could be relevant?"

"The mental health expert for the defense presented a theory of 'altruistic killing.' Killing for the good of the children. Anything that supported that would have been relevant."

"But that theory was bogus."

"I haven't said that," Daryl insisted.

"Was it bogus?"

"I'm not going to offer an opinion."

I took a different tack. "You said the first statement you made to the police was the only full, accurate account. Nothing you would add?" Daryl shook his head. "I was fresh from the fire. And I was surprisingly accurate."

Once again I was losing the fight to get Daryl to come clean. I went for broke: "Given that you deserve to die, given that the state has condemned you, why not make it easy and kill yourself? Why this struggle?"

"It's not that easy," said Daryl quietly.

"If you could, you would?"

"That was the original plan. Others in this unit—even those with false hope, meritless claims, or flat out liars—deep down they're aware of their guilt. But they feel justified." Daryl paused. "But in order to assert that justification, they'd have to abandon their claims of innocence. And they're too caught up in their web of deceit. They're being taken advantage of, pumped up with false hope. And they've sold out to their appellate attorneys."

"That's all very interesting, but why didn't you kill yourself?"

"There's a tendency to want to get the last shot in," Daryl explained. "While they're dragging you to the proverbial gallows. Get that last shot in."

"If the Governor offered you a commutation tomorrow to life in prison, would you accept it?"

"No."

This was the closest Daryl ever came to telling me he wanted to die. "You wouldn't accept it because you don't deserve it? Or because you don't want the life that would await you here inside?"

"It would be selling out." Daryl knit his brow. "I'm still a citizen of Tennessee. They do some things right. They're a little slow in the capital litigation department, but I guess they're doing the best they can."

"As a citizen of Tennessee, you approve the sentence of death."

"No one is here for littering. I'm not holding the state of Tennessee against the wall, saying, 'Commute me or face perpetual litigation.' I'm not doing that."

"You were judged by a jury of your peers?"

"Probably more accurate to say 'a cross-section of the community.' It's difficult to find someone with my background."

"Any part of your military background help you to . . . ?" I stepped gingerly on forbidden ground.

"Everybody in the army was trained to fire a gun. How much of an expert do you need to be to fire at point-blank range?"

"Do you believe in an afterlife?"

"Sure."

I've asked convicted murderers this question many times over the years. "Yeah," said one particularly vicious killer after detailing his many brutal crimes. "I do believe in heaven and hell."

"And where will you be going?"

"Heaven. They taught me when I was young, as long as I embrace Christ any time before I die, I go to heaven. No matter what I done. So someday, maybe I'll be lying in a pool of blood. And I'll embrace Christ." Devout Christians inform me this distorts church doctrine, but as long as killers *believe* their road to salvation and permanent happiness in the next world lies open to them, the fear of God will not deter them.

Could a man who premeditatedly killed his four children ever hope to enter the pearly gates? "Hell is a relative term," Daryl explained. "And depending on the quality of your life on earth, you may not realize you're in heaven. Some guys here had it so bad that this is a relief. I've lived in a garage with no heat. I've also stayed in four-star hotels in Germany and dined at five-star restaurants. So, as far as whether death row is living hell, well, don't try this at home. You're smiling."

"I was asking about an afterlife."

"The *living* hell question is the one I pondered."

I took a stab at Daryl's real motives for "volunteering" to die, turning his wry humor serious. "Do you see waiving appeals on the basis of the memory of your children as potentially contributing to the state of your soul after you're dead?"

"Everything you do contributes to the state of your soul after you're dead," he responded solemnly.

"So that you may be improving your afterlife by ending this life?"

"I'd rather not soil it by endless and frivolous appeals."

"Soiling your life?" I repeated Daryl's words to him, astounded that a man who deliberately killed his four children could see his own life as still unsoiled.

"Sure." Daryl paused and spoke carefully: "I could produce a petition with a few hundred meritless claims—typed up really nice—referenced, cited, footnoted, and it would all be meritless, frivolous, or an outright lie. There's no honor in that. And I'm not subscribing to someone else's concept of honor."

"Is there honor in being executed?"

"There's honor in taking responsibility for your actions and not blaming them on someone else."

"So being executed is an honorable death?"

"It depends upon your perspective."

"Your perspective," I demanded.

"I wish things had worked out. But apparently they didn't."

"The ancient Greeks and ancient Hebrews independently embraced 'blood pollution,'" I said.[3] "Unpunished crimes would pollute the community." I looked Daryl straight in the eyes. "Are we polluted as long as you're alive?"

"I think that's an archaic way of describing it," he replied, wincing. "If society doesn't respond appropriately within the standards of moral decency, they'll invite further attacks. If you let a guy go, chances are he's going to do it again."

"They wouldn't be letting you go," I said quietly. "They just wouldn't be killing you."

"They'd be giving me a discount. Life has to have value to society," Daryl continued. "I don't think you can attach a money value to life. I don't think you should be able to buy your way out of it. If you don't have an excuse, by taking a life, you're sacrificing your own. Retribution is the sole purpose of the death penalty. And what more can you take from someone than their life?"

"Your execution would give value to your children's lives?"

"It will *acknowledge* it."

Emile Durkheim, the great nineteenth-century sociologist, added this newest justification for punishment: its expressive function—*denunciation*.[4] Speaking for the community, the people's representatives denounce the murderer, declaring him no longer fit to live. States such as New Hampshire execute no one. Yet thus far, that state clings tenaciously to the death penalty, perhaps as the best way to denounce our worst criminals. The execution ritual gives us the final occasion to denounce the condemned.

Daryl had added his own twist to the expressive function of his execution: "It would *acknowledge*" the value of his children's lives. "There should be no doubt that I was aware of the value of my children's lives before I killed them. If I weren't aware of the value, it never would have happened."

"I can't make sense of that statement," I said, aghast. "I can't even begin to comprehend that statement."

"The theory of the defense was 'altruistic killing,'" he reminded me.

"But that's bogus."

"Why do you keep saying that?" Daryl snapped, obviously irritated. "The state's theory was that I did it to spite my wife. You can accept that, but *that's* bogus."

The jury that sentenced Daryl to die and Tennessee courts that affirmed that death sentence agreed with the prosecution's theory: Daryl Holton murdered his four children for the *pleasure* of revenge. To get back at his ex-wife, Crystal, for taking the children from him, for living with another man.

"What's your theory?" Daryl challenged me. What *was* my theory? "I've been accused of being a racist," he continued. "Of killing my daughter because she was biracial and I was not the biological father. But *that's* not true!"

"The claim that it was an altruistic killing was *not* bogus?" I asked, demanding clarification.

"I don't think so. The defense psychologist got it right. I just didn't support his testimony."

"So then, why *do* you deserve to die?" *The* question again. And again Daryl retreated for legal cover.

"Because, 'the aggravating circumstances outweigh the mitigating circumstances.'" He smiled. "It's easy to remember."

"Yes it is." So easy to remember and difficult to apply.

"We're talking about the value of my children's lives," Daryl insisted.

"There are other people involved," I countered. "Their mother, their grandmother. And the children themselves. Why should Daryl Holton's evaluation trump everybody else's?"

"I'm the one on trial," Daryl snapped, then hesitated. "You're asking me to justify my actions."

"Or pronounce them unjustifiable!" I insisted angrily.

"I won't do either. I've never doubted my justification of what happened. The mental health expert polished it up."

So Holton *did* claim that he killed the children for their own good. Surely eight years later he must see this "altruism" as grotesque egotism and selfishness. "Looking back at it, you still feel the same way?"

"I probably should have abandoned the insanity defense. My story was presented to the police. I don't think a six-figure trial was necessary." His great regret: the unnecessary expense of his trial, not killing his children. Daryl Holton reached safe harbor, once again, by applying legal hindsight.

This moment I wanted to punish him badly—to strip him of his self-righteous justification. I wanted him to suffer the deepest pain of remorse. If Daryl would not emotionally or morally confront his killings, if he continued to divert the conversation to the law, I would, if I could, destroy his self-respect by means of the law, making it a question of justice, that delicate intersection of law and morals. "Did the jury miss the just outcome?"

Daryl dodged this easily. "You're asking me to intrude on the jury's discretion. I won't do that." Daryl, the Sophist, defined justice as whatever the jury decided.

"Did the O.J. jury make a mistake?" I demanded.

James Bragg largely set my views on the O.J. Simpson verdict. A product of the inner-city streets, Bragg and many of his school buddies ended up together inside Lorton Central. They became prisoners; he became warden. We hadn't spoken in a couple of years, but the night a jury found the former football star "not guilty" of a double murder that almost everybody then and today believes he committed, I called Bragg.

"Brother Rob, calling about the O.J. verdict."

"Well?" I asked, awaiting Bragg's colorful condemnation.

"They did the right thing."

"James!"

"The LAPD framed a *guilty* man. You can't let the police get away with that," said Bragg, himself a former DC homicide detective.

"The O.J. jury did not make an accurate determination," Daryl admitted. "But the jury is entitled to nullification." Jury nullification bedevils strictly rule-bound justice, as it suggests the rightful power of a jury to ignore the evidence and find against the facts in the defendant's favor for higher reasons. This hearkens back to Aristotle's idea of equity, that sometimes the strictest justice is the greatest injustice.

"The jury is entitled to nullify," declared Daryl. "The defendant is not entitled to it. I have no problem with the verdict. They did the best with what they had," he insisted. "The state has assured me that they have given me *all* exculpatory evidence," Daryl continued, dripping with sarcasm. "And the defense attorneys assured me they gave me *everything* they had. Since there is no more, the verdict is right."

"You have something no one else has. You understand what really happened." I looked at Daryl. "Were you sane, that moment?"

"I'm not going to answer that."

"Because you can't?"

"Because the ultimate issue is for the trier of fact."

"Frustrating," we both said, exactly in unison. Daryl broke the silence. "They've got me in a bind—he says with shackles on. You're asking me the right questions, but you're also asking me questions that can give me problems."

He wouldn't reveal himself further. I started to call it quits and say goodbye for good to Daryl Holton.

"What can I wish you? I wish you dead?"

"That's the nicest thing anybody has said to me in years," Daryl smiled. And got serious, or maybe he had been. "I hope you appreciate that I wouldn't clutter a courtroom with frivolous issues."

"I do appreciate that. What I think doesn't matter, but I think you deserve to die," I said, looking at Daryl sincerely, the oddity of it all striking me as I said it. "I think it's right that they execute you. I think it honors your children's memory."

Daryl Holton quietly absorbed this verbal blow from a person he'd spent six hours with over two days. We got up, awkwardly, facing each other, with Daryl chained and helpless.

"Thank you," I said.

"Thank *you*," said Daryl. "I appreciate the conversation."

"Should I get them to open the door?"

"Yes, I forgot to bring my keys with me," Daryl quipped. And with that, we shook hands, and Daryl shuffled from the room to the sounds of an officer yelling, "Clear the pod!"

As I left Daryl, a strange beat with peculiar rhythms piqued my curiosity somewhere in the distance. Although he hardly shared my mission, Burton Mixer, my prison guide, smiled and walked me down a hall and into a room. Condemned murderers, armed with heavy wooden mallets and sharp chisels, pounded on leather, there in the Tennessee death row's arts and crafts room! Michael Bane put down his mallet and looked up, smiling as I entered. "This is a purse," he explained to the camera, taking a break from chiseling a large letter S. "For my daughter, Sherri." Next to Bane, his coffee. Around him, guys quietly into their leatherwork.

I looked around. Flashes of fluorescence reflected off racks of sharp metal tools. I'd seen my share of confiscated prison shanks. Prisoners fashion weapons from razor blades melted into toothbrushes, from tightly wrapped newspaper with sharpened Plexiglas blades, from windowsill strips, etc. Years earlier, an attacker had slit Bane's throat with razor blades embedded in two Popsicle sticks. But here in Tennessee's death row arts and crafts room, open and exposed, rows and rows, in three trays, each one already sharpened: Instant Shank—no scraping necessary! Of course you can't order weapons from the commissary. Yet.

I looked up from my extended video close-up of this potential weapons cache and caught Bane watching me filming. *It's too big a price*, his drooping but smiling eyes told me.

Even those who deserve to die still remain human beings, of course. We do owe them some relief from the tedium of heavy labor at leatherwork. So, in one corner of the arts and crafts room, a large-screen color TV broadcast the NFL game. "That's a big TV," I said aloud to no one and everyone.

A condemned killer defensively took up my challenge. "They think we got it made, up here."

"And what would you say?" Could he feel my anger and disgust? He was armed, I wasn't.

"I'd say I'd trade places with them," piped up another condemned killer. *Trade places with the victim*, I seethed silently. Don't despair. At this moment, these condemned killers did in fact suffer inside that arts and crafts room. There was no escaping it: Their beloved Tennessee Titans were losing, 24–12.

19

A ONE-MAN CHAIR

"I'M AN ATTORNEY IN NASHVILLE; I UNDERSTAND YOU spoke to Daryl Holton," said a voice on my school answering machine. Only now does it strike me that Kelly Gleason did not say, "I represent Daryl Holton." Daryl had told me he considered Kelly Gleason his adversary.

I returned Gleason's call. Her voice had an edge, which didn't surprise me. Over the years, several defense attorneys have groused that I'd spoken to "their" clients without permission. Some have threatened to contact the bar association. The Code of Professional Responsibility only prohibits *opposing counsel* from contacting a client, not research journalists who happen to be law professors.

Kelly Gleason asked for a copy of the videotape. I refused. Would I be sharing it with the prosecutor? I didn't plan on it. Her voice changed. "Did Daryl tell you he wants to die? He's never told me that."

I didn't know how to answer. I decided not to answer and quickly ended our conversation. Now what to do? Sharing the video with the defense or the prosecution might affect whether Daryl lived or died. Officially, of course, I was neither Daryl's defense attorney nor his prosecutor. Morally I was evolving into a little of both. Daryl's actions spoke remorse; his statements denied it. His killing horrified and repulsed me; his intelligence and humor drew me in. What would Daryl want me to do?

Burton Mixer, death row's counselor, arranged a phone call with Daryl. I nervously babbled, ending with the question: "Do I turn over the videotape to the prosecutor, the defense, or neither? I'm not bound by your wishes, but I want to know them." I paused.

"You just said a mouthful; that comes from your being a professor." That good-natured put-down. Almost every law professor with any insight should suspect he or she talks too much. My sense of justice should guide me, Daryl counseled.

"Do you consider Kelly Gleason your counsel?"

"I don't consider them my attorneys, but I don't have a choice. I would like to defeat them but fair and square on level ground." Daryl clearly wanted to end the conversation. "Mr. Mixer now has his hands around my throat," Daryl joked. "So, go ahead, use our conversation for everything it's worth. But keep it fair."

Daryl refused to sign the slew of petitions that Kelly Gleason filed in his name. He would not become the tool of lawyers. "They consider the appellate process to be a team effort," he complained when we first met. "'We're all in this together; we're going to fight the death penalty together.' And I stood up, 'What's all this "we" stuff? It's a one-man chair.' A team effort? No. This is *my* right to appeal."

Appellate attorneys on a mission might toss the defendant off the team, Daryl complained. "They say, 'We'll let you know what happens when we're done.' And if the defendant persists in getting in the way, defense attorneys threaten to unleash the 'competency bomb'—have the court declare the condemned incompetent." The law says that in order to forego appeals, you must be competent: able to make a rational choice. Appellate attorneys attempted to ensnare Daryl in a catch-22: Choosing to forego appeals by itself demonstrated his irrational incompetence to forego them.

While Daryl battled his lawyers in a fight to the death, we began to correspond. "Reviewing our conversations at length leaves me more intrigued and puzzled," I wrote him. "I should have pressed you to resolve the tension between a commitment to equality under law—treating like cases alike—and at the same time to particularized justice, which treats each individual person and situation uniquely."

I expected a response to that initial letter, but hardly Daryl's detailed critique of US Supreme Court jurisprudence, beginning with *Furman* and *Gregg*. "Equal protection principles apply not only to defendants but also to victims and society as a whole," Daryl's letter declared. "Justice for a victim might be thought of as the fulfillment of a belated duty by the State, the State's primary duty being protection." Daryl embraced the great trade—protection for obedience—as an article of faith. Only he extended the government's covenant to include a belated duty to the dead victim it had already failed to protect. "The death of the victim" did not "diminish the duty to deal with the perpetrator," his letter continued. "The duty is to the memory of the victim."

Society's original failure to protect the victim created its new obligation to punish the killer. "All victims (indigents, miscreants, and affluents) are entitled to the equal protection of due process," Daryl proclaimed. For the murdered victims, equal protection really amounted to equal *prosecution*. If we cherish each person's uniqueness and realize each situation's uniqueness, we can never tell whether like cases have been treated alike. No judge should ever second-guess the jury, Daryl insisted. No appellate court could possibly review a jury's death sentence for consistency. Thus, Daryl concluded, "*bona fide* equal protection required the death penalty be *sought* in all first-degree murder prosecutions with an aggravating circumstance. Prosecutors do not do that."

A prosecutor might forego seeking death for obvious reasons: to avoid the expense of a weak case or where the victim's family opposed it. Or where the killer did not seem to be the worst of the worst, considering his life's good deeds or bad luck. Daryl rejected all classic mitigation such as horrible background, abuse as a child, or general good character. Mitigation, he insisted, should play no part at trial or capital sentencing. Instead, appellate courts and governors should use mitigating evidence much later to reduce a jury's death sentence.

Daryl made me reconsider equal protection of the dead by the living. Once he declared it, it seemed so obvious to use "equal protection" to link society's failure to protect dead victims with its obligation to punish the living.

Daryl Holton certainly had practiced as he preached. With his own life at stake, against the strong advice of counsel, Daryl steadfastly refused to put on mitigating evidence at trial. It took the jury just two hours and fifteen minutes to sentence him to die. Appellate attorneys now cited his failure to present mitigating evidence to attack that sentence. But as Daryl's letter clearly revealed, his choice to forego mitigation supported his well-considered general jurisprudence. His appeal to human dignity moved me, until he reminded me what this was all about: "Eight years ago, I killed my four children by shooting them in the back."

I put down the letter. He never denied killing his children. But after all this time, so matter-of-factly to put it in writing, without pain or shame.

"I wish I had asked you whether the deaths of your children could have been avoided, and how?" my letter admitted. "I do not understand why your evaluation of the children's lives—notice I don't say '*your* children'—takes priority over their own evaluation and life force?"

"Not to worry; I noticed you didn't say 'my children,'" Daryl replied in the margin. "But I know you meant my children. Candor Alert! Professor Blecker, let's talk about you. I understand a natural human desire for retribution. . . . However, when someone tells me that they feel wronged if another member of their society is wronged, then that sounds . . . well . . . contrived. Passion, as I understand it, comes from the heart not the head. It sounds as if you are espousing a fervor that you think you should have rather than one you actually feel. Sort of like the difference between the war in Afghanistan and the war in Iraq. Your expressed desire to see others suffer, without having been directly violated yourself, sounds morbidly perverse. You might want to get that looked at."

So Daryl dismissed my retributivism as phony, dismissed my intuition that he deserved to die, dismissed my fury, my hatred stirred by his children's voices, demanding justice. I vowed to show him that my feelings ran deep. "Perhaps you just try to encourage debate as liberal arts professors often do," Daryl continued. ("I did not place any emphasis on the term liberal.") He attacked my "expressed desire to see offenders suffer. I fear you have run up against that wall known as the 8th Amendment. The ban of cruel and unusual punishment" would not "bar the death penalty. It just means you can't enjoy it," Daryl closed his jurisprudential analysis. "It is meant to be a relief, not a sport."

A relief, not a sport. Eventually, I would come to appreciate how profoundly this applied to Daryl's own feelings toward his children, even as he killed them. Daryl would force me to feel this distinction as the state of Tennessee prepared to kill him.

In May 2006, in *Holton v. State of Tennessee,* a decision without precedent, the Tennessee Supreme Court found for Daryl by officially finding against him. The state high court held invalid all petitions unsigned by the condemned unless the defense independently established the petitioner's incompetency. "The Court found in my case, that refusing to meet with attorneys did not indicate incompetence. You need more. Whether it's drooling, or hanging from the rafters," Daryl explained. *Holton v. Tennessee* not only rejected all petitions in Daryl's name but also dismissed all Daryl's state attorneys, including Kelly Gleason. Thus the court ended all state appeals.[1]

Daryl supported Tennessee's move to reset his execution date, but he still had to contend with Steve Ferrell, his *federal* appellate lawyer. So this tangled legal procedure continued with Kelly Gleason, Daryl's *ex* state defense attorney, now unofficially coordinating with her federal counterpart. The Tennessee Supreme Court next rebuffed the federal defender, setting Daryl's death date as September 19, 2006.

"So, the Tennessee Supreme Court gave you a principled victory," my follow-up letter congratulated Daryl on his new death date. "Would you like to have another on-camera conversation if I can make it down there?"

"Damn! Does that mean I have to dust and sweep?"

20

DEAD RIGHT

IN THE BEGINNING OF AUGUST, STEVE FERRELL, THE FEDeral defender determined to save Daryl from himself, located a psychologist, Dr. George Woods, who could find Daryl incompetent to waive appeals. Corrections summoned Daryl for the doctor's visit, but he refused to discuss his case with Dr. Woods. The good doctor still concluded that Daryl suffered from post-traumatic stress disorder along with depression. This mental health expert suggested the real possibility that witnessing the deaths of his four children had so permanently traumatized Daryl as to make him incompetent. It seemed like a variation of the classic story about the defendant who kills his mother and father and then begs for mercy because he's an orphan.

Dr. Woods's submission moved a federal district court to appoint its own expert, Dr. Bruce Seidner, to examine Daryl. The court ordered a hearing two weeks before Daryl's scheduled execution.

Kelly Gleason contacted me. Daryl wanted me to know he'd been transferred to Brushy Mountain for his federal competency hearing. I chortled at Dr. Woods's ridiculous characterization of Daryl as incompetent, but Kelly Gleason assured me she too believed it. Then she stunned me: "Daryl Holton is one of the most ethical people I've met in my life." Was she serious? Absolutely, she assured me.

Kelly would not reveal much more about Daryl, so I asked her about herself. Her first capital client, she recounted, raped, sodomized, and disemboweled a 60-year-old virgin. Kelly saw the crime scene photos and then met the killer. "He's a human being," she soon discovered. But how could she put her mind, her energy, her soul in the service of such a monster? "My job is to care about people no one else cares about." I wanted to understand her perspective, but she wanted to talk about Daryl's view of me. "Daryl thinks you're 'a sheep in wolf's clothing,'" said Kelly. "But I insisted you are a wolf."

Steve Ferrell must have spent Labor Day weekend feverishly preparing to keep Daryl alive. At the hearing, Dr.Seidner recounted his many hours reviewing Daryl's records, interviewing correctional officers, and finally the two days spent with Daryl himself. All the evidence showed Daryl competent. Only Dr. Woods, "a lone standout," still suggested Daryl's incompetence.[1] Actually, Ferrell had found someone else to join Woods. On September 5, only hours before the hearing convened, Ferrell submitted Kelly Gleason's newly sworn affidavit. A dedicated capital appellate defense attorney, Gleason probably lost sight of the degree to which her feelings and ideology had colored her conclusions. In any event, she had sworn to a court she believed Daryl "incompetent" and without a "rational understanding" of "his legal options."[2] The judge may have sensed that this highly competent, compassionate defender disserved herself by this sworn opinion. Kelly Gleason, I'm sure, would tell it differently.

From start to finish, however, the judge simply ignored her affidavit, relying instead on Dr. Seidner's report and his testimony. "Nothing in the Riverbend record suggest[s] incompetence," Seidner declared. "No objective evidence I could find would suggest a mental disorder or defect."[3] Daryl did have a "credible history of depression," but "nothing suggest[ed] that he does not have a rational process. . . . He has no unusual beliefs about death and fully understands the legal reasons for and consequences of his execution and death. He is not overborne by guilt, delusion or irrational thinking. His adjustment to death row has been as good as one could expect."[4] The doctor had found Daryl "fully competent" to make a rational choice to forego further appeals. Yet as Seidner observed without elaboration, Daryl was no "volunteer." He had refused to express any remorse whatsoever, whereas death row "volunteers" traditionally seek to die as a release for either their all-consuming guilt or unbearable life on death row.

Ferrell took his last desperate shot and thoroughly cross-examined Seidner. "What is your definition of rational?"

"There needs to be an intellectual capacity to differentiate between options. Sufficient memory to hold information. Good reality testing."[5]

No help there.

Ferrell refused to give up, pressing again and again, but Seidner held his ground. "If a defendant in Mr. Holton's situation says he has options and the options he chooses or argues for are non-existent, would that be delusional?"

"It depends. If one of the options is 'the Starship Enterprise is going to teleport me at the last moment,' *that* would be delusional."

"In the end, you don't know what he believes his options are?" Ferrell concluded, desperately attempting to end on a doubtful note.

"That is correct."[6]

The court addressed Daryl directly: "I don't think anybody in this courtroom who has seen or heard your testimony could doubt that you have the ability to reason and think rationally," the judge declared, totally rejecting the sworn testimony of Woods and Gleason. "There may be those who disagree with your decision, but it is not up to them to make the decision for you. It is your decision and yours alone to make. I am going to dismiss the petition."[7]

Daryl had won! He was free to die in two weeks.

21

WHOSE VOICE?

"SEPTEMBER 19. IS THE DATE REAL TO YOU? DO YOU EX-pect to die on that day?"

"Pause for effect?" Daryl quipped in the margin of my letter he returned to me. "Don't be so dramatic."

"Does life get clearer in meaning? Does it get more or less precious? Do things come into focus?" my letter asked. "Do you count the days? With anticipation, fear, longing, dread?"

"Ask me when the order dismissing the federal *habeas* petition becomes final."

"At this point is death a penalty? Or is the thought liberating? Are you focused on the final ritual? Are you composing a final statement? Do you feel relieved, at peace?"

"This sounds eerily like an inquisition," Daryl chided. "Although I could probably use the practice, it's late."

Tennessee prepared to execute Daryl in less than a week, and I still didn't understand his story. Did he kill the children from revenge? If so, feeling no remorse would make it worse. Or did Daryl kill them from an insane delusion that they were better off dead? Not commanded by God or the devil, like Andrea Yates believed, but doing what he thought best, for *them*. Delusional filicide—purely from selfless love. Arguably insane and not responsible. Or some complex mix? Worst of all, like Susan Smith, did he kill his children not for their own good, but selfishly for his own? In her case to have an affair, in his to end his pain and frustration at having them alive but removed from his life?

Although we'd had this dialogue by letter and phone, we hadn't seen each other face to face in the year since we first met. Now that Daryl's death date was only days away, I wanted a chance, one last time, to clear it up. I pride myself on not being a Sophist. I hope that's more than clear by now. Every question does not have two sides. Danny Rolling, Charles Manson, and their kind deserve to suffer and die for their crimes. I feel certain. But both sides of the death penalty debate must be heard and taken seriously. Thus, I have always co-taught my death penalty course with leading abolitionists—for several years now with Kevin Doyle, chief of New York's capital defenders, until he argued himself out of a job by convincing the New York Court of Appeals to strike down that state's death penalty. Look around at colleges and law schools, dominated by death penalty opponents: Do those abolitionist professors integrate a retributive perspective supportive of the death penalty into their courses? Anyway, I assumed Daryl had cut off contact with Kelly Gleason, his former defense attorney. That left me, alone, as the only professional-lawyerly voice from the outside still communicating with him. And I was telling him to die.

So I called the person Daryl most respected, Professor James Liebman. Liebman chuckled at Daryl's claim to have read his two-volume treatise including all the footnotes. That would make Daryl one of only three people to have done this, including Liebman and his coauthor! And Liebman confided doubts about his coauthor. Jim Liebman came to my office, watched video clips of Daryl, and videotaped a message I would play for Daryl at our meeting on death row.

By this point I had myself become the subject of a documentary. Ted Schillinger, the director, insisted on filming my visit with Daryl. Due to die in a few days, Daryl obviously would not be the documentary's focus. Three in the room would destroy our one-on-one intensity. Daryl and I might play to the director. Ted assured me he would set up the camera and then step outside, leaving Daryl and me to ourselves.

Daryl entered, in chains. With his head almost shaven, and obviously thinner, he had noticeably aged in the ten months since we first met.

"Long time no see," he said.

"You've been a good correspondent," I said truthfully, as Ted set up the camera.

"I have a lot of questions about you," said Daryl, not returning the compliment.

"If this documentary comes out later, some might protest I manipulated you. So what *are* we doing?" Of course in the deepest sense, I wasn't quite sure myself what I was doing. Why was I there, really? To say goodbye, to find out the truth? To make Daryl feel and show remorse before he died? I did feel the human intensity, meeting with a man I had come to care about, now scheduled to be killed in a few days.

Of course Daryl wanted to discuss the appellate process that consumed his life these last several years. Truth be told, I cared relatively little about legal process and have minimized it here. Before he died, however, Daryl would recount his great victory in *Holton v. Tennessee.*[1] "The public defender office assumes they have a duty to file on behalf of everyone condemned to death. It's not only a statutory but an ethical duty. But I actually read the law."

"That's not fair," I mock protested.

"That literacy thing comes in handy now and then," Daryl shot back. "So it turns out they're merely supposed to be *available*—ready, in case *you* decide *you* want to file a postconviction petition. So the state attorney general was arguing my position. See, I'm still a citizen of the state. That Second Amendment may not be fully mine, but I still have rights."

Our conversation had begun, with Daryl renewing his constant complaint about defense attorneys using him for their own agenda. "You're an attorney, too," said Daryl. "Let me point that out. You ask the right questions, rather than some fuzzy warm human interest questions."

"I don't want to mislead you. Over the past year, my involvement has grown beyond mere professionalism," I admitted.

"Fondness or repulsion?" asked Daryl, smiling but probing.

"No—well, yes," I stammered with truthful ambivalence.

"I can trust that. It's American to be curious," said Daryl. "I'm not special or unique," he insisted. "I'm just different. Notoriety comes with receiving four death sentences. It's easy to get caught up in feeding the media, just to keep the cameras coming down—if you have a starving ego, if you like that infamy."

"You said you were looking forward to being 'yesterday's news.'"

"That's what tends to happen after an execution. Or if you're found incompetent. You disappear from the news into a mental health facility."

"Can that await you?" I asked, imagining a fate neither of us wanted for him.

"There's always that possibility. The lawyers always have a second bite at the apple. So you have to watch what you say. I saw this battle coming a long time ago. I never wanted to give the attorneys ammunition to challenge me. So I declined their visits, and I really had to limit my conversations with other inmates and guards."

Declining to move to less restrictive levels, treating officers with respect but making no conversation, Daryl Holton's notorious and "odd" antisocial behavior—he called it "asocial, not antisocial"—now suddenly made sense. But the federal lawyers just wouldn't let go. "They're arguing the stress of a controlled environment," aka "death row syndrome."

Death row syndrome claims that life on the Row awaiting execution tortures the condemned into submission. His own death becomes a refuge and release from this living hell. Europe created that claim in 1989, in *Soering v. UK,* when the European Court of Human Rights refused to honor an extradition treaty with the United States on the grounds that "the very long period spent on death row in such extreme conditions with the ever present and mounting anguish awaiting execution"—separate from the death penalty itself—constituted "cruel, inhuman, and degrading" punishment.[2] Abolitionist American psychologists readily amplify the claim that maximum security and especially the Row psychologically depresses, damages, and distorts the capacity of the confined to make rational choices.[3] Daryl's real fear of "institutionalization," where prison becomes too comfortable, completely negated the death row syndrome that his lawyers threatened to claim.

"Is this stressful?" I asked Daryl.

"I do dread the sight of attorneys coming down the hallway," he deadpanned. Depressed? "There's a lot that disappoints me." But Daryl did praise Dr. Seidner, the court-appointed evaluator, as "thorough." By observing closely and administering psychological tests, "he practiced his art." "The MMPI [Minnesota multiple personality inventory] indicated that I have a personality disorder: 'Schizoid and narcissistic.' Those terms used to bother me. 'Schizoid'—all that means is 'loner.' I'm always honest when I take it, and I consistently score as schizoid or as a loner. 'Are you generally around people that you don't want to be around?'" Daryl repeated the question from the exam. "I'm living on *death row!*" I couldn't help but laugh. "There are 14 million people in the state of Tennessee," Daryl smiled, "who would rather not be associated with the people I live with. Two-thirds would prefer not to have them breathing. So I don't feel too bad about preferring my own company."

"Could you have manipulated the test?"

"Lying would require an enormous amount of energy," Daryl replied. But he did refuse to answer one question on the MMPI. "And I told the guy I would leave this one particular question blank. When you answer 'true' it automatically pops up on the psychopathic deviance scale that you're *paranoid.* You have to answer 'true' or 'false.' And the question is, 'Someone is trying to kill me.'"

I burst out laughing and felt thoroughly ashamed for losing sight of the seriousness of it all. But asking the condemned on death row whether someone is trying to kill him to prove him paranoid—too much.

"Someone trying to kill you, Daryl?"

"They claim they are. I've had my doubts. But I haven't had this much control since trial." How were other condemned inmates reacting to his volunteering, thus making it easier for the state to execute them next? "The ones that have approached me say they realize it's my decision. Of course there's jealousy. Because some guys here don't get media coverage. They're just hard to love."

These child killers—these sadistic, murdering rapists—so hard to love. "'Schizoid and narcissistic.' Do you love yourself?"

"I respect myself. The expert described me as someone who considered myself as having high morals."

"Kelly Gleason said, 'Daryl Holton is one of the most principled people I have ever met.'"

"She also said I was one of the most irrational people she's ever met."

"Would you characterize yourself as a moral person?"

"I've tried to be. I try not to do things just because I can."

"Can you understand how the People of Tennessee can hate someone who murdered his four children?"

"Yeah, but how many of these people who are so angry ever knew my children?" Silence would have settled in here, but Daryl pressed to bridge the gap between us. "You would obviously not trust me if I told you I loved *your* children."

"But would you trust that I hate that you killed your children?" Why had I veered off from telling Daryl that I hated *him,* instead of telling him I hated what he'd done? Was I falling prey to "progressive" cant: "A person is more than their worst act"? Was I signing up for the religious "hate the sin, love the sinner"? I despised what Daryl had done. I repeatedly told him he deserved to die. Because I hated *him* for what he had done. Sometimes I had to remind myself that I hated him. Always, he insisted, I had to tell myself that I loved his children.

"Can I feel your pain? Can you feel mine?" Daryl challenged.

"I can feel your children's."

"Can you?" He looked at me, incredulous. "I think you're feeling what you think you should feel." We had come full circle, returning to Daryl's accusation in his first letter to me.

"Help me understand." I took a breath, and we started down this long, winding road, presumably for the last time. "You murdered your four—you *killed* your four children—let's not put the legal label on it because after all if it is the product of insanity, it's not murder—"

"Don't patronize me!" Daryl snapped, with obvious irritation. "Just say it."

"OK. You killed your four children, you say, because they were living with an alcoholic mother who was not taking care of them in a roach-infested apartment in a bad part of the housing projects, sending them to school, unwashed, uncared for, neglected. And you decided they were better off dead than living in that situation. Is that a fair characterization so far?"

"Yes."

"At trial you raised an insanity defense," I continued. "A mental health expert testified that you had committed an 'altruistic killing.' This was the first time you ever heard that statement, but when you heard it, it rang true to you."

"You'd be hard-pressed to find me embracing the concept. An altruistic killing would be a selfless killing."

"So it was not selfless?"

"The state's theory was that it was motivated by revenge," said Daryl, diverting me again.

"Which you've rejected!"

"I do reject that. The original plan was suicide." Daryl showed irritation that I was confounded. "Are you asking, was I being altruistic then?"

"Yes." This could be the moment of truth. I stared at Daryl like a poker player waiting to see whether his opponent would go all in.

"Let me ask you this, and I don't want to open any doors to your personal life," said Daryl. "I'm not even going to ask, 'Do you love your children?', because if you have children, I believe you do. *Why* do you love your children?" Daryl had completely and unexpectedly turned the tables.

"I only have one child. I do love her. I love her because . . . I, I, I love her," I stammered. "Do I know why I love her?" I stopped, feeling the love, but failing to grasp how exactly this played in Daryl's argument. Do we love our children selflessly? And what does that mean? The honesty between us oddly compelled me to concede something. "I do see some part of my love for her as egotistical. Is this what you're getting at? You want an admission from me. I do partly see my child as an extension of me, and since I love me, I love her. I love her for some qualities she has that I admire," I continued. "I love her because she's enabled me to see life through her eyes. I love her because she's now produced grandchildren whom I adore. I love her, just instinctively. Yes, I do love her."

"I can feel like you do," said Daryl. "But I can never understand the full depth of your love for your child. You can't find the words to express it. Same for me. There's just no way I can tell you how I loved my children." Daryl paused for a moment, then continued. "But if they're an extension of yourself, then that's not selfless, is it?"

"No. I admit that some part of my love is selfish."

"I don't have any problem admitting that to you," Daryl echoed. Suddenly he was making us no different from each other. I flashed back to

Johnny Allen defending hired killers and getting me to imagine I might hire one to avenge the killing of my family: "We the same, Rob. We just do it in different ways."

"But you expressed your love for your children by killing them," I protested.

"Yes." I stared at Daryl's eyes, searching for tears or mist showing remorse. Finding none, my indignation and anger welled up. Daryl seemed to sense it. "The hardest part, and I'm not going to even try, is attempting to convince someone that I loved my children," he said wearily.

"And looking back on it, ten years later, you still think that killing them was the appropriate expression of that love?"

"I wish things could have been different. I wish there had been other options. But acknowledging that there actually were other options, I'm just not going to do that."

"Because it's too painful?"

"It's just not a good idea," Daryl said in the frustrating way he had of shutting me down. "We're not there yet," he added, suddenly stirring my hope.

I had planned to save until the end an all-out frontal attack on Daryl's defended self-righteousness, using excerpts from the police tapes.

"I'd like a 15-minute break," Daryl said. "Right now might be a good time." We had less than two hours left. Liebman's video plea would take 20 minutes just to play.

"I thought I might show you something." Daryl patiently waited while the computer booted up.

A still image popped on the screen. "Is that Professor Liebman?" Daryl asked, busting my surprise. I don't know how he could have known or guessed. For the next 20 minutes, hunched over the screen, straining to hear over the din of the air vent, Daryl watched and listened to his legal idol and guru.

"Hello Daryl, I'm Jim Liebman. Even though we've not met, I feel a connection to you. Robert told me about your having read the book. I brought a copy; I thought I would autograph it and give it to Robert to double the weight of his luggage." Liebman paused a moment, then spoke his real purpose: "What's taking place in your own life—it's a momentous occasion, certainly for you. The first thing I should say to you is that I respect the decision that you've made."

Ah, that old chestnut. When Liebman first uttered it into the camera, I smiled at his tactic. After a defense attorney has argued his client's innocence at the guilt phase of a capital trial, he or she now faces the same jury that convicted the defendant of first-degree murder, a jury that has, in effect, just called the defense lawyer a liar. During the penalty phase, that lawyer must now beg, cajole, and plead with the jury to spare this convicted murderer. Most defense attorneys consider it a blunder to argue residual doubt about guilt during that penalty phase when the jury's choice has been narrowed to life in prison or death. Often the defense will substitute a different attorney to plead with the jury. But an awkward transition from guilt to penalty still confronts the defense. How can they challenge the verdict, insisting the jury made a mistake, while begging that jury for mercy? Thus this standard penalty phase opening: "We *respect* your verdict."

And so Liebman insisted he "respected" Daryl's choice to die. "A human being expresses their humanity by making choices. And living with the responsibility for those choices." How ironic, that choosing to kill his children could somehow express Daryl's humanity, although dying for it might be different. "It's a great and wonderful thing," Liebman continued, "for a person under lock-down 23 hours a day, in the most solitary situation, to be able, despite everything, to have the capacity to make choices." Liebman instinctively conceded Daryl's competence for rational choice, the very point that Kelly and Ferrell seemed to deny.

"If you can stand the presumption, I want to be sure that in making the choice you're making, you consider what you have to offer to other people. You're a very smart, very thoughtful man. You've made a huge impression on Robert, and that kind of power, thoughtfulness, responsibility, and morality, is a gift that a choosing human being thinks about using in some way."

Liebman appealed to Daryl as principled and unselfish. "That's not to say that you won't die. That's not to say that the verdict that the state of Tennessee has imposed on you won't be carried out—because as you say, the likelihood is that it will be. But in the meantime you could be doing things that nobody else could do, or choose to do, that could mean so much to others. I've given up trying to change anybody's mind. But I do want to ask you as a choosing human being, to make sure that you're making a choice consistent with your beliefs about the way you should behave in the world." He barely knew Daryl, yet somehow Liebman knew to go for Daryl's soft spot—consistency.

"And maybe I'll just close on that point since you have reached out to me in this funny way, as lawyer and law professor and writer. Tennessee has imposed this verdict on you. And if that verdict stands, there's no reason why, from your perspective, the state should not take your life. I understand that completely. But the law of Tennessee, in fact the law of the United States, is that before they *do* take your life, the courts and society and community have gone through a process of making sure that you are the right person to execute.

"So to the extent you're taking your morality from the law, you have every right to go through the process and let the courts decide whether everything was done properly in your case." Liebman pitched it to Daryl perfectly. If you want to let the law take its course, if your morality *is* legality itself, then allow the appellate process to determine the right result. You impede the law by not allowing it to cast its gaze fully on your case. "So if you're making that choice because you think you need to do what the law says, I'm simply telling you as a lawyer and law professor who's studied this that I disagree. The law actually gives you the right to put the state through its paces.

"That's not to say that you need a lawyer to make claims you don't think are valid," Liebman continued. "But you have the ability and the right"—he might have said "responsibility"—"to take the state through that process yourself in whatever way you want. Whether or not you do that is important to me. It's important to justice." Liebman's skill in arguing for Daryl's life on Daryl's terms left me awestruck. This skilled capital defender closed his low-key personal appeal to judge, jury, and the condemned rolled into one: "As I said, whatever choices you make, I respect those choices. And I am pleased that you read my book, that it made an impression upon you, and that you've reached out to me through Robert. So thank you very much. I certainly will be paying attention to what happens to you over the next couple of weeks."

And then, on camera, he signed the volume: "To Daryl Holton, with respect and admiration. James Liebman."

During these 20 minutes, Daryl mostly remained expressionless. The disc ended, and Daryl nodded and looked up. "You know how you imagine someone—that's how I imagined Liebman."

"When you hear his voice saying, 'Don't go forward,' does it make a difference?"

"Can I answer that question when I come back?"

We signaled the officers. And Daryl left to get something to eat.

A half hour passed. Where was Daryl? Had he gotten caught up in some bureaucratic tangle? Perhaps he'd had enough. Would I never get him to reveal his true motives? For whose sake had Daryl killed the children that night in the garage? For whose sake would we kill him? To allow the general public, especially the victims' family, to feel satisfied at justice? Do we punish the murderer for his own sake, to let him find expiation, make it right with whatever God or the hereafter? Or, in the end, do we do it for the victims, to offset the harm and help restore the balance? It sounds so metaphysical, and yet for us retributivists, it feels so real.

More time passed. No Daryl.

He suddenly appeared with his own gift to me: a thick envelope full of his legal papers, the formal record of his drawn-out battle with the lawyers. "Who knew that inaction would require so much effort," Daryl chuckled at the irony of his whole legal struggle.

Daryl would have happily spent this last hour together in abstract debate about jurisprudence, but I forced us back to that night he killed the children, insisting his motive in setting out to kill the child of his ex-wife's new lover had to be revenge.

"Put yourself in my shoes at the time," Daryl said. "If you had just killed your four children and want revenge, how hard would it have been for you to continue through with your plan?" I had no answer. Unnerved, I couldn't, or wouldn't, put myself in his shoes. "It's a relief that you *don't* understand— that you can't put yourself in the situation," Daryl consoled me.

"Why plan to kill a child that was not your child?" I demanded.

"I don't know; I really don't know. It looks like revenge," Daryl finally conceded.

"You were looking to get back at your wife by getting back at her lover," I insisted. "Because you were killing *his* child."

"OK, yeah, OK," Daryl admitted. "But then it didn't happen. I had the opportunity. But it just didn't happen." Why not? "You're asking me to explain insanity," Daryl declared, coming as close to pronouncing himself insane to me as he ever would.

This last hour we spent together strangely blended calm discussion and passionate attack. "How *could you* kill four children you loved?" I snarled at one point with rage and contempt.

"If you've ever been to the dentist and come away still numb after being anesthetized. That's how I felt," Daryl replied. Before, during, and after. "All over dentist-type numb."

Daryl came full circle, revealing to me as he revealed to the police that night exactly what he felt at that moment: He felt nothing. Does the absence of feeling make him insane? Psychopaths apparently feel nothing as they inflict pain; that depraved indifference to human life and suffering separates them from us.

I didn't buy this "all over numbness." Literally, he felt nothing? Daryl admitted to a sense of dread as he watched the children play at McDonald's because "I knew what was coming." Nevertheless, "there was no turning back," Daryl insisted.

I threw everything I had at him. But Daryl would not show pain or express remorse. "I won't roll out the red carpet so you can march in and exploit my emotions," he countered. "I am vulnerable, very vulnerable. I'm just not going to let you in."

"I don't want to exploit, I want to explore," I lied. I did want him to ache with remorse. "It hurts," Daryl admitted.

That admission stunned me. "Does it? 'Cause you don't show it. Other than this unpleasant situation where someone like me tries to pick the scab—"

"Are you kidding," Daryl shot back. "You're a breath of fresh air. You really are. And that's odd sitting across the table from somebody who wants to see me dead. I actually consider you a friend, as odd as that may sound."

Odd and very unnerving. I refused to acknowledge our friendship, but even as I let the silence suggest I didn't care about Daryl, he suddenly seemed shaken, wounded, and weary. After one more round of sustained pummeling, he paused, looking at me, pain flickering in his eyes. "What else?" he asked quietly. Nothing really.

We said goodbye. I confessed to Daryl that as much as he deserved to die, I could not personally flip the switch. "That's because you're emotionally involved." Daryl smiled. I understand why, in federal prisons, and increasingly on state death rows, they transfer the condemned to a separate location for death watch and execution. The staff there hadn't interacted with him for years on the Row. They would not be emotionally involved in killing a man they had come to know. "You *shouldn't* be able to pull the switch," Daryl consoled me. "And if you can't enjoy it, it's not cruel." Was he talking to himself as much as to me?

For almost five hours, I had jabbed at Daryl inside Tennessee's death row at Riverbend, trying to get through his defenses. I had come here this last time to extract his dying confession, to convince Daryl he had been lying to himself and me. His mass murder could not be a selfless act of love. I hit Daryl with evidence from his own lips, undermining his claim to a purely selfless motive: to spare the children their miserable degraded lives. I tried to force him to confront his own selfishness. To feel the anguish of real remorse. I came at him with everything I had. He wobbled, but he did not go down.

And when time ran out, Daryl pronounced himself bad at goodbyes. He urged me to "relax" and examine my own motives. We rose. "Later," he said with that wry smile, and started moving away. I couldn't or wouldn't call him my friend. I told him repeatedly I wanted him dead. I acted cold and stern and unforgiving. And yet, in this, our last moment together, I instinctively patted Daryl on the shoulder. Our visit had ended. He shuffled out of sight, shackled, leaving me drained and exhausted.

22

WHY AREN'T YOU DEAD?

FIVE DAYS LATER, SEPTEMBER 18, KELLY SENT ME UNSET-
tling news. Daryl might not die that next morning. After years fighting and
finally defeating his lawyers' attempts to appeal in his name, at the last moment, Daryl on his own suddenly appealed to the US Supreme Court. He
had no problem with the death penalty for crimes of this type, Daryl assured
the Court. Nor did he claim newly discovered evidence of his innocence. But
ironically, Daryl explained, with all those lawyers attempting to act in his
name, he had never gotten his day in court. At trial, counsel had argued insanity *and*, over Daryl's vigorous objection, diminished capacity. But, Daryl
insisted, either he should be held fully responsible or not at all. By arguing
diminished capacity, Daryl's lawyer had signaled Daryl's sanity to the jury,
undermining his insanity defense.

Furthermore, Daryl pointed out, Tennessee violated the US Constitution by requiring *him* to prove the very diminished capacity that should
never have been raised in the first place. By placing the burden of persuasion on the defendant to show insanity and diminished capacity, the state
had violated the Constitution's requirement of "proof beyond a reasonable
doubt of every fact necessary to constitute the crime."[1] Because diminished
capacity negated the intent necessary for first-degree murder, Daryl argued,
in effect Tennessee had presumed him guilty and required him to prove his
innocence.

Finally, by insisting on including their own pet claims, however absurd,
incompetent appellate counsel forced on him had stripped him of his right
to appeal on only those issues he chose. Of course Daryl had allowed the
statute of limitations to run on *their* claims. Intentionally so. Otherwise he
would have been forced to join his own legitimate appellate issues with their
frivolous ones. Now legally liberated from the lawyers, although barred by

the statute of limitations, Daryl could for the first time have his own appellate issues considered.

Daryl's constitutional claim and cases he cited struck a nerve. Nowhere does the Constitution specifically command the presumption of innocence or proof beyond a reasonable doubt of guilt. Ironically, this bulwark of protection for defendants, which forces the government to establish guilt to a near certainty, replaced an even more defendant-friendly biblical "any doubt" rule. The problem that Daryl identified has long divided the Court: Do we violate the presumption of innocence by presuming sanity, or full capacity, and requiring a defendant to rebut that presumption by showing it more likely than not that he was insane, under the influence of passion adequately provoked, or of diminished capacity? For three decades, in criminal law, I've assigned a string of cases and attacked the Court for its incoherent and at times flatly contradictory doublespeak.

Reading Daryl's petition, I began to fantasize . . . I would act as Daryl's counsel, help him vindicate his claim. Together we would force the US Supreme Court to decide definitively whether a state could require a defendant to prove facts in his favor. . . . But here my fantasy shattered upon the ugly realization that I would become just one more lawyer using Daryl and his case as a vehicle to promote my own agenda, a means to my ends, not as an end in himself. This, he long claimed, his lawyers had done to him; this, I claimed, he did to his children. And now I would do it to him.

About noon on September 18, 2006, 13 hours before Daryl's scheduled death, the Federal Sixth Circuit Court of Appeals stepped in and issued a stay. Jennifer Smith, Tennessee's deputy attorney general, now suddenly became Daryl's real adversary and desperately tried to get the US Supreme Court to revive the impending execution.

I stayed awake, waiting for word. Two hours after Daryl was due to die, I received an email from Kelly at 3:13 a.m.: "I am very tired and relieved." The US Supreme Court upheld the stay. Tennessee would not kill Daryl anytime soon.

"September 19, 2006. Well that's a date I hadn't been expecting to put on a letter to you," I wrote Daryl, overnighting his legal papers back to him. I had a hundred questions, "but for now, this is to say I don't believe justice has been done yet. Welcome back to the land of the living. And why aren't you dead?"

I felt angry and manipulated. Daryl had conned me. I needed to see him as principled, a man who would die for his code. I knew I'd miss him. But now that he had spared himself, my righteous indignation flared. I wanted him dead. Why had he played me? Why, after all these years, suddenly pick up his appeals? Daryl would never explain it in a letter. So a week later, I forced a telephone call.

"You told me a story, Daryl. And I believed it. About a man who killed his children and then intended to kill himself. But he didn't. *He* wants to live! Then he claims he will allow the law to take his course and kill him. But at the last moment, he picks up his appeal. He wants to live!"

"It's a natural reaction," Daryl said flatly.

"My family and friends think I'm blind to you. How could I not see this guy as a selfish coward, they ask? Are you a selfish coward, Daryl?"

"Are we talking about then or now?"

"I was invested in seeing you as principled."

"Don't paint me as valiant. Not someone who killed their children. If you can put yourself in the same situation and the same thing happens to you, what do you do?" he demanded.

"If I were who you've presented yourself to be, I would have brought a TV set and watched it with them in the garage. I would have turned on the gas, gently eased them out of suffering and pain. And died with them."

"Hmm. You really shouldn't be handing out parenting advice." Why did he change his mind? "You can't say I changed my mind. I just never told you what was on my mind."

In attacking Daryl, I completely botched the logic of his petition. "You haven't practiced law in a while, Professor," Daryl observed with obvious disdain. "Read the God-darned *habeas* petition."

"I did."

"Well, then get someone to explain it to you who knows the law." Daryl had every right to belittle me when I mangled his legal claim. I deserved this and more but didn't realize it at the time. Impatient and weary, Daryl explained it simply, once again, and added one more claim: The carbon monoxide from the kerosene heater in the garage where he slept may have poisoned his mind and destroyed his judgment.

Daryl found my legal analysis shockingly confused and my repeated attempts to get him to express remorse most irritating of all. "Do you recognize now, it was a horrible thing to do?"

"Have I ever disputed it?"

"You've never acknowledged it. That what you did was horrible, horrific, horrendous, morally despicable. I've never heard you say you regret it." Pause. "Do you regret it, Daryl? Looking back at it, do you regret that you murdered your four children?"

"You want me to try to mitigate the deaths of four children?" Daryl shot back, artfully turning the tables on me.

"I'm asking you to take responsibility. To understand the enormity. Not just that four children are dead, but that four *innocent children who didn't deserve to die* are dead!" All the anger at Daryl, the fury that he could sleep well at night, his self-righteousness, all the frustration poured out as I verbally attacked him, babbling a mile a minute. He waited until I came up for air.

"Are you trying to retry me?" he demanded.

"I'm trying to get you to try yourself."

Daryl must recognize killing his children as a monstrous and despicable act. Why else voluntarily stay at level C, shackled all the time outside the cell? "I might have a bondage fetish," he quipped. His humor only stoked my fury. How *could* he still insist on his right to kill the children?

"Do you really believe I thought it was a right, rather than a responsibility?" Daryl demanded.

"Don't we have a moral right to do what we have a responsibility to do?" I countered. The question stopped him. And he diverted the conversation. "I don't think you got what you came for."

"I never get what I came for; that's why I come back." I calmed down and turned back into a researcher. "What was death watch like?"

"Pure adrenalin. It wasn't unpleasant. I didn't see the chair. Slept ten hours each night; slept like a rock. I kept the TV off but an oldies radio station on. During the day I was drinking a lot of coffee and chain-smoking. They have to hand you a cigarette and light it for you, so I kept one lit all the time. There's an officer who sits there and writes your every movement. I told them, 'There's a time and place for everything—the time to be solemn will be here sooner or later, but there's no need for it now.' I kept up a constant barrage of trivia." One-liners came: "I asked the chaplain, 'If a really religious Texan declares holy war, is that called a Yee-haad?' That was original." Daryl chuckled, remembering another humorous moment. "They came to me Monday morning—I'm supposed to be executed on Tuesday at 1 a.m. Asked me if I wanted to order commissary—I said no thanks."

"How did you find out they weren't killing you that night?" I asked.

"The death watch staff came to tell me they were taking me back to the unit."

"What did you say when you heard it?"

"'I shaved my legs for this?'"

I suppressed a laugh. "How did you feel?"

"A little chilly with my bald head in the cool evening air."

"Disappointed or relieved?"

"Curious. I didn't know who had stopped it."

"Daryl," I said with obvious irritation, "what do you *want* to happen here? What's your goal?"

"To read all the papers and filings." Daryl seemed to have new respect for Ferrell, the federal defender. "We're buds, but we're adversaries." But Daryl clearly had enough of me. "We're running out of time. I was expecting more."

"What were you expecting?" I asked.

"'Why are you still alive?'"

"Why *are* you alive?" I spat his question back to him.

"It's natural for humans to struggle."

"If you have to go through this again—"

"I'm planning on it—"

"Best guess: Will you be executed?"

"Yeah, I think I will."

"And so you're now captain of your own ship. Is that satisfying?"

"No. Because I'm not the only boat on the water, Dummy."

23

TURNING GREY

I HADN'T TIME TO DWELL MUCH ON DARYL BECAUSE OF battles looming in New Jersey and Illinois. The New Jersey death penalty "study commission"—carefully selected to provide cover for an abolitionist governor and legislature—invited me to testify at its next live hearing and submit a written statement in advance. As the lone death penalty supporter from the academy, I raced the clock to review every page of prior testimony, responding to a hundred unchallenged claims from earlier witnesses. Three weeks after my unpleasant telephone conversation with Daryl, I appeared at the state house in Trenton before an obviously abolitionist commission, one that in theory possessed an open mind. Opponents packed the house, wearing T-shirts and buttons denouncing death as punishment. But they sat quietly as I warned the commissioners, "You do not make your decision in a vacuum. Consider the alternative." I urged them to investigate the actual quality of life for those who serve life without parole. "If you saw what I saw, it would appall you." I closed my oral testimony, imploring them to reject the simple options. "You have a rare opportunity to debate and deliberate, to refine the statute, limiting it to only the worst of the worst."

"Is the 'worst of the worst' in your view, an objective or subjective determination?" Commissioner Robert Scheinberg challenged me.[1]

Here we were again, back with Plato and the Sophists. "I believe that there is a moral fact to the matter—that this is not all just a matter of opinion. Even if you abolish the death penalty, most of us will still agree that some murders are worse than others. Boundaries may be subtle and difficult. But just because I can't tell you exactly where the worst of the worst becomes merely horrible, I can identify clear cases: The robber who sticks up a 7-Eleven and shoots the clerk who grabs for his gun, absent other aggravating circumstances, clearly does not deserve to die. Charles Ng who maintains a torture chamber in his basement, kidnaps women with their children, videotapes their torture over weeks, exposes them to unspeakable misery, rapes, and then murders and mutilates them clearly does deserve to die. They don't inhabit the same moral universe." Objectively.

"I hear you say that the possibility of executing an innocent person is the cost of doing business if you want to uphold the death penalty," demanded Yvonne Segars, New Jersey's public defender. "Yes or no?"

"No." I paused. "The remote, remote possibility of executing an innocent person is the cost of doing *justice*. It's not the same thing."

"The point is innocent," she insisted.

"You will expose your innocent children to a minuscule risk of death for your own convenience. Surely justice is a higher value."

New Jersey would never execute anyone as long as its liberal state supreme court routinely struck down death sentences, insisted Commissioner Kathleen Garcia, the survivors' advocate. "I have as much compassion for the perpetrators as they had for their victim. But when is this cruel hoax over for the survivors?"

Never, really. But better false hope than real despair. "Look into the conditions of life without parole and you'll realize it's yet a crueler hoax," I replied and started detailing various perks for lifers when Reverend William Howard Jr., the chair, exercised his prerogative and prevented me from more fully driving the point home.

My claim that the worst killers often experience the best lives inside must have irritated abolitionist commissioners because they invited ranking corrections officials specifically to rebut it at their next hearing. What was the "meaning of life without parole?" Commissioner James Coleman asked James Barbo, corrections director of operations. Barbo recounted a Sunday afternoon watching inmates take "their monotonous walk" to dinner. "Their hair turned grey, just like mine did," he observed. It was an odd metaphor to capture the "debilitating" life in prison. We all get older, at least those of us fortunate enough to live out our lives. Our hair turns grey if we are lucky enough to keep it.

"I can personally think of nothing more horrific than contemplating and enduring the process of growing old in a maximum-security prison," Gary J. Hilton, acting commissioner of corrections, reassured the commissioners.

Really? Can't imagine anything worse than living your life in prison? How about being raped, then tortured to death, before you reach your sixteenth birthday? How about being robbed and then herded into a freezer, watching, terrified, as the two killers massacre your coworkers, knowing you're next? Somehow I'd rather grow old, my hair turning grey, reading, watching TV, and playing cards in prison. I suspect he would, too.

On January 2, 2007, the so-called "study commission" sent their thoroughly biased final report to the legislature, nearly unanimously calling for abolition and completely ignoring any possibility for refinement or reform. The final report carefully skirted retribution after summarily dismissing it up front, completely ignoring the question of justice. Locally and internationally hailed as comprehensive and complete, the commission's report avoided the moral complexity of the great debate. Unbalanced and biased, it did not even mention any alternative to abolition or standing pat.

The commissioners hadn't entirely ignored my testimony, however. Apparently stung by my protest that "well-behaved" first-degree murderers, based solely on their "good" behavior inside, might end up in a medium security prison with a life of relative leisure, the commission recommended and the legislature enacted legislation abolishing New Jersey's death penalty and replacing it with "life imprisonment without the possibility of parole, *to be served in a maximum security facility*."[2] That last part, little noticed or commented on, mandated perpetual maximum security for the worst of the worst regardless of any security risk they might no longer present. The Garden State had taken a small but significant step. The past *would* count, forever.

New Jersey had abolished the death penalty based on the big lie—that day after day, inside maximum security prisons, convicted killers serving life without parole suffered as much if not more than if they had been condemned to die. I prepared to rebut this lie under oath in Illinois.

My first speech before the Association of Government Attorneys in Capital Litigation had resulted in artifacts and access to Oklahoma and Tennessee. After a follow-up talk at their annual convention the next year, an Illinois capital prosecutor invited me to testify as an expert witness in the upcoming trial of Juan Luna for the Brown's Fried Chicken Massacre—the second-worst mass murder in Illinois history after Richard Speck.

Speck, the infamous rapist-murderer of eight student nurses in Chicago in 1966, had given me grounds to protest during the Vietnam War that we were killing the wrong people. In 1967, a jury took 49 minutes to sentence Speck to death, but the US Supreme Court eventually reversed his death sentence on the strength of its *Witherspoon* decision that jurors with religious or moral qualms about capital punishment could not be automatically excluded.[3] Illinois had resentenced Speck to 1,200 years in prison, where he died in 1992 from a heart attack.

A year later, in January 1993, two men walked into a Brown's Chicken restaurant in Palatine, Illinois. Although employees had already bagged the garbage and prepared to close for the night, the new franchise owners accommodated these last-minute customers. One man ordered and ate some chicken, and then both announced a robbery. They herded all seven employees into the restaurant freezer. And there they massacred them. The investigation yielded no useful fingerprints. The chicken yielded no useful DNA, but Illinois lab technicians froze and stored the chicken anyway. One hundred investigators from several police agencies followed dead ends for months.

Three years later, a post-mortem Stateville prison videotape publicly surfaced of Richard Speck snorting cocaine and sporting breasts he'd developed through prison hormone treatments. The public rage grew as Speck declared to the camera, "Hell, if they knew how much fun I was having in here, they'd let me loose." Speck removed his silk panties to engage in oral sex on tape with a fellow prisoner. "It wasn't their day," Speck declared about the eight nurses he'd killed. So Illinois's worst mass murderer returned to stoke the public's fury. But its second-worst mass murderers remained at large as a hundred investigators dwindled to four.

With the new millennium approaching, doubts about the death penalty spiked nationally. A Northwestern University journalism class discovered that Illinois was preparing to execute Anthony Porter for a murder he probably never committed. Porter, a gang-connected street robber, had preyed on others in the same park where the robbery/murder took place. But that thuggish callousness hardly qualified him to die. And so, shaken by the pending execution of an "innocent" man, on January 31, 2000, Republican governor George Ryan threw in with the abolitionists, announced an Illinois death penalty moratorium, and established a death penalty study commission.

Three months later, armed with improved techniques, Illinois crime lab technicians retested the frozen chicken from the restaurant massacre and extracted a good DNA sample.[4] Unfortunately, the profile failed to match any known criminal in the database. The next year, a wrecking ball turned the restaurant into a parking lot. But still the second-worst mass murder in Illinois history remained unsolved.

Nine years had passed. The frozen chicken yielded one murderer's genetic print. But the cold case remained in deep freeze. Until one day, in April 2002, a woman revealed a secret she said she could "live with no longer." Her former boyfriend had confessed to her the night of the massacre. The police took swabs from James Degorski and Juan Luna, the other person she identified. Luna's DNA perfectly matched the chicken. In custody, both men confessed.

In January 2003, after two years of finding fault with the death penalty but not finding one innocent person living on death row, Governor Ryan's commission issued sweeping recommendations to narrow the aggravating factors and prevent executing the innocent. Some proposals went too far. The commission would eliminate death as punishment for killing children and redefine torture to require that the killer took pleasure at inflicting prolonged pain and suffering. How would any prosecutor prove that? Besides, a depraved indifference to a victim's suffering should suffice. Other proposed reforms did not go far enough. Murdering in prison would still qualify for death, thus singling out prisoners for special protection but not children or other vulnerable victims.[5]

Mired in scandal and maladministration at the end of his term—with friends and associates already under federal indictment for selling commercial licenses to unqualified drivers, including one who crashed a truck he couldn't drive and killed six children—Governor George Ryan found himself serenaded by abolitionists who assured the politician that greatness could still be achieved (not to mention big bucks on the lecture circuit). Having forced the victims' families publicly to air their pain again and beg for the justice they had long been denied, the governor ignored his own commission's proposed reforms. Instead, as adulation poured in from world leaders, in a legal but morally indiscriminate act of executive prerogative, Governor Ryan commuted all 163 death sentences, and to the adoring cheers of abolitionists who lit up the Coliseum in Rome and nominated him for the Nobel Peace Prize, the governor emptied Illinois's death row.

Some justice did prevail here, however, when Ryan eventually served time in federal prison for corruption. Meanwhile, under a new administration, prosecutors sought the death penalty against a new crop of killers and gradually repopulated Illinois's death row. Now, with Juan Luna's capital trial only months away and his guilt clearly established, Illinois prosecutors invited me to testify as an expert witness. The jury would almost certainly convict him of first-degree murder. At the penalty phase, the defense would probably call Roger Cowan, an ex-warden, to assure the jury that inside prison, a lifer suffered daily. Cowan had already testified to this fact in another capital case. In fact, this retired warden's résumé brazenly listed his current employment as "professional witness."

I agreed to rebut his testimony on one condition: I would not get paid. How could I accept money to help get someone killed? The prosecutor gets paid, the state's psychiatrist gets paid, but I'd be damned if I'd ever become a "professional witness." The state's attorneys, of course, readily agreed to that demand. I would document life inside every Illinois maximum security prison and submit a report with a video collage to show the jury. I couldn't wait until they cross-examined me under oath.

The Illinois Department of Corrections hardly wanted a professor-videographer probing their prisons, but once Judge Vincent Gaugen signed an order commanding it, they had no choice. So while Daryl Holton fought to prove himself competent to die, I began documenting life in general population inside Illinois's maximum security prisons to rebut the big lie that life inside was worse than death itself.

24

SIX FEET OVER

"THERE'S NOTHING DANGEROUS ABOUT THIS PLACE," James Perruquet assured me at Stateville. "A little kid could walk through this place." As a teenager, Perruquet had sexually abused and then tortured to death a 14-year-old boy. Eventually released on his seventh trip before the parole board only to murder again, Perruquet detailed his daily life without parole. "I wake up, clean myself. My cell mate goes to work—I don't go to work until 1 p.m. So I have the cell to myself. Flip on TV, see what's going on, check out the news in the morning. I'll turn on the radio, listen to some music while I'm cleaning up. About an hour before work I watch *Who Wants to Be a Millionaire?*, try to answer the questions. Then I go back to the news until I work in the kitchen. I'm out on the line serving everybody. Then I go back to the cell house, take a shower, go in and watch some prime time. I like *24*, *Lost*, *Prison Break*. Now everything's coming up with their season finales, and I'm just trying to determine which one I want to watch the most. So I watch. And go to bed." With no lights-out policy, he could, if he wanted, watch late night TV. Although Perruquet enjoyed his weekend handball games, he did have real grievances: There's too much chicken; the meat and vegetables taste overcooked. "I'm a Bears fan; I'm a Bulls fan," he explained, covering football and basketball. How about baseball? It wasn't easy being a Cubs fan while locked up for life, Perruquet complained. His prison job schedule forced him to miss too many afternoon games.

Fortunately for Perruquet, prisoners no longer cared what crime a guy committed on the outside. "We're all the same in here. We all look at each other the same." Of course prison did have its own class structure. "Like out there, you've got your lowlifes, your middle, and your upper." Perruquet considered himself "middle class. I got myself a job, a little money. I don't go around wishing I had stuff. I'm just living the level life."

"Safeville," that's what they call Stateville, Dary Lewis agreed. "Quite a few people call it that. Cook County Jail, that was a rough joint, a lot tougher than Safeville. Another common perversity of our criminal justice system: Jails usually house arrestees awaiting trial, whereas prisons house convicted felons. And yet daily life inside prison beats life inside jails for those we still presume innocent. Take the penalty.

Lewis's routine resembled Perruquet's: "Wake up, clean up the cell. Watch my soap operas. *General Hospital.* Every day—religiously." How else to amuse himself? "We get *Playboy* and *Penthouse.*" That surprised me. "As long as they're not hard-core. No penetration. At rec, I walk around, talk, play ball, cards. Play for fun. Talk shit." Dary chuckled. Sports? "Die-hard Bears fan—that's my team. When they flying, I'm riding with them. When they're sinking, I'm with them too." Smiling as we talked, Dary characterized this prison as "the best punishment to make me suffer mentally."

These brave souls on the inside, along with many millionaire retirees outside, somehow manage to survive the "suffering" of daily soap operas and playing cards. "You need to do something to deal with the pain," Lewis countered earnestly. Even better than TV, reading did it for Dary. "My physical being may be trapped here. I can go nowhere. But mentally, I'm as free as a bird."

Who could better explode the myth that lifers had it worse than the condemned than recently condemned prisoners themselves, now released from the Row? "When they announced that commutation on TV, I was overjoyed," Howard Wiley recalled at Pontiac, the next Illinois maximum security prison I visited. "Sometimes when I talk about it, I get teary eyed. Because when you are facing death, everything else just vanishes." Wiley had spent 13 years on death row for killing three women in an apartment. "Some people would say life in prison is worse than death. That is not true. I've experienced death row. Every morning I woke up one day closer to being executed," Wiley grimaced. "One guy did tell me, 'I'd rather be dead. George Ryan didn't have to save me; he could have let me get executed.'"

"Did he kill himself?" I asked.

"No, he's still running around here," Wiley replied, barely suppressing a smile.

"Why?"

"That's what I asked him. Why don't you buy yourself an extension cord and go hang yourself?"

Of course you can find exceptions, but perversely, as Wiley observed, "Life in the penitentiary *preserves* you. You don't get older, as people would in the street. You get plenty of rest, you're not drinking, no access to drugs, you stop smoking."

Prisoners preferred life to death, and yet ironically, as I first discovered in Florida and later had confirmed in Oklahoma and Tennessee, life on death row had its advantages over general population. "On death row you get a shower every day, go out every day, have a cell to yourself," explained Jimmy Pitsonbarger, another former condemned inside Pontiac whom Ryan commuted. "I have more movement over here, but I had more peace of mind there. If I had my choice of either place—" Pitsonbarger breathed deeply, his earnest eyes and quiet demeanor hardly suggesting his murderous crime spree in three states. "It would probably be here. If I'm going to face death, I'd rather do it like every other human being, not knowing when it's coming." However, as Timothy McVeigh declared, scoffing at his own pending execution, "At least I know when I'm checking out." But Pitsonbarger disagreed. "I would rather be on death row to do my time, but not to die."

Of course, for those lifers lucky enough to land in a medium security prison, daily life in gen pop hands down beat life on the Row. "One year after being convicted of mass murder but spared the death penalty, the prisoner here can have all day Saturday and Sunday free to play on the ball field, six hours of visits every weekend, phone lists of ten people, good food— chicken and ice cream," I had complained indignantly to Warden Steve Beck at Mack Alford Correctional Center, aka "Stringtown," Oklahoma's medium security prison.

"Yes, conceivably," Beck agreed matter-of-factly.

"And that doesn't offend you?"

"It's not my place to be offended," Warden Beck answered breezily, brushing aside my question.

"Well it's mine," I insisted, my voice cracking with indignation at what I'd seen. "It's morally wrong. I know this like I know my hand has five fingers."

Unlike Sergeant Rushton, Beck didn't resist. "Certain crimes the person *should* be made to pay every day. But I'm not here to punish. My *professional* opinion is whatever I'm tasked to do by my superiors. If my task is to tie them to a pole and horsewhip them every Monday morning, they'll be horsewhipped every Monday morning. But I'm professionally tasked to provide recreation. We have a confined, violent clientele here. They're going to do something with their time. Now then, do I want them playing softball, or do I want them fighting officers? I want them playing softball. As the warden I certainly do. Like any job, I have to do certain things that I don't like doing."

"Are you glad you've become numbed to injustice?"

"When I know an inmate has done something terrible, I get a feeling. But I don't let it show. Some manslaughters, in their situation, I'm not sure I wouldn't have done the same thing. But this guy kills a man and his wife, drags them out in the field, and sets them on fire. . . . Go hang him from a tree."

"You can't!" I snapped back. "The Constitution and the courts won't let you."

"Exactly!"

"But don't let him play softball and eat ice cream," I yelped. "That *can't be* the only alternative."

"What am I going to do with him?"

"Make life as unpleasant as you can. Legally. Even if you endanger your staff slightly more. Instead you sacrifice justice for fear." Even as he defended against my attack, the warden seemed to invite it.

"As Steve Beck, if I had my way, we'd have a lot of ropes hanging on those trees. As the warden I'll have them climb the ropes for exercise." Beck laughed heartily.

"I enjoy the day," said Robert Pitts, a pleasant, cocky prisoner searching for the right words to describe his life inside the Turney Center, Tennessee's medium security prison.

"You're in for murder. Want to tell me about it?"

Pitts smiled at my invitation. Had he planned on stabbing to death the victim of his burglary?

"No," he explained. "That happened spontaneously."

"Why'd you stab her?"

"I stabbed her *because* I didn't know if she would die from the hits that I already administered to her with a lead pipe I found in her yard. And I thought this here might kill her."

"Did she resist?"

"No."

"Then why kill her?"

"Because . . . I wanted to make sure I received a life without parole sentence," Pitts explained in his matter-of-fact drawl. My shock must have shown. "I was homeless, and I couldn't think of doing anything except committing crime." Pitts had worked "a regular job for eight years," but he "got fed up with it. So with the knowledge that the American justice system would give me a life without parole sentence for first-degree murder, that's what I did. I knew all I had to do was murder a person. So that's what I did."

"Why her?" I demanded.

Pitts laughed. "I don't know. As far as her deserving anything, that might be something for God to answer."

"Wasn't the death penalty a risk?"

"I thought about that. Living on the streets was a risk. I was eating out of trash cans; I didn't feel good a lot of time. I wasn't getting the nutrients like a well-balanced diet."

"And you get that here?"

"Hell yeah! They feed us like bulls. God, it's so much better here."

"Ever think about the killing?"

"A little."

"Does it bother you?"

"Nope." I admired his honesty and detested his truth. "Why did she have to die?" Pitts repeated my question to him. "I sinned. And I'll burn in hell for that." I hoped that thought terrified him. No such luck. "I would not want to go to heaven," Pitts insisted. "I hate God. I would much rather burn in eternity than be around Him for one second. The devil is my master." Pitts chuckled. "I'm the same as everybody else," he continued. "I'm out for myself. The Bible tells me I am a wretched sinner that will not receive salvation. So if you know who you are, why not just be who you are?" He laughed heartily.

Did Pitts have to kill his victim? "Couldn't you have gone to a shelter?"

"I've been to shelters. Shelters aren't me. Prison is much more me."

Later, videotaping Pitts shooting pool, I did observe a genuinely anguished moment as he agonized over a difficult bank shot. Vicious thug. Spending life like this, lucky guy. Took the penalty.

In the weeks following my visits to Stateville and Pontiac, I sketched out my testimony, captured and cut footage to show the Luna jury. At first I toyed with the idea of fashioning a generic collage of best bits from Oklahoma, Tennessee, and Illinois. Taken together, they would give the jury a comparison between daily life inside prison and death row.

My chance encounter with Turney Center's prison rock band—they called themselves the Death Puppies—would make the Luna jury stop and consider the real alternative to a sentence of death. Right before meeting Pitts, I had heard a throbbing, driving beat. I stood just inside a small room, my eyes fixed on long-haired convicts in torn T-shirts screaming into microphones and enthusiastically blasting away on drums and electric guitars, until my ears rebelled and drove me from their practice session. I found out later that one of the band members had murdered an entire family.

The highlights reel would definitely include the Riverbend commissary. Officer Robert Pollock ran that operation and proudly carried out his mission. When I walked into a prison commissary the first time, bright colors assaulted my eyes. Rows and rows of sodas, coffee, tobacco, shampoo, Vienna sausage, peanut butter, beans, mackerel, cheddar cheese, hot sauce, Bumble Bee tuna, Hershey's with almonds, Skittles, soups, mouthwash, Vaseline dry skin therapy, styling gel, Metamucil.

"I notice the items are dated."

The commissary chief lit up. "We don't send anything back there that's out of date," he insisted.

"You ever run sales?" I asked, irreverently.

"Yes. We had some cookies close to being out of date. They had stopped buying them." Pollack contemplated this still unexplained mystery. "So we marked them down! And they sold!"

"Does it bother you to supply cookies to rapist murderers?"

"It's not my place to judge them. I didn't put them here. It's just my job to make sure they have fresh goods."

And, of course, Unit 6, my last stop that initial trip to Riverbend when I first met Daryl, absolutely must make the final cut. Regardless of his crime or sentence—even life with no parole—a well-behaved prisoner in general population could work his way there. The jury would see gleaming weight machines, the near-NBA-regulation-size basketball court with its highly polished wood floor. But most unsettling of all, the softball game played on a manicured field with white-lined base paths and prisoners all in uniforms—baseball uniforms! One guy smacked an inside-the-park home run. "Walk, walk," his teammates called out merrily, allowing their hero of the moment to circle the bases triumphantly, greeted at the plate with high fives. Of course when home run hitters swung for the fences, they had to clear the barbed wire that topped them. But inside the park, moment to moment, these guys played.

This composite prison experience would most dramatically give the lie to the claim that life inside was worse than death. Oklahoma State Penitentiary's warden's assistant, Lee Mann, would sum up the video simply and close the show: "We make it easy for them because it's easy for us when it's easy for them."

Any history, documentary, or nonfiction account including this one, by necessity, selects, juxtaposes, and compresses the stuff of everyday life. Yet it purports to be truth. But I realized that defense attorneys would pounce on a multistate video as proof that Illinois prisons were too harsh to yield such scenes. So in the end, I restricted the Luna jury video collage to Illinois. My camera struck pay dirt there recording prisoners "shopping" at the commissary—that's what the commissary sign said—according to the prison's posted rules. Convicts merrily called out their orders, while officers swiped a host of grocery items across cash register scanners. A typical supermarket, only it's inside a maximum security prison. As a receipt prints, cut to prisoners sauntering out, with sacks of goodies slung over their shoulders, laughing.

I hoped the jury would get the irony of a prison library's "true crime" section.

Donald Hulick, the thoughtful, earnest warden at Menard, would act as voice over, explaining his "mission" in terms by now familiar. Of course, punishment played no part. "It's my responsibility to get over to that commissary, make sure the people who shop on Monday or Friday get granola bars or noodles. We try to make certain that every offender has the same opportunities. We make sure their privileges are provided to them."

The jury must see Illinois prisoners playing ball and clowning around in the modern barbershop while others worked in industry, all with Hulick's narration: "If their institutional adjustment has been excellent, they can be placed in one of those prized assignments."

"Will his past crime influence the quality of his life?" I asked.

"No." Then the warden corrected himself. "In some cases, someone with a life sentence can be preferred for assignments."

"So ironically, those who commit the *worst crimes outside* might even have a better chance at the *best life inside*."

Hulick hesitated. "I guess based on what I just said, yes. That is ironic, but it's true."

This video collage and my live testimony would mark the first time, probably, that an expert witness would rebut the life-is-worse-than-death claim to a capital jury. Although the video failed to convert *New York Times* chief legal correspondent and columnist Adam Liptak from abolitionist to death penalty advocate, it did move this excellent journalist—who routinely subordinated his personal views to an informed public's right to hear both sides—to fly to Chicago to cover Luna's penalty phase.

I had carefully rehearsed my statement to the jury: People experience punishment differently. You imagine how you would feel locked up for life. We imagine life without parole, where you never see the light of day, as a living hell. The defendant did a terrible crime; therefore, he receives a terrible punishment. But that's not prison. The nature of the crime will be completely severed from the experience of the punishment. If officers tried to punish, they'd risk their own safety and ruin their career prospects. Instead they insulate themselves psychologically from the inmates' crimes, not consulting a prisoner's record, and embrace a mission statement that tells them their job is not to punish.

I'd close at Illinois's medium security prison, Danville, where Luna, if he got lucky, might live out his later years. "When I was transferred here, I was given a key to my own room," lifer Watson Gray would explain. "It took me awhile to get used to that. You could close your door." A man's cell became his bedroom. Not the place that confined him, but a safe refuge. And right outside the cell, guys hung out all day in the communal room, playing chess, checkers, or cards. "Life inside is what you make it," Gray would guide them. "Even though you're written off and removed from society, there's still opportunity for you. Simple pleasures. Going out in the fresh air and the sunshine." The pictures would prove the truth, but Watson's narration would drive it home. "Nobody enjoys serving life, but it depends on how you live it. Think of this as a city and yourself as a citizen of this city."

"So life, even in a maximum security prison, significantly beats—"

"Being dead," Watson laughed heartily. "Significantly."

"As long as you're six feet above ground and not six feet under, you got a chance," Howard Wiley from Pontiac would soothingly sum it up.

As expected, the jury convicted Juan Luna of mass murder. Now came the penalty phase: Should Juan Luna, who cold-bloodedly murdered seven terrified employees inside the Brown's fried chicken joint that night, live this life or die? Which more nearly approached justice? Life or death? As expected, Roger Cowan, the ex-warden turned professional witness, testified to their bleak life inside, bolstered by a $200-an-hour defense psychologist who characterized prison life as "excruciatingly psychologically painful."

Minutes before my time came to testify, the prosecutors chickened out and canceled me and the video. The crime itself, they claimed, rendered my testimony unnecessary and potentially counterproductive if the defense, as expected, made my pro–death penalty views a diversion.[1] I suspect but cannot prove the prosecutors wanted to protect corrections from the defense assault over why I, but not they, documented life inside.

Without this powerful footage, the defense got the last video plea: Luna's child on tape pleading with the jury to spare his father. Even so, the jury voted 11–1 for death. Illinois requires a unanimous verdict, however, and when the lone stealth juror refused to budge, with the weekend approaching, the rest of this sequestered jury caved in and voted life without parole. Had the jurors seen my prison video, would none have held out? So Juan Luna got life—a life the defense laughingly claimed as worse than death. And still I hadn't gotten my chance to rebut the big lie.

25

DEATH WATCH

I HADN'T THOUGHT MUCH ABOUT DARYL HOLTON IN THE months following his last-second stay of execution and our unpleasant follow-up phone call. He'd conned me, and his life left a bad taste. I long since shifted my focus to losing battles in New Jersey, then Illinois. But one day a letter arrived from Daryl. "I feel compelled to write and at least offer an explanation based admittedly on hindsight. Given the tone of our last conversation, I understand if you're not interested." After reading US Supreme Court briefs in a "minimally similar" competency challenge, Daryl feared the Sixth Circuit would stay his execution, he explained. Thus, he petitioned the Supreme Court to demonstrate his competence to file a petition. Daryl had no "delusion that the Court would grant relief. The points were purely academic. The Supreme Court denied my petition without comment. WHEW! So that's it in a nutshell. I understand if you could care less. I've thought of our conversations and wondered how you are. The hair has finally started to grow back on my lower legs. I'm still bald but not a Buddhist. Drop me a note if you can."

I ignored Daryl's letter for several weeks. But eventually I replied. "One part of me is definitely disappointed in you for being around to read this letter and in me for writing it," I confessed while acknowledging Daryl's damned clever explanation for picking up his appeal: He filed to live so that he could die. "This death penalty focus wears me down—I'm really tired of it," my letter truthfully admitted. "But the need for justice and the naïve belief that it's possible in this world drive me on."

Daryl wrote back immediately, expressing delight at our renewed contact and surprise that New Jersey ever had a death penalty as everyone there was insane and therefore constitutionally exempt. Daryl sent me a one-act play he'd just written, spoofing me. "Not much new to report here," he said but added a P.P.S.: "Oh, almost forgot. The state filed a motion to reset my execution date."

"So how's this for self-centered arrogance?" my return letter began. "I'm sitting here, drinking my Poland Spring water, deeply conflicted between wanting justice and having you around a little longer to give me shit. So I woke up early this morning thinking about you being killed at the end of the month, at last for real, and I feel lousy. I hope you put me on your visitors' list. But what's left to say?" my letter confessed. "I'm planning on going down there execution night to mingle among the protesters outside and say to the chanting mob—'Look, oppose the death penalty, but don't claim he didn't make a knowing choice.' And so I'm getting psychologically geared up to see justice done and freed to start making sense of this strange interlude. When suddenly, popping onto my computer screen, news that the Governor has imposed a 3-month moratorium on all executions. And again I'm feeling unhappy, but this time because you'll be alive, and once again justice won't have been done. I'm tired of this damn roller-coaster. And how absurd, how screamingly absurd, that I'm complaining to you!"

Once again, everything was on hold while the Department of Corrections devised a new execution protocol. In spring 2007, few people expected Tennessee to execute anyone any time soon. But only a few days after the commissioner submitted revised procedures to the Governor, Tennessee executed Philip Workman. Workman's case disturbed me. According to the prosecution, he had killed a police officer in a shootout during a botched robbery attempt. Workman's advocates have raised questions as to whether, in fact, one police officer tragically and accidentally shot and killed the fellow officer during the shootout. Perhaps eliminating the felony murder aggravator while employing residual doubt might have spared this condemned man—not an upstanding citizen but not the worst of the worst. In lieu of his final meal, Workman requested a large vegetarian pizza be delivered to the homeless. Corrections refused, but the night Tennessee executed Phillip Workman, sympathizers sent hundreds of pizzas to homeless shelters.[1]

The punishment of death hung over Tennessee's death row. The state immediately moved to reschedule Daryl's execution. "So it's for real," I wrote Daryl that night, not knowing that a few hours earlier, Daryl officially declared that he did not oppose the state's motion to reset an execution date. Daryl's new date: September 12, 2007, 1 a.m. Daryl's death suddenly loomed once again.

As August wound down, the Department of Corrections shut down all media access to death row. I could only visit Daryl as a personal visitor. Somehow the man with a near-photographic memory repeatedly forgot to put me on his visitors' list. It usually takes six weeks to add a visitor, Mary Dennis, the warden's assistant, informed me. And Daryl was due to die much sooner than that. "The warden may allow expedited procedures," I told Daryl. But he must request it. Daryl took pride in never asking or receiving special favors. "Unless you'd prefer I not visit. Your call. Last chance."

"Give it a try," said Daryl simply.

I received the visitation application form and quickly filled out the standard stuff—name, address, telephone, date of birth, race, eye and hair color. I chuckled at having to circle my "complexion": "Black, Dark Brown, Dark, Fair, Light Brown, Light, Medium, Medium Brown, Yellow." And then the problem: RELATIONSHIP TO INMATE. Tucked among 24 options—Aunt, Brother, Cousin, Daughter, Father . . . the one single nonfamily choice: Friend. Obviously I wasn't Daryl's relative, but "friend"? The form warned that all questions must be answered. Worse, this document, once submitted, would become "a public record."

I'd be damned to officially declare myself the friend of someone who murdered his four children. I sat and stared at the form, put it aside for an hour, then picked it up again. My "friend" Daryl Holton? I crossed out "Friend," added "Acquaintance," and risked the visit.

If they didn't kill Daryl this time, they probably never would. And then what? We'd keep up a lively correspondence, and I'd become his lifelong buddy? I vowed that this visit, if they allowed it, would be goodbye. Either way, alive or dead, after September 12, Daryl and I were done. Would I tell him to his face? Or better yet, simply let his death date arrive, knowing he'd be dead to me thereafter? But why visit one last time, if not to say goodbye truthfully?

Maybe it should have been déjà vu, visiting Daryl once again, right before his newly scheduled execution. But this time it felt different, going in alone without camera or recorder. They had just moved Daryl to death watch, the last stop before the chair. Thick Plexiglas separated us at first, inside this tiny visiting cell. But that quickly melted away. Daryl seemed calm but not lethargic. "Last year I was running on adrenalin," he explained. Now that he'd shed his lawyers, Daryl saw the clear path to the finish. Did he believe Tennessee would kill him in less than three days? "I have fewer doubts," he said cautiously, so as not to jinx it.

Last year I wanted him to feel pain, express remorse, reveal his true motives. This time it felt wrong to attempt further progress with that project. Slightly stiff at first, we allowed the block of time together to dictate its own rhythms, going in and out of heavy stuff, at will, without notice or set-up. I hoped it wouldn't feel like that final awkward hospital visit with the dying when you pretend it's not happening and don't know what to say. But Daryl quickly put me at my ease, bringing me up to date.

"Tobacco here is the new pot." The prison had gone smoke free. Daryl had quit without a problem. "But I now have new company on level C." He smiled at the thought of model convicts, found with tobacco, losing their privileges. Daryl seemed to forget that as of a few hours ago, after eight years there, he no longer lived on level C. Now he lived on death watch. One step closer.

Daryl proudly shared the details of his latest victory over defense law-yers, state and federal. Most of it I knew. Most of the rest, dry and legal, few of us would find interesting. But I was here for him. Or so I had convinced myself. Besides, it was amusing to hear Daryl retell it. It seems that "some ignorant clerk" fashioned Tennessee's execution manual as a "cut and paste job." Thus, before *lethal injection,* the manual required a prisoner's head must be shaved and sponges must be soaked in solution. Daryl wondered ironi-cally whether he too might qualify for a shave and a sponge, although he had chosen the electric chair. Anyway, that cost Tennessee three months to fix.

Daryl continued to fill me in on "current events." "I think my scalp burns for five minutes. Lawyers can skew that to challenge electrocution." He wanted to refuse an autopsy but feared some defense lawyer would somehow use that as new evidence of Daryl's incompetence.

"Do you expect to feel pain?" I felt self-conscious at my tone, lest Daryl wrongly sense I wanted him to suffer in the chair. I didn't, although some might.

"Not a lot. A minuscule amount more" than lethal injection he said, matter-of-factly. He seemed so calm. "Oh, I get irritated by the little crap," Daryl replied jovially but then became serious. "It will be a relief," he assured me, about Monday night's scheduled execution. "I don't have to worry about my laundry on Tuesday." I laughed.

"Is it a release, a relief?" I asked seriously, wanting to explore the mean-ing of death with a condemned man really facing it.

"It's an exit," said Daryl with that gleam in his eye. "There's more op-portunity in death than there is on death row. No closure there."

"Are you looking forward to it?"

"Yeah," he said. I couldn't read him. "I'm also looking forward to the next episode of *Law and Order,* but I guess I'll have to skip that!"

Our conversation was chaotic. Daryl flashed back and forward. "If my trial lawyer had been better, I would have gotten here a lot sooner," he said ruefully. "But I wouldn't have told my story."

"Have you now?"

"No, not yet. The attorneys make their points, the media theirs."

"Can anyone ever tell your story?" Daryl nodded. And pointed at his visitor. "You."

Kelly insisted what I suspected—I still didn't really know his story. So I decided to use this opening to pick at a scab I had intended to let scar. "I've got to ask you one last time. Why did you plan to kill your wife's—"

"*Ex*-wife's new boyfriend's daughter," Daryl corrected me wearily, with obvious annoyance.

"How was this even arguably 'altruistic'?"

Silence. I assumed Daryl, disgusted, waited for me to switch subjects. How many times would I ask this? The moment grew embarrassing. I waited for him to decide on the right verbal cut to disparage my stupidity or stubbornness.

"The little girl could have been motivated by revenge," he said quietly. I couldn't believe my ears. "If someone else raised your children—" he started to explain. "If they started calling somebody else Daddy—" Then he stopped. "The planned killing of the little girl was revenge," he conceded quietly.

What about the children he *did* kill? Would Daryl's well-defended explanation all unravel? Daryl seemed ready finally to clear it up. "Your children *are* you." He saw I didn't get it. "I was saving myself. Like a bear caught in a trap, gnawing off his own limb to get out of that trap. I killed them because I had to. Life is a trap. Everything was about and for my children. And anything was better than what was going on."

"Anything was better?" I gently prodded him with his own words.

"I still don't see better options. I wish I could have found another way." Daryl looked up at me—looked me right in the eyes. "You're looking for remorse," he said quietly, "but you're not getting it." The silence between us sunk in, as his words echoed and my resentment built. "Why *would* I express remorse to you? You have some illegitimate emotional investment in my children who you never met. It's one thing to act from a civic sense of duty. But your imagined emotional connection to them is unreal, unhealthy, and illegitimate."

We had come full circle from that first meeting. Daryl had struck back as pugnaciously as he ever would. We sat and stared at each other. I felt sorry for him. Then I hated him. Why would he not show remorse? Why did I need that? Why do most of us need other people to express remorse? Did I need Daryl to really feel the pain, or was it enough to show it?

Johan Huizinga, in *Homo Ludens*, teaches that society tolerates its cheats more than its spoilsports.[2] It pardons hypocrites long before it forgives revolutionaries. At least the cheat or hypocrite acknowledges the legitimacy of the game and its rules and later, once caught, apologizes for violating them. The spoilsport or revolutionary rejects the game. As long as you will bow and scrape, pretend to abide by the rules, apologize and express remorse, and swear to be good in the future, we feel less threatened and hate you less. Studies show that capital juries credit killers' expressions of contrition.

Why did I hate Daryl this moment? Because he would die without the decency at least to fake remorse and regret? Or did he simply not hurt enough, not feel pain he so richly deserved? I don't know, but that moment when he defied the gods of decency and stuck to his guns, I did despise him.

Was I just another Sophist, content with appearances? Or did I need Daryl emotionally to suffer for his monstrous deed, to face what he'd done, as a step toward his real redemption? Worse than a Sophist, was I a sublimating sadist, transferring my sadism onto society's detested object? Difficult and deep questions about pain and punishment can divide us starkly or subtly, but mostly they lay unexposed and unexplored, overlooked and overshadowed in the death penalty debate itself. I cared so that Daryl be killed without pain while I so badly needed him to *live* with it. Pain he would feel. Pain he would then show.

Apparently Daryl did not feel this huge gulf growing deeper than ever between us. These past two years, he'd repeatedly overlooked or gently chided me for gratuitous unwarranted attacks any time I needed to distance myself from him. Prove to myself I wasn't like him. We're harder on ourselves, our own, some of us. "I would much rather be tried by a white jury than a black one," Itchy had insisted, surprising me years earlier. "A black juror feels like he must distance himself from me—make the statement 'I'm not like him, he's nothing but some shit.' Black jurors will convict faster and sentence harder."

Daryl repeatedly forgave me my trespasses. But I could only imagine forgiving Daryl if I knew he would not forgive himself. Kant supported the justice of executing repentant and unrepentant killers alike: If a murderer comes to repent his criminality, he becomes a better person for embracing a value system that now condemns him. While his crime would pain him more, his punishment would pain him less. He knows he gets what he deserves. The unremorseful killer feels no pain from his crime, and thus his punishment pains him all the more. Each more nearly gets what he deserves.[3]

"Do you think about it?" I asked quietly.

"It's detrimental to dwell on it. I know that's what you'd have me do," said Daryl quietly, looking at me.

Suddenly I felt ashamed of myself, trying to make him feel miserable, here on death watch. Then and there I stopped. Perhaps he felt a sudden relief from my releasing nearly two years of pressure.

"My children had a doomed existence," he said flatly.

It was well past noon. I felt grateful corrections had melded Daryl's last two permitted outside visits into this one extended. Later I realized they probably accommodated themselves. On death watch, corrections seeks to keep the condemned calm. Not let him brood and become agitated. Death watch has deeper meaning as ritual and routine. Officers on death watch, Robert Johnson observes in *Death Work*, remain "emotionally aloof," "civil but impersonal," providing the condemned "company but not comfort."[4] While I shifted uncomfortably in this narrow, low-set visitor's seat, conscious of the scene, my surroundings, and my place in them, Daryl, obviously animated, clearly enjoyed our time together. In the warden's eyes, as Robert Johnson suggests, I too had become like the chaplain, "an honorary member of the execution team."[5]

Time passed quickly on death watch with Daryl. Our conversation wove in and out. Much of it I've forgotten. I remember we did talk gallows humor. "Three death row inmates were scheduled to die," he recounted. "On their last night, the warden presents them a bottle, which they break, and out pops a genie. 'Usually I give the condemned three wishes, but since there are three of you I'll give you one wish each.' The first wished for girls and landed in the Playboy mansion. The second wished for home and found himself with his family. The third, a little slow, shrugged and looked around, feeling lonely in the empty room. 'I wish my friends were here with me.'"

The medical technician startled me, slipping into Daryl's cubicle to check his "vital signs." What grand irony. Always respectful to staff, Daryl submitted. His blood pressure, 108/69; his pulse, 76. A bit racy, Daryl remarked.

Self-effacing and casual about death, Daryl strangely focused on himself as an object of bureaucratic scrutiny. Ironic, constantly to monitor and measure the vital signs of the soon-to-be-killed. His real vital signs could be found in the Governor's heart or briefs filed by lawyers determined to make a last-ditch effort to save Daryl from himself. The nurse left. Time was running out. I looked at him. I had no idea what to ask next.

"Why did you hit Crystal?"

"Kayla had to be told I was not her natural father. The kids at school would taunt her with it. She had to be prepared. My ex-wife did not want to deal with it. But one day she says, 'Your Daddy does not love you anymore. Because you're not really his.' And I slapped her senseless. Crystal told Kayla

I didn't love her. I never could forgive that." He looked at me sadly. "I'd rather think about the good stuff."

"Like what?"

"Clowning around with them. Making up lyrics—'His name was Steven. He was a terrorist.'" [sung to *Copacabana*] Daryl choked up very slightly. "I wish it had turned out better." It almost had turned out better, Daryl explained. "I got custody of the boys in '92. I got us passports." Daryl broke off from that thought. "If she didn't abuse them. . . ." He paused—stuff was going on inside him obviously that I should let bubble out. Daryl filled in the pause dutifully. "It was the lesser of two evils."

"Was there a moment? When you absolutely knew what you would—"

"Yes. My ex-wife allowed me over to see the kids. They were sleeping when I got there. I went upstairs and as I bent down to kiss him, two roaches crawled across my six-year-old's face. When I bent over and saw those roaches, my stomach recoiled. I knew *what* I had to do. I didn't know when. The second week after I move out she meets her boyfriend. By October she moved in with him. Got an order of protection keeping me away from my children. Told me I would never see the children. You each have something in common," Daryl said dryly. "She also encouraged me to kill myself.

"I was seeking relief. Not satisfaction," he continued, separating his own lethal motivation from my retributivism. "The death penalty should afford society relief."

"Not satisfaction at seeing justice done?"

Daryl shook his head. "Society is too prone to excess to seek satisfaction. Only for relief. To return to normalcy."

So here at last, I guess he had confessed his true motive. Daryl killed his children to get relief. Relief from his guilt and frustration at their squalor and neglect, relief from his feeling of impotence to do anything about it.

"If you go on the spectrum from pain to pleasure," Daryl continued, "you've gone through relief to get to satisfaction, and then eventually pleasure."

Daryl killed his children for relief. Not ultimately for their sake, but for his own relief.

And now, ten years later, facing the executioner once again, "How do you feel about dying?"

"Relieved."

Not satisfied, not pleased, but relieved to die. And how should we feel about his dying?

"Relieved but not happy," Daryl said simply, with deep, appealing symmetry.

"But why should *we* not feel satisfaction at justice being done?"

Daryl shook his head. "That smacks of sadism. You should feel relieved. In your words that you've removed the pollution. But not happy."

We were coming to our end. We both had the sense it was time to say goodbye. I turned it to execution night.

"You know I'll be down here."

"Not for my sake."

"No. I want to be at the vigil. Show them some clips of you."

"Don't turn anti–death penalty," Daryl ribbed me. "TCASK can be very persuasive." TCASK, the Tennessee Coalition Against State Killing, would coordinate the vigil and protest outside the prison.

"Anything you want me to tell anybody?"

"Tell Liebman I appreciate his work. If you meet Justice Scalia, tell him he rocks." He paused. "Children are not a *public* resource," Daryl insisted again. "Good luck."

Corrections had come in to escort Daryl. The death watch officers suddenly seemed so removed, showing neither pity nor anger. Daryl, always polite and quiet, here seemed more alive than they. We rose, and he surprised me by pressing his hands to the thick Plexiglas that separated us. Right out of the movies. "Stay out of trouble." Daryl turned away, then turned back. "Talk to Kelly, she needs it. And watch out at the vigil. They'll drop hot wax on you. They're big on candles."

Daryl walked away. I watched, stood up alone in my cubicle weak-kneed, and walked out of Riverbend, dreading my return a few days later, execution night.

26

KILLING THEM SOFTLY

BY THE TIME DARYL REJECTED THE NEEDLE AND CHOSE the chair, lethal injection had become a national center of controversy. For centuries, governments tortured their condemned criminals. In the United States, this land of liberty, punishment long ago morphed from inflicting bodily pain to depriving convicted criminals of freedom, matching units of time spent in prison to the seriousness of the crime. During the Enlightenment, as Foucault recounts in *Discipline and Punish,* "one no longer touched the body, or at least as little as possible, and then only to reach [the soul]."[1]

Except for the death penalty.

In the new republic, James Madison, the father of the Constitution and moving force behind the Eighth Amendment, supported capital punishment as a range of more or less psychologically painful methods. A particularly egregious murderer knew he faced not only death but afterward his corpse's dissection or public display, to be picked at by the birds. Thus, the death penalty for the founding generation, as Stewart Banner reminds us, provided "government officials with gradations of severity above and below ordinary execution."[2]

During the next few decades, progressive Americans considered crime as "more like disease than like sin." Treatment replaced punishment as the enlightened response. The nineteenth century saw a rising middle class with a new "aversion to the sight of death. Disease and dying moved away from homes into hospitals. Cemeteries moved from urban areas to garden-like spots, far from living people." Only the "vulgar mob" enjoyed watching the infliction of pain.[3]

The invention of anesthesia recast pain as largely avoidable. Electrocution and gas replaced hanging, by and large to avoid pain. Then lethal injection replaced them both, to end all pain, even in the punishment of death.

At every opportunity we banished pain from our sight; we professionalized and bureaucratized its infliction in private settings. The intentional infliction of pain, and with it punishment itself, became a sight and act to be avoided—a source of shame.

With the decline of public executions and the rise of prisons run by professional bureaucrats, as Foucault observed, punishment—increasingly "abstract"—became "the most hidden part of the penal process." In the modern bureaucratic prison, "the pain of the body itself no longer [became] the constitutive element of the penalty. Far from the art of unbearable sensations, punishment has become an economy of suspended rights."[4] These days, with corrections embracing their primary mission as safety and security, punishment has become the art and economy of suspended *privileges*. The public has largely accepted this transformation as inevitable, but it could have been and still can be different.

In 1890, the US Supreme Court had allowed New York to substitute the electric chair for hanging—a case involving Thomas Edison's attempt to discredit as deadly George Westinghouse's alternating electric current.[5] Since then, the Court hadn't confronted the constitutionality of death as painful punishment. Legal challenges to lethal injection now worked their way up to the high court. Although the US Supreme Court eventually refused to strike down the needle as unconstitutional in *Baze v. Rees,* Michael Morales's pending execution in California helped launch the intense scrutiny.[6]

Morales volunteered to do a favor for his gay cousin, jealous of his bisexual lover's girlfriend. Morales carefully planned and rehearsed how to use a belt to strangle Terri Winchell, 17, by all accounts a lovely girl who sang in the church choir and saw the best in people. But the belt broke as Terri struggled for her life. So Morales grabbed a claw hammer and beat her 23 times, ripping the flesh from her face. Then, feeling it "a shame to waste a good piece of ass," Morales dragged this innocent girl, face down, across a road and into a vineyard, where he stripped off her clothing and raped her. Then he stabbed her four times in the heart and stole 11 dollars, which he spent celebrating that night on beer, wine, and cigarettes.[7] If lethal injection worked as designed, Morales would die painlessly. If the executioner botched it, this sadistic rapist-murderer might suffer deservedly excruciating pain for a couple of minutes.

"Let us consult the human heart, and there we shall find the Sovereign's right to punish," Beccaria declared tellingly.[8] Intuitively and emotionally, I feel certain we have the right, if not the responsibility, to painfully punish monsters such as Morales because they deserve it. We rightly hate—yes, hate—Morales, Manson, Speck, and others like them. Fitzjames Stephen, the great English judge and historian of the criminal law, declared it "highly desirable" to design punishments "to give expression to that hatred."[9] Even the anti-retributivist Beccaria supported the emotional, intuitive basis for punishment. This same great utilitarian—resolutely opposed to capital punishment—nevertheless asserted the right to *painfully* punish an armed robber who hurt his victim. Moral intuition, written in Beccaria's heart, dictated that some violent criminals deserved violent punishment, painfully inflicted.[10]

Can a painless, consciously pleasant death be inhumane precisely because it lacks any pain? Some retributivists insist that punishment, including death, can sometimes be so *inadequate* as to fail the victims or their surviving loved ones. Embracing human dignity as our primary value, retributivists like Adam Smith emphasize "a humanity . . . more generous and comprehensive," opposing the "compassion we feel for a particular person, a more enlarged compassion . . . which we feel for mankind." In summary, unwarranted "mercy to the guilty is cruelty to the innocent."[11]

Retributive justice, it seems to me, sometimes requires intentionally inflicting a quick but painful death on a person who intentionally or with a depraved indifference made his innocent victims suffer before they died. Abolitionist critics may find this especially repulsive. And if they have their way and abolish the death penalty worldwide, looking back on it someday, these sentiments may sound primitive and outside the limits of humane discourse. By that point, no longer considering a quick but painful death as possible punishment, we may also reject as inhumane punishment a long, unpleasant life.

Michael Morales may deserve more pain than he can physically tolerate. It would violate the Constitution and our own human dignity to kill him as he deserves to die. Would it defile human dignity, however, intentionally to inflict on him a quick but painful death? You shrink in horror at these suggestions? But let us see where your moral logic takes you and us along with you. The American Association of Jewish Lawyers and Jurists *amicus* brief before the Supreme Court claimed Talmudic support for "*the most beautiful death* possible."[12] What could this mean, practically? A BBC documentary, featuring former British defense minister Michael Portillo's search for an ideal execution method, proposed breathing nitrogen, where the condemned would die in a state of euphoria.[13] Why not? Why merely a painless death? Why do we not owe Michael Morales and other sadistic rapist-murderers a "beautiful death," a euphoric death? A Glasgow television critic called me "the scariest man I have ever seen on TV" for protesting that "painless" does not always equal "humane"—that some people, but not Daryl, deserve a quick but painful death.[14]

Lawyers on both sides of the lethal injection controversy, along with the US Supreme Court justices, seemed to take it as given that wherever practical, human dignity always supports the least painful punishment. The actual constitutional challenge before the Supreme Court, therefore, avoided my call for Morales's quick but painful death. Instead, abolitionists challenged lethal injection because it *risked* an *unintended* painful death. Other times they argued about the constitutional *appearance* of a painful death.

Twenty-five hundred years ago, the Sophists championed appearances against Plato who insisted on reality beneath appearances. Oddly, much of the controversy over painful punishment replays this ancient controversy: The debate not only revolved around how a botched execution might cause the condemned a painful experience but also how his dying would *appear* to observers. A single, massive, lethal dose of anesthetic alone—the new lethal injection—will render the condemned killer unconscious and impervious to all pain. But without the paralytic agent, a body's nervous reaction would give a painfully false appearance of pain. However, an improperly administered anesthetic, followed by the paralytic agent, would produce but mask real pain and suffering, which the condemned, now paralyzed, would experience but could not publicly express.

Thus, he would die *apparently* peacefully while *really* suffering. When it comes to lethal pain and suffering, must appearance match reality? Does the Constitution demand truth in dying?

Nothing could be more perverse and unjust to a real utilitarian than causing the condemned to suffer an agonizing death, all the while appearing to die peacefully. Punishment should never be more painful than it appears. To the contrary: All punishment, including death, should *appear* much more painful to observers than it *feels* to criminals because as Beccaria explained, "the severity of punishment [is] intended more for them than for the criminal."[15]

Chief Justice John Roberts supported the state's self-professed good motives for the paralytic agent—to spare witnesses discomforting appearances—even if that risked actual pain to the condemned. Beccaria would have found this perverse, that "dignity" might justify a real risk of painful death in order to avoid a messy-looking painless one: "The degree of the punishment," Beccaria declared, "ought to be so contrived, as to have the greatest possible effect on others, with the least possible pain to the delinquent."[16] Bentham took the appearance-reality gap to its logical conclusion, proposing the government stage phony hangings, secretly sparing the condemned.[17] Let the public be conned.

And the condemned? Some older guys accurately anticipate what's coming. "I already know there ain't no pain," Gary Welch explained to me on Oklahoma's death row. "I've had three operations. They can cut your legs and your arms off, cut your bones in two when you're under that, and you don't know nothing about it. Anybody that's worried about, 'Is there any pain?,' I tell them right quick, 'You can't fight Sodium Pentothal. They may get a few jerks and dying quivers out of you. Old Painless—that's what I call the executioner, it's so damn quick and smooth. 'Come on, Gary, Old Painless is waiting on you!'"

Lethal injection strikes me as wrong, ultimately, not only because it might *arbitrarily* cause pain but also because it certainly causes confusion, conflating punishment with medicine. Publicly opposing this method of execution, I found common ground with Professor Deborah Denno, a leading abolitionist scholar who relentlessly attacks lethal injection protocols as haphazard. Although Denno vigorously opposed all capital punishment, we both agreed that the firing squad, among all traditional methods, probably served us best.

But Tennessee didn't offer Daryl that option.

Because he killed his children when Tennessee used the electric chair, the state allowed Daryl to choose the chair over the needle, thus avoiding *ex post facto* constitutional challenges to inflicting a punishment not in effect when he committed his crime. The legislature probably assumed that everyone given that choice would choose injection. But Daryl chose electrocution.

By choosing the chair, Daryl had avoided this lethal injection legal controversy only to stir up another one. The US Supreme Court long ago had found the electric chair constitutional but hadn't revisited it since. Some state supreme courts had recently struck it down. In the days immediately preceding Daryl's death date, media attention focused on Daryl's chosen method. Why had he selected the chair? To draw attention to himself, to create controversy? To avoid it? To delay his execution or ensure it? Perhaps Holton was masochistic and showed, by choosing the chair, his own incompetence to waive appeals.

Daryl explained it to me simply during those four hours we spent together on death watch. "When you consider purchasing a suit hanging on the rack, you check the price tag. If it's worth what the tag says, you take it to the checkout. At the cash register, you don't ask for a discount. I knew the price for killing my children. Electrocution. I was prepared to pay the posted price then. Now that I'm about to check out, I don't get a discount."

27

BEARING WITNESS

"HOLTON DID NOT REQUEST A SPECIFIC LAST MEAL BUT ate what was served to other inmates," a voice intoned. "A couple of hundred yards from the prison, at a large enclosed field, protesters have begun to gather for their vigil." And here am I, sitting at an empty Formica table, already set for tomorrow's continental breakfast, in this fluorescent motel lobby, alone, face-to-face with Tennessee TV's 10 O'Clock News.

The lead story, eclipsing that day's special election for mayor of Memphis: "Only hours before Daryl Holton is scheduled to die in the electric chair, 78 lawyers have filed an *amicus* brief on behalf of the Tennessee Bar Association seeking to halt his execution."

Daryl believed he'd finally rid himself of unwanted legal interference. Even Steve Ferrell, the federal defender, had peeled off. But now, last minute, a new slew of lawyers tried to stop Daryl's execution. These self-proclaimed "concerned members of the Tennessee bar" petitioned the state supreme court to "exercise its inherent authority and withdraw its order of execution." Why? "The specter of excruciating pain and certainty of cooked brains and blistered bodies" violated the state and federal constitutions, they claimed, quoting the Georgia Supreme Court, which had outlawed electrocution in that state.[1] The condemned faced "the most horrible way to die possible," potentially analogous "to being burned alive at the stake."[2] Daryl failed to comprehend this, they insisted, "misunderstanding the physics of electrocution as his chosen method, erroneously believing he will die instantly and painlessly." It made no difference "that Holton apparently wants to be electrocuted. It is *this Court*—not Daryl Holton—which has the ultimate power to determine whether electrocution comports with the standards of decency in Tennessee."[3] By citing the Tennessee Constitution, the lawyers invited the state high court to banish the electric chair in the state and insulate that decision from US Supreme Court review.

Did Daryl know this new crop of lawyers still fought to keep him alive? Would he be spared yet again? The breaking news: "The long saga, off again on again scheduled execution of Daryl Holton at 1:00 a.m. Central time, apparently is on. The Tennessee Supreme Court has refused to step in and stop it. . . ." The execution would move forward. And what the hell was I doing in the lobby of a budget Nashville motel watching TV?

I strode toward a field, my daughter's video player inside my briefcase, loaded with a disc of Daryl clips. "Children are not a public resource. . . ." I figured that would start an interesting conversation with the protesters. It felt wrong to secretly record these people. And I certainly couldn't explain that I was wired. Odd, all those years ago, on the opposite side of this scene supervising undercover investigations as a special prosecutor; now *I* was the undercover agent. Field lights in the distance made it feel like a 1960s happening. This whole circus atmosphere disgusted me. Approaching the entrance to the protest, I switched off the hidden microphone the documentary director had hidden under my belt.

A bearded, burly man blocked my way at the narrow enclosure to the fence. Someone would be out soon to speak to me. People passed by in wool coats and sweatshirts, nodding to the gatekeeper. Most carried blankets; a few carried lawn chairs.

Reverend Stacy Rector, executive director of Tennessee Coalition Against State Killing (TCASK) approached. She politely put me in my place. "We know your views. We don't want to be preached to." I wouldn't attempt to convert anybody, I assured her. I would simply join them for a moment to commemorate Daryl Holton's execution. "Would you like to know better the man whose death you protest?"

She instructed me to wait and returned to the group inside the enclosure, where 50 yards away, people mingled in little clots. Candles flickered, slightly out of place in the field still glowing with the last remnants of the day's light. People milled about; I could see someone tuning a guitar, but I couldn't hear notes. A microphone waited, ready for later. "TREAT THE ILLNESS DON'T KILL THE PERSON," a sign read. These good, kind, gentle folk, coming out to protest this chilly night in flannel and wool. This whole scene took me back to my college days. Back then I occupied their ground. I wanted their fellowship, these abolitionists.

"I'm getting bad vibes here," the burly gatekeeper growled, still blocking the entrance. "I'm sure if my dog were here, he'd bite you." So even the gentle folk have their tough. "I'm not interested in a group hug," Daryl's voice echoed from our first meeting. "I don't want to become part of the col-lective." I looked longingly at the group, gathering together inside. A candle flamed here and there. The guitar strummed. I stood there, waiting for the reverend to return and invite me in, longing for their companionship, want-ing to sit among them and light a candle.

Reverend Stacy appeared. No one wanted to see the video. If anyone changed their mind, they could join me outside the enclosure and watch it with me. "But part of me belongs with you, in there," I protested. "At least let me sit silently among you and light a candle for Daryl." Stacy nodded, apparently agreeing.

Suddenly Department of Corrections security showed up. "You can't go in there," a beefy security director instructed. "Alright?"

"I've earned the right to light a candle."

"I'm telling you, you're not going in there, alright?" security insisted, obviously irritated. "We don't want any incidents."

"What are you afraid of?" I protested. "That I'll attack them? I'm un-armed and outnumbered." He glared at me, unamused. "Are you worried they'll attack me?" The warden had allowed me to walk unprotected among condemned killers. But those abolitionist protesters—there's real danger lurking there. "*She* said it's OK." I turned to Reverend Stacy for confirma-tion. "No," he said.

"But she said so."

"It wouldn't be a good idea," Stacy declared simply, disavowing her invitation.

"It's right that I be there," I yelped, my voice cracking, not yet realizing how odd that I'd managed to unite corrections and TCASK in common cause: keeping me from the enclosure.

"I told you, you're not going inside that fence, alright?"

"The warden has extended me every courtesy; I don't want to prove a problem," I assured him. "But it's *not* alright." It was so not alright.

"Your place is out there," he said, pointing to the open field behind me. My place? Alone, outside the enclosure? But then I noticed I wasn't alone. A few yards behind me, two protesters stood side by side, holding up their own sign. It probably said "Fry Him" or something equally repulsive. My place couldn't be with them. "Must we remove you?" security asked firmly but without hostility. "If you step inside, we will."

What about freedom of association? But then, too, TCASK members didn't want to associate with me. I promised not to go inside and stood there. Stacy was gone; Burly hadn't stayed to gloat. I stood alone at the mouth the enclosure, watching more candles lighting, listening to softly sung group hymns. Were they singing, "This land is your land; this land is my land," or did I imagine it?

I suddenly realized that if Daryl could be in two places at once, strapped to the chair ready to die, and at the same time out here, Reverend Stacy and the Burly Beard would have banned him, too, from their vigil.

I looked at my watch. 11:30. An hour and a half to go. By this time they've shaved him. Was he anxious? Did he wonder how the chair would feel? We know that electricity seeks the path of least resistance, which may be the skull and skin with its exposed nerve endings, and not the brain or heart. Witnesses at an electrocution have seen flames and smoke and smelled burning flesh. Daryl might be about to cook alive, perhaps even conscious during his violent agony. Probably not, but we might never know. Had he taken the sedative they'd offered him? What was he thinking? How was he feeling? The thought of Daryl's flesh burning made me sick.

If I couldn't talk to Daryl, I needed to talk about him. Banished from the vigil, I approached the two protesters, a man and woman, on "my" side of the fence, holding their sign: "An eye–4-an-eye." I tried to explain Daryl to them: "I've gotten to know him. And there's some part of me that's going to miss him. Because I don't see him simply as the monster that you understandably see him as." And they looked at me like I'm from Mars. "On balance I want him dead too. That's why *they* won't let me go inside."

"It's like a cult," she said. "They're brainwashing everyone in there."

"I hope you understand that Daryl favors the death penalty."

"Do *they* understand that?" she demanded, nodding at the protesters.

"I don't know. They won't let me inside to talk to them."

So here am I, complaining to the fry-them-all set that their enemies won't let me join in song and protest and then assuring them that even the arch-evil Daryl would stand with them if he could. But I'm completely blind to this bizarre irony, to the different emotional languages we speak, too caught up in the moment to begin to comprehend the gulf between us and the twisting meanings of this whole scene. Instead I pushed on. "Daryl admits his killing was selfish. He said he felt like a bear caught in a trap who in the end will gnaw off a part of his own body."

"Did you ever tell him that he's not a bear?" she said bitterly. "That we don't eat our own eggs when we know they won't hatch?"

"No, but I did tell him I found him utterly selfish." As much as I was talking to her about Daryl, I was really talking to Daryl again, one last time. "It's complicated," I insisted. "In the end, if I have to be standing with *them*," I said, nodding to the still swelling group inside the enclosure, "or you, I'm standing with you. But I do admit there's a part of me that's with them. It's easier for you to see him as this one-dimensional monster who killed his children," I admitted. "But I've come to know him. There are worse cases than Daryl."

"I know," he chimed in, looking at me. "My father was killed in 1987 by a minister. He was killed in a church. He was decapitated, and the church was set on fire."

"And they cut off some pieces," she added, "because he had some tattoos. And do you know the only thing saved him from getting away was the fact that he turned himself in."

"My father was known to be a drunk. And the man that led him to Christ was the same man that shot him in the back. Cut off his head, decapitated his arm."

"Drained his blood because he had been a butcher," she added.

What the hell was happening here? Who were these two, dragging me into their bizarre world?

"Rolled his body up in a piece of carpet and set the church on fire in downtown Nashville," William completed the story. "So the way I feel about it, if you got blood on your hands, I don't think you should have a jail cell to support you. If you're man enough to commit the crime, be man enough to pay for the crime," he said with that simple folksy assurance, sounding a little like Daryl in different dialect.

"That's kind of how I feel about Daryl," she replied. "He said he killed his kids 'cause they weren't living the kind of life he thought they should live—"

"The kids were stinking, made fun of, and the six-year-old had roaches crawling across his eyes," I explained.

"But you can fix things like that," she insisted.

"You are here representing the children?" I asked.

"That's what I'm doing," she said.

"I'm here to represent the people who aren't here," William agreed. These plain folk humbled me. You know, the kind we intellectuals dismiss as simple, clinging to their guns and God. George Washington believed that any choice could be explained to the people. And once they understood, they would inevitably do the right thing. These untutored folk passed sophisticated moral judgments with developed clarity.

"You don't see the mother on the news," she observed.

"Nobody seems to know where she is. Daryl was disappointed—"

"That it didn't have a bigger effect," said William, probing Daryl's reaction while condemning it.

"I think so." And I recounted the details of that night, as Daryl had explained them to the police. These two, at least, allowed me to present Daryl's case to them. TCASK had refused. "When I asked him how he felt while he did it, his answer was, 'I felt numb.' Nothing in him snapped, nothing like that."

"Well I hope after that—" She looked at me, trembling, and continued quietly and sincerely. "And I took to heart everything you say." Her eyes began to fill with tears, her voice quivered. "I hope no part of his body feels numb tonight. I hope he feels every single shock that goes through his body. And I hope it takes him the longest possible time to die." I was stunned.

"I *do* agree that some people deserve to die painfully. But not Daryl. Daryl arranged for them to die with a smile on their face. Instantly."

"That's about as sick as he is," growled William, glaring at me while tears rolled down her cheek. She sobbed quietly. "For you to stand there and try to say that it was OK for him to kill his kids—"

"That it was OK!?" I spat his words back at him. "I *said* that he didn't deserve to die *painfully*."

"He arranged for his kids to die with a smile on their face," William growled.

"Instantly! And not in pain."

"That's about as sick as he is."

"That doesn't mean it's OK! *She* said she hoped he dies painfully with extended suffering."

"He does deserve to die painfully," William insisted firmly. "If it was my choice it would be right out here, from a rope hanging from a tree."

"Do you distinguish Daryl from someone who rapes and tortures children before he kills them?"

"Have you ever been raped?" she turned to me, anguish and anger written all over her face. "I have. By someone in my own family. I wish they would take him and drag him behind a truck," she sobbed. "You have no idea what it feels like."

Should I back off and allow her to suffer? "Rapist-murderers do deserve to die painfully," I agreed.

"You don't think that shooting kids—" William tried me again. "To be as sick-minded and telling them to stand back to back, 'Daddy's got a surprise for you.' And then to shoot your kids, you don't think that he deserves to die for that?"

"Not *painfully*," she corrected him.

"I want it to be as painful as possible," William insisted.

"I am *definitly* in favor of pain," she added, completely composed now. "And I'd like to leave it on that note."

"Well I'm glad you're here," I said truthfully. "I'm glad somebody's on this side of it. Unfortunately, the press will cover it that everyone was there to protest—"

"I don't care how they cover it," she said quietly. "I'm not here for that."

"I understand you find a lot of what I say repulsive." I usually reserve that line for the abolitionists.

"I've given you my position and you've given me yours. I took to heart some of the things that you say," she assured me. "But it's the picture of the kids that I can't get out of my head."

"I can't either," I agreed and explained that Daryl had planned to kill himself.

"Too much of a coward," William snarled with contempt. "The man that killed my father hung himself. With a computer cord. He was on death row 16 years when he died."

"Would you be out here if it weren't for your father?"

"I would be," both insisted simultaneously.

"These people over there," William said, nodding to the crowd inside the enclosure. "None of them have ever probably had anything real extreme happen in their life."

"That's not always true." I defended TCASK's sincere abolitionism. "It doesn't matter if it's the devil, it doesn't matter if it's Hitler. For them the issue—"

"Are there Jewish people over there?" she cut me off.

"Probably," I said. "Why does that matter?"

"'Cause you know, people are so against Hitler. and if it were back in the day, and he was alive—"

"There are Jews against the death penalty, even for Hitler," I told them.

"Now that's a tall argument."

They're about to kill Daryl within an hour, and we're standing here talking about Hitler. These two had had enough of me, and I of them. I looked at the group inside the enclosure, clustered together, their candles lit now by the tens. 12:30 a.m. And Daryl, my friend—my acquaintance, Daryl. What was he thinking; what was he feeling?

I walked to the fence and peered over it, not conscious that at this moment, I was literally on the fence, caught between two worlds, feeling at home in neither. Only later did I fathom the ironic twists of this night. How I started out prepared to reveal Daryl to plant doubt in abolitionists convinced he should not die at all, only to end up attempting but failing to plant doubt in those already certain he should die in pain.

As I moved toward the enclosure, trying to soak up their candlelight, straining to catch their strains, thoughts of Daryl began to flood me. "I am taking responsibility," his voice whispered again, "no more nor less than what's mine. . . . You make it sound like punishment. . . . It's proportionate to the crime I was convicted of." Memories of our conversations popped up and then receded as a mist rose and the hymns grew fainter.

I stood at the open gate, one foot inside the enclosure, the fog rolling in, dimming the harsh light that flooded their vigil. To them I was polluted and polluting. They did not want me on their ground. Not as a missionary, not as a messenger. I inched forward, into the mouth of the enclosure, toward the group. This moment made me flash back to the Lorton Central gym that night at the fights, where I felt drawn to Johnny and bolted from my commanded spot. There the joint pulsed with energy, and that fence restraining the mob inched toward me. Here the fence was fixed, and with fog thickening, the mob receded. There I fled from the spot to join Johnny. Here, also feeling alone and vulnerable, I strained to stay fixed, one foot literally on either side. "Who knew that inaction would require so much effort," Daryl's voice filled me.

The fog thickened, the candles diffused into a distant glow. Not for the children; not for Daryl. For whom did those candles burn?

Daryl Holton requested David Raybin, a former prosecutor who helped draft Tennessee's death penalty statute, to witness but not impede his execution. Raybin later recounted how Daryl took the dead man's walk with "dignity," shuffling to the execution chamber. They seated Daryl in the chair. His eyes were shut for the next ten minutes as they fastened the straps and belts, placing soaking wet sponges between the metal contacts and Daryl's bare ankles. "This," Raybin wrote, "was the torment. The sensation of wetness, leather, and a dozen hands about his body must have been maddening. While the guards knew what came next, Daryl had no way of knowing and, I am sure, thought every moment was his last."[4]

Pure rhetoric. Daryl knew he would make a final statement, and the curtain to the witness room had not yet been raised. By all accounts, Daryl started to hyperventilate, whether frightened as Raybin assumed or, as I suspect, to induce lightheadedness to make a smoother transition from this world. Tennessee's new execution protocol did not cover hyperventilation. The warden ordered the straps loosened and waited for Daryl to catch his breath. Meanwhile, Raybin left the chamber and slipped behind the curtain, on the other side of the window facing the execution chamber where the witnesses waited impatiently. I had been part of that scene with Demps. Ushered in, sitting in silence, staring at the curtain, sitting in quiet suspense.

1 a.m. approached. Again my stomach churned. "Do you expect to be executed?" I had asked Daryl. "Eventually, but I have my doubts." Would there be another stay? Standing out there alone, one foot inside the enclosure, thoughts, memories flowed, flicking moments one place to the next. "This is my problem. This is my business with the state of Tennessee. I'm not some vehicle for someone else." Had Daryl become my vehicle? "If I'm executed I don't want to hear a damned thing from the state of Tennessee; we're done," Daryl insisted that first meeting. I'd never told him that last visit, *Live or die, Daryl, we're done.* I felt pangs of remorse toward the man who never expressed remorse for killing his four children. As I imagined Daryl in the chair, no anger welled up at this condemned man.

When the blinds inside the death chamber opened at 1:09, Daryl already sat in the chair. Daryl looked "almost like a young child buckled into a car seat," declared abolitionist witness Dan Barry in his Sunday *New York Times* front-page column. "He yawn[ed] a wide-mouthed yawn, as though just stirring from an interrupted dream, and open[ed] his eyes."[5]

Warden Ricky Bell asked Daryl whether he had any last words. Daryl had told me twice his last statement would be two words. He had considered but rejected reading something from John Milton's *Areopagitica*. Written in 1644, the title means "things to be said before the Areopagus"—that ancient, high court in Athens that tried premeditated murder. What might Daryl have said before the highest court? "Good and evil in this world grow up together, almost inseparably," Milton declared in this essay against censorship. "And the knowledge of good is so involved and interwoven with the knowledge of evil, and in so many cunning resemblances hardly to be discerned." Good and evil were "out of the rind of one apple tasted." But this would be *my* dying declaration drawn from the Areopagitica: "When God gave him reason, he gave him freedom to choose." I could only guess what Daryl would have said.

When asked whether he had a final statement, Daryl mumbled two words: "I do."[6] Nothing more.

Officers placed a sponge soaked in saltwater on Daryl's head. Then they added a "leather cranial cap lined with copper mesh inside." Salt water streamed down Holton's face, soaking his shirt. Raybin imagined the electric chair here "weeping tears for its victim."[7] Trying to dry him, an officer apologized for the drip. "Don't worry about it," Daryl consoled him, to the end considerate of the staff.[8] Meanwhile, media witnesses discussed and settled on Daryl's last words—"I do"—but couldn't figure out what they meant.[9]

They blindfolded Daryl, covered him in a black shroud, and connected the cable to the bottom of the chair. Without warning at 1:16 a.m.: BANG!

As 1,750 volts shot through him, Daryl's body tensed, his back arched up, hands gripping the chair, body straining against the straps. After 20 seconds, his body fell like a sack back into the chair. Fifteen seconds later the second jolt. No sound, no blood, no smell of burning flesh. All witnesses, including Kelly Gleason, believed Daryl died instantly and painlessly. Then they waited five minutes by the clock. "Ladies and gentlemen, this concludes the legal execution of Daryl Holton," came a voice over the loudspeaker. "The time of death, 1:25. Please exit."

Here at the mouth of the enclosure watching the protesters, at this moment I felt alone. *Don't they realize we need to do this?* And the pair behind me. *Don't they realize how careful and discriminating we must be?* I turned to look back at those two wounded souls, huddled together this night to bear witness to justice. Gone. At the vigil, the fog so thick, impossible to make out anything but one broad candle glow. The glowing spot in the distance faded. Protestors begin to file out of the enclosure, carrying blankets, walking by me. Daryl was dead. It was over.

28

THE 13TH JUROR

BUT OF COURSE IT WAS NOT OVER. IT STILL ISN'T, AT LEAST not for me. The first few days after Daryl died, I checked my mail anxiously for that letter he must have written to me in his final hours: "By the time you read this I will be room temperature" (his phrase) it would begin, characteristically wry. In it, Daryl acknowledges his monstrously selfish motives and makes it right between us. "I do. I feel remorse. I do," the letter would close.

Kelly emailed me that morning. Daryl died quickly and apparently without pain. She knew Daryl had urged us to meet, but that's the last thing she needed. What do I think his last words meant? Perhaps Daryl played a joke of self-reference with "I do": I do have last words and these are they, "I do." Most observers think he simply reaffirmed his wedding vows. But Daryl also said "I do" to the police: I do understand my rights. And to the courts that found him competent: I do wish to forego my appeals.

Like Socrates in the *Crito*, Daryl had refused to escape his own death sentence, once issued, not because he necessarily agreed with it, but because he embraced the legal process that declared it. So to the law itself, perhaps Daryl delivered his final, consistent message: I do honor, cherish, and obey you.

Each day at school I checked my mailbox. No last letter from Daryl yet. At some point, missing letters must be presumed dead. I couldn't shake Daryl. So I began to rummage through a long-neglected bulging manila envelope at the bottom of my filing cabinet. I reread our letters to each other, understanding better the arc of our relationship and Daryl's constitutional jurisprudence. I came upon a transcript of an early social services "parental evaluation" Daryl had sent me. At the time, I only glanced at it, then stuffed it, barely read, in the oversize folder. Daryl never referred to it again. But I carefully read the evaluation a couple of weeks after they executed Daryl for killing the children he claimed to love. It told a troubling tale.

"Mr. Holton revealed judgment and healthy priorities and insight to the feelings of his children," the report declared, with biting, posthumous irony. Daryl's sentence completion displayed stress and fear:

1. The happiest time . . . is spent with my children

10. My nerves . . . are numb after 1 month without my children

23. My mind . . . is on hold until my children return

"Mr. Holton accepted complete responsibility [for] his children," the detailed evaluation concluded. "In addition to taking on new roles as a father, he also pursued a career in computer science, thereby improving himself as a parent. Moreover, he continues to provide for his family without apparently any child support from his previous wife. However, Mr. Holton encouraged the children to have equal access and interaction with Crystal. Thus revealing concern that the children develop a relationship with their mother."

The report recommended a case worker "assist Mr. Holton in obtaining food stamps, etc. and encourage him to accept those services rather than feeling that all of the burden is his." And it concluded that Daryl should be reunited with the children as soon as possible. But as Crystal had been abandoned as a child, and then periodically abandoned her children, *she* shouldn't be trusted alone with them!

This, in effect, Daryl's "last letter" to me, engulfed me with remorse and guilt. Daryl Holton had fought a desperate but losing battle to keep the family intact, while their mother abandoned him and them. He desperately tried to keep his children well fed, clothed, housed. He cared for them and deeply cared about them. Had Tennessee implemented its own recommendation and reunited him with them, Daryl might well be alive, caring for children he loved, and not killed because he "took care" of those same children we would not let him love.

The jury, of course, never heard this argument, now playing in my head.

Had I totally misjudged Daryl? Had the People of Tennessee executed a loving father who cracked under the pressure? He was no Charles Ng, maintaining a torture chamber in the basement, videotaping his own sadistic blood lust. Nor was he Danny Rolling, a serial rapist-murderer. In the aftermath of his death, I felt a need to cling to Daryl's goodness. I felt suffused by his best light.

So I reread our letters, reviewed our conversations, reevaluated our relationship, and saw how many times I fell short. How many times I failed to engage him, nastily disparaged his honesty. Every once in a while Daryl would complain that I failed to uphold my end of our exchange. But overall, Daryl's forgiving nature, his affable manner, made me feel ashamed, while his professed principles took on new meaning. Daryl *did* love his children. He sacrificed everything for them, asking only that they remain a meaningful part of his life. And then he sacrificed them. Did the jury ever truly judge Daryl Holton's moral culpability?

I've always thought my own birth date metaphorically appropriate. Janus, the two-headed month, makes January 31 the most forward day from which we still can look back. Daryl claimed he really never had his day in court. How could he, with trial or appellate counsel forced upon him, pursuing their own agenda? Now that Daryl was dead, I tried to look back and judge him in a neutral light, legally and morally, to reach a verdict, acting as the more fully informed juror Daryl Holton never got to have.

A jury in a capital trial, Daryl insisted, should be allowed to consider only three justifications or excuses: self-defense, insanity, choice of evils. Obviously self-defense did not literally apply to Daryl. Nobody threatened him with unlawful, deadly *physical* force. Self-defense could operate here only metaphorically—if Daryl killed because it was necessary to save his psyche, his sense of self.

Almost every state recognizes a defense of insanity. But, again, Daryl did not fit the profile. He knew the nature and consequences of his conduct. He carefully planned and methodically killed his four children. Although suffering from depression, Daryl certainly knew what he was doing, and that society prohibited it. So he knew what he was doing, and he knew what he was doing was wrong.

We've advanced beyond this. The Model Penal Code and the states that follow it would excuse him if mental defect makes him lack "substantial capacity" to "appreciate" all this. Suffering from bouts of depression, sleeping in his uncle's garage, breathing in carbon monoxide from that kerosene heater, feeling "all over numb" as he killed his children, although he knew what he was doing, Daryl Holton arguably lacked substantial capacity to *appreciate* what he was doing was morally wrong. Some states embrace "irresistible impulses" as a source of insanity. Daryl may have been driven to kill them to avoid the pain of living without them and the thought that they would call someone else "Daddy." But was his an irresistible impulse or simply an impulse he chose not to resist?

Much as I tried to press him, Daryl had refused to reveal his sanity or insanity. Sometimes I thought he evaded this issue to prevent defense attorneys from seizing on his own statements to keep him alive. Other times I thought him modestly disavowing his own right or capacity to decide. Mostly

I thought he hid the truth. Looking back, Daryl's refusal to declare himself sane or insane seems more radical. He wasn't avoiding the truth. There simply was no truth, no fact independent of that jury's decision. The jury found him sane. Therefore, he was sane. Man the Measure. The Sophists win.

If Daryl was sane and did not act in self-defense, this left only his final justification for killing the children—the defense of "necessity" or "choice of evils," also a classic justification. By consistently regretting the "necessity" of his choice while displaying no remorse, Daryl seemed to claim this defense. The defense expert who testified at trial that Daryl killed "altruistically" in effect tried to combine insanity and choice of evils. But as Daryl himself finally revealed, he acted selfishly, like a bear caught in a trap gnawing off his own paws. Daryl killed the children to remove them as an immediate source of his anguish. "Enough." This may have been the lesser of two evils, but only for him.

In the end, I see Daryl as more Susan Smith than Andrea Yates, killing not for their sake, but for his own. So, on balance, if I'm the thirteenth juror, I console myself that legally Daryl committed unjustified, unexcused, aggravated criminal homicide. But was it first-degree murder? Was he rightly condemned to die? After Daryl's execution, I felt the need to reconsider what Daryl so vigorously sought to hide from the jury: mitigation. Traditionally, murder becomes manslaughter or first-degree murder becomes second-degree murder when a person snaps and kills in the heat of passion or under the influence of an extreme emotional disturbance. Although Daryl didn't snap, *suddenly* crack under pressure, or kill in a furious assault, still he might qualify for mitigation. We no longer call it "the heat of passion." As Daryl described it, he felt "locked in," "numb." When they executed him, he probably also felt numb. Under stress, I too often feel distant and drained of emotion. Under pressure, I myself get tired and disengage.

I believe Daryl did kill under the influence of an extreme emotional disturbance. But I cannot accept the influence of that disturbance as reasonably explained. A reasonable passion may always be self-contradictory—like a round square. But suppose sometimes it does make sense. If Daryl had killed Crystal, his ex-wife, who first abandoned their children and then ripped them from his life, I could mitigate that intentional killing from murder to manslaughter. But, on balance, I cannot reasonably explain how the disturbance influences him to kill the children. In summary, because Daryl's killings were not justified, excused, or adequately mitigated, on balance, the jury correctly convicted Daryl of four counts of first-degree murder. But were they right to condemn him to die? Did the aggravators outweigh all the mitigators?

Four children.

What is specially aggravating about children as victims? Their innocence, the lost potential? Yes. And more. Are some victims more valuable than others? Abolitionists often attack those victim-centered aggravators: the elderly, children, police officers. Do we not violate our fundamental commitment to equal protection under law by aggravating for certain victims? Do we not thereby imply that other victims—convicted murderers turned prison snitches, for example—have less value? Retributively, we do correctly aggravate for killing children and other "vulnerable victims" because the killer demonstrates his special selfish cowardice by preying on them. Hugo Bedau and other great abolitionists embrace this special horror at killing the helpless, rejecting the death penalty itself as the most inhumane exercise of power over powerlessness.[1]

Daryl not only killed children; he killed his *own* children. Does this aggravate or mitigate? Both. I completely reject Daryl's characterization of children as a family resource. Yet random killings do seem especially aggravated because the killer had no connection to the victim. In the end, for me, Daryl's plan to kill another man's child strictly from revenge acts as the real aggravator. But can we fully condemn a person for imagining, planning, and setting out to do what he later renounced before doing it? No forgiveness or mercy here?

Capital statutes command us to balance mitigating circumstances against the aggravators. Daryl mostly kept mitigators from his jury: He had no prior criminal record; he served in the military long and honorably; he was a devoted father. After the killing, he turned himself in and cooperated fully. Daryl would count none of this, but an emotionally informed jury should have counted it for what it was worth.

And then, too, Daryl lived in prison as singularly reliable, respectful, and cooperative, a model inmate. He kept to himself and threatened no one. Some states such as Texas make a big deal of this and require the jury to find him a "future danger" before they sentence him to die. But morally, retributively, this too counts for little. The most vicious bullies on the street, once captured, often become cowards inside, cringing sycophants and snitches. Although Daryl posed no *future* threat, we justifiably kill him, if at all, for the sake of the past. "The voice of your children's blood cries out. . . ."

Odd that I never asked myself the obvious question until after Tennessee executed Daryl, and my co-teacher Kevin Doyle confronted me with it in class: Did the voice of his children cry out for Daryl's blood? "Daddy, we love you," they had written, right before he killed them. Where's the evidence that his children would have wanted Daryl dead—their father whom they loved and trusted? If his children could come alive and look down on Daryl strapped to the chair in that chamber, would they have said, "Throw the switch"? Would they have killed him for killing them? Who knows?

On balance, do Daryl's motives mitigate? He sought relief in killing his children. Exactly the same kind of relief he conceded society should feel in killing him. "Solace in the face of suffering," Marvin Henberg calls retribution.[2] When Kelly Gleason called Daryl the "most principled person I ever met," I chortled and choked. But Daryl did prefer death to dishonor. He would rather die than make frivolous appellate claims. He could have pled guilty and gotten life. Perhaps he could have defeated his death penalty at trial; certainly he could have delayed it on appeal. In the end, Daryl Holton died a martyr to his own jurisprudence—yes, a martyr, and a mass murderer.

"With all that's happened," the police asked Daryl the night he turned himself in and confessed, "what should be the outcome? What type of punishment do you think—" Only when it came time to suggest society's appropriate response did Daryl refuse to cooperate. "That question I have to wait on. That answer could be used against me." The police probably assumed Daryl meant his answer could be used to seek his death. But now I wonder if he feared his answer could be used to keep him alive. Or perhaps Daryl meant, "I deserve whatever punishment a jury says I deserve."

"I want to pursue the truth and present the facts as they happened, with no exaggeration," Daryl had confessed to the police. "I want to tell my story and be done with it." The jury would find the facts and apply the law. This became Daryl's hope, his credo, for a decade as he struggled with a legal system that seemed determined to subvert its own commands.

Daryl's attempt to reveal his truth fell on deaf ears, including mine. I disavowed my friendship with a man who declared me his friend, a person I gratuitously and too often acerbically wished dead. The months that followed Daryl's execution filled me with guilt and doubt.

As the thirteenth juror with my own very high burden to persuade myself to a moral certainty that Daryl Holton deserved to die, I state for the record: I am convinced to an absolute certainty he did it and convinced beyond a reasonable doubt that altruism was not his primary motive, nor revenge his exclusive motive. In the end, I do believe he loved his children. Only a little less than he loved himself. I also remain convinced beyond a reasonable doubt that Daryl's planned killing of little Kiki Rhodes showed a spiteful, wanton, depraved indifference that on balance makes Daryl deserve his fate for killing his children.

I remain convinced, but not morally certain, that he deserved to die. Taking into account the pressures and Daryl's demonstrated sacrifice and love for the children and family, I have a lingering doubt, and therefore as a juror knowing what I know, and am likely ever to know, I would spare his life. Countless times, I have reevaluated myself and my commitment to the punishment of death. "Killing and dying do not come easily to full human beings," Robert Johnson rightly declared in *Death Work*.[3] I still feel certain that rapist-murderers, serial killers, and mass murderers generally deserve to die. I am convinced to a moral certainty that a humane society by making their lives miserable before blotting them out more nearly approaches justice than if it provides them first-run movies and sports to watch and play. I believe, and want to believe, that Daryl had a painless death. I believe in the end that he felt as he insisted we feel—relieved but not happy. But I feel neither relieved nor happy. Daryl Holton was an extraordinary human being. Yes, a human being. He was brilliant and insightful with a wry sense of humor. Wherever there's a death penalty, the people must realize that not every condemned murderer is a one-dimensional monster to be killed at whim with no loss. Daryl has taught me much; I will miss him. Abolitionists believe that we retributivists cannot feel the humanity of those we condemn. I regret the many times I gratuitously accused him of lying to me, and himself. I'm glad I energized him. For in the end, although I crossed it out publicly, and it makes me very uncomfortable to say it here, Daryl Holton became my friend.

"There's a tendency to want to get that last shot in," Daryl explained. Perhaps that's why I cling to the memories, or the memories cling to me. Daryl's voice calls from the ground. I cannot get closure. I so want to hear Daryl calling to me from beyond the grave. "We're done. Lighten up. Move on." Yet his death haunts me still; a death I called for and support, with residual moral doubts. Perhaps we did make a mistake by executing Daryl Holton. It disturbs me deeply. But in the end, it remains a price I'm willing to pay for justice.

There really was no good ending. Not if Daryl lived, nor if he died. What irony. The guilt, regret, and remorse I sought to elicit from him, he ended up producing in me. I may never have gotten him to tell his story. But if you've read this far, I imagine you've long since realized, he got me to tell mine.

PART V

FIGHTING FOR THE FINISH

29

NO WORD FOR IT

"I AM WRITING TO YOU BECAUSE MY FAMILY WAS MUR-dered in July 2007," began an emailed letter that appeared in my mailbox in February 2011 with the all too familiar "DEATH PENALTY" as the subject line.

In 2007 the public reacted with shock and fury at the news: Two men broke into the Petit home in quiet, suburban Cheshire, Connecticut. First they bludgeoned Dr. William Petit with a baseball bat and tied him to a pole in the basement. Steven Hayes raped and strangled Jennifer Hawke-Petit, Dr. Petit's wife, after forcing her to withdraw $15,000 from the bank. His younger accomplice, Joshua Komisarjevsky, sexually abused Michaela, Petit's 11-year-old child. After keeping the girls separately tied to their beds for hours, these monsters poured gasoline on and around Michaela and her 17-year-old sister Hayley and burned them alive. Dr. Petit escaped as his house went up in flames and his family's rapist-murderers fled.

"The first defendant was sentenced to death last year," Dr. Petit's letter continued, "and the second defendant goes on trial this fall." Jury selection would start next month. "The C[onnecticu]t legislature voted to abolish the DP in 2008, but Gov. Jody Rell (R) vetoed it, and the legislature never attempted to override it despite 2/3 pluralities in the House and Senate. They have decided to try and abolish it again this year. I have been pro-DP as an adult even before what happened to my family. I believe it is the only justice available in many cases." Dr. Petit asked me whether I would testify before the legislature.

"First, last, and foremost—please accept my condolences," I replied. "Like so many others, I feel saddened for your loss and suffering and en-raged at the killers."

"I had just finished reading your article, 'Less Than We Might: Meditations on Life Without Parole,' when your email arrived," he replied the next day. "I thought I was hearing myself speak." A couple of days later, at Dr. Petit's request, we spoke on the phone. Three and a half years had passed since that night they raped and killed his family. Petit's measured voice still showed the pain. "There's no word for losing your children," he said sadly. "Lose your wife and you're a 'widower,' lose your parents, you're an 'orphan.' But your children—there's no word for it."

What's in a word? So much, really, when your child has been murdered. Petit told me how he had struggled to convince the judge to use the girls' names. "In court, even today, they talk of the 'alleged murder victims.' I'll drive them to the cemetery; then we'll see how alleged they are." Petit revealed the pain that media accounts can cause over time. "First it was 'Jennifer Hawke-Petit, Haley and Michaela.' Then it was 'Jennifer and her daughters.' Then 'the Petit family' and finally 'the Cheshire murder victims.' Their names are gone. They have become the detritus of history." Petit fought relentlessly to ensure that Hayes and Komisarjevsky, his family's killers, would die. He also established a charitable foundation to help keep alive the names and memory of Jennifer, Hayley, and Michaela. "Everyone around here remembers Michael Ross," Petit complained. "Who remembers the names of his victims?"

Most everybody in Connecticut did remember Michael Ross. And many also recalled the abolitionist federal judge determined to keep him alive. Ross had murdered eight young women, including two teenagers. The prosecutors who sought his death felt certain; the jurors who unanimously sentenced him to die felt certain. The courts, including the US Supreme Court, concurred that this mass-murdering rapist could constitutionally receive society's ultimate sanction.[1] But 11 hours before this sadistic serial killer would finally get his due, one man, US District Court Judge Robert N. Chatigny, stopped it. "He [Ross] never should have been convicted." Let that sink in. "Or if convicted," the Chief continued, "he never should have been sentenced to death because his sexual sadism . . . is clearly a mitigating factor."[2]

The *Diagnostic and Statistical Manual of Mental Disorders* defined a sexual sadist as "a person sexually aroused by recurrent intense fantasies of non-consenting victims' psychological or physical suffering (including humiliation)."[3] If the sadist feels distressed by these fantasies, even if he doesn't act upon them, he becomes officially labeled a "sexual sadist" and deserves help. But if he does act on these fantasies, and he rapes, tortures, and then kills his victims, I'm convinced he deserves to die. Most of us are.

But we were not the Chief. "Michael Ross may be the least culpable—the least—of the people on death row," Judge Chatigny proclaimed. If Ross picked up his appeals and returned to death row, "He would be the subject of ridicule. He is effectively boxed in now," Chatigny empathized. What compassion that a man who put eight women in coffins should himself feel "boxed in." But what if Michael Ross made a knowing, intelligent, and voluntary decision to die? Then "God love him," declared the Chief.

God love him? *God damn him.* If there is a hell, may he burn in it. Ross's attorney, T. R. Paulding, a death penalty opponent, believed an attorney should serve his client's ends. But not the Chief. "If I were his lawyer, I'd be in his face," Chatigny scolded. But the judge did not stop there. "You better be prepared to deal with me. I'll have your law license."[4]

Under threat of professional death, T. R. Paulding caved. And the People watched helplessly as Chatigny, abolitionist hero, single-handedly ground the gears of justice to a halt. In the end, Chatigny was reversed on appeal, and Connecticut did kill Michael Ross, the state's first execution in 45 years. "Unquestionably the world would be a better place without Michael Ross in it," my *Hartford Courant* op-ed closed. "Then, too, the federal bench would probably be a better place without Judge Chatigny on it."[5] Chatigny's eventual nomination for elevation to the Second Circuit Court of Appeals faced a firestorm of protest, leading him to withdraw.[6]

"Who remembers the names of Ross's victims?" Dr. Petit had asked.

"Remember. Remember Dzung Ngoc Tu, 25; Tammy Williams, 17; Paula Perrera, 16. Debra Smith Taylor, 23," my op-ed concluded. "Remember Robin Stavinsky, 19; April Brunais and Leslie Shelley, 14; and Wendy Baribeault, 17. Imagine the lives they never led; remember how they died."

Dr. Petit and I met in New Haven. Of course I grieved for him—how this man must have suffered. But he had also become a powerful national symbol, that rare survivor who devoted himself to advancing capital punishment. I came with a list of questions. Did the killers' remorse or regret count for anything? Would Jennifer, Hayley, and Michaela have wanted Hayes and Komisarjevsky killed? I doubted the defense would dare ask this. The prosecution, too, might avoid this question, but the answer counted heavily with me. Had Petit made a covenant with Jennifer, Hayley, and Michaela? Did he resent it when people told him to live in the moment?

Petit remained silent as I read aloud my questions: If the state did kill his family's murderers, what should they feel as they die? How should they live until they die? I looked up at him. I hadn't yet earned the right to ask the last question on the list: Do you feel guilty that you escaped and lived while your family died? Our meeting included Professor Jeff Meyer, Petit's legal adviser. On advice of counsel, Petit declined to answer any questions. The judge had issued a gag order, and Dr. Petit expected to be a witness at Komisarjevsky's upcoming trial. At least that's the reason he gave. Could it be that he didn't want me probing wounds that would never heal but had formed at least a superficial scab? Anyway, he would not open up to me, but he assured me again that our views on punishment dovetailed. So we focused on the upcoming legislative hearings.

Connecticut's death penalty statute, of course, needed refinement and revision. And abolitionist witnesses deserved rebuttal. For the next several weeks, I once again pored over transcripts of prior hearings and offered Connecticut's joint judiciary committee a blueprint to refine and restructure their state's death penalty statute. I won't detail those proposals here. I have already urged many of these reforms upon you, including the elimination of aggravated felony murder (see Appendix B).

Experience had taught me that no single day's hearings would produce a committee proposal to radically refine a death penalty statute. Instead, the legislators would focus on keeping or killing the death penalty. I hoped to convince abolitionist-leaning legislators to keep death as punishment because their alternative—Life in Prison without Release, as Connecticut called it—failed even more miserably. I had to show them that a lifer's life in Connecticut resembled Oklahoma, Tennessee, and Illinois.

Dr. Petit proved invaluable, contacting key legislators who persuaded corrections to grant me immediate access to their prisons but without a video recorder. Nothing surprised me that day I spent researching the range of lifestyles that convicted Connecticut murderers might experience. "We're in the management business. We don't judge inmates," the warden explained in now familiar terms about life at MacDougall-Walker, a maximum security facility where condemned killers would most probably end up if the legislature abolished death row. Then on to Osborn, a medium security facility, where the best-behaved convicted murderers could eventually land. "I'm not concerned with what their crime was," the deputy warden there explained. "I'm concerned with their institutional adjustment. We're not here to mete out justice." All too familiar. "You'd think a level reduction would bring a better level of comfort," the deputy warden continued, "but it doesn't. It brings you a better level of security." In fact, perversely, MacDougall-Walker, the more "secure" maximum security prison, had air conditioning. Osborn had none. And while both facilities were heated, frigid air penetrated the windows of the medium security prison whereas maximum security MacDougall-Walker, better insulated, offered the prisoners greater comfort during the New England winter.

"You're talking to the wrong person," the deputy warden in charge of programs replied when I complained that a prisoner's crime had no connection to his prison experience. Apparently he had no sympathy for my position. But later he clarified it. "When I said, 'You're talking to the wrong person,' I meant you should talk to the legislature. If they enact a law that tells who and how to differentiate, we'll do that."

"The *legislature* must distinguish," Brian Garnett, the public information officer and my guide, concurred. "Don't expect us to do that on our own." All these years I had been complaining about the wrong people, to the wrong people. We need to convince legislatures to link crime to punishment.

In the four weeks between Petit's first contact and the joint judiciary committee hearing, I worked night and day to do just that, submitting *The Road to Consider,* a 27-page, single-spaced manifesto that analyzed and criticized the anti-retributive perversity of Connecticut's—and the nation's—mal-administration of justice.[7]

Let the punishment fit the crime. People have mouthed this philosophy for millennia and seemingly still believe it. Today, death penalty opponents claim life without parole (LWOP) as their genuinely fitting substitute punishment for the worst of the worst. These abolitionists embrace LWOP as cheaper, equally just, and equally effective—a punishment that eliminates the state's exercise of an inhumane power to kill helpless human beings who pose no immediate threat. Furthermore, they insist, LWOP allows the criminal justice system to reverse sentencing mistakes.

But LWOP cannot substitute for the death penalty. Connecticut's mission statement, typical of corrections throughout the United States, said it all: "The Department of Corrections shall protect the public, protect staff and provide safe, secure and humane supervision of offenders with opportunities that support successful community reintegration."[8]

Safety, security, protection. Nowhere does that statement so much as mention *punishment.* The mission statement guides the administration. The simple, disturbing, paradoxical fact is, *inside prison, it's nobody's job to punish.*

A better name for a sentence of LWOP might be "death by incarceration," abolitionists have insisted, using artful but misleading rhetoric to support the substitution of life for death.[9] True, almost all aggravated murderers sentenced to LWOP will die *in* prison. But almost none will die *because* of prison. We all live condemned to die somehow, somewhere. Some of us will die in old age in our sleep, or watching television, or taking a bath. Should we call these closing scenes "death *by* sleep," "death *by* television," "death *by* bathing?" Or is it simply about *where* we die? "Death by home," "death by hospital," "death by bowling alley," "death by incarceration." The rhetoric obscures the reality.

The question of justice—whether LWOP can morally substitute for the death penalty—depends not on where these vicious killers die but on how they live before they die.

"If Jennifer Hawke-Petit, 17-year-old Hayley, and 11-year-old Michaela could somehow watch what happens to their rapist-murderers, spending their lives in prison without parole, would they feel satisfied that justice was being done? Although the more heinous crimes generally do carry *longer* prison sentences, the most vicious criminals serving life sentences for the worst crimes often have the best jobs, best hustles, and easiest lifestyles." In short, inside prisons, daily life mocks justice: *Those who deserve it most suffer least.* As long as the Department of Corrections and its staff believe that "what a man did out there is none of my business—how he acts inside determines how he'll be treated here," the people will never have justice.

Under a section titled "Special Punishment for the Specially Heinous," my statement called for a punishment more nearly fitting the crime: "This legislature should specify that harsher punishment shall attach *on death row.*" And if Connecticut did abolish the death penalty, the statute should continue to single out the worst murderers for the worst punishment. "The legislature should specify that all those serving life without parole must do their time *entirely* in a maximum security prison. *Where* the worst murderer serves a sentence, however, does not determine *how* that person experiences daily life inside. That uniquely harsh punishment should be *experienced* uniquely. *A person who rapes and murders a child should by statute be perpetually confined in the most punitive setting allowed by law.*"[10]

Later on, my written statement drove home the point again: "If this state does abolish the death penalty, the legislature should replace it with life without parole *in a special punitive setting,* reserved for the worst of the worst. The condemned should serve their sentences under conditions no better than what the Department of Corrections designates as punitive segregation, presently reserved for inmates who violate internal administrative prison rules." Thus, if it did abolish the death penalty, Connecticut should also abolish *mandatory* LWOP for murder, "saving it only for those aggravated murderers found specially to deserve it. They should be punished every day, and reminded constantly of what they did and why we're doing what we're doing to them."

30

THE HERSHEY BAR

THE RULES GOVERNING THE LEGISLATIVE HEARING AL-
lowed anybody who registered in person that morning to testify sometime
during the day, but only for five minutes, unless legislators chose to ask follow-up questions. The order of witnesses would be randomly generated. I
had to leave my wife in the lurch to testify. We had agreed to babysit the
grandchildren, and she felt ill. How could I complain to Dr. Petit, who no
longer had a wife or children and would probably never have grandchildren?
I hoped to get an early number. No such luck.

Petit "drew" the first slot. That pleased me, of course, but I suspected it
couldn't be random. Petit spoke straightforwardly and soberly. It didn't matter what he said or how he said it. Everybody in the chamber knew what he
had suffered. His was the face of justice calling for death as punishment. As
a compromise to sway legislators sympathetic to the power of his appeal, the
proposed bill would abolish the death penalty, prospectively only, reserving
life for *future* first-degree murderers. In theory, Steven Hayes would remain
on death row, still subject to execution. And Joshua Komisarjevsky, once
convicted and condemned, would join him.

But what were the odds that courts and a future governor would ever
allow a state to kill a person for a crime that could no longer get death? "I
know you can't say with certainty," Senator John Kissel pressed Professor
Jeff Meyer, Petit's adviser, testifying on his own that day. "But would you say
it's more likely than not that [prospective repeal] could form the basis of a
successful appeal for those ten on death row right now?" A simple yes would
do. But the professor displayed that annoying trait all too characteristic of
academics who can't or won't simply admit the obvious. "I can't say it's more
likely than not," Meyer equivocated. "I can say there are very substantial
arguments." When his turn came to testify, Barry Scheck of course pounced

on Meyer's admitted uncertainty. Scheck called it "a fool's errand" to assess it "more likely than not" that either the Connecticut Supreme Court or US Supreme Court would strike down prospective repeal. "Professor Meyer gave the only honest answer," Scheck insisted. "We don't know."[1]

Want to bet?

Kevin Doyle, formerly New York's capital defender, conceded publicly that he would be "shocked" if Connecticut ever executed anyone once it abolished the death penalty prospectively. And Professor David Dow, Director of Texas's Innocence Project, called executions "highly unlikely" after prospective repeal. But, Scheck insisted, "I've learned humility about this process." Barry Scheck has been accused of many things—I've not heard humility among them.

"Life without parole is considered by many a worse sentence," Scheck assured the legislators, knowing full well that the US Supreme Court had held otherwise. And since many consider life worse than death, the skilled rhetorician continued, "You won't get fewer guilty pleas if you eliminate capital punishment." Clever but counterfactual. The vast majority of murderers do not consider life inside worse than death. "You're going to be shocked," Scheck, the Sophist assured his rapt audience. "If you abolish capital punishment prospectively only—other than the difficulty of the Connecticut Supreme Court dealing with the pending cases—if you do it, people are not going to even really notice the next day." And he laughed.

"You're a scholar," Senator Edward Meyer, an abolitionist and Professor Meyer's father, said to Scheck during follow-up Q&A. He cited Justice Harry Blackmun's famous "I shall no longer tinker with the machinery of death."[2] "Do you know the context in which he made that statement?"

"Justice Blackmun came on the US Supreme Court a firm supporter of capital punishment," Scheck replied, completely distorting the truth. "And he reached the conclusion that he didn't believe [in] the journey [of] the Supreme Court."[3] I sat there, knowing I wouldn't get my chance to rebut this falsehood for many hours. "I yield to no one in the depth of my distaste, antipathy, and, indeed, abhorrence for the death penalty," Blackmun had declared early on, dissenting in *Furman*. "It serves no useful purpose . . . violates [my] childhood's training and life's experiences."[4] Justice Blackmun always detested the death penalty. He made it clear that he'd vote against it as a legislator and commute sentences if he were a governor. But as a US Supreme Court Justice, he believed in each state's right to decide for itself. Only when Blackmun came to believe it impossible to combine the constitutionally mandated fairness with consistency in its administration did he finally vote to outlaw death as punishment. Characterizing Blackmun as a "firm supporter" of capital punishment who later saw the light hardly contributed to the "honest debate" that Scheck claimed to embrace.

Let me be clear. I respect Barry Scheck enormously for his tireless and effective effort in founding and running the Innocence Project. Every true retributivist must be profoundly grateful to him and other lesser-known, dedicated public defenders who spend their careers protecting the innocent against false conviction and wrongful punishment. But I also knew from our public appearances together that Scheck will, when he thinks it serves the cause, amplify doubt and spin.

Although the judiciary committee officially restricted each witness to a five-minute opening statement, somehow Scheck's had gone on for nearly 20 minutes without interruption. During a break, I complained to Representative Gerald Fox, the committee co-chair. He assured me that when my turn came, the committee would allow me at least equal time. Fox kept his word.

After sitting for hours through an avalanche of abolitionists, my chance finally came around 10 p.m. Weary legislators wanted to go home; a couple had already left. "If the courts struck down a prospective death penalty repeal," I assured the committee, then those currently on death row would be released to general population to serve life without parole. "The question has come up over and over again today, what is [that] life like?" I knew. And now so would they. "One month after being sentenced to life without parole for the rape and murder of a child, that person will be outside his cell, free to shower, talk on the phone, play with others, rec indoors or out, ten to twelve hours a day. Every day—for the rest of his life. Ten to twelve hours a day! Within one month of being sentenced to life without parole for the rape and murder of a child. You tell me this is justice.

"Ask yourself, 'Why is there no punishment?' I'll tell you why there's no punishment in Connecticut, and no punishment in Tennessee, Oklahoma, Ohio, Florida, and other states I've visited. Because not one word in any department of corrections mission statement in the United States of America mentions the word 'punishment.' Not one. Officers say, 'It is not our job to punish. It is our job to keep the people of Connecticut safe, keep the inmates safe from each other. And help those preparing to go outside to reintegrate into society.' But for those who are never going outside, still no part of their mission is punishment. . . .

"There's an interdisciplinary arts program, including dance, poetry, sculpture. More prisoners want to get into it than there are spaces. Do they take those who murdered and raped children last? No! You submit a portfolio; it's on the basis of talent. Everything is future oriented. Life begins when life begins. At day one, inside.

"And you ask the officers, 'Is this justice?' Answer—'Justice is not my issue.' 'Is this punishment?' Answer—'Punishment is not part of our mission here. The judge punishes them.' Don't take my word for it. Tour the prisons. You're the legislature. They can't deny *you*. Ask the questions I asked: 'Is it your job to punish? Is there any different lifestyle for those who committed the most serious crimes?'"

I told them of my visit to death row, which housed Steven Hayes, the Petit family murderer. "I peeked into Steven Hayes's cell to see this man who raped, who doused them with gasoline and lit them. He was sleeping. On his desk, a Hershey bar. On the empty bunk above him, bags of potato chips and other goodies from the commissary. All these little pleasures in life. This is not justice.

"You've heard retribution disparaged here—punishing people because they deserve it. 'We swear forever, we will not forget, we will not forgive!'" I looked at the legislators. "If you reject retribution, you cannot support life without parole! Life without parole makes a covenant with the past: 'No matter how much this person may change, no matter that he no longer poses a danger; that he regrets and feels remorse—we forever commit ourselves, never to forgive, never to forget, never to release. Life without parole is retributive to the core.

"You heard the claim, 'You can only get the justice you can afford.' That demeans the capital defenders of Connecticut. But you *do* only get the *privileges* you can afford. From the first day on death row, if you have the money in your commissary, you can get a color TV. It may take months or years in general population if you're a drug dealer, or a car thief. But if you raped and murdered a child, if you've got the money, that TV is yours, from day one.

"If the legislature wants to do something about unequal justice, mandate that commissary privileges aren't a function of how much money you have. Your life inside should reflect the seriousness of your crime. In short," I urged the legislators, "especially if you abolish the death penalty, you should designate a special form of punishment for the worst of the worst of the worst." I had gone on awhile and was obviously tiring. Representative Fox graciously asked whether I would take questions.

"From your perspective, is life without parole not justice?" challenged Gary Holder-Winfield (D), vice chair of the judiciary committee and a leading abolitionist. "So what will you do to him past a life sentence without parole?" Senator Edwin Gomes (D) followed up on Holder-Winfield's challenge. "Torture him?"

"No. I'd have a special prison based on the nature of your crime. A special prison with permanent punitive segregation [PPS]." If this book makes a difference, if we come to our senses, those who seek a morally acceptable substitute for the death penalty, who remain committed to making the punishment fit the crime, may adopt something like this. Obviously we need collective wisdom to carefully design and fully implement such a punishment, but let me briefly sketch the outlines of PPS.

The worst of the worst of the worst should be specially convicted and, in a separate penalty phase, specially condemned by a jury to suffer this fate. Beyond a permanent loss of liberty, life should be painful and unpleasant, every day. We should house those condemned to PPS in a separate prison and permanently subject them to the harshest conditions the Constitution allows. Specifically, they would eat only nutraloaf, a tasteless patty, nutritious enough not to foreshorten their lives but offering no sensory pleasure. We should keep their visits to the constitutional minimum, and none would be *contact* visits, ever. These aggravated-murderers would never touch another human being again. They would labor daily, and exercise. But they would not be allowed to play.

These most heinous criminals would never watch TV and, of course, no Internet. They would get one brief, lukewarm shower a week. Photos of their victims would adorn their cells—in their face but out of reach, reminding these condemned killers daily of their crimes.

PPS could sustain a connection between crime and punishment. Every corrections official working in the PPS wing should be required to read a description of the crime of everyone punished there. We should of course tolerate no abuse of these prisoners, no beatings or sadism from officers. But no conviviality either. Officers should be proper, but distant and cold. For PPS, corrections' mission should be punishment. *Those most vicious predators punished by perpetual punitive segregation would never receive better food, housing, or medical care than we allow our innocent poor outside.*

As it reconnects crime to punishment, PPS clearly separates LWOP from ordinary life sentences. We should reserve this hopeless, bleak experience only for the worst of the worst of the worst. No "three strikes and you're PPS." No "drug kingpin and you're PPS." PPS should never become a default sentence, as LWOP has become in many states that abolished parole for all murder. Only if they deserve PPS by their extreme callousness or cruelty should they receive it.

But then, why confine PPS to murderers? It feels right, retributively, to limit death as punishment to aggravated murder or attempted murder—to do to him what he did or would have done to his victim. But why not extend PPS to the most callous and vicious white-collar criminals? Does Bernard Madoff come to mind?

"As one of three generations of Madoff victims and a criminal law professor who calls for proportional punishment—no more nor less than deserved," my letter to the *New York Times* began, "I read with concern reports claiming that Mr. Madoff received the 'maximum.'"[5] The brother of Bernard Madoff's father-in-law, one my father's dearest friends, got special dispensation to allow our family to invest with Madoff, although we hardly met his financial threshold. Madoff's "risk-free arbitrage," one of his ranking employees explained to me, produced that steady income. And so the mantra in our family: "Don't worry about the grandchildren's tuition; there's Madoff."

For 30 years my father meticulously recorded every transaction from his monthly statements, religiously paid all taxes from each year's capital gains. And then, December 11, 2008, the news broke: Madoff was a fraud. Our taxes had been real, our principal, our family's gain over the years—worthless. Needless to say, I have little love for Madoff. When the *New York Times* reported in July 2009 that Madoff had received "the maximum," I knew he would experience nothing like it.[6]

Madoff's letter to his daughter-in-law describing his life in prison later confirmed it: "It has the look and feel of a college campus with lovely lawns and trees. I live in a dorm (one story) with 24 other guys with plenty of privacy. I can come and go pretty much as I please with no lock ups. I have a clerk's job, and everyone treats me with respect and great friendship. I have loads of friends to talk to even if most are covered with tattoos. As you can imagine, I am quite the celebrity and am treated like a Mafia Don. They call me either Uncle Bernie or Mr. Madoff. It's really quite sweet how concerned everyone is about my well-being, including the staff. It's much safer here than walking the streets of NY."[7]

I knew something like this was coming when the feds sentenced him. That's why I wrote that letter to the *New York Times*, hoping they'd select it from the avalanche of Madoff haters. "We focus too much on the duration rather than the intensity of his prison sentence," my letter insisted. "Because he inflicted pain and suffering on unknowing victims in order to achieve an undeserved lavish lifestyle, every day in prison for the rest of his life he should clean toilets. Then and only then will we victims come close to being satisfied."

The Times contacted me. They were considering my letter for publication. Would I agree to edits? They suggested some good, tiny changes, and also would cut all reference to the victims' satisfaction. OK. And no cleaning toilets—"inappropriate." How about "every day in prison for the rest of his life he should *do lowly tasks*," the editor suggested. "Do lowly tasks" didn't quite capture it for me, but we compromised at "clean latrines."

How many lives Madoff ruined? His son, and others, killed themselves. My father, a hard-working, honest man, 102 years old, has lost a substantial part of his life savings. And to make it worse, someone on the inside cashed checks from my Dad's nonexistent account, so the government refuses his claim and he's gotten back not a penny. While I do detest Madoff, this vile creature doesn't deserve the death penalty.

An ultra left-wing colleague's reaction probably surprised me most about the whole episode. This bleeding heart who never said a kind word about punishment, never showed the slightest anger at any criminal, a proselyte for restorative justice, sent me an email after the *New York Times* published my letter. My proposal didn't go far enough, she insisted: Bernard Madoff should clean toilets—*with a tooth brush!* Ah, if only.

"I walk the track each day and also started pumping iron," Madoff's letter continued. They have plenty of recreation here. Two baseball fields, volleyball, handball and racquet ball, bochi [sic], horseshoes, outdoor and indoor basketball courts. Twelve pool tables, pottery and art classes, etc. I have been asked to teach a business class once I get settled in. I have been so busy that I have not even been watching T.V. Well, that's enough about me," Madoff closed his cheery letter. That's more than enough about Madoff except to protest. Put the death penalty aside, consider the greed, the callous indifference to lives he ruined—you tell me this life in this prison for this man is justice!

PPS for Madoff? Perhaps.

PPS should not cost much more than LWOP does today. And while satisfying society's need to justly condemn and punish, PPS should also most effectively deter would-be monsters. Under the banner of PPS—the new life without parole—abolitionists who know that evil exists and vicious people may sometimes deserve to die but who can never trust the government to kill its own citizens could unite with reluctant death penalty advocates, haunted by sentencing mistakes or racial discrimination.

PPS should never be inflicted because a person, juvenile or adult, has become incorrigible—not subject to change or development. The perpetually dangerous must be incapacitated, but PPS should be reserved only for the deserving. With PPS, we make and keep an unbreakable covenant with the past.

"So, no, I do not advocate torture," I told Rep. Holder-Winfield, meeting his challenge at the judiciary committee hearing.

Our dialogue continued late into the night—their questions, sometimes pointed, always thoughtful, ranged over a host of issues including Senator Michael McLachlan's invitation to explain how polls undercount support for life without parole. "Abolitionists are fond of saying, 'If only the public were informed at how ineffectual the death penalty is, they'd reject it,'" I said. "If only the public were informed as to how non-punitive life without parole is, they would rise up and oppose it. The poll questions obscure the crime. How about 'For those who rape and murder a child, which do you prefer, death or life without parole?' And the questions don't give any real sense of the punishment. The public doesn't understand the crime to which they're responding; and they don't understand the punishment they're supposedly preferring."

The committee's abolitionists brought the discussion back to human dignity as if it were their issue. "You've said some people should die painfully." Representative Fox challenged me to defend this.

"The Eighth Amendment unquestionably outlaws torture. There's no room for disagreement historically or morally. But somebody who rapes and murders a child, who pours gasoline—" I choked for a moment, conscious that Bill Petit sat 12 feet behind me "—deserves to die in pain. He does not deserve to drift off in a dreamy state. He does not deserve to go out in an opiate haze. Not given what Steven Hayes did. A quick but painful death. And don't execute them randomly. *Worst first.* Steven Hayes gets an accelerated process." I wanted to say Hayes and Komisarjevsky. But Komisarjevsky had yet to be tried, and technically at this moment, although doubtlessly guilty, legally he had to be presumed innocent.

"Does it demean us, and you, to ask for the death penalty as revenge?" fellow supporter Representative Al Adinolfi inquired, giving me yet another chance to distinguish retribution from revenge.

"Some people deserve to die, and by killing them we acknowledge the free will that produced the monstrous acts they committed. If we just treat them as things—throw them away, keep us safe, and don't care what happens to them, then we demean ourselves. The death penalty *acknowledges* their responsibility," I insisted, using Daryl's word. "Steven Hayes dies because of the vicious choices he made." I thought again of Dr. Petit a few feet behind me. "Also because of the victims' horrible experience. But not only that. I haven't lost sight that these murderers are human beings," I assured the committee, and talked of Daryl.

"Back on the issue of punishment," Senator Eric Coleman redirected me, initiating the most pointed exchange of the night. "Could it be that officials in Departments of Corrections throughout the nation perceive the loss of liberty and incarceration as inherently punitive?"

"Yes. And that's why they use the phrase, 'A person doesn't come here for punishment; he comes here *as* punishment.'" I told these legislators how, inside Lorton Central, I'd watched the Super Bowl with 12 convicted murderers. "I realized that if you told them they had three hours of freedom and could go anywhere they wanted, many would have stayed right where they were. In front of their color TVs, cartons of cigarettes bet on the game, with their buddies, cheering. Life takes on new pleasures. Someone who rapes and murders a child. Someone who immolates them before he kills them—" I winced in pain and fury "—shouldn't have Hershey bars. Isn't that obvious? I guess not to you."

"That's not obvious," Sen. Coleman countered. "That's so trivial to me that it's preposterous to even talk about it as a pleasure. So what if he has a Hershey bar?" Coleman pressed.

"So what?" I growled indignantly, conjuring up Steven Hayes. "He shouldn't experience that sweetness, that delicious taste of chocolate. He should never have a contact visit. He should never be able to touch another human being."

"That's different," the Senator cut me off.

"You agree with that?" I challenged.

"I'm not saying I agree with it. But it is certainly different than seeing a Hershey bar lying on his desk."

"He should never get the pleasures of food; he should never see sunlight; he should never see flowers."

And so our spirited dialogue continued, to the groans of witnesses still scheduled to speak and the chagrin of a dwindling audience, except perhaps for those watching it broadcast live on Connecticut public television.

Driving home in the early morning hours, I felt exhausted but exhilarated. I had talked of Tennessee's arts and crafts room, Ohio's death row basketball league, of Itchy, Bennie Demps, and Daryl. These weeks, these years of searching and researching had culminated here in Connecticut in a thoughtful, if sometimes heated, extended discussion before concerned, well-prepared legislators determined to do the public good as they saw it. I supposed my testimony hardly affected them. But an email from Dr. Petit the next day, thanking me on behalf of Jennifer, Hayley, and Michaela, brought me to tears.

31

IN A PERFECT KINGDOM

ELEVEN DAYS LATER, ON MARCH 18, 2011, JURY SELECTION began in the Komisarjevsky trial. Judge Jon Blue figured that phase alone would take three months. Because the judge had already presided at Steven Hayes's trial, the defense urged him to remove himself, or at least move the trial from his New Haven courtroom. Denied. They urged him to sequester the witnesses, including Petit himself. Dr. Petit had attended every day of the Hayes trial, turning away when the jury viewed photos of the charred ruins of his daughters' beds. Petit's visible anguish, the defense argued, must improperly sway a jury. But Judge Blue ruled that the doctor, as much victim as witness, had a right to attend the trial. Motion denied. Preliminaries complete, jury selection began.

Many trial lawyers—prosecutors and defense attorneys—believe that jury selection largely determines the outcome of a capital trial. Obviously prosecutors must weed out those who never would vote for death—not even for Hitler, or the devil himself. Hopefully these abolitionist jurors reveal themselves and the judge would strike them "for cause." If not, prosecutors should sense potential jurors' firm rejection of death as punishment and use one of their 40 discretionary or "peremptory" challenges. For their part, defense attorneys seek to unearth and eliminate the "killers"—those jurors who automatically vote death for *every* convicted murderer, regardless of the circumstances of the crime or background of the defendant.

But here symmetry breaks down. Whereas a single undetected "killer" could not by himself contaminate an entire jury, one "stealth" abolitionist juror who escapes the judge and prosecutor's radar can, by holding out, single-handedly undermine a consensus in those jurisdictions such as Connecticut that require a unanimous jury verdict for death. Thus, I urged the Connecticut legislature to substitute 11–1 or 10–2 for unanimity. However, our deep cultural preference for acquitting the guilty rather than convicting the innocent does have special force in capital trials: We should much rather a jury sentence to life someone who deserves to die than sentence to die someone who deserves to live.

Although a judge should dismiss automatic lifers and automatic killers, difficult problems remain, with the vast majority of potential jurors whose feelings fall somewhere between. In several cases, the US Supreme Court tried to strike a humane constitutional balance. Its most famous early jury selection case, *Witherspoon* (1968), held that excluding all potential jurors who express "conscientious objections to capital punishment" would leave a jury "uncommonly willing to condemn a man to die," thus violating the defendant's Sixth Amendment guarantee to a trial by an impartial jury. Jurors could be excluded for cause only if they made it "*unmistakably clear* that they would *automatically* vote against capital punishment without regard to any evidence that might be developed at the trial."[1]

But that standard, the product of late 1960s liberalism, proved far too skewed against death as punishment in the modern era. "What common sense should have realized experience has proved," the Court declared 17 years later. Many potential jurors "simply cannot be asked enough questions to reach the point where their bias has been made 'unmistakably clear.' They may not know how they will react; they may not be able to articulate it, or they may wish to hide their true feelings."[2] Thus, in *Wainwright v. Witt* (1985), the Court issued its current corrective, permitting the state to exclude potential jurors "whose views would prevent or *substantially impair*" their ability to vote for death. The Court later made it clear that a trial judge should also dismiss as "substantially impaired" all those pro–death penalty jurors who would *automatically* vote death for all first-degree murderers without regard to mitigating circumstances. Somehow judges and opposing counsel, through questionnaires and live exchanges with potential jurors, would try to weed out all those "substantially impaired."

I've never selected a jury. But attending AGACL's capital prosecutor training institutes, learning defense strategy from Kevin Doyle, reading practice manuals, and watching a small sample of jury selection in a New York capital case, *People v. Webb*, taught me how much the US Supreme Court's jurisprudence—easy to respect but difficult to apply—dominates the selection process.

Christopher Webb stood accused of breaking into his victims' apartment and then shooting and killing the mother and wounding her pregnant daughter, who lived but miscarried. "Death is not a punishment," declared potential juror no. 68. "When you put him to sleep you put him to rest. We all have to die, one way or another."

Should the defense try to get rid of these punitive jurors, all too eager to convict and punish defendants by sentencing them to life? Where guilt was a foregone conclusion, it might be useful to have one juror, steadfastly determined to stick it to that convicted murderer by giving him life. The judge excused no. 68 for cause.

In order to gauge potential jurors' reactions to life or death as punishment, the lawyers treated Webb's indictment as if it were established fact. "If you found that Mr. Webb had broken into an apartment, killed a woman and shot another, causing her to miscarry," the prosecutor asked a potential juror, "could you sentence someone like that to death?"

"Sure, if he's guilty."

"Could you see a situation like that as life without parole?"

"Objection. I have a problem," declared defense counsel. "It's already stated as a crime."

"Could you keep an open mind?" the judge asked, focusing on the sentence rather than defendant's guilt in the first place.

"I'd have to hear the case. But the way [the prosecutor] described it—it would be death." Excused for cause.

"My church has not *per se* preached against it," another potential juror declared. "But overall I'm not here to judge. I am against the death penalty in principle."

"Assume Mr. Webb has been found guilty," the defense gently prodded this potentially sympathetic juror. "If the facts of the case were bad enough—"

"I would base my decision on the crime itself. I can keep an open mind." Clearly under *Witherspoon* she can't be excused for cause. It's not "unmistakably clear" that this potential juror will "automatically" vote against death. But *Witt* makes us decide whether a person who insists she's against the death penalty in principle but claims she can keep an open mind counts as "substantially impaired."

"You are saying contradictory things," Judge Anne Feldman declared.

Now the defense attempted to get this sympathetic juror to agree at least to "consider" death as punishment. "The prosecutor has told you about the facts of the case—a young woman nine months pregnant shot, her mother killed . . . . Those are the facts of the case the prosecution will try to prove to you. That Mr. Webb pushed his way into an apartment . . . ." Sitting through this for several hours, I saw how often lawyers on both sides virtually conceded the defendant's guilt before the trial even began.

Some determined lifers or killers exposed their bias, but many others posed a difficult challenge. "The same crime deserves the same punishment, no matter what the background," declared a potential juror, articulating the basic principle of equality under the law. She would not allow her personal feelings about the defendant's background or lifestyle to affect her judgment of guilt or desert, she insisted. Justice must have no respect for persons, we declare. "That woman holding the torch in New York harbor with that god-damn rag around her eyes," as Lorton prisoner Pete Arnold described his composite American symbol. Blind justice—our ideal, throughout—except in the penalty phase of capital trials. Excused for cause.

I came to appreciate the inexact art and science of selecting a capital jury—how rarely would bias be "unmistakably clear." How difficult if not downright impossible to apply the Supreme Court's jurisprudence and de-termine who really had an "open mind." Worst of all, how grueling for Dr. Petit to sit there, hour after hour, day after day, watching the process to select 12 persons and six alternates who would decide life or death for the man who raped his 11-year-old child and murdered his family. "No Jurors Picked for Komisarjevsky Trial on First Day," a headline read.[3] The judge excused 18 people who claimed financial hardship and 17 others who admitted they could not be impartial.

Looking to understand jury selection better and hoping to help relieve Petit's tedium, I enlisted him to act as my eyes and ears in the courtroom. Whenever potential jurors claimed "life is worse than death," Petit's emails informed me, the judge directed them to consider death the more severe sanction, cutting off all discussion. Sometimes the prosecutor, other times the defense struck these jurors.

While Petit did his best to see legal justice done day after day inside that New Haven courtroom, I did my best to use his family's tragedy to alert the public to the fraud committed in their name. Gustavus Adolphus Col-lege invited me to deliver one of two keynote addresses at their Thirty-First Annual Mayday Peace conference. Opposing me: "the Mother Teresa of the abolitionist movement," Sister Helen Prejean, author of *Dead Man Walking*, whose portrayal won Susan Sarandon the Oscar for best actress.

I hoped we would engage in constructive public dialogue rather than debate. Alas, Sister Helen's busy schedule, "her people" informed the hosts, did not permit a public exchange. I offered to make myself available whenever she was available. Her busy schedule still somehow precluded it, the conference organizers told me, obviously embarrassed that Sister Helen would not share a stage with me but unwilling to criticize their star attraction.

The fliers declared it: Sister Helen would give the morning address in the chapel—"Dead Man Walking: The Journey Continues"—detailing a parent's ascent in forgiving the murderer of his child. I would give the afternoon keynote, "The Worst of the Worst: How Should They Live, Why Should They Die?," in the auditorium.

I knew what to expect from Helen Prejean. I'd twice witnessed her entertaining and polished stream-of-consciousness storytelling. How she unwittingly became involved with the abolition movement, accompanying the condemned, and afterward the victims' family, on their journey from hatred to love. Since she had no intention of engaging me, she didn't need to know what to expect from me. The night before our talks, however, news broke that no one expected. President Barack Obama announced it: American special operatives had killed Osama bin Laden!

"A life sentence is for real," Sister Helen assured adoring students who packed the chapel. A convicted murderer serving life without parole "will pay every day of his life," she declared, using standard abolitionist hyperbole. "I don't see the sense in killing people to say that killing people is wrong. . . . Whenever a uniquely precious unrepeatable human being is killed, it's always the worst of the worst," she insisted with that indiscriminate symmetry that destroyed all distinction between a mass murderer and those of us who would kill him in response. "Killing is wrong, no matter who does it—me or you all." Sister Helen's smooth and folksy rap elicited the usual laughter and applause. I sat up front in the audience chafing at the bit to engage her. During Q&A, somebody asked Sister Helen how she felt this day after the American people learned we had killed Bin Laden. "I don't feel safer," she replied, avoiding the retributive question of desert. After the thunderous applause that greeted her talk, Sister Helen generously carved several minutes from her busy schedule to sell and sign books.

"Sister Helen told you this morning of a father's journey," I began my afternoon talk. "I would like to recount a different father, a different journey. . . . A summer evening in Connecticut, July 2007. Jennifer Hawke-Petit and her daughter leave their local Stop & Shop with the ingredients for the family Sunday dinner. Michaela, the 11-year-old vegetarian, loves to cook for the family. Next month, her 17-year-old sister, Hayley, will start her freshman year at Dartmouth and then hopefully on to medical school to help research a cure for MS. Michaela prays the research will help her mother, Jennifer, who suffers from incipient MS. As they exit the supermarket, lurking in the shadows, Joshua Komisarjevsky trails mother and daughter to their upscale house. . . ." I detailed that horrible night to make sure the killers' viciousness sank in. How after sexually abusing Michaela,

Komisarjevsky took four cell phone photos of his terrified, helpless victim. "Bound and tied to their beds, lying there for six hours before Komisarjevsky doused them in gasoline." Imagine their terror. Somebody lit the match; 17-year-old Hayley, burning up alive, broke free from her restraints. In an attempt to save her younger sister, she died of smoke inhalation at the top of the landing. Eleven-year-old Michaela burning alive, still tied to her bed, also eventually choked to death on the smoke. "Do you doubt, can you doubt that these monsters deserve to die?"

And how should they live until they die? "Sister Helen says she feels no safer that Osama is dead; only 16 percent say that his death makes us safer. But what percent felt *satisfied?* Not safer but satisfied?" How much more satisfying, I insisted, that Bin Laden wasn't instantly obliterated by a missile launched from a drone. We imagine that moment, when Bin Laden confronted our young soldiers sent to keep our covenant with the victims at Ground Zero—"We will not forgive; we will not forget."

Surprisingly, many liberals echoed this sentiment. "I don't want closure. I want memory, and justice, and revenge," the acid-tongued *New York Times* essayist Maureen Dowd began her very next column, "Killing Evil Doesn't Make Us Evil." "Liberal guilt may have its uses, but it should not be wasted on this kill-mission," Dowd continued. "The really insane assumption behind some of the second-guessing is that killing Osama somehow makes us like Osama, as if all killing is the same."[4]

"Perhaps the people of Connecticut will someday kill Steven Hayes and Joshua Komisarjevsky," my Gustavus talk concluded. "I doubt it. But if they do, on that day we will reaffirm, with a sense of satisfaction, relief, and renewal, what President Obama declared the other night, announcing Bin Laden's death to the American people and the world: 'We will be true to the values that make us who we are.' And on nights like this one we can say to the families who have lost loved ones to this terror, 'Justice has been done.'"

When I returned to the guest house from my talk, who did I find all packed but still lounging around and amiably chatting? Yes, of course, the saintly Sister Helen. Somehow her too busy schedule had allowed for her lecture, a book signing afterward, lunch, and an afternoon at leisure, but not one minute of public dialogue between us.

As prosecution and defense continued their protracted struggle to pick Komisarjevsky's jury, legislative leaders lined up support for the judiciary committee's abolition bill, while polls showed almost 80 percent wanted Hayes and Komisarjevsky executed. The Connecticut Assembly's overwhelming Democratic majority stood ready to abolish the death penalty with the Governor's support. The state Senate seemed evenly divided 18–18, the abolitionist Lieutenant Governor poised to break the tie.

But Dr. Petit begged senators not to complicate Komisarjevsky's upcoming trial by prospectively abolishing the death penalty. A jury would find it difficult to condemn a person who would only face life, had he killed the same way today. Petit's determination paid off. Edith Prague, a Democratic senator who earlier voted for repeal, announced, in deference to Petit, that she would vote against repeal this year. "They should skip a trial and hang Komisarjevsky by his genitals from a tree," the feisty state senator declared, giving the media their story for the day.[5] So repeal efforts died in the Connecticut legislature, at least for that year.

As jury selection dragged on, I broke from grading 540 final essays briefly to accompany Petit on his grinding trek. I hoped in some tiny measure to help relieve the tedium and take a turn at the vigil. At 9:58 a.m., two minutes before court's scheduled start, I burst into the New Haven courtroom and flopped into a seat reserved for the jury panel. An officer politely invited me to choose any other seat in the nearly empty courtroom. Two prosecutors sat at their desk, waiting. A computer but no lawyers sat at the defense table. Jeremiah Donovan, the avuncular and experienced defense attorney, entered, spotted me jotting down notes, and introduced himself. The jury panel would soon arrive, he told me. They would be most interested in seeing Komisarjevsky. I also wanted to see this monster up close.

Joshua Komisarjevsky walked into the courtroom, looking serious but not frightened, dressed in a black suit, black shoes. His buzz cut made him look different from his pictures. Komisarjevsky greeted his attorney, sat down, and began to look through some papers. Our eyes never met, but I tried to direct my hatred to the back of his head.

The jury panel entered. After a friendly greeting and some inspiring comments about the jury's role in our system of criminal justice, the judge called panelists individually. The first juror couldn't speak English. Excused. "I can't see myself sentencing anybody to death," declared another. Excused. And so it went, with the usual assortment of citizens revealing themselves, more or less. "In a perfect kingdom would there be a death penalty?" the defense was fond of asking. "If 1 is very much against the death penalty and 10 is very much for it, where would you place yourself?" This single question most succinctly probed a juror's bias. As you might expect, the vast majority of jurors who sat answered "5." But Petit told me that some who said 4 and even 3 but no 6s or 7s sat. When Petit arrived, I moved my seat next to his, closer to the jury panel but farther from Komisarjevsky.

One particular panelist, Ms. E., a Veterans' Administration psychologist who supervised a research study to help people cope with chronic illness, sensitized me to a key problem. "I don't know that I could sentence a man to death," she admitted. "It was despicable, and that poor family suffered so. But I don't know that I personally could sentence a man to die." You might think that *Witherspoon* settled it. Be gone, lifer. Of course the defense badly wanted her. "Could you answer a series of questions accurately," Donovan asked her, "if they amounted to sentencing a man to death without actually doing it?" She paused and reflected. Could she answer a *series* of factual questions, knowing they added up to death? "Yes." I didn't believe her, although I believed she believed she could. The judge seemed unwilling to dismiss her for cause.

"Do you have personal feelings concerning the death penalty?" asked the prosecutor, trying to demonstrate Ms. E.'s substantial impairment. "You said you could answer certain questions, but didn't know if you could sentence someone to death."

"I couldn't just answer one question—life or death. But I could answer questions, knowing the result is death." She paused. "I'd have a sense of discomfort, but answering questions would put distance."

What mechanisms we employ to emotionally distance ourselves from the results of our own choices. Disavowing responsibility, deadening yourself to the consequence of your actions while acting as an instrument of a state that kills, we've seen that before. The clerks who stamped the papers that helped move lines of people destined for the Nazi death camps hardly pulled the switch that released the gas that killed the innocent millions. Ms. E. could create a distance, she declared. She could abstract herself from the consequence of her own decision. She could, she insisted, make herself believe that responsibility lay with the law and not her personally.

Judge Blue mostly allowed the lawyers to run jury selection, but here he stepped in: "The question will be, 'Do the aggravators outweigh the mitigators?' Can you answer that objectively, knowing the result would be death?" How inviting to say, *Yes. I can follow the law even if I disagree with it.* Sitting there, I realized the judge had allowed it to get too abstract. The prosecutor should press her directly: *Can you be responsible for putting someone to death? You will be responsible—can you be responsible? Can you vote a person to die?*

Instead, the prosecutor went back to the old standard: 1 to 10, "if 1 represents 'totally against the death penalty,' where would you place yourself?" Take a guess—what did this psychologist answer? "4." Was she being honest with herself? When push came to plunger, regardless of what the law called for, she said she personally could not vote for a man to die. That's not a four.

At this point, the prosecutors asked the judge for a moment to consult. And they walked over to Dr. Petit. The defense had their professional jury consultants. The prosecution had Petit. The prosecutor asked the lone surviving victim whether he felt comfortable with this potential juror deciding the fate of a man who raped his daughter and killed his family. The victim, or at least a loving survivor, *should* actively participate, if he or she wishes, in selecting the jury. Survivors should get a voice, not a veto. I agreed with Petit's judgment. Ms. E. should not sit. And so she left the courtroom. But the subtle question left its mark: Can we sensitive, intelligent human beings separate ourselves from our own instincts and emotions?

Should we even try?

32

EVERYWHERE ELSEWHERE

EVERYONE KNEW THE JURY WOULD CONVICT KOMISAR-jevsky. Most everyone also predicted they would sentence him to die. The defense, of course, tried to pin it on Hayes. He alone started the fire that killed the girls to eliminate his DNA from the crime scene, they claimed. Josh never killed anyone or expected it to happen. But tests revealed gasoline on Komisarjevsky's clothes. And Michaela had bleach on hers, proving that Komisarjevsky too worried about his DNA on the victim. After deliberating eight hours over two days, the jury convicted Komisarjevsky on all counts. Now they would determine whether he lived or died.

Or so the jury must believe.

In *Caldwell v. Mississippi*, the US Supreme Court's 5–4 decision held that a prosecutor could not tell a capital jury that ultimately the defendant's fate rested with the appellate courts. "You are the judges and you will have to decide his fate," the defense attorney had argued, begging the jury for mercy. "Your decision is not the final decision," the prosecutor countered, assuring the jury that courts would review and could overturn their death sentence. But "there is no appellate mercy," a US Supreme Court plurality insisted, striking down Caldwell's death sentence. Jurors who simply wanted to denounce the murderer might feel free to condemn him to die, relying on appellate judges to backstop them. Those same appellate judges might feel bound by the jury's original judgment, although they too preferred a life sentence. Thus, "a defendant might be executed, although no sentencer had ever made a determination that death was the appropriate sentence."[1]

In short, responsibility might lie everywhere elsewhere.

The British psychiatrist R. D. Laing coined that catchy phrase, "everywhere elsewhere."[2] Keeping true to his idea, I imagine two strangers on a cruise, falling in love in the moonlight. On their return, they announce their engagement. Grandma believes this man will make her darling grand-daughter miserable but does not want to meddle. The bride's mother sizes up her future son-in-law as a mismatch, but her daughter looks so happy. The groom regrets the whole thing, but the wedding has seemingly gathered unstoppable momentum. In the light of day, the bride-to-be regrets her rash affair but would never break her mother or grandmother's heart. And so they go to the altar with their love everywhere elsewhere—in other words, nowhere.

In state after state, I've discovered responsibility for punishment resides everywhere elsewhere. Corrections officers insist the judges' punish, the judges pin it on the legislature, and legislators look to corrections.

The Eighth Amendment requires "accurate sentencing information as a prerequisite to a reasoned determination of whether a defendant shall live or die," the Supreme Court insists.[3] I agree. But shouldn't a jury fully prepared to take responsibility for deciding between life and death appreciate the real "meaning" of its choice—the day-to-day experience of life in prison?

At Komisarjevsky's penalty phase, the defense argued he was "doomed from birth." They listed 43 mitigators that caused Komisarjevsky to do what he did. He was "biologically predisposed" to mental health problems, raised in a "conservative evangelical Christian community" that shunned psychiat-ric or medical intervention. He was sexually abused by a foster brother. His grandfather, his drum teacher, and his church mentor all died when Josh was 14. He had eight known head injuries. In short he was abused as a child and dominated as an adult.[4]

Komisarjevsky's penalty phase forces us back to the classic, insoluble conflict between free will and determinism. One part of me knows, believes, *must* believe that people choose to do what they do. I choose to write these very words that you will choose to keep reading I hope. And yet, at the same time, genetics increasingly suggests that we are biologically predisposed, born with different temperaments and tendencies. Psychology informs us how, as children, our personalities are (de)formed by persons and events beyond our control. Our value systems are shaped by mentors supplied by chance or circumstance.

"I came up like the average ghetto child," Lorton prisoner James L. explained to me.

"My mother surviving off that welfare check and what we all could put together by begging. I remember going to bed so hungry I had to drink water to stop my stomach from bubbling and cracking. All these extension cords everywhere. Iron board hooked to the television, the television hooked to the fan. Something always missing. We pay the gas bill, that mean the electric was off. We pay the electric; that mean the rent didn't get paid. If we ate good, the telephone man missed his money.

"I hated not being able to have the things I wanted. Live across from people getting out of their station wagons with big shopping bags of food every week. I come home. Nothing to eat. I can't curse out my mother for not having any food, so I might go down the street and bust the store window and laugh. Let me make somebody else miserable. I might take a cat and put a string around his tail and wing it around.

"'Yowwwwwwwww!' That's how I feel motherfucker. The same way I'm doing you, that's the way they doing me. So I came up knowing how to survive. How to get money. How to get over, how to lie with a straight eye. And how to be tough and rough."

The child is the father of the man. Is it any wonder that James L. became a criminal? And yet—and yet, his older brothers and sisters did not.

Street killers' early childhood memories both flesh out and defy the stereotypes. One murderer's mother was a missionary and a nurse, his father a preacher and a mailman. Though some were physically abused, some were lovingly cared for, even spoiled. Older siblings or friends initiated some into crime. Others came upon it themselves.

Thousands of hours over a decade inside Lorton prison, where convicted street criminals spilled their guts, severely tested my belief in free will. "What made me *go into* crime?" Lorton inmate Leo Simms chuckled, repeating my early naïve question. "I was already into crime. From day one. My environment, my neighborhood, my family. I didn't consider it crime. You know when you say 'crime'—I heard the word. . . . We ate and slept, and drank and wore crime. When I'm sitting on the steps and the man came up with a pan of steaks and Mama bought them, that was crime. She cooked them and put the onions on them, I'm eating crime. I'm doing just what I came up to do. I didn't *get* into it; I was *born* into it. And if the word 'crime' came along with what I was supposed to do, then that's what it was. To do and to have and it's 'crime.'"

First Amendment absolutists foolishly claim that media does not create or contribute to violence. The Lorton generation imbibed the TV series *Miami Vice* and the movie *Scarface*. These kids worshipped and fantasized themselves as the film's Tony Montana, ruthlessly rising from rags to riches, killing anybody in his way. Some became distorted versions of the villains—to them heroes—they lionized. Today's little mass murderers in the making have new and different media. How could a person spray shoot a crowded movie theater in Colorado? Or walk into an elementary school in Connecticut and open fire, killing the principal, six teachers, and twenty six- and seven-year-olds? My guess: They went through those motions a hundred times with violent video games. Took that weapon in their hands and electronically killed their simulated victims over and over. And felt pleasure or, eventually, all over numb, like Daryl. Even worse than physical access to weapons, we give our children psychological access to the methods and motions of mass murder. Abolitionists look in the wrong place when they claim we numb ourselves by singling out the worst of the worst of the worst, and through a long, drawn-out, expensive ritual, we try, convict, revisit, and eventually kill one. Our video game industry breeds a generation of killers.

Reggie Brooks, another Lorton prisoner, scoffed at deterrence as "a foolish concept." Reggie's deterministic "slot theory" explained how things really work. "For example, hustling drugs. The guy who brings it in, gives it to one guy on the street. That guy has eight different people working for him. Suppose he gets busted. He's moved out. One of those guys working for him moves up to fill his slot. It becomes automatic. The fact that one guy's been busted, that he faces 15 years in prison, has nothing to do with anything. It's about slots. You move in, and you move up. Everybody's looking to move to a higher slot, in the straight life and the hustling life."

But science and social science explain only so much. We retributivists, including Leo Simms himself, still believe in free will and personal responsibility. And we still pursue justice. "How can a person be the product of genetic and biological predispositions, early childhood personality (de)formation, adult influences and pressures, and at the same time be held fully accountable for his criminal choices," my *Hartford Courant* op-ed asked the opening day of Komisarjevsky's penalty phase.[5] We retributivists need free will. Without it we cannot blame or punish. Society in general needs free will. Without it we cannot praise or reward. Yet science advances relentlessly, more accurately explaining and predicting behavior, correlating it with chemical changes in the brain.

On December 9, 2011, the jury unanimously sentenced Joshua Komisarjevsky to die. Dr. Petit of course thanked them. This was not revenge, he declared: It was justice. The Komisarjevsky family, who had stood by Joshua, testifying on his behalf, issued their own revealing statement: "From the very beginning, we have spoken out about the horror of the crime and taken the position that whatever verdict the jury reached was the right verdict. With today's jury decision, our view is the same. The crime was monstrous and beyond comprehension. There are no excuses."[6]

While Connecticut refused to abolish its death penalty in advance of Komisarjevsky's trial, Illinois did abolish its own. I thought back to my brief visit there to the Row. "I was already commuted once before by Governor

Ryan back in 2003," a voice called out to me as I walked down the hall by his cell with my video camera. Illinois's death row looked like the rest of the prison wing, except the condemned had single cells. "What does it serve me to be put back on death row again?" he complained.

I looked up at the name tag—"Urdiales." I peered into his cell. "*People* magazine?"

"Yeah. *L.A. Sun Times. Rolling Stone.*"

"What did you do?"

"What do you do when you're on death row?"

"How many?"

"Enough to get me here."

Andrew Urdiales—the ex-marine turned serial rapist-murderer who terrorized Orange County, California, for years before torturing and killing even more women in Illinois—kept the conversation going. "More than two people, and what was that other aggravating circumstance they got me on? Damn, I forgot." Urdiales did remember the eight women he'd raped and killed well enough to describe each in detail to the police. Poor Andrew Urdiales, complaining about his hellish, hopeless life on death row: "It's boring. You just kinda sit around all day. Watch television. We go outside to the yard a few days a week. We have showers. We get mailed books, magazines. But mostly boring."

The day after Illinois abolished the death penalty and released him from his living hell, California prosecutors moved to extradite Urdiales to stand trial on five counts of capital murder—one for each woman he killed there. Last I looked, he's still a lifer at Pontiac. I do hope his boredom has been relieved somewhat in general population where he can now enjoy his shopping.

Since Illinois abolished the death penalty, it hadn't mattered after all that I never got to testify in Juan Luna's trial.

Ironically, by condemning Komisarjevsky to die, the Connecticut jury removed the last political obstacle to abolishing that state's death penalty, albeit prospectively only. Early in 2012, the legislature went through the motions of a hearing, but everybody knew it was a done deal. Abolitionists now had the votes in the Senate. Hayes and Komisarjevsky would remain on the Row, for now. Most of us feel confident Connecticut will never kill them.

Day after day during jury selection, Dr. Petit had sat within striking distance of Komisarjevsky. At lunch break, I told Petit how much I admired his strength and resolve. I also wondered aloud at his remarkable restraint. "Nothing anyone could do to your family to make you want to kill him?" Johnny Allen had challenged me years before. How could Dr. Petit sit there, day after day, 25 feet from the man who bludgeoned him with a baseball bat, who sexually abused and killed his 11-year-old daughter, with nothing between them except a waist-high wooden railing, easily vaulted, and one bored court officer, half nodding off? "How can you do it?" I asked him as we walked back to court. Petit shrugged. "What else am I going to do?"

Suppose the doctor had taken the law into his own hands by vaulting that barrier and strangling or stabbing to death the man who bludgeoned him and burned up his family? Who could blame him? What right-feeling person would argue he was no better than the man he killed? The public would cheer, but prosecutors must present a case against Petit to a grand jury. To vindicate the law. Would they refuse to indict him? And if *People v. Petit* did go to trial, would any jury unanimously convict him of murder? Would they find him justified, or at most guilty of manslaughter, for intentionally killing under the influence of reasonably provoked passion? Petit would do no more than a year or two.

How can we not admire Dr. Petit, who lost so much and tried to make good come from evil by establishing a charitable foundation in his family's memory, dedicated to eradicating disease, protecting women from violent crime, and offering them increased opportunities in science? How could we not extol the virtues of this law-abiding citizen who suffered so much? We do admire greatly how he kept his dignity and somehow summoned the strength all those years to bear witness to justice, tirelessly restraining the tide of abolitionism. Wishing him all anonymity and peace in the years to come, still I cannot imagine living with myself, knowing that my family's vicious killers got to live out their lives, playing, watching TV, and eating Hershey bars. As a constitutional historian and criminal law professor, of course, I can't possibly argue for vigilantism. But as a human being, I do confess. God forbid this happened to my family, if I had the opportunity, I hope I'd have the guts to kill him myself.

And take whatever came behind it.

"Russell Peeler had an 8-year-old and his mother killed to eliminate the child as a witness; Todd Rizzo used a sledgehammer to beat to death a 13-year-old boy simply to know what it felt like. These condemned killers can now look forward to their release into general population where their crimes will be forgotten and consciously ignored by officers and prisoners alike, eager to make the best of their lives, day to day," my lead op-ed in the *Hartford Courant* reminded the people of Connecticut, right before that state's Senate formally voted to abolish the death penalty.

New York had virtually ignored my plea for real *punishment* of life in lieu of death. New Jersey tacked on a last-minute amendment mandating those sentenced to life without parole serve their *entire* sentence inside a maximum security prison. However tentatively, that state had broadened the focus beyond the length of sentence to call for a more restrictive *quality* of life inside. In Connecticut, I had pounded the point repeatedly before the judiciary committee, urging permanent punitive segregation in my prepared statement and at length in live testimony. The committee majority seemingly ignored that plea and simply moved an abolition bill to the legislature.

"Steven Hayes and Joshua Komisarjevsky deserve to die. If the state keeps them alive, they deserve to live miserably, forever condemned, segregated, and denied the perks and privileges of daily prison life. . . . The end of death as punishment does not end, but opens a conversation," my media plea concluded. "What should the punishment of life feel like day-to-day, when we can no longer kill those who most deserve to die?"

The next day I received an odd anonymous message assuring me my perspective had not gone unnoticed. Two days later, at the last moment and without explanation or advance notice, the Connecticut Senate tacked on an amendment to its abolition bill: LWOPers would forever serve their sentence in a specially designated separate prison wing *under the same conditions as punitive segregation, forever denied contact visits,* with no more than two hours of recreation a day.

I felt I did my part to keep my covenant with Jennifer Hawke-Petit, Hayley, Michaela, and others similarly situated in graveyards across the United States. Connecticut has not fully embraced PPS. But even as they abolished death as punishment, Connecticut's legislature took that most welcome but unusual retributive step toward a perpetually unpleasant *punishment of life.*

PART VI
FORGIVENESS AND REDEMPTION

33

I CAN LOOK YOU
IN THE EYES

WE EXECUTED TWO CONVICTED MURDERERS THE NIGHT
of September 21, 2011. One surely deserved to die. The other—well, that
was Troy Davis.

Troy Davis's death caused a worldwide firestorm of protest. Abolitionist
media outlets played it up and made it simple: A black man killed a white
off-duty police officer. No physical evidence connected Davis to the crime.
Corrupt cops manufactured evidence and coerced witnesses; a jury convicted
and condemned Davis to die. But as his execution date approached, seven of
nine witnesses recanted, and yet somehow America's racist criminal justice
system ignored overwhelming evidence of innocence and railroaded an innocent black man to his death.

In 1968, this outrage might have caused race riots and mass destruction—20 years later, it might have produced mass demonstrations led by
organizers such as Reverend Al Sharpton coordinating street protests with
shouts of "No justice, no peace." By 2011, the United States had elected a
mixed-race president, and the leaders of a matured civil rights movement
had largely gone mainstream. Troy Davis's recent execution did, however,
move Reverend Sharpton's organization, National Action Network, to invite
me—the token death penalty supporter—to publicly discuss the Davis case
at its House of Justice in Harlem. It helped, of course, that Michael Hardy,
Sharpton's counsel, had been my student in criminal law. Knowing I would
face a hostile crowd and determined to discover how we could have executed
someone under those circumstances while the Komisarjevsky penalty phase
wound down in Connecticut, I focused on Troy Davis, one of the two we
killed September 21.

But, as I reminded the audience that day in December, "One surely deserved to die."

Early morning, June 7, 1998. James Byrd Jr., a 48-year-old black man walking home from a party in Jasper, Texas, accepted a ride from three white men: Lawrence Brewer and his fellow racist prison buddy, John King, and Shawn Berry, the driver, who knew Byrd from around town. Instead of taking Byrd home, the three decided to have some fun. They drove the victim to a remote county road, beat him severely, urinated on him, chained him by his ankles to their pickup truck, and dragged him three miles along an asphalt road. Byrd struggled mightily to keep his head up, as the road ripped his flesh and sheared his elbows to the bone. Finally, this unspeakable torture ended, when a drain pipe decapitated the helpless victim. A southern jury condemned Brewer and King, two well-known white supremacists, for torturing a black man to death.

The day before his execution, Brewer told a local radio station he had no regrets and would do it all again. He did, however, manage to make a minor contribution to justice by ordering a lavish last meal, which he then refused to eat. That waste moved the Texas Department of Corrections to abolish special last meals for the condemned. So Texas executed Lawrence Brewer a few hours before Georgia killed Troy Davis.

Troy Davis had come close to the needle before. Confronted by doubts of his guilt, the US Supreme Court issued a last-minute stay and ordered a federal district court to conduct an extraordinary hearing. Davis's defense team could offer any evidence of his innocence. That hearing lasted several days, and Judge William T. Moore Jr. meticulously analyzed the evidence in his 172-page opinion.[1]

"I appreciated this invitation," I told the Harlem audience, "and thought I owed it to you to carefully consider and digest the evidence. I owed it to you, as you owe it to yourselves to be informed as to what happened at the bus stop that night, and since."

Preparing for this talk, I carefully read the court's detailed analysis, contacted prosecutors and appellate lawyers who handled the case to discover that the abolitionist media had spun the facts. True, no physical evidence *directly* connected Troy Davis to the shooting of Officer Mark MacPhail. But ballistics evidence established that shell casings from an earlier shooting that day—Davis was convicted of shooting that man in the face—matched casings from the murder weapon in the MacPhail shooting. Of course it was *possible* for Davis to have handed off the gun to his confederate, who later shot the bullet that killed MacPhail. A suspicious shirt later turned up in Davis's washing machine. That also could have been handed off after the killing. But the media misled the public by flatly declaring that "no physical evidence" whatsoever connected Davis to the killing.

But hadn't seven witnesses who originally identified Troy Davis as the shooter since recanted? Not exactly. Four eyewitnesses actually saw the shooting. One stuck to his original testimony despite repeated pressure by the defense. Another gave an affidavit she refused to swear to. Another recantation did not actually contradict the trial testimony: It declared only that now, years later, the witness could no longer swear to the earlier contemporaneous testimony identifying Davis as the shooter. And the fourth and key witness, Dorothy Ferrell, did directly recant, claiming she lied at trial because the district attorney promised her favorable treatment on her own charges. But curiously, although "she should have been Davis' star witness," the defense team left her sitting in the hall right outside the courtroom and "kept her from testifying" lest she be subject to cross-examination under oath.[2]

A jailhouse snitch did recant his own "completely fabricated" trial testimony that Davis had confessed to him in jail. But his lies so clearly contradicted everyone else's account at trial that no jury could have given it much weight originally.

And the racism that so infected the criminal justice system? It turns out that seven of twelve jurors who convicted Davis and condemned him to die were black. And the "racist" cops who supposedly manufactured evidence and coerced witnesses? Two of those local police officers were black, one an ordained minister. I dug further. If the national and international media raised such a hue and cry, I could only imagine the local media. But I discovered another inconvenient truth: The two Savannah African American newspapers—*The Savannah Herald* and the *Savannah Tribune*—each published a single op-ed piece from an NAACP representative decrying Davis's execution. But neither ran a single editorial opposing it on their own. "We didn't want to take a position," an editor explained to me. Why not? "It was just not something we wanted to get involved with." Could it be that the locals knew Troy Davis had more than once earned his street name, "Rough as Hell"? In its third hearing, the parole board—the final executive word in Georgia—two blacks and three whites moved Davis forward to execution, apparently without dissent. True, a white D.A. had initially prosecuted Davis. But Savannah's newly elected black district attorney, having publicly distanced himself from the controversy, nevertheless, out of sight of reporters, appeared before the parole board to support the state's case for execution.

"So I can look you in the eyes," I told the almost all-black audience at the National Action Network, "and tell you with a clear heart and soul:

I am convinced beyond a reasonable doubt that Troy Davis killed Officer MacPhail. I am convinced beyond a reasonable doubt that the police did not coerce testimony. Davis's supporters (including Reverend Al, but I didn't have the guts or bad manners to single him out) have created a disinformation campaign, pressured witnesses to recant, and greatly exaggerated the possibility of Davis's innocence in court and the media."

Judge Moore did not find Troy Davis guilty of murder. He did not determine "whether a reasonable doubt exists in light of the new evidence." The Supreme Court had not given him that job. Judge Moore found only that Davis had failed to demonstrate "a clear probability that any reasonable juror would have a reasonable doubt about his guilt." As Judge Moore restated the legal standard, "Mr. Davis must show by clear and convincing evidence that no reasonable juror would have convicted him in the light of the new evidence."[3] Troy Davis did not come close to meeting that burden. The judge's detailed analysis still convinced me (and the judge) beyond a reasonable doubt that Troy Davis murdered Officer MacPhail, who bravely came to the aid of a helpless man being beaten at a bus stop. Davis clearly failed to satisfy even the lower burden he would have imposed on himself.

But the judge did signal in a footnote that he had a *residual* doubt: "Mr. Davis's guilt was proven at trial beyond a reasonable doubt but not a mathematical certainty. However, Mr. Davis does not challenge his conviction based on residual doubt. Nor can he, as such a challenge appears foreclosed by Supreme Court precedent."[4]

"I also look you in the eyes and tell you that although I feel certain that some people deserve to die, I would not have executed Troy Davis," I admitted to the audience. Although the prosecutors did meet their burden of proof for *convicting* Davis of murder—proof beyond a reasonable doubt that he did it—they failed to meet the correct burden of proof for executing him. So I would have convicted Troy Davis again. But I am left with a *lingering* doubt about his innocence. A doubt not strictly rational but real. And I have a moral uncertainty that he deserved to die.

"In an agitated moment, he shot Officer MacPhail, stood over him and shot again. For that, Davis deserved to spend his life in prison. But this killer did not inhabit the same moral universe as monsters who rape and then murder children, or hired killers or serial killers. "Davis was not Brewer dragging James Byrd to his agonizing death. We must be convinced with no lingering doubt about a person's guilt before we execute him. We should be convinced to a moral certainty that he deserves to die. With Troy Davis I am neither."

Outnumbered 5–1 on the panel that day and speaking early, I expected a vigorous counterattack from the speakers who followed. No panelist, however, challenged me on the facts—not one. A fellow panelist did criticize me for focusing too much on the specifics of the Davis case, although that was the announced topic of the panel. Afterward, most heartening of all, several members of the audience approached me. One told me he agreed with me, "but I can't say it in this crowd."

"I disagree with you," declared another, "but I admire your courage to walk into this lion's den. You sure tamed them lions." He laughed, and we shook hands.

Race, racism, and the death penalty deserve an extended and serious treatment rather than the brief mention here. In summary, however, my experience and exposure to black inner-city street killers and their families, as well as leading studies, lead me to conclude that today we are no more likely, and probably slightly less, to execute a black death-eligible murderer than a white one. Studies have also shown in the modern era, on average, it takes longer to execute a black condemned killer than a white one. Some of this stems from the odd but undeniable fact that white condemned killers much more frequently waive their appeals—become "volunteers"—than do black ones. I have my theory why but cannot prove it.

Although we much more readily execute murderers who kill white victims than black, that hardly shows, as abolitionists who cry "racism" often claim, that society "devalues" black life. To the contrary, as I discovered from listening to black killers and their families, often that disparity shows just the opposite. Prosecutors usually consult the victim's family before deciding whether to pursue death. Black-on-black murders often result from drug deals gone bad or inner-city gang violence. Often these victims' families decline the death penalty. They know their child was "in the game." "Everybody knows that drugs breed bodies," the Lorton prisoners confirmed. Rather than compound the tragedy, recognizing that their own lost child could well have been defendant as victim, they vote to spare the killer. This hardly shows these survivors devalued black life. To the contrary, they continue to value it, including the life of the murderer himself.

Opinion polls typically force respondents into a simplistic "yes" or "no" when they ask, "Are you in favor of the death penalty for someone convicted of murder?" In one leading poll, black respondents twice as frequently as whites showed their more nuanced view by refusing the "yes" or "no" option and writing spontaneously the only morally proper response: "It depends." While a majority of African Americans do oppose the death penalty, public opinion polls consistently show substantial support, 40 to 45 percent within the black community. Since most killings are same race, prosecutors from poorer, minority counties will count the difficulty and expense in getting a jury drawn from that community unanimously to vote death. Thus, this district attorney will less likely prosecute capitally. In the end, most of the "race of victim" effect turns out to be geography (i.e., county to county variability). Within any given county, killers of white victims no more frequently receive the death penalty than killers of blacks.

The United States must face its shameful history of racism. Historically, worldwide, racists have used capital punishment to oppress minorities and suppress their struggle for human dignity. Relatively speaking, however, during the post-*Furman* modern era, the American death penalty with its heightened standards of due process and appellate review stands as a bright spot in the struggle for racial equality.

And yet, I'm convinced that racism still perniciously infects critical aspects of the death penalty while substantially contributing to the disproportionate black population serving life or condemned to die. Felony murder acts as the most common death penalty aggravator, with robbery the most common felony. Minorities disproportionately commit robbery—not surprisingly as economic circumstance correlates with race. Thus, the robbery aggravator, whether consciously or not, creates the great racial disparity, where approximately 6 percent of the population—black males—constitutes 42 percent of death row.[5] As Justices on both sides have agreed, "racial bias" becomes "most striking" in the "midrange" cases such as felony murder.[6] If states would only "narrow the class of death-eligible defendants" to those "categories of extremely serious crimes for which prosecutors consistently seek, and juries consistently impose the death penalty without regard to the race of the victim or the race of the offender," then "the danger of an arbitrary and discriminatory death penalty would be significantly decreased, if not eradicated."[7]

Again, limit the death penalty to the worst of the worst of the worst—Charles Manson, Danny Rolling, Jeffrey Dahmer, Richard Speck, Michael Ross, James Brewer, Charles Ng, Joshua Komisarjevsky, and Steven Hayes—whites mostly, by the way—and racial disparity greatly diminishes.

But it will not disappear.

A more pernicious racism operates below the surface of the criminal justice system. Almost no one talks of it. Studies show that juries will more frequently convict blacks with darker skin tone and "stereotypical" African features. Judges give them longer sentences on average than blacks with more stereotypically white features. This largely unconscious but real racism pervading black and white communities continues unchecked and difficult, if not impossible, to eradicate.[8]

In the end, however, "Troy Davis's execution hardly stands for racism or railroading an innocent man in the face of overwhelming evidence of his innocence," I declared in print.[9] "Instead the case stands for a deliberative mix of executive, legislative, and judicial responsibility, state and federal. It stands for the people's purest representatives—the jury, a majority black— sentencing him to die." The abolitionist pack that cries wolf here does itself and us a disservice by numbing us to real problems of race and innocence.

The day after Georgia executed Troy Davis, September 22, 2011, friends and family held a memorial service for Itchy. This man, who controlled the Lorton Central gym and law library, became ravaged by Alzheimer's, got transferred to a prison hospital and dropped out of my life. I felt sad delivering his eulogy, recounting how Itchy got his name as a child, for mistakenly using poison ivy as toilet paper; how 14-year-old Itchy had become Washington, DC's "colored" spelling bee champion. I talked of Itchy's transformation, how he dedicated himself to saving a generation of at-risk or imprisoned youth. Among the attendees, hobbling on crutches and emaciated, Leo Simms, Itchy's closest prison buddy, still lived. Also honoring him in death, a few of Itchy's street women, now middle aged. Itchy's son, David Brooks, aka "Little Itchy"—a name he detested—sought to embody his father's spirit by establishing a program to train and employ inner-city high school kids as lifeguards at local pools. Young David desperately strove to get Itchy "compassionately" released to die free on the outside. I never told him I hoped he failed.

David Leon Brooks, this brilliant tough guy, or what was left of him— the "living legend" who shared his life with me and saved mine—deserved to die in prison.

The past counts.

34

NONSENSE ON STILTS

"CRIMINAL JUSTICE SYSTEMS OPERATE OUTSIDE PUBLIC scrutiny," the invitation from Germany began. "Except for prominent cases (e.g., the controversial death sentence of Troy Davis in Georgia; the trial of Oslo killer Anders Breivik; state compensation to convicted child murderer Magnus Gafgen in Germany)." I knew about Troy Davis, of course; the world knew about Breivik, the Norwegian mass murderer who in 2011 gunned down dozens of young victims on an island. But who was Gafgen?

Magnus Gafgen, a German law student, couldn't wait to live the lifestyle of a successful lawyer. So on September 27, 2002, he kidnapped 11-year-old Jacob von Metzler, the youngest son of a prominent Frankfurt banking family, and dropped a note at Jacob's home, demanding one million euros for the child's safe return. Only if the kidnappers left the country with the money would the parents ever see their son again, the note insisted. Three days later, at 1 a.m., the police watched a man collect the ransom at a rural train stop. They tailed him, finally arresting him that afternoon at the Frankfurt airport as he prepared to flee.

At police headquarters, informed of his right to remain silent and consult a lawyer, Gafgen refused to reveal the child's exact location but did tell the police that another kidnapper had hidden the boy in a hut by a lake. Early the next morning, fearing for the child's life, Wolfgang Daschner, deputy chief of the Frankfurt police, ordered Detective Ortwin Ennigkeit to threaten Gafgen with torture and, if necessary, actually to torture him in order to rescue the kidnap victim. The detective refused to obey, on the advice of intermediate superiors, who instead suggested they confront Gafgen with the boy's parents. Daschner commanded Ennigkeit again, noting in the official police log the circumstances that justified his order. The police commander emphasized that he would threaten torture solely to save the child's life and not to further the investigation. So the detective threatened Gafgen with torture by a specialist trained to inflict severe pain and leave no marks. Ten minutes later, Gafgen confessed. He had strangled the boy almost immediately. He took the police to Jacob's body, hidden under a jetty at a remote pond.

In April 2003, Gafgen challenged his prosecution. By threatening him with torture, the police, he claimed, had violated his constitutional rights under Germany's Basic Law, along with the European Convention on Human Rights. Balancing the police's "serious violation" against "the severity of Gafgen's unlawful conduct," the trial court allowed criminal proceedings to continue.[1] The court, however, excluded Gafgen's coerced confession but did allow the victim's body and the kidnapper's tire tracks at the pond to count as evidence against him. Now faced with this overwhelming proof of his guilt, Gafgen confessed again at trial, he insisted, to try to make amends. The court convicted Gafgen of kidnapping and murder and sentenced him to life in prison, characterizing the killing as especially grave, thus eliminating any presumption of parole after 15 years.

Gafgen immediately appealed.

Meanwhile, the scene shifted as the cast of defendants changed. In December 2004, a German court convicted the two police officers: Daschner, the superior, for ordering the threatened torture, and his subordinate for threatening it. The court rejected the classic defense of "necessity": Conduct that would otherwise constitute a crime becomes legal when, according to ordinary standards of intelligence and morality, it clearly avoids a greater harm. Most of us intuitively support private citizens and public officials who transcend the law in an emergency they did not create. On balance we choose the "lesser evil" for the greater good. Recall, Locke called it executive "prerogative."[2]

But citing Article 1 of Germany's Constitution—the most fundamental guarantee of its Basic Law—the Frankfurt regional court held that by threatening torture during Gafgen's interrogation, the police violated his dignity. The court declared "absolute" the duty to protect every person's human dignity. It allowed "no exceptions or any balancing of interests." The court did note mitigating factors: The police acted from good motives (to save the child's life) under extreme pressure and exhaustion in "the very tense and hectic situation."[3] Also, the officers had already suffered professionally: Daschner had been transferred to the Ministry of Interior, and Ennigkeit was removed from further criminal prosecutions. Nevertheless, the court convicted the police officers of coercion. And imposed a suspended

fine of 3,600 euros on the detective who threatened torture to save the child
and 10,800 euros on the deputy chief who ordered it.

A year later, Gafgen, the kidnapper-murderer, sued the State of Hesse,
demanding compensation for his psychological trauma. Separately Gafgen
appealed his murder conviction to the European Court of Human Rights
in Strasbourg, citing the police interrogation as a violation of the European
Convention that absolutely prohibited torture.

On June 1, 2010, the 17-judge Grand Chamber of the European Court
of Human Rights issued its judgment. Every judge agreed. The police had
violated the International Convention: "No one shall be subjected to torture or to inhuman or degrading treatment or punishment." There would be
no exceptions, the majority declared, "*even in the event of a public emergency
threatening the life of the nation*" (emphasis added).[4] Think about that. The
police acted improperly although motivated to save a child's life. They would
have acted wrongly to threaten torture in order to save 10,000 lives! "Even in
the most difficult circumstances, such as the fight against terrorism," there
could be no "inhuman or degrading treatment or punishment" that "arouses
in its victims feelings of fear, anguish and inferiority" or "drives the victim
to act against his will or conscience." Poor Gafgen, forced to feel fearful and
anguished, having had his "moral resistance" overcome, then acting against
his own conscience by revealing the location of the child he kidnapped and
killed. This "absolute" right not to be treated inhumanely "does not allow
for any exceptions or justifying factors or balancing of interests," Europe's
highest court insisted.[5]

Furthermore, Germany had not done enough to prevent other such
outrageous violations. Both police officers had been convicted and removed from their posts. But following his transfer, the Interior Department
had promoted Daschner to chief of technology. Nor had German courts
awarded Gafgen monetary compensation for the violation of his rights.
Ordinarily the European High Court would defer to the national courts'
choice of sanctions. But here, in a rare moment, the Court actually found
a particular punishment too *lenient*. Of course this "too light punishment"
label was attached not to the child killer but to the police who did what they
could to save the life of his victim! And because Germany's punishment
was too light, its ferocity at the police officers too little, its compensation to
poor Gafgen not yet tendered, the Grand Chamber perversely but officially
conferred on this murderer the label he had earned—"victim."

The court next turned its attention to Gafgen's murder conviction.
International conventions guarantee everyone a fair trial. "Torture or ill
treatment" should never yield proof of the victim's guilt. Otherwise, we

"legitimize" the police's "morally reprehensible conduct" and "afford brutality the cloak of law."[6]

Clearly the threat of torture alone had caused Gafgen to confess, which then led the police to the boy's body and Gafgen's tire tracks at the site. Only after the trial judge admitted this irrebuttable evidence of guilt over Gafgen's strenuous objection, did the killer confess again. Thus, if the absolute prohibition on torture truly banned "fruits of the poisonous tree," Gafgen's murder conviction could not stand.[7] He would be entitled to a new trial. Without the body or tire tracks, Gafgen could be convicted only on lesser charges of kidnapping, subject to a maximum of 10 years in prison.

The majority couldn't stomach this outcome. Who can blame them? So they weaseled out of their own "absolute commitment" by holding that Gafgen's "inhuman treatment," while violating the Convention on Human Rights, did not amount to torture. "Inhuman treatment falling short of torture" allowed them to consider competing interests, the court declared. Furthermore, the right to a fair trial—unlike human dignity—was not absolute.

"There is no doubt that *the victims of crime* and their families as well as the public have an interest in the prosecution and *punishment* of criminals" (emphasis added).[8] So by the court's own declaration here, the dead victim, little Jacob, separate from his closest survivors, continued to have an interest in the murderer's punishment. So true. So rarely acknowledged by courts, especially European courts. But if Gafgen's conviction really rested on tainted evidence, unconstitutionally obtained, how could it possibly stand? Here the Grand Chamber pulled off a grand fudge.

Once the trial court admitted the boy's body and Gafgen's tire tracks, Gafgen had "voluntarily" confessed again at trial. At the time, Gafgen insisted he was freely confessing from remorse and to take responsibility for his offense. That second confession alone convicted Gafgen of murder, the majority now declared. The trial court had merely used the tainted physical evidence not to prove his guilt but only to test the truth of his second, uncoerced confession. Thus, Gafgen had received a fair trial. Pure sophistry—"nonsense on stilts," in Bentham's telling phrase.[9] In less refined circles, we call it "bullshit," but necessary bullshit to keep Gafgen in prison for life.

The Grand Chamber's six dissenting judges called them on it. They would have retried Gafgen, excluding the physical evidence along with his confession! But the majority held, 11–6, that Magnus Gafgen, victim and murderer, would not get a new trial. Of course we cheer the result. But the logic and lip service to the "absolute prohibition" against inhuman treatment only weakened its effect. Obviously driven to achieve justice in the particular case, the majority had in effect overridden the general prohibition of its most Basic Law. And that's exactly what the police had done, only their motive was to save a child's life rather than serve the investigation that would lead to the killer's punishment. That's what Dr. Petit declined to do, leaving Komisarjevsky to his legal fate.

The police alone got punished for stepping outside the law in an emergency.

Actually the German public also paid a price. In April 2011, a Frankfurt state court finally awarded kidnapper and child killer Magnus Gafgen 3,000 euros ($4,250) because, as the presiding judge declared, Gafgen had suffered "serious rights violations."[10] The state must pay—some small part of every citizen's taxes would go to him. Ironically, having set out to achieve a comfortable lifestyle, Gafgen would in the end get his wish, albeit in a German prison.

35

THE CHANCE TO SOMEDAY

ALTHOUGH THE GAFGEN CASE CAUSED A FIRESTORM OF protest in Germany, grabbing headlines and the attention of the European public, somehow I had never heard of Magnus Gafgen. Few Americans had. I would never have known about him except for that invitation from the University of Heidelberg to speak at their annual symposium on "Morality and Criminal Justice."

I knew next to nothing about postwar German law, its Constitution, its values. In truth, I knew relatively little about the whole European system of criminal justice. Of course I'd heard the constant call of abolitionists and self-styled progressives for the United States to follow Europe's lead and abolish the death penalty. Rarely did they extend that call publicly to urge that we "follow Europe's lead" and also abolish life without parole. In determining the meaning of "cruel and unusual" punishment, the US Supreme Court has sharply split over whether Europe should count. When majorities in *Atkins* and then *Roper* declared the death penalty unconstitutional for all mentally retarded murderers and all those under 18 at the time of their murders, they cited abolition "by the leading members of the Western European community."[1] Justices Scalia, Thomas, and Rehnquist "rejected out of hand" counting "the subjective views of five Members of this Court and likeminded foreigners."[2] But the majority declared repeatedly that a European consensus informed, although it did not constitutionally "control," the justices' own "independent judgment."[3]

Retributive advocates of death as punishment may vigorously oppose exempting all 17-year-olds from the death penalty and yet embrace the majority's international perspective as guidance toward moral fact. Deciding moral limits to punishment, we do rightly consult the enlightened views of Europeans.

While the Court split over Europe's relevance, every Supreme Court Justice in *Roper*—majority and dissent—ignored the profound distinction between laws, treaties, and conventions officially enacted by government elites and the moral sense of the people they supposedly represent. The Justices simply morphed "international law" into "the overwhelming weight of international public opinion." Even Justice Scalia fell into the trap, equating "the *laws* of the rest of the world" with "the *views* of other countries and the so-called international community."[4]

Consult the *People* of Europe, Asia, Africa, or South America. Give them the facts of real-world cases and not a simple, distorting, abstract question such as "Do you support executing juveniles?" Ask the world community about Kenneth Loggins and Trace Duncan, whom Alabama had condemned. Both 17, Loggins and Duncan picked up Vickie Deblieux, hitchhiking to her mother's home in Louisiana. They took her to a secluded spot and, after throwing bottles at her as she tried to escape, tackled her and then kicked and stomped on her for 30 minutes. Loggins stood on Vickie's throat until she gurgled blood and then exclaimed, "Okay, I'll party." They threw Vickie into their truck, stripped her naked, and played with her lifeless body—at one point inserting a beer bottle into her vagina. When they had finished, they threw her body off a cliff. Loggins and Duncan later returned to the crime scene, further mutilating Vickie's corpse: stabbing and cutting her 180 times, removing a portion of one lung, and cutting off her fingers and thumbs.

Ask the People, here, there, and everywhere, "What do *these* two 17-year-olds deserve?" Give the "world community" the facts of these crimes and ask them to make the real choice: Keep these young monsters alive and in prison? Allow them to read, watch TV, exercise outdoors, enjoy snacks, watch movies, play basketball, and softball? Or condemn them to die and kill them? Then let's determine where lies the "overwhelming weight of international opinion."

We celebrate a teenager who dashes into a burning building to save a neighbor's children. We don't dismiss this courage and heroism as the product of a not yet fully formed personality or immature sense of invincibility. If we rightly praise our best young adults, why not condemn our worst?

I had sworn never to set foot on German soil. The rest of the world might forgive the Germans for the Third Reich; I never would. "What purpose does the criminal justice system serve?" the Heidelberg invitation read. "Is European criminal justice too lax? American criminal justice too severe? Are there moral objections to the idea of punishing people? Has criminal justice evolved away from retribution? Is there a moral obligation to punish?"

How could I refuse such an invitation to make the retributive case to German youth? I would teach classes and engage in public dialogue with Andrew Hammel, an American abolitionist, now a professor at a German university. I would confront young Germans about their nation's Nazi past. I would confront them about their pacifist present. I would urge on them a more retributive future.

A growing divide between punishment in the United States and milder treatment in continental Europe developed over centuries, as James Whitman recounts in *Harsh Justice*.[5] German prison administration traditionally protected the dignity of high-status prisoners, exempting them from painful and degrading punishments such as mutilation and flogging. Political prisoners served their time in separate "fortress prisons" where they maintained their privacy, dressed elegantly, prepared their own meals, received visitors, and expected deferential treatment by their jailors. Whitman details how Europe evolved by abolishing degrading low-status punishment, eventually elevating common criminals' prison experience to match that traditionally reserved for elites.

Adolf Hitler did time as a high-status prisoner during the Weimar Republic, and yet the Nazis campaigned against "liberal" punishment philosophy, rejecting rehabilitation and insisting primarily on deterrence but also retribution. Imprisonment, as the 1934 Nazi policy statement put it, should be "*something nasty that makes them hurt*."[6] A painful experience, prison would deter others and compel convicts to "atone for the wrong they have done." With popular backing, the Nazis insisted on a punishment philosophy consistent with "healthy popular instincts." Although Nazi courts handed down 30,000 "judicial" death sentences, their "larger machinery of human destruction" essentially "swallowed up" judicially ordered capital punishment. The Nazis entirely eliminated prisoners' rights, using prisons and concentration camps to repress and exterminate.[7]

Immediately after the war, defeated and shamed, German elites desperately sought to distance themselves from their nation's collective atrocity. Germany adopted a postwar constitution, its Basic Law, enshrining "human dignity" as *the* absolute, transcendent value, binding forever all branches of government. Their new Basic Law abolished the death penalty, making Germany the first European country to outlaw capital punishment. The German far right welcomed abolition. The Allies would hang no more Nazi war criminals and might someday release all they had already imprisoned. Postwar German liberal socialists saw the 1930s and 1940s as proof that the People, driven by emotion, would support inhumane brutality if given the chance. With concentration camps freshly haunting them, the European left, especially in Germany, rejected the National Socialist emphasis on deterrence and retribution, returning to a tradition of rehabilitation as punishment's primary purpose. They also returned to traditionally European, top-down, "rational" criminal justice policy, well insulated from popular control. Educated experts would craft criminal legislation. Corrections officers—civil servants—with considerable job security and some prestige should implement penal policy. Retribution would be no part of their mission.

Although the German Criminal Code generally called for relatively short sentences by US standards, murder still brought a sentence of life in prison based on the killer's motives and state of mind. Presumptively the court would grant parole after a lifer had served 15 years, as long as "the particular *gravity of the* convicted person's *guilt* does not require its continued execution" (emphasis added). In short, in defining the worst of the worst and specifying the length of their punishment, the German Criminal Code remained retributive.[8]

Within limits.

In 1977, the German Constitutional Court used the claim that "life is worse than death" to strike down life without parole. The Constitution, declared the Court, conceives of all "human persons as spiritual-moral beings endowed with the freedom to determine and develop themselves." No matter who they are or what they've done. "The state must regard every individual with equal worth." Each person must be allowed "to shape his own life." Of course, "every punishment must justly relate to the severity of the offense and the guilt of the offender." But the court held it "cruel, inhuman, and degrading" for the state "to deprive persons of their freedom without at least providing them with the chance to someday regain their freedom." The German Constitutional Court declared ever-milder punishments as "the wave of the future."[9]

So Germany broke with the past. Once the length of the sentence had been set, largely on retributive grounds, "resocialization" constituted the primary purpose of prison administration. Life inside for the worst of the worst would demonstrate a German focus on dignity. The new German Prison Act's strange provision, the principle of *Angleichungsgrundsatz,* or "normalcy," grates on our retributive sensibilities: "Prison life must resemble as closely as possible life in the outside world." As scholars and courts carefully worked it out, all prisoners would work for decent wages, accumulate unemployment insurance, and annually earn three or four weeks of "paid vacation"—just like ordinary citizens in the outside world. Even lifers could take vacations—inside the prison of course—but free from responsibility.[10]

Citizens expect privacy and respect. Thus, Germany largely abolished prison uniforms and cells with bars or peep holes. Guards should knock before entering, addressing prisoners respectfully at all times. Prisoners, too, had a right to conjugal visits and romantic relationships with outsiders. In summary, no matter what crime they committed, no matter how long their sentences, convicted criminals should be treated like any other citizen.

But not always. German law strictly prohibits personally insulting speech. But when prisoners accused their judges of being Nazis or called prison officials "cretins" or power hungry "perverts," the Constitutional Court gave them greater leeway before their words amounted to "gross insult." Thus, prisoners remain freer than officers or ordinary German citizens to hurl insults.

Prison administrators must protect prisoners' privacy, dignity, and autonomy. They must also enhance each prisoner's prospects of social integration, prison's primary purpose. As a prisoner began his sentence, the administrator would design a written reintegration plan. Kant famously insisted that we must never make a person a means to our ends. We must always treat him as an end in himself. The Germans take Kant to heart. Forced resocialization—we might call it "rehabilitation" in the United States—that coerces or compels a prisoner to substitute new skills and values for dysfunctional criminogenic ones seemed to violate the Basic Law's first specific guarantee: "Every person shall have the right to free development of his personality."[11] Pondering these apparently contradictory commands, German criminologists and law professors distinguished "resocialization" from "rehabilitation." Rehabilitation connotes treating and curing a sick offender, whereas resocialization signifies a neutral process that restores to offenders their law-abiding relationship to society. And lest they violate a criminal's freedom to develop as he will, academics insist that prisoner administrators must consult each prisoner in designing a resocialization plan, but the criminal may refuse to cooperate in it! Thus, the prison administration should "stimulate and encourage" prisoners but never impose or compel them to resocialize.[12]

This academic-inspired, legally codified German prison utopia ran into stiff resistance from individual German states that actually administered life inside prison. They demanded that public safety also count. But the majority of experts insisted that resocialization remain the primary if not exclusive purpose of prison. Although retributivists failed to have punishment included in the Prison Act, higher regional courts, sharing instincts that German (and many American) criminal law professors largely lack, supported administrators' refusal to release lifers convicted of "inconceivably cruel murders of Jews during the Third Reich." These courts held that the gravity of the original offense *could* continue to matter with "particularly heinous" crimes. The criminal academy protested, but a majority of the federal constitutional court supported sometimes making the past count.

The *War Criminal Case* (1986) involved a former Nazi official, 66, sentenced to life imprisonment for sending 50 people, including pregnant women and children, to the gas chambers of Auschwitz and Birkenau. Twenty-two years later, prison administrators approved that prisoner's release. But the Frankfurt Regional Court overruled them because of the atrocity of his crime. Although the constitutional court unanimously affirmed his continued imprisonment, it emphasized that the seriousness of the crime must be weighed against the human dignity of the offender and warned that as the offender ages, the past recedes as justification for imprisonment. Regional courts expanded this retributive permission to consider the gravity of the offense before release for all lifers who committed especially heinous crimes. But German academics continue to embrace resocialization as the only rational purpose of prison.[13]

Understandably nauseated by its past, and seeking the world's forgiveness and its own renewal, Germany attempted to rehabilitate itself by categorically rejecting most everything the Nazis embraced. It enshrined human dignity. The Nazis had relied on popular feeling; the new government would rely on experts' detached rationality. It abolished the death penalty, when one poll showed 77 percent of the public supported it. The Nazis had degraded whole peoples as subhuman and then set out to exterminate them in prisonlike concentration camps. Postwar Germany rejected all degrading punishment, rejected the very idea of moral inferiority or second-class human beings, insisting that even the most vicious or sadistic criminal, however dangerous, still possessed as much dignity as anybody else. Insisting that criminals and free citizens should as nearly as possible live the same lives, German criminologists rejected all status differentiation between more or less serious criminals. Desiring to be altogether forgiven, the German elite forgave all others. They sought to distance themselves from irrational passion and embraced abstract rationality, failing to recognize that ideology no less than emotion produced the Holocaust. Branded as evil, the Germans rejected the very notion of evil.[14] Desperately in need of forgiveness and rehabilitation, Germany embraced those ideals. To avoid self-hatred, it rejected hatred itself.

So I flew to Heidelberg with this awkward message: You rejected death as punishment because you killed millions of innocents. Now substituting abstraction for emotion, you look down on us retributivists. Substituting analysis for anger, conflating punishment with reward, you have assumed a new sense of superiority, all in the name of human dignity.

Germany, you overreacted.

36

A TRAMP ABROAD: HEIDELBERG

"ROB, LOOK, IT'S YOU!" MY WIFE JOLTED ME OUT OF MY stupor in the back seat, near the end of our car ride from the Frankfurt airport to Heidelberg after the overnight flight. I lazily opened one eye. There it was—a large bus stop poster bizarrely displayed my picture—*Robert Blecker Wants Me Dead*. Ted Schillinger's scrupulously fair documentary commercially premiered at the Village Cinema in Greenwich Village to mostly good reviews, although the *New York Post* critic did call me "an arrogant fool" for attempting to decide who should live and who should die: "I always thought that God, not some deluded law professor, made such decisions."[1]

How strange and exciting opening night to cradle my granddaughters, Isabella and Chloe, outside in front of that poster under the theater's marquee. How disconcerting three years later to enter a foreign city, especially one so charming as Heidelberg, only to confront again my own picture on wanted posters at the outskirts of town.

The next morning, I met with Professor Gerhard Dannecker before appearing at his class. The Professor assured me that while the German academy largely rejected retribution, some supporters remained, mostly in hiding until they achieved full professor status. That night the German-American Society aired the documentary, setting out 75 chairs for the anticipated audience, then another 75 as people poured in, and another, and another, until several hundred people packed the room that officially held 500. Some sat on the floor and on radiators, others turned away at the door. What a startling contrast to nearly empty theaters in the States! But here students had a rare opportunity to hear the other side, largely forbidden among the German educated elite.

The next day I visited the prison in Heidelberg, literally a stone's throw from town. A prisoner's crime, the officer in charge explained, had no bearing here. No surprise. That day's meal, prepared in the prison's modern kitchen—pork steak, red cabbage, potatoes—sounded good, unless of course you were a vegetarian. But vegetarians had their own menu. For the rest, meat four times a week, fish on Friday. Officers ate the same food as the prisoners. Furthermore, my host boasted, the prison adhered to the strictest hygienic standards, "better than fine restaurants." Here, as in maximum security prisons, prisoners had flat-screen TVs in their cells, with remote control and a PlayStation.

In Germany today, in order to keep medical costs in line, specialists operate within a strict budget for ordering or conducting sophisticated tests and procedures. When a physician exhausts that month's budget, patients must wait. Delay, of course, may endanger your health. But everybody waits. Except prisoners. When doctors treat inmates, the sky's the limit; no budgets constrain them. So violating the principle of "normalcy," prisoners get *better* medical care than ordinary citizens, with a better doctor/patient ratio than in the outside world. Got a serious medical problem in Germany? Take the penalty.

My guide surprised me, describing the maximum security prison he'd recently left after 30 years. Lifers there did live differently than other prisoners: "They have a larger cell, since they will be here for a longer time." And they worked better jobs—cleaning offices, cooking and handling food, or acting as shop foremen. Of course not every officer met every ideal of prison administration. "We know we should knock before entering," he confessed, "but it's not always done." I noticed an ashtray in a prisoner's room of this no-smoking facility. "You wouldn't tell a person he can't smoke in his own bedroom. We do not look upon him as a prisoner, but as a man who needs help," my host summed it up. "The length of the sentence expresses the evil of the crime. It's not my job to add to his punishment; my job is to help him live afterwards. I have sworn an oath to the German Constitution. Besides, it would only make my life harder to make his life harder."

I went directly from the prison to meet with three distinguished German criminal law professors. My host shared his latest meta-study of deterrence studies, full of statistics and far removed from the reality of crime or punishment. These academics seemed mystified that a criminal law professor would actually visit a prison. What could that experience possibly teach me about the theory of criminal law? Our time together felt formal but polite. Their sense of human dignity seemed so abstract. "You must think me primitive," I said before our meeting broke up. The long embarrassed silence confirmed it. "I hope by the time you visit next, your views have changed," declared my host. Professor Marcus Englerth, who accompanied me and would moderate my public dialogue the next day, also sensed their disdain. I felt much more at home among the German students.

The next morning's class, a mixed graduate/undergraduate constitutional law course, stirred up deep emotions. Students there, like students most everywhere, hadn't done their homework and weren't prepared to discuss assigned excerpts from my writing. "Alright, then, let's talk about Gafgen," I suggested, attacking the Grand Chamber's opinion as "indefensible." Better to kill a million children than threaten a kidnapper with torture? Were they serious? "The police did the right thing," I insisted.

"What about Gafgen's human dignity," a German youth protested. I smiled inwardly. Here was the moment. I flashed back to war movies and wished that somehow all those Nazis in hell could witness this Jewish American retributivist engaging their grandchildren in the classroom on their home soil. "You advocate the police to violate his human dignity?" the student persisted.

"Whatever dignity a child killer may possess surely yields to the dignity of the child he has kidnapped and killed," I countered. "We are not all equal, not all equally worthy of concern and respect. We show our healthy respect for human dignity by doing what we can to save that child's life, even at the cost of threatening to torture his kidnapper." Dozens of students vigorously knocked on their desks—a German signal of approval. It startled me, this sound that rose and crested, but continued, then died out. "Many of you apparently agree. But let's count the other side. Who believes the police violated Gafgen's dignity and should be punished? Who would spare Gafgen from being convicted and punished as a murderer?" Many youths banged on their desks. But we had the clear majority. After class, several students thanked me for expressing opinions they had never heard spoken openly in public, especially by a professor. Others vigorously disagreed. We pledged to continue our conversation.

I opened that afternoon's public dialogue with Professor Andrew Hammel by briefly explaining and advocating retribution, distinguishing it from revenge and relating a criminal's moral blameworthiness to the punishment he deserves. "The past counts," I insisted.

The European criminal justice system "won't give up on anyone," Hammel replied, characterizing the "German approach," unlike mine, as forward-looking, "noble and inspiring," "profoundly hopeful—you could also call it naïve."

"In the US, rehabilitation has become a terrible failure," I replied, citing Itchy's observation that lessons you learn in 25 years inside prison, you forget in 25 days on the street. But "our main difference," I explained to the audience, "lies in how to deal with those people who have done incredibly vicious things"—those people who should never be released, "whose human dignity" Europe and Hammel were so concerned with promoting. We hear about Europe's "mild system of punishment, its humane system of punishment." But was it justice?

Anders Breivik killed 77 people—hunted them down and killed them. First Breivik set off a bomb at Oslo's government district, killing eight. Then he opened fire at the summer camp of the governing Labor Party's youth wing, stalking and killing another 69 victims mostly in their teens and early 20s. Breivik killed them, he insisted, to help resist political parties that welcomed Muslim immigrants.

Under Norwegian law, "Breivik faces a maximum of 21 years in prison," I reminded the German audience. "How humane, how dignified," I dripped sarcasm. "If someone murders children, if somebody methodically hunts down and kills 80 people, I *feel certain*—not just rationally, but *really* certain—that he deserves to be in prison for the rest of his life if we do not kill him. He should never be free. I don't care who he becomes. We make a covenant with the past. He shall never be free again. And while he lives out his life in prison, he should not be watching flat-screen color television, treated to delicious food, contact visits, and playing sports with his guards.

"If you don't understand this, if you don't feel this, if your intuitions don't tell you this, I can never persuade you. But my suspicion—more than a few of you feel certain I am right. Your culture cannot shame you out of feeling those feelings. But the elites in German society have shamed the people out of expressing their true feelings, have suppressed those feelings, and devised a prison system in which the quality of life inside, for the worst of the worst, is simply unjust." Apparently the audience applauded more vigorously than pleased the videographer. The posted YouTube version cuts off applause here—and once again later—obscuring communal support for retribution.

A *Time* magazine article detailed life inside Norway's newest prison: "The facility boasts amenities like a sound studio, jogging trails and a free-standing two-bedroom house" for inmates' overnight visits. "The most important thing is that the prison looks as much like the outside world as possible," its architect explained.[2] Thus, trees obscured the 20-foot security wall, whose top had been rounded off. "The cells rivaled well-appointed college dorm rooms, with their flat-screen TVs and mini-fridges. Every 10 to 12 cells share a living room and kitchen." The good news: Breivik wouldn't end up in that community setting, a Norwegian newspaper reported. Fearing for his safety, authorities intended to keep him segregated from other inmates. But heaven forbid this mass murderer feel lonely. "We are planning a professional community around him," declared the prison director.³ "Together they would play chess and volleyball. In Germany you're not allowed to say, 'I personally think Breivik should be strung up from a tree,'" Andrew Hammel candidly admitted in response. "I think he deserves to die—metaphysically," he continued. "He's about the guiltiest criminal ever. Only I don't think the state has a right to kill him. [Applause] I just don't trust the state enough to do that. It's really hard because Breivik is so heinous. But we're not going to sink to his level. We protect his human dignity not for his sake but our sake. We treat him better than he deserves because of what it says about us as a society, about our ability to overcome these completely understandable and natural feelings of vengeance and hatred.

"If you have a set of principles by which society operates, then they are going to be tested by cases like Anders Breivik," Hammel continued. "And that is where, as we say in America, the rubber meets the road. Why do a majority of Norwegians accept the fact that Breivik will go to a relatively luxurious prison life for only 21 years? Because their culture has reduced their instinct for violent retribution or cruel punishment." (I would substitute "dulled their instinct for justice," but I let it pass.)

"That is a sign of growth and cultural maturity," Hammel continued. "So although I have nothing but contempt for Breivik, I'm actually proud that Norway has stayed its hand." Once again, vigorous applause greeted him.

"I accept the accusation that Germany, from a retributive perspective, underpunishes people," Hammel continued later in the same vein. "I would rather a state gives people less punishment than they deserve than routinely give people more punishment than they deserve. So I'm OK with the German public's will for revenge, or retribution not fully realized. Sixty-five to 70 percent of Germans themselves say their criminal justice system is too lenient. And I accept that democratic deficit—that failure to reflect the will of the people—as an appropriate price to pay for having a humane criminal justice system."

"We *should* err on the side of innocence and human dignity," I agreed. "Our very harshest punishments, such as the death penalty or life without parole, should require a higher burden of persuasion than ordinary punishments." And I urged on this German audience the now familiar "no residual doubt of guilt combined with an intuitive non-rational moral certainty that he should die." "But I am certain, as a human being who happens to be a retributivist," that somebody who methodically murders dozens of children and young adults "should not live a life thereafter, day to day, that resembles as nearly as possible the life he would lead were he free and blameless."

"What would your idea of an appropriate punishment be?" Hammel challenged.

I ticked off nutraloaf and outlined permanent punitive segregation for Breivik or Gafgen. "Life should be unpleasant, forever."

"If we are all influenced by society and educated by everyone around us," an audience member challenged, "how can we determine how much responsibility we have for what we do, and how much responsibility society has for what this person does?"

"That's the right question. We've been wrestling with this for centuries. From a strictly scientific perspective, we are all caused to do what we do. And punishment merely testifies to our present ignorance. Once we get more sophisticated, we may understand why every criminal committed every crime. Punishing him, hurting him will become a primitive vestige," I conceded to the Heidelberg audience. "On the other hand, you all sit here—I don't believe you believe your biological predisposition and your upbringing have drawn and driven you to this spot. That at this moment you are incapable of being anywhere else or doing anything else.

"If we all are caused and not responsible, then punishment disappears. But notice what else disappears with it. We cannot justify celebrating great achievement. That too becomes a function of biological predisposition, psychological formation, etc., etc. But the German Basic Law itself guarantees the right of individual choice in personality development. Kant declared it life's great paradox—to accept that we are all subject to the laws of nature and science, caused to do what we do. And at the same time, but in a different sense, we freely willing agents author our own behavior. So we do punish vicious criminals. But of course, we must pour our resources back into inner-city schools, keeping them open 24/7, providing good meals, good counseling, places of refuge for these kids to escape from a deforming environment inflicted on them that they never chose." Swat the mosquitos but drain the swamp. "If that seems paradoxical to you," I insisted at Heidelberg and still do, "it is."

"The stereotype—and I like stereotypes, they're time savers," Hammel followed up: "An American sees a homeless disheveled person with a shopping cart full of rags and says, 'What's wrong with that person?' A European sees that person and asks, 'What's wrong with us?'"

The moderator, Markus Englerth, returned to Gafgen, turning the tables on Hammel. "What would *you* consider appropriate punishment? How much longer should we imprison him? He has converted to Christianity. He's written a book, *Alone with God*. He's showing utter remorse. If he's been rehabilitated already, how much longer should we keep him?"

"He's in prison for 25 years. That's what a special life sentence for a particularly grave crime means in Germany," Hammel replied. "That's a reasonable punishment for his disgusting and vicious, greed-motivated crime." Spoken like a retributivist. But if he truly reforms, why keep Gafgen one moment beyond the need for public safety or social reintegration? No sooner had Hammel's anger surfaced than he suppressed it. "Many prisoners turn to God to get a chance at early release. But I've met many prisoners who I think have made a thoroughly sincere transformation. And that is a complete and utter victory for society. Because society has reclaimed a human being and brought him back into the fold. Exactly what a criminal justice system should aspire to. After Gafgen serves his 25 years, he should be able to rejoin society. A win-win situation and the system working at its best."

37

RIGHT BODY,
WRONG PERSON

THE OTHERS HAD SPOKEN OF GAFGEN'S APPARENT RE-
morse and transformation. Twenty-five years listening to convicted killers
and officers have sensitized me to the difference between remorse and regret. Almost always, well into a life sentence, a convicted killer feels regret.
He comes to understand his own life as wasted in prison. He comes to regret
the effect on his family, who must watch him grow old inside. That's regret.
That's not remorse.

Should it matter whether the killer regrets his own "mistake"? Does
his sorrow make him less deserve to die? Should it move us to free him any
sooner? Utilitarians count a killer's regret, if only to predict his diminished
dangerousness. Those who do not regret what they did remain more likely to
do it again. But we retributivists care, if at all, only about his feelings toward
his victim, as we act on our own. Long ago this civilization abandoned the
belief that an offending limb or weapon deserved its own punishment. We
would not extinguish or permanently banish the finger that squeezed the
trigger, but rather the selfish cruel personality that directed the finger to
squeeze the trigger and laughed as the victims begged for mercy. Today we
condemn the *person* to death or to life without parole. The body gives us the
only way to get to that soul.

He may no longer be a threat. But that's hardly a reason to spare or
release him. A sadistic killer lies completely and permanently paralyzed—
dependent on our care and medicine, docile, bordering on inert. The helpless body of this vicious killer poses no conceivable threat to anybody. Should
we spare this shattered frame while the vicious person still lives, seething,

within it? As Kant said, we honor his humanity. We put him on trial and punish him.

But suppose the aggravated murderer poses less danger now because he has "learned his lesson"? Suppose by the time of his sentencing, the killer really regrets the killing? Genuine regret—"I was wrong in doing this"—may mean no more than "I did it wrong, inefficiently, unnecessarily." Or "it wasn't worth it." Suppose by living the nightmare that society imagines prison to be, this terrified, condemned, or permanently caged killer acquires a healthy respect for the law, which he will demonstrate, as Itchy explained, "by staying out of its way."

A vicious killer, now more skillful and wary, hardly gives us reason to suffer him to live, much less live free. The retributivist emphatically denies any relevance of this "regret." We can only hate him less—perhaps enough to let him live or free him—if we are assured he has come to hate himself more. We need the killer not only to regret his past mistake; we need him to feel genuine remorse.

Inside Lorton prison, prisoners opened up to me. I found many who truly regretted their killing. It simply wasn't worth it. But I also found genuine remorse among convicted killers, sometimes for murders no one knew they had committed. Reginald B., a naïve, patriotic kid sent to Vietnam, found himself in combat after only three days of in-country training.

"All this shit is going off around—boom, dtdtdtdtdtdtdt!—all the small arms fire, grenades. I urinated on myself. I was just that scared. And later on when all the commotion was over with, a guy in my company came over to me. 'I pissed on myself; can I get another pair of pants?' I asked him. I'm green, I don't know.

"'No, you stuck with them pants till we go back in.' When we finally go back in, I'm still shaking. The brother took me under his wing. He gave me a pill. 'This make you feel alright.' So after a few minutes I start mellowing out. They call it Benactol. And from Benactol I graduated to reefer, and hash, and opium, and then a brother out of California gave me some heroin. And that was the top of the line drug for me.

"You had to numb yourself, with all the shit that's happening around you, man. You're sitting around and your buddy showing you pictures of his baby, letters from his old lady. Turn around to reach for your canteen; you turn back and his brains is in your lap. And then when you come in from the bush, you don't know who's who. You sitting at the bar drinking, it could be a girl bringing you the next drink with a grenade. There wasn't no clear lines. The whole goddamn place was a war zone. Going through these things, every day, every hour, every second, you had to numb yourself.

"I think every GI got his own personal My Lai. We been out in the jungle for 18 days. I ain't changed clothes in that time; had no water to wash my body. It's hot as a motherfucker. And we're sweeping an area, looking for a ranger team that supposed to have reported in, three or four days prior. I'm in tall elephant grass, breaking this goddamn bush. And I come into a clearing. When I start stepping, I feel something squishy up under my boots. I look down. Here in six little neat piles are human innards. You know, the intestinal tract, the hearts, in six little neat piles. This is Charlie's sign saying, 'This is your people.' This squishy fucking feeling, to step in and smell that—

"When we get back to the firebase, we had a three day stand-down. Usually, the hootch girl, Mama Sang, who come in to clean up, bring our dope. This particular day Mama Sang don't come in. So now we got to go down the hill, to a little town they got set up down there to serve the GIs. Beer, pussy, dope, whatever.

"So I go down there. I'm pointed to a kid. And I go up to him. And I got this beard on my face and I'm stinking. I got a problem, and I got my .45 on my hip. I just want my dope and go on back. So I say, 'Boy Sang, you got cum sa?,' which means 'You got some dope?'

"'No, no GI. No got cum sa, me not got cum sa!'

"So I say, 'You telling a lie.' I take my hand out of my pocket. Show him I got a lot of money. I ain't coming to take his dope. We carry on this conversation for less than five minutes. I'm getting pissed off at this little motherfucker. Why he won't sell me this dope? Ain't nobody out here, but some Vietnamese. Other soldiers, they going back up the hill to camp. So I grabbed him in the collar, and take him into some bushes. And I throw him on the goddamned ground. I pull out my .45. 'You give me cum sa!'

"Boy Sang crawl up to me and grab me around the knees. And he's holding me, crying, and running off in Vietnamese—I don't know what the fuck he's saying. He's begging me for his life. So I cocked my .45 and I put it right at the front of his forehead. 'Me no got cum sa.' He's crying. But I'm thinking about the guts that I stepped on out there, all the rest of this shit. It don't justify what I'm preparing to do, but it all came into play. 'No got cum sa.' Lying his little ass off. I blow his motherfucking head off. And walk away. Don't give one second thought about it. He's a kid; maybe 12 years old. I mean that .45 exploded him.

"I can't get away from it, even to this day—shooting that little Vietnamese boy, just because I could. No other reason. Just because I could. Wouldn't nobody say nothing about it. There are a lot of things I want to bury in my subconscious and have it stay there. That's the number one thing I wish I could erase."

Most of those who genuinely regret their killing refuse to dwell on it, insisting they've learned from their mistakes and are ready to move on. "Since I done it, I ain't going to cry," explained Anthony C. "I mean it ain't no sense crying over spilt milk," Joe W. agreed. "I don't regret what I've done because I can't change it," said Tyrell B. "I can't push back the hands of time. But I can learn." European criminologists support this attitude as constructive and appropriate: Learn your lessons, don't repeat your mistakes—socially reintegrate. To the forward-looking cost/benefit set, our retributive irrational covenant with the past to justify punishment seems pointless and cruel. Besides, psychopaths incapable of true empathy— glib chameleons who readily inflict great pain on others to avoid the slightest discomfort to themselves—can display remorse on demand. They simply fake it. Society has always treated its hypocrites more gently than its revolutionaries. Except for suicide, how can we rely on outward signs of remorse?

Can a person's will to live make him deserve to die? And why should we care how the killer feels *now* about his own actions and attitudes back then if we really condemn and punish the *person* who killed? After decades in prison, older murderers disavow their detested youthful bodies and selves. Eventually a certain comfort and relief accompanies their sense of metamorphosis.

"I am so glad I am no longer that person," Homer Berwell told me. "I have killed, and I know what it is. The death of your adversary will not satisfy your hatred. Christ said you can pay it off in love," said Burwell, a Lorton prisoner in his late 70s serving out a life sentence. "If I had to now, I'd rather be killed than kill."

Sometimes it's easy to keep detesting these killers into their old age. The media helps America renew its Charles Manson hatred and fascination every few years when he comes up for parole, taunting the public with those frenzied eyes and that swastika carved into his forehead. It keeps fresh our outrage at the ritualistic killings he commanded. When producers at A&E interviewed me for their remake of the 1995 Manson *Biography* and a new *Manson Women* bio, it felt mildly satisfying to call Manson "scum and pure evil" to the camera, although they'd probably cut that—only they kept it in the documentary remake that aired on the Biography Channel. "Nobody is born evil," psychologist Barbara Kirwin insisted in this documentary. "Evil is a long time in the making."[1] Assuming evil does exist, and she conceded it did, are we certain no baby already possesses a genetic predisposition to cruelty, sadism, callousness? Some young children raised by loving parents seem inexplicably to display a cruel viciousness that makes us shudder.[2] How ambiguous to declare, "It's not their fault."

Charles Manson made it easy to keep hating. The teenagers who killed for him posed a more complicated problem and resulted in a delayed but more complex documentary. Thirty years later, Leslie van Houten and Patricia Krenwinkel, soft-spoken, intelligent women, fully owned up to their despicable past and seemed thoroughly remorseful. Their many good deeds over four decades in prison attest to their genuine transformation.

One part of us simply condemns them without reservation—how could they have surrendered themselves to Manson's control and kill perfect strangers? "I came of age in the late '60s—sex, drugs, rock and roll. And we were searching. Searching for people who seemed sure. And Manson seemed to be sure," the documentary has me insisting. "Do these women really regret what they did? Are they transformed people?" It seemed so with Van Houten and Krenwinkel. When the California Supreme Court declared the death penalty unconstitutionally cruel and commuted the women's sentences to life, Van Houten explained, they began to face their crimes. Periodically they went before parole boards, and routinely those boards denied parole—in Van Houten's case, in June 2013 for the twentieth time. Susan Atkins, another member of Manson's "family," suffering from terminal brain cancer and expecting to die within months, petitioned for compassionate release. The parole board denied it, and she died in prison.

"Rehabilitation is rare—it's real but it's rare," I declared in the documentary. "I've done my best to carry myself and live my life in a way that other people aren't harmed," Leslie van Houten declared truthfully, and with quiet, understated dignity.[3] So what's the solution, or proper resolution? "We cannot and should not forget the past," my voice intones over the women's pictures and closing credits. "The victims' blood cries out to us. And it always will."

Searching for genuine remorse among convicted killers these decades, I found it rare but real. Wayne M., 25, had run away from home with a buddy ten years earlier, then run out of money, and found himself with his friend's gun in his hand, failing twice to summon the nerve to rob. On the third attempt, he recalled, "I went to a car, stuck the gun through the window. I never held a gun before that night. I'm shaking, trembling, sweating. Before I could even get words out my mouth, the gun went off! I stood there in shock. Because, oh my God! It was never supposed to happen like that. Shocked because I had just talked to my mother and she said, 'Just tell me where you're at; I'm coming to get you.' But my own pride, my own arrogance—'I'll find my own way home.'

"So the gun went off and I'm standing there and could not believe what happened. But it was real. He died 48 hours later. I think about how much did he suffer? Because we put him out of the car on the street. And we drove off." Wayne fled back home to Delaware, where he was arrested, extradited, and charged as an adult. With his codefendant prepared to testify against him, he pled guilty to second-degree murder.

Of course Wayne regretted his murder from the moment the gun fired. But he didn't focus much on his victim until that next September when the anniversary approached. "I started waking up three in the morning, sweating. I would wake up from the dream where he was in it, asking me one question, 'Why me?' Every night. I can't live with myself for what I've done. Disbelief. Shock. Fear. I thought so much about who he was. Didn't know. Don't know.

"I saw my own death in his face. I looked in his eyes; they were glossy, watery. And that same question always. 'Why me?' I can see in his eyes the mystery, the knowing, the confusion, the concern—why me? All these years I haven't been able to answer." Wayne gulped.

I waited, wanting to hear more. But all I saw were his moistened eyes. He had drifted. "So you woke up that September 12 and it hit you? What were you feeling?"

"Uncontrollable remorse. That the only way I would live with myself is kill myself. The only way that this crime will ever be equated is if I died too. That if I took my life, then I could say on a silver platter to his family, 'Is this enough to make you understand that I am sorry?' Within a week I tried. Dynatabs. They put you to sleep. I had about 30 of them, took all them at once."

"What's the last thing you thought about right before you took them?"

"That the only thing I could do to compensate his family was take my life. Nothing else could be said; no time could be served. Took me 20, 30 minutes to go out."

"What did you focus on?"

"Death. Seeing him after. Getting to know him. Tell him I'm sorry. They tell me I had an asthma attack and went into convulsions and that's what alerted people. They rushed me to the hospital, pumped me out with charcoal. I'm sitting there in that hospital bed, with that tube running down my mouth, getting ready to go back to the DC jail. 'Damn, damn, damn! Why me? Why did I live? Why can't I die?' Then I find out later that those who commit suicide don't go up to heaven."

Wayne's real remorse moved him to join his dead victim. But he lived to tell of it. The retributivist demands the remorse be not only real but also sustained. "The anniversary of his death I honor every year. I don't eat; I don't work. I don't talk to nobody. I don't do anything. I just think about him. People that's locked up with me say, 'You're crazy, man.' I just look at it as trying to find answers to something that I done.

"But I can't bring him back," Wayne said with anguish. "I can't talk to him. If you don't know him you really can't get familiar with him. I don't know him to love him. I don't know him to respect him. I don't know him to understand him. I try." He paused, tears rolling down his cheeks now. "I look at that day as a day of remembrance, a day of reaffirming that I'll never do nothing like that again. In my mind I have a conversation with him."

"What does he say?"

"The same question always. 'Why did you do it? Why me?'"

If we do allow a killer's remorse to incline us to mercy, unpleasant facts intrude. Studying and listening to convicted killers for years, I've learned that while remorse cannot be forced, it can easily be faked. Prisoners preparing to go before parole boards rehearsed for me their "remorseful" selves, carefully constructed and completely phony. And those who do genuinely feel it may find themselves unable to express it. Wayne eventually went before the parole board. When they asked him how he felt about the crime, he sat there, unable to speak. "It felt like I had an asthma attack. Gasping for breath and words. Leaving myself dumbfounded. Not knowing what to say, but knowing what I feel. Every word I had thought about saying lost me. I answered with a handful of tears." The parole board turned down his bid for freedom. "They gave me a five-year hit. Come see them in two thousand something."

I wonder where he is today.

A truly remorseful killer fully absorbs his own offense, not only its consequences to himself but also to the victim and the surviving family. Genuine remorse demands deep and abiding pain, every day he lives. Self-loathing should set in. He should turn on himself, detesting his own villainy, relieving his self-hatred only through self-annihilation. Perhaps these suicides end it well, no longer bad enough for us to kill or good enough to live.

But a person can be eradicated in different ways.

After decades of appeals and delays, we may commit yet another kind of mistake: Having rightly convicted and sentenced a killer to die, we may wrongly kill him, falling prey to mistaken identity in the deepest sense. I had pondered this in 1998 when an international media storm broke as Texas prepared to execute Karla Faye Tucker. Fifteen years earlier, 23-year-old Karla Faye, while high on drugs, brutally murdered two victims with a pickax. She felt a sexual rush, she admitted, while she gouged the flesh from her first victim.[4]

Then she embedded the pickax in the chest of her second victim, a terrified witness hiding under the bed covers. In the 15 years since her horrific murders, Karla Faye claimed to have found Christ. And she never lost her good looks. All cultures, probably, associate beauty with goodness: "The hand that hath made you fair hath made you good," declares Shakespeare's Duke.[5]

Would Texas execute this born-again Christian beauty? Almost everyone wanted to believe in her transformation, including me. "We may be killing an innocent person," I declared on TV. "The person Texas would kill has long since escaped. Right body; wrong person." I felt unexpected warmth from the host, until I added, "So the lesson we learn from this: Kill her quickly while she still deserves it, before she has had time to escape."

The Supreme Court rightly forbids us to execute a murderer simply to incapacitate him. Society can construct escape-proof prisons that will reliably confine them. But if we wait too long, we cannot prevent the *persons* of the prisoners from escaping the bodies we still confine. A personality transformed replaces the one we failed to kill. By the time we do execute him, or decades later when we still keep him caged and try to punish him, it is too late. We can only inflict the pain of death or life on a different person than the one who, decades before, squeezed the trigger and laughed. By delaying too long, we allow the selfish, heartless, vicious, cruel, sadistic killer to escape justice. We substitute an older look-alike to receive our punishment and become his dead-double. There's metaphor in this, but then science can never fully account for a "person."

"Remorse is relatively rare," I insisted to the German youth in Heidelberg. "It can easily be faked, and it can never be forced." But however rare, it can be real.

Much later that night, at a student party in a relaxed setting, German students approached me. Now I reversed roles in our Q&A. "What did your parents and grandparents teach you about the Holocaust?" I asked. "What did they say at the kitchen?"

"Mostly they avoided it. Or they blamed it on others," several students agreed. But two youths told it differently. "Before she died, my grandmother gave me a present she had hidden from the family in a small box. It was a medal. She was a nurse and saved some people after a bombing raid." She paused. "So the Nazis gave her this medal. As a hero of the Third Reich. She was so proud, but she was also deeply ashamed. She wanted to destroy it, but she couldn't. And she gave it to me before she died. I still have it."

"How do you feel about it?"

"Proud. And ashamed, like her."

In an inverted way, we retributive advocates of the death penalty or PPS should feel our own kind of ambivalence. Proud that we still care about justice, proud that we keep covenants with the past, and yet a little ashamed that we feel satisfaction, however deserved, at the pain and suffering we would cause another human being.

"My grandfather was a high-ranking SS officer," another student confided in me. "My parents say they didn't know it. But he had a special tattoo. They knew his brother ranked high in the SS. After the war, my great uncle fled to Chile. My grandfather admitted he was a member of the party, but he had to be to practice his profession as a pharmacist. But then, a few years later, he too fled to Chile."

"Do you feel responsible?" She shrugged. "How do you feel about being German?"

"We're taught not to *feel* German. We're European. We don't wave the German flag at football games."

"I wish the world would stop looking at us as Nazis," another youth protested. "It wasn't me. I didn't kill the Jews. My grandparents—my great-grandparents, perhaps. But not me, not my friends here, not our generation. We are not guilty. We were not responsible. I mean we *all* have responsibility to make certain that genocide never happens. Everybody," he insisted and repeated it later in an email. "We, Germans, have greater sensitivity, yes. But no greater responsibility."

A couple of students approached me, tentatively. "Can we ask you a question? Did you mean what you said, today at the end? Did you really mean it?"

I did. As our public dialogue concluded, the moderator asked me for a one-minute closing statement. I had no idea what to say. But words streamed from my lips with a life of their own. All these weeks preparing, saturating myself in a different way of seeing the world, then these last few days with German youth led me to close by making a statement I would never have thought possible: "I grew up knowing and believing from my parents (and not even understanding what I was knowing and believing) that this evil, vicious person Adolf Hitler deserved to die. The question since then has been, Who else? I believed the German people were evil. I've come to Germany and seen a people who felt guilt. Asked the world to accept them, allow them to make a clean break with the past. Prove they had a much better value system than what [their nation] perpetrated on the world. And so I close after my visit here, hoping the debate continues about punishment. I hope you give the retributive perspective its due. But I also hope there always remains disagreement, always serious resistance not only to the death penalty but to retributive instincts. And I cannot imagine a people who I would more want, and more trust to make that argument on behalf of human dignity, on behalf of rehabilitation now, than you."

38

THE UGLY MIRROR

AFTER MAKING MY PEACE WITH A LIVING FRAGMENT OF German youth and before returning to the United States, I visited a site of the dead, the memorial constructed at an equal opportunity hell—the German concentration camp at Flossenburg. "Work shall make you free," the famously cynical Nazi slogan on the stone pillars greeted prisoners as they entered the gate. Flossenburg prisoners, barely clothed, worked as slave laborers in nearby quarries. At the end of a grueling day, prisoners carried back to camp the bodies of their weaker colleagues, fellow prisoners literally worked to death. This relentless, backbreaking labor—hauling stone twelve hours a day six days a week, in every weather, with a single break for a bowl of thin soup and perhaps a few scraps of bread—killed thousands. Photographs of the camp and oral testimony of survivors reveal to us visitors, decades later, the brutal regime of this SS work camp, operating according to its mission statement: These prisoners would be "annihilated by work."[1]

Annihilated by work. Here, no metaphor necessary: death by prison.

The Republic of Germany maintains this memorial to cruelty, acknowledging a national inhumanity: "Violence permeated every aspect of the camp and determined daily life for prisoners," declares explanatory copy, highlighting horrific photos. "The SS harassed and humiliated inmates, and subjected them to constant and indiscriminate violence. This arbitrariness heightened the inmates' feelings of powerlessness." Sadistic guards forced prisoners to stand rigidly at attention, betting on who would fall down dead first, or collapse and be killed, our guide explained. Flossenburg initially housed prisoners of war or political prisoners, along with some common criminals formally tried and sentenced. Once the Jews swelled the ranks, the SS took special pleasure at inventing new games, a guide informed children on a school trip to the site. "Guards forced groups of prisoners to dash across a yard to a far wall. The winner might receive an extra crust of bread. The loser would be torn to pieces by the guard dogs. This amusement efficiently separated the most and least fit to work."

In January 1941, when nearly 600 Polish prisoners arrived from Auschwitz, Flossenburg's mission moved beyond supplying stone to aid in the war effort. The next month, "the SS began targeted annihilation of this group." After the evening roll call, guards brought prisoners selected for execution to the detention barrack, where they spent their final night. The following morning, the execution commando shot and killed them next to the crematorium. "In programmatic fashion, the SS murdered Polish concentration camp inmates, foreign forced laborers, Soviet prisoners of war, the elderly, sick, and infirm."

As the pace of executions increased, the single crematorium couldn't dispose of the dead. So the SS stacked the bodies, doused them in gasoline, and burned them. (At least they reserved their gasoline for their dead victims. Hayes and Komisarjevsky torched the Petit children alive.) Many prisoners condemned to death at Flossenburg awaited their fate in "the Bunker"—a makeshift death row—alone in dark rooms, with no food for days until the SS killed them. Flossenburg, like most prisons, also had a "punitive segregation" building where the SS inflicted special punishments on those who violated prison rules. Here, the Nazis starved and "abused" their prisoners—the memorial mercifully left the precise abuse to the imagination.

Flossenburg also housed high-status prisoners. The SS hanged leading members of the German Resistance there, including Pastor Dietrich Bonhoeffer, one of the few Protestant theologians who actively opposed National Socialism from the beginning, along with Major General Hans Oster, who led the failed plot to assassinate Hitler in 1944. Their "trials" included no witnesses, no defense, and no formal record for appeal. Otto Thorbeck, the reliable Nazi judge, sentenced them to death; the SS hanged them at Flossenburg the next day. After the war, Thorbeck practiced law in Nuremberg. In 1955, a German court convicted him for assisting in murder and sentenced him to four years in prison, but two years later, the federal constitutional court reversed the conviction, holding the Nazi regime had the "legal" right to execute "traitors."

The Sophists won that one.

Although the Nazis formally executed 1,500 death sentences at the camp, the vast majority of the 30,000 prisoners who died at Flossenburg— men, women, and children—died by degree, "one day at a time," from disease, starvation, or exhaustion, as the population swelled to more than 15,000.

"One thousand men in 200 beds. Murder and whips—hunger our constant companions," a survivor wrote at the time. "More than 100 people die every day—perishing in the lavatories on the concrete, or on the ground outdoors. Never before has humanity been forced to endure so much suffering as here—terror—beatings—mental and physical anguish. But stay strong—time has almost run out for the guilty and their crimes."

"Hundreds were responsible for the crimes committed at the Flossenburg concentration camps," the memorial's text declared. "But only a few were charged and convicted of their crimes." The German postwar government began a reparations process, inviting survivors to seek compensation. "How can I accept money for the death of my father?" one survivor asked me and any other visitor who pushed the button to listen to his plea. "I need the assistance. I'm not afraid to say that I do need it. But how can I say that my father was worth this much?" Today, abolitionists extol the virtue of "life in prison *plus* restitution to the victim's family." Do they realize the emotional toll it takes to receive support and perversely feel grateful for "compensation" from the killer? This anguished survivor, who would not profit from his father's extermination, concluded my time inside the memorial, which was closing for the day.

Outdoors, I walked among the victims' graves grouped by nationality and religion, staring at Flossenburg's crematorium, the dissection table, walking the execution grounds, conjuring up photos of skeletons in rags with stripes, of survivors recounting their tortures, in their native German, Polish, Czech, or Russian with a quiet English voice-over, and like most other visitors, tears stung my eyes. I burned with anger and cried for those poor, suffering dead souls.

Was it any wonder that post-war Germany, liberated from their collective sadism or brutal indifference, now instituted a new regime, including prisons with good food, medical care, modest labor optional, and recreation? Having crammed thousands into cramped barracks designed for one-tenth that number, do we now wonder why the Germans insist on prisons with single, spacious cells? Having once inflicted sadistic guards to humiliate the prisoners, is it surprising they now demand prisons that never degrade the people they house? I detested what Germany had been and greatly admired this nation, 70 years later, for presenting the unvarnished horror to their school children and the world so they would witness and remember.

Flossenburg acted as my ugly mirror, reinforcing several lessons during my 25 years searching for justice. Today's European and American criminal justice systems largely sever crime from punishment. The Nazis did too. The vast majority of prisoners they humiliated and killed were never formally charged, convicted, or sentenced to prison or death. The Nazis mostly punished their victims for who they were, not what they'd done.

To make greater sense of Flossenburg, I read Victor Frankl's *Man's Search for Meaning*, which recounted this Adlerian psychoanalyst's own experience as a prisoner in the camps. Frankl's account detailed the arbitrariness of life and death in the prisons. Guards quickly sorted new arrivals, making snap judgments. Those incapable of working, Frankl recalled—the sick and elderly, mothers with young children—were immediately marked for death and sent to one line, handed a bar of soap, and marched into a gas chamber marked "bath."[2]

For a moment I considered this possible shred of decency within the Nazis's vicious and degrading extermination plan. I imagined these filthy, ragged victims smiling in momentary relief as they walked, unsuspecting, into their death chamber. Then I realized that brutal efficiency, not compassion, motivated this deceit: The bath soap prevented resistance and made mass murder go smoother. I felt ashamed that I once mitigated Daryl's mass murder, when he explained to me how he lured his unsuspecting children into their death chamber and lined them up, two by two, with the promise of a Christmas surprise so they too would offer no resistance.

Lucky enough to have escaped immediate death and fighting to survive in prison while searching for life's meaning in this brutal setting, Frankl recounted his own physical suffering at the hands of sadistic guards bent on punishing this exhausted, starving prisoner for not working beyond his capacity.

But Frankl locates his most degrading moment while resting on his shovel, when a guard happened to look his way. The officer didn't think it worth his while to chastise or beat Frankl, whom he assumed was loafing, but instead "playfully" threw a stone his way, as if "to call a domestic animal back to its job, a creature with which you have so little in common that *you do not even punish it.*"[3] Oddly, Frankl confirmed what we retributivists insist, sometimes to the derision of abolitionists. Our determination to punish shows we continue to take seriously the punished as a human being; we continue to feel him worth despising.

"One literally became a number," Frankl explained. "Dead or alive—that was unimportant. The life of a 'number' was completely irrelevant." Again, this struck me as oddly metaphorical for contemporary prison administration. The punishment now, like the person then, has gotten completely subsumed in a number—21 years for Breivik. The number, an abstraction, has become the punishment. "What stood behind the number," Frankl observed, the person within those "skeletons disguised with skin and rags" being worked to death, "mattered even less."[4] Perversely, 70 years later, with prisoners in their comfortable cells enjoying PlayStations and flat-screen TVs, at work or play but confined in prison, in the United States no less than Germany, the number of years alone matters. The murderer's *experience as punishment* matters not at all.

Frankl concluded his journey as I conclude mine, rejecting murder under cover of imprisonment, rejecting sadism and torture under cover of punishment, and most of all despairing at the rampant randomness of pain and suffering, administered by the hand of man, more or less wholly disconnected from whatever might be deserved.

We have much to learn from Europe and some to teach it. The United States vastly overpunishes relatively trivial crimes and relatively trivial criminals. It banishes and marks them for life and then releases them, unprepared, into a cold or hostile world. Europe vastly underpunishes the worst of the worst of the worst, rejecting justice as an unworthy goal of prison. "It is now far more likely," Fitzjames Stephen declared more than a century ago, "that people should witness acts of grievous cruelty . . . with too little hatred than that they should feel too much."[5] How challenging to strike a balance in the end between giving people what they deserve and giving vent to the same ugly impulses that make them deserve it.

We punish much too much and much too little. We administer prisons that completely separate crime from punishment. We administer executions that sever the connection between killers and their victims.

For whom do our candles burn?

If the European Union breaks up or the European elites forgive their own past sadistic impulses and cowardice, if this generation's leading liberals and progressives at home and abroad come to their senses, abandon abstract ideology, and embrace democratic legitimacy, then perhaps for the worst of the worst, once again the punishment will more nearly fit the crime. Until then, those of us who search for justice as deserved punishment must find our way among the People.

Although brutal murderers may enjoy long lives while our memories of their suffering victims decay, many abolitionists, especially devout Christians today, maintain their own moral equilibrium through faith that justice will be done in the hereafter. This belief may console them, and the need for justice may incline a victim's survivors to their religious beliefs, seeking as they do solace in the face of suffering. It would console me to believe that all murderers someday face ultimate justice. But ours is a secular society that separates church and state. We, the People, must commit ourselves to human justice in this world, here, as if there is no hereafter.

Searching for justice, I've tried my best to understand crime and punishment, as deeply as I could, from all points of view. Good, sensitive abolitionist scholars, defense attorneys, and activists have earned my gratitude and respect. Of course I feel kinship to that small band of capital prosecutors and scholarly retributivists fighting tirelessly for justice, like Sisyphus pushing condemnation up the mountain, denied by abolitionist courts at every turn. Both sides have taught me, informed me, and made me pause. Knowing many of these murderers, I cannot dismiss all of them as monsters or the products of forces beyond their control. They remain human beings. Capital defenders have treated me well, I think, because I've taken that trouble, like them, to find the humanity even in killers. As human beings worthy of concern and respect, sadistic or callous killers deserve to suffer but only in proportion to their moral blameworthiness. And here, at last, we part company. In our desire to see the guilty suffer, are we retributivists merely sublimating sadists? After knowing them, it does sometimes become more difficult to hate. I do admit to feeling kinship with, yet separate from and—dare I say it—better than the worst of the worst.

After all these years among them, I still strongly believe on balance that some people do deserve to die, and we have the obligation to execute them. I know to a moral certainty that some people deserve to be punished and others rewarded for their choices and actions. I also feel certain that we become worthy of the title "humane beings" only if we sometimes punish, sometimes reward, sometimes treat, and sometimes assist. And if that time comes, when a "progressive" Supreme Court holds we can no longer constitutionally kill the worst of the worst of our worst, then justice demands we should punish them for the rest of their lives.

And if the day arrives, not long after, when neurobiology rebuts classic retributivists along with contemporary German constitutional commitments to every citizen's freedom to develop their personhood, when science conclusively banishes free will as illusion and teaches us that no one deserves blame (or praise), then we will have separated our sense of self from a traditional core that kept us free. We will have become a culture much impoverished, one that has broken faith with the past. And human dignity, as most retributivists and abolitionists know it today, will have vanished.

I hope not. But meanwhile, whether we occupy common ground or find ourselves still separated by an unbridgeable moral gulf, I appreciate that you have journeyed with me to this end.

APPENDIX A

COUNTERING THE ABOLITIONISTS

THEIR ARGUMENTS, OUR REPLIES

FOR CENTURIES, BOTH SIDES HAVE THRASHED IT OUT, EVEN AS they complain there's nothing more to be said about capital punishment. But this topic has hardly been exhausted. We just feel exhausted hearing the same arguments over and over. Below, find ten common attacks on death as punishment and effective counters. Instead of rehashing what has been said, let's move the conversation forward beyond these.

1. HYPOCRISY

We say "Thou shalt not kill," and yet we kill. Many variations and bumper stickers: "Why kill to show killing is wrong?" **We devalue life by taking it.** The state adds another murder with capital punishment. So-called right-to-lifers display inconsistency if not hypocrisy when they oppose abortion yet support the death penalty. All human life is sacred.

Countering the Claim

Sometimes **only by killing the worst killers can we achieve justice**. Far from hypocrisy, responding in kind connects us to our deepest intuitions. Metaphors illuminate our instinct for justice: "Fight fire with fire. Give a person a taste of her own medicine." Retribution, the conscious return of pain for pain—literally "payback"—partakes of a deeper human instinct developed into systems of punishment and reward. We celebrate by repaying pleasure with pleasure. We punish by inflicting pain. The claim of hypocrisy proves too much: **By imprisoning kidnappers, do we devalue liberty?** And when we fine a thief, do we devalue property? Sometimes only death as punishment, a like-kind response to murder, accomplishes justice. Besides, "thou shalt not kill" mistranslates the Bible, which really commands "thou shalt not commit murder." Right-to-lifers who support the death penalty emphasize the sanctity of *innocent* human life.

For those in the pro-choice movement who support a woman's right to kill an innocent unborn child, yet oppose society's right to kill an adult vicious predator, whose life is sacred?

2. HUMAN DIGNITY

a. Religious: Who are we, mere mortals, to judge? **Only God has the right to take life.** We can count on justice in the next world.

Countering the Claim

If God does work justice in the next world, it will be the only true justice. But constitutionally in this secular society, we separate church and state. We commit ourselves to **pursue justice in this world** as if this is all there is.

b. Secular: Intentionally putting to death a person who does not immediately threaten us **violates human dignity.**

Countering the Claim

We death penalty proponents claim **human dignity as** our **primary focus**. By taking the killer's life, we acknowledge and keep alive the *victim's* dignity—her voice, her memory. Beyond that, we essentially acknowledge the killer's dignity by holding him responsible and punishing him. We take his liberty, then forfeit his life as something of great value. Those who would substitute life without parole for the death penalty fail to acknowledge the full value of the killer's—and more importantly, the victim's—life. Abolitionists who would "throw away the key" cease to care about the killer as a human being whom we continue to care about. If he is sane, adult, and fully responsible, we want him fully punished. We want him dead.

3. MISTAKE

To err is human: Any government program, designed by politicians, administered by bureaucrats, will inevitably execute innocent people. All other punishments can be reversed once we discover error. We cannot afford to take the risk that the government may execute innocent people. **One innocent person executed condemns this unnecessary punishment as morally despicable.**

Countering the Claim

We constantly and unnecessarily endanger our own lives and our families as we drive cars and cross streets. Many times a day, we risk the lives of those we love for the sake of convenience. **Surely then, we will occasionally risk the lives of those we detest for the sake of justice.**

Killing an innocent person remains our criminal justice system's worst nightmare. Thus, true retributivists join in supporting the mission of the Innocence Project. Ironically, the prospect of death radically reduces the odds of mistake, calling forth advocates for the accused while lifers rot in prison largely unattended. Our best and brightest—pro bono attorneys from big law firms with endless assets—zealously defend those sentenced to death. Death as punishment should require extraordinary burdens of persuasion: no lingering doubt of guilt and a moral certainty that death is deserved. We should refine our capital statutes and continue to make extraordinary efforts to reduce factual error to near zero; at the same time, we insist that not all mistakes are equally tragic. **In the end, we must risk a minuscule possibility of error for the near certainty of justice.**

4. EXPENSE

The Death Penalty costs way too much. It drains budgets. No rational person can defend the unnecessary, astronomical expense of investigation, trial, appellate litigation, and maintaining death row. That money could be put to much better purposes, such as crime prevention and victim compensation.

Countering the Claim

The people who complain about expense increase it. Much can be trimmed. Of course, if abolitionists grind the system to a standstill by frivolous appeals, the cost per execution becomes infinite. Intuition tells us it should be cheaper to kill a prisoner than to cage him for life. But studies standardly confirm that super due-process does cost more. Those studies rarely include the hundreds of thousands of dollars in trial and appellate costs saved each time an accused aggravated murderer pleads guilty and accepts life without parole to avoid the death penalty. Nor do opponents typically include the increasing geriatric costs society faces as the lifer population ages. **Punishment, however, should never be measured or meted out according to economic expediency. In the end, it may cost more to punish more severely. Who ever said justice was cheap?**

5. DETERRENCE

a. The death penalty deters no one from murder.

Countering the Claim

Of course it does. Employing this simple, silly argument, abolitionists make it more difficult on themselves. Both life and death as punishment deter imperfectly. "Capital punishment has obviously failed as a deterrent when a murder is committed," declared the Royal Commission: **"We can number its failures. But we cannot number its successes.** No one can ever know how many people have refrained from murder because of the fear of being hanged."[1]

b. The death penalty deters no better than life without parole. Abolitionists
need only show that death does not deter more effectively than life without parole. All other things equal, the less punishment the better. Many leading, sophisticated, statistical studies show death deters no better than life in prison. The statistical case has never been made. No evidence exists for the death penalty as a superior deterrent.

Countering the Claim

Human nature, "the whole experience of mankind," suggests otherwise, countered Fitzjames Stephen, the great jurist and historian of the criminal law. It's difficult to demonstrate that death most "effectually" deters simply because it is "in [it]self more obvious than any proof can make it.... 'All that a man has will he give for his life.'" In prison, "however terrible, there's hope."[2] The "no evidence" hyperbole should not be taken seriously. I know of killers who killed in Washington, DC, but not in neighboring Virginia or Maryland solely because those states had the death penalty. Other anecdotes support this. Of course suicide bombers and other self-destructive murderers can't be deterred, nor can many passion killings. But common sense dictates that, on balance, the terror of death exerts a superior deterrent effect, also subconsciously "building up in the community, over a long period of time, a deep feeling of peculiar abhorrence for the crime of murder."[3] "The weariest and most loathed worldly life," Shakespeare declared, "is a paradise to what we fear of death."[4]

Logically, psychologically, anecdotally, and perhaps statistically, death remains the more effective deterrent than life. Besides, polls show the vast majority—supporters and opponents—don't find deterrence their primary issue.

6. THE COMPANY WE KEEP

Why is the United States the only democracy with the death penalty? Are we proud of the company we keep? **Iran, North Korea, China.** Those who largely share our values, such as Europe, Canada, and Australia, reject the death penalty as barbaric. Why should the United States not follow Europe's lead and abolish capital punishment?

Countering the Claim

We also associate ourselves with **Japan, India,** and much of the Caribbean. In a democracy, the popular will of the electorate should translate directly into law. Yet every European country *abolished* the death penalty in the teeth of overwhelming *popular support* for it. In Poland, support still hovers around 75–80 percent. Somewhere around half the Canadian people, after all the education and shaming, still support the death penalty. A majority of the British still support the death penalty, as do the Czechs. European *elites* overwhelmingly oppose the death penalty. They've also managed to abolish life without parole, allowing mass murderers like Anders Breivik to be sentenced to 21 years for killing 77 people. Bottom line: **Today, the United States stands as the only leading Western democracy still acting like a Western democracy on this issue.** In any case, if the European Union fractures, some parts of Europe will rejoin us.

7. APPARENT MAJORITY SUPPORT

It vanishes in the United States, **polls show**, when the people are given the specific option of **life without parole.** The public, when it really considers the alternative, does not clearly support the death penalty.

Countering the Claim

The standard poll question, "Which do you prefer for murder, the death penalty or life in prison with absolutely no possibility of parole?" doubly elevates support for life. Most citizens equate "absolutely no possibility of parole" with "absolutely no possibility of release." But a future governor may commute the LWOP sentence; a future legislature or court may follow Europe's lead and abolish life without parole as unconstitutional. The poll question also fails to make plain a real aggravated murder and/or the real nature of the alternative. **Suppose instead we asked: "Which do you prefer for a serial killer who rapes and murders children: death, or a life watching television, playing sports, going to therapy and arts and crafts with free medical care inside prison?"**

8. A LIVING HELL

a. Death row is torture. Prisoners constantly suffer while waiting to be executed.

Countering the Claim

Life on the Row day to day often feels no worse and sometimes much better than life inside general population. Prisoners have an incentive to behave; a group ethos prevails. The condemned use standard psychological coping mechanisms to make life on the Row more pleasant.

b. Life inside is worse than death. The prisoner dies one day at a time. He is sentenced effectively to life and death in prison.

Countering the Claim

Clever rhetoric, replacing the obviously ridiculous "death by prison." Lifers give the lie to the claim: LWOPers generally thrive in general population, often living the most privileged lives inside. **Few lifers commit suicide,** although they can. Give us this day our daily day. Inside or out, we all live until we die.

9. RACISM

a. Disproportionate representation of blacks on the Row. Black males make up 6 percent of the population and more than 40 percent of the Row.

Countering the Claim

Blacks commit a disproportionate number of death-eligible killings but constitute a smaller proportion of the most despicable killers. **The discriminatory effect of black overrepresentation on death row rarely results from discriminatory intent.** Robbery, the most common aggravator, correlates heavily with race and class. As Justice John Paul Stevens famously observed, confine the death penalty to the most culpable only, and the disparate racial effect largely disappears. Refine and redefine the death penalty. **Get rid of the felony murder aggravator.**

b. The death penalty devalues black life. The death penalty is more likely for a black defendant and much less likely where the victim is African American.

Countering the Claim

The race of the killer will not dictate the odds of his getting death. Studies almost uniformly confirm it: This most pernicious racial discrimination has long since disappeared. A black defendant is no more likely (and probably slightly less likely) to be sentenced to die than his similarly situated white counterpart. But studies consistently show that juries sentence killers of black victims to death less often. That hardly proves racism. Most black victim cases involve black killers, and most of those take place in counties where prosecutors rarely seek the death penalty. An inner-city black victim's family opposes death typically because they continue to see worth in all black life, including the killer's. Within a given county, it generally makes no difference if the victim is black or white. **The race disparity turns into a geographical effect with**

different counties' prosecutors going for death at different rates under the same state law. Whether states should impose uniform capital prosecutions across counties remains an open question. The real but hidden racism discriminates against skin tone and stereotypical African features. This pernicious bias infects the black as well as white community and skews the entire criminal justice system.

10. IT'S JUST WRONG

Argue all you like, we're still sure.

Countering the Claim

At last we reach common ground. **We too feel just as certain.** Although intuitions drive us to opposite conclusions, **we agree that feelings matter. And moral facts exist.** It's always wrong to kill unnecessarily. But where they deserve to die, killing the worst among us becomes a *just* wrong.

APPENDIX B

A MODEL DEATH PENALTY (PERMANENT PUNITIVE SEGREGATION) STATUTE

JUSTICE ALWAYS REMAINS A WORK IN PROGRESS. STANDARDS OF decency continue to evolve and not always toward greater leniency. This proposed model statute builds on centuries of others' insights that underlie my decades investigating and testifying. My blueprint surely can and should be refined, but I'm convinced it improves on current codes. This proposed statute *eliminates* some standard aggravators—notably felony murder and premeditation—in order to more clearly isolate and *punish* most severely *only the worst of the worst*. Should legislatures adopt some variation of this statute, moral logic dictates they reevaluate those condemned presently on death row. Governors should commute to life without parole those condemned whose murders do not meet these criteria. The rest should be executed more quickly, worst first.

AGGRAVATED FIRST-DEGREE MURDER

Whoever intentionally or with a depraved indifference to human life kills another human being with one or more of the following aggravating circumstances commits **Aggravated First-Degree Murder** and becomes eligible for a punishment of death (or Permanent Punitive Segregation—PPS). A convicted murderer can only be condemned to die (or PPS) if a **unanimous jury** finds at least one of the following aggravating circumstances beyond a reasonable doubt:

I. AGGRAVATING CIRCUMSTANCES

A. The killing was **especially heinous, atrocious, or cruel.** This includes but is not limited to situations where:
    1. The **killer exhibited pleasure** in **inflicting extended pain and suffering,** or
    2. The **victim** was **tortured** before being killed. Torture includes the infliction of physical or mental pain and suffering beyond what is necessary to kill. Rape or other violent sexual abuse constitutes torture.

B. The **victim** was **especially vulnerable** because of age or physical or mental condition.

C. The murderer killed **law enforcement or emergency medical personnel because of that status.** This includes jurors, prosecutors, and judges as victims killed to prevent a verdict or to retaliate.

D. The murderer was a **serial killer.** A serial killer has killed or attempted to kill a total of three or more people on three or more unrelated occasions.

E. The killing constituted **mass murder** (i.e., the defendant killed four or more victims in a single incident).

F. The killer was a **contract killer or paid assassin.**

II. AGGRAVATING MOTIVES may sometimes overlap with aggravating circumstances. But the jury may specifically find any of several motives that alone shall aggravate the murder and may make it death (or PPS) eligible. Each motive includes but is not limited to primary examples that follow it.

A. **PECUNIARY:** The killer was a **paid assassin** or otherwise killed primarily for pecuniary gain.

B. **GREED:** The murderer had the victim killed **to collect insurance or inheritance.**

C. **BIAS:** The murderer **killed because of the victim's race, religion, national origin, sexual orientation, gender identity, or expression.**

D. **EXTRAORDINARY SELFISHNESS:** The defendant killed an **unresisting robbery victim or** person who happened to **witness the defendant's crime.**

E. **CALLOUSNESS:** The killer **knowingly endangered several persons.** (This particularly applies to terrorists and mass murderers.)

F. **SADISM: The killer relished inflicting pain.**

THE PENALTY PHASE

PURPOSE: To present all relevant mitigating and any other aggravating factors revealing the killer's character or circumstances of the offense that may move a jury to spare or condemn. *Experience demonstrates that we can never completely list in advance* the nature or weight of *all morally relevant aggravators and mitigators.*

In the penalty phase, each side shall have great leeway to present evidence. Only if the judge finds the evidence irrelevant beyond a reasonable doubt shall he or she exclude it. The rules of evidence shall not apply during the penalty phase.

BURDEN OF PERSUASION IN THE PENALTY PHASE:
A jury **may** sentence the defendant to death (or PPS) only if:

A. **At least 10 of 12 jurors are convinced with no residual or lingering doubt of** the convicted murderer's **guilt** of aggravated first-degree murder,

B. Upon full and fair consideration, these 10 jurors agree **beyond a reasonable doubt** that **aggravating circumstances clearly outweigh mitigating circumstances,** and

C. These jurors are convinced to a *moral certainty* that **the convicted murderer deserves death (or PPS).**

But if upon full and fair consideration of the character of the convicted murderer and circumstances of the murder a **unanimous jury** concludes with no residual or lingering doubt that he did it, and to a moral certainty that he deserves it, they **must** sentence that convicted murderer to death (or PPS).

During the penalty phase, **the defense may renew its challenge to facts the jury has already found beyond a reasonable doubt by its guilty verdict.** The jury shall be specifically instructed that, although it already found all facts necessary to convict the defendant of first-degree murder beyond a reasonable doubt, it may yet have a **lingering doubt about** the defendant's **guilt and the facts on which they rest. The judge shall also instruct the jury that, notwithstanding their certainty of guilt, they may have** a **moral doubt** about the appropriate **punishment.**

MITIGATING CIRCUMSTANCES

Mitigating circumstances include but are not limited to:

A. The **defendant's childhood**, especially as a source of abuse or character deformation.

B. The **defendant's motive or delusions**.

C. The **defendant's mental state:**

1. Killing under substantial **stress, passion, or provocation** (although insufficient to mitigate murder to manslaughter).

2. Killing under the influence of **substances** voluntarily taken, but only if defendant shows he had no reason to believe he would act aggressively or violently while under their influence.

D. The defendant's prior **good deeds**—personal sacrifices and past accomplishments, including service to the family, community, or the nation.

E. The defendant's killing was **out of character**.

F. **Anything else** bearing on the defendant's character or circumstances of the offense that might move a juror to spare rather than condemn.

VICTIM IMPACT STATEMENTS

During the penalty phase, the Defense should attempt to humanize the defendant. Anyone, including the convicted murderer's friends or family, may recount his or her good deeds or emphasize the killer's own traumatic suffering or abuse as a child. The jury can view the living defendant in court. Thus, to help the jury strike a moral balance in deciding life or death (or PPS), the People may call the victim's family and friends as witnesses to humanize the victim and communicate their own sense of loss, aided by photographs or other video images. As the US Supreme Court has held, survivors may express no opinion on the proper sentence.

Regardless of how the survivors feel, the *victim's* opinion of the killer's fate *should* count. Thus, a reliable **living will** or **declaration of life** shall be admissible in the penalty phase. As long as evidence clearly supports it as the authentic views of the victim, a signed and dated or videotaped statement such as:

I hereby declare that should I die as a result of a violent crime, I request that the person or persons found guilty for my killing not be subject to or put in jeopardy of the death penalty under any circumstances, no matter how heinous their crime or how much I may have suffered.

OR

I hereby declare that should I be killed under circumstances that constitute aggravated murder, I request my killer shall be put to death.

Once victim character evidence is raised, either side may present written evidence that the victim either supported or opposed the death penalty with such qualifications as the victim made apparent during her or his life. The judge shall examine such evidence from either side, out of the presence of the jury, and shall admit it only if it clearly and convincingly shows that the victim would have supported or opposed the death penalty (or PPS) under the circumstances of the particular killing. The judge should inform the jury that they are not bound to effectuate the victim's living will but should give it substantial weight.

CONDITIONS ON DEATH ROW/PPS

Those condemned to die or to PPS shall be permanently housed in a separate prison [wing], with their daily conditions no better than prisoners already subject to punitive or administrative segregation for the worst prison infractions. Specifically, within constitutional bounds, those condemned to death or PPS shall have only the minimum constitutionally mandated exercise, recreation, phone calls, or physical contact. They shall not be permitted any communal form of play.

Their sole food shall be nutraloaf, nutritionally complete and tasteless. Photographs of their victims shall be posted in their cells, out of reach, in visibly conspicuous places.

EXECUTION PROTOCOL

Death shall be by firing squad or other constitutional method that makes it clearly punishment and not medicine. A member of the victim's family may choose the method of execution among the constitutionally permissible options.

Before (or after) the condemned makes a final statement, the victim's family may display a brief audiovisual memorial of the victim's life and may also include crime scene photos and scenes from the victim's funeral, burial, and gravesite.

Executions shall be public.

IF THE U.S. SUPREME COURT EVER HOLDS IT CONSTITUTIONAL:

A. The **minimum age** subject to death or PPS **shall be 16**, with a strong, nearly irrebuttable presumption against death or PPS at 16, diminishing until 21.

B. **Attempted** first-degree aggravated murder **may qualify** for death or PPS, especially when coupled with sexual assault.

APPENDIX C
A CORRECTIONS MODEL MISSION STATEMENT

THE DEPARTMENT OF CORRECTIONS SHALL MAINTAIN SAFE AND secure facilities that restrict prisoners' liberty more or less according to the seriousness of their crimes as well as the threat of future harm they pose and prospects for their rehabilitation.

The Department of Corrections shall protect the public, protect staff, and provide humane supervision of prisoners with opportunities and programs that meaningfully support successful community reintegration for those offenders sentenced to a term of years or life with a possibility of release.

For those prisoners sentenced to death, permanent punitive segregation, or life without parole, the department shall administer punishment—an unpleasant, restrictive daily regimen designed to continually convey society's intense disapproval of the crime and the criminal.

APPENDIX D
US SUPREME COURT HIGHLIGHTS

HUNDREDS OF US SUPREME COURT DEATH PENALTY DECISIONS have shaped the progress and revealed the meaning of cruel and unusual punishment under the Eighth Amendment. Highlighting three dozen or so cases shows the Court's complex and erratic attempt to constitutionally reconcile diverse states' sense of justice with uniform constitutional guarantees.

Before the modern era, the Court had already wrestled with the question of how much punishment the US Constitution tolerates. The justices could not "define with exactness" "cruel and unusual" punishment. But in *Wilkerson v. Utah* (1878),[1] the Court did "safe[ly] affirm" that the Eighth Amendment outlawed torture and all other punishments "in the same line of unnecessary cruelty." In addition to torture, the Court also outlawed punishments that were "by their excessive length or severity ... greatly disproportioned" to the crime. The very thought of these punishments would make any person "of right feeling and heart shudder" (*O'Neil v. Vermont,* 1892).[2]

"The punishment of death is not cruel," the Court explained further in *In re Kemmler* (1890),[3] upholding the newly invented electric chair. But punishment does become "unnecessarily cruel" when it involves "torture or a lingering death—i.e., something more than the mere extinguishment of life." Still, the Court could not precisely pin down the meaning of the Eighth Amendment because as it explained in *Weems v. United States* (1910),[4] "the clause" was "progressive" and "may acquire meaning as public opinion becomes enlightened by a humane justice." Human dignity underlay the Eighth Amendment, the Court insisted in *Trop v. Dulles* (1958).[5] And to serve human dignity, "the Eighth Amendment must draw its meaning from the evolving standards of decency that mark the progress of a maturing society."

Punishment's modern mantra was born.

In deciding between life and death, judges had great "discretion" and could draw on an infinite variety of facts and circumstances, the Court held in *Williams v. New York* (1949).[6] "Individualized punishment" should "fit the offender and not merely the crime." History had taught a profound lesson: It was simply "beyond present human ability" to "identify before the fact those characteristics of criminal homicides and their perpetrators which call for the death penalty" and to "express these characteristics in language which can be fairly understood and applied by the sentencing authority."

Thus, the Court held in **McGautha v. California (1971)**[7] that "sentiment and sympathy" could guide a jury's decision to impose life or death. Because no formula was possible, capital sentencing juries could exercise "standardless ... untrammeled ... absolute" discretion without violating due process of law. So constitutionally, no standards need guide a jury's discretion.

Yet the very next year, in **Furman v. Georgia (1972),**[8] in nine separate opinions, the US Supreme Court, 5–4, struck down capital punishment as administered across the United States. A death penalty "becomes 'unusual,'" Justice Douglas declared, "if it discriminates against a defendant by reason of his race, religion, wealth, social position, or class or if it is imposed under a procedure that gives room for the play of such prejudices." Thus, all death penalties administered "arbitrarily or discriminatorily" became unconstitutional. As long as the state imposes death on "a capriciously selected random handful," Justice Stewart famously observed, the penalty without standards becomes "cruel and unusual in the same way that being struck by lightning is cruel and unusual."

Forced to empty their death rows, bolstered by popular support for death as punishment, 35 states immediately enacted new capital statutes to meet the Court's constitutional demand of guided discretion. "We now hold that the punishment of death does not invariably violate the Constitution," the Court declared, upholding Georgia's and Florida's new statutes, which listed aggravating circumstances in advance and provided for a separate, second sentencing trial. Furthermore, the legislature need not "select the least severe penalty possible so long as the penalty selected is not cruelly inhumane or disproportionate to the crime involved" (**Gregg v. Georgia, 1976**).[9] "*Furman* is satisfied when the sentencing discretion is guided and channeled" (**Proffitt v. Florida, 1976**).[10]

At the same time, the Court, 5–4, struck down other states' new statutes that eliminated arbitrariness by making death a *mandatory* penalty for certain crimes. "Death is different from all other sanctions in kind rather than degree," the Court declared in **Woodson v. North Carolina (1976).**[11] "The fundamental respect for humanity underlying the Eighth Amendment requires consideration of the character and record of the individual offender and the circumstances of the particular offense." Even a precisely worded first-degree murder statute with a mandatory death sentence fails to provide juries with a "meaningful opportunity" to consider possibly relevant mitigating factors, the Court held in **Roberts v. Louisiana (1976).**[12] Thus, as Justice White noted, dissenting, "States are constitutionally prohibited from considering any crime, no matter how defined, so serious that every person who commits it should be put to death regardless of ... his character." The sentencer must be allowed to consider "any aspect of a defendant's character or record" and any "circumstances of the offense" the defendant might offer to support imposing a sentence less than death. Essentially, as the Court declared in **Lockett v. Ohio (1978),**[13] the state must allow the defendant to raise all "relevant mitigating circumstances." The sentencer may determine the weight to be given relevant mitigating evidence, the Court held in **Eddings v. Oklahoma (1982),**[14] "but they may not give it no weight.... *Lockett* requires the sentencer to listen." A defendant must be allowed to show that he has behaved well while in prison awaiting trial, the Court held in **Skipper v. South Carolina (1986),**[15] and thus "would not pose a danger if incarcerated rather than put to death." Other post-crime evidence may also be relevant. A jury must be allowed to hear that a defendant's accomplice received a life sentence (**Parker v. Dugger, 1991**).[16] Or that the murderer has undergone a "post-crime character transformation" (e.g., a religious conversion in prison) (**Brown v. Payton, 2005**).[17]

Although the defendant can introduce any mitigating circumstances the jury will weigh against the aggravating circumstances, the state may choose not to provide standards to guide the jury in weighing those mitigators against aggravating circumstances as long as "any decision to impose the death sentence be and appear to be based on reason rather than caprice or emotion" (*Zant v. Stephens*, **1983**).[18] A judge may instruct the jury not to be swayed by "mere sentiment, conjecture, sympathy, passion, [or] prejudice" because, as Justice O'Connor declared in her concurring opinion, ultimately the sentence imposed at the penalty phase should reflect "a reasoned moral response to the defendant's background, character, and crime" (*California v. Brown*, **1987**).[19]

Of course the defendant has no constitutional obligation to put on any evidence during the guilt phase of his case. But the Court in *Walton v. Arizona* (**1990**)[20] upheld a state's right to impose a burden on the defendant to prove *mitigating* facts. Furthermore, as the Court held in *Kansas v. Marsh* (**2006**),[21] a state may require the *defendant* to persuade the sentencing jury that the mitigators outweigh the aggravators.

One thing united the fractured court in *Furman:* Every justice personally rejected retribution as a wise reason to punish. Yet increasingly after *Furman* the Court did employ retribution to *limit* capital punishment to certain kinds of crimes and criminals. Although rape was "highly reprehensible" and "short of homicide, the ultimate violation of self," the Court in *Coker v. Georgia* (**1977**)[22] characterized death as "grossly disproportionate and excessive punishment" for raping an adult woman. Furthermore, based on a national "consensus" and its "own independent judgment," the Court, 5–4, later also held death unconstitutional for the rape of a child. Although child rape "may be devastating," a majority declared in *Kennedy v. Louisiana* (**2008**),[23] in terms of "moral depravity" [and] injury, [it] cannot be compared to murder." The death penalty should not be applied where the victim's life was not taken, the Court held, but expressly left undecided the question of "treason, espionage, [and] terrorism."

Nor was death a constitutionally valid penalty for a getaway car driver in a robbery gone bad. When we impose the death penalty, a person's punishment "must be tailored to his personal responsibility and moral guilt," the Court held in *Enmund v. Florida* (**1982**).[24] Condemning a person "who neither took life, attempted to take life, nor intended to take life ... does not measurably contribute to the retributive end of ensuring that the criminal gets his just deserts." For a few years it seemed as though only a defendant who intended to kill the victim could be punished with death. But in *Tison v. Arizona* (**1987**),[25] the Court upheld the death penalty for a major participant in a felony who did not kill or intend to kill but did display a "reckless indifference to the value of human life."

So who were the worst of the worst? Could they be simply described? The US Supreme Court struck down Georgia's "outrageously or wantonly vile, horrible or inhuman" aggravator, involving "torture" and a "depravity of mind." According to that definition, any juror could find every murder "outrageously or wantonly vile" and, moved by emotion rather than reason, exercise unguided discretion in violation of *Furman* (*Godfrey v. Georgia*, **1980**).[26] Nor did "especially heinous, atrocious, or cruel" adequately narrow the class of "death eligible" and adequately guide the jury's discretion (*Maynard v. Cartwright*, **1988**).[27] As applied to defendants who randomly kidnapped and shot in the head a young off-duty marine, leaving him blind to wander in the desert for several days and "ultimately die from dehydration, starvation, and pneumonia," the Court apparently corrected course once again in *Walton v. Arizona* (**1990**),[28] upholding the state's "especially heinous, depraved, or cruel manner" aggravator. And a clear majority of the Court later upheld Idaho's "utter disregard for human life" as applied to a serial killer who had "shot, stabbed, beaten or strangled to death" at least 11 victims in seven states. Death could be deserved for killers who evidenced "the highest, the utmost callous disregard for human life, i.e., the cold-blooded, pitiless slayer," the Court observed in *Arave v. Creech* (**1993**).[29] A state "could treat capital defendants who take pleasure in killing as more deserving of the death penalty than those who do not." And Idaho could include those "who kill without feeling or sympathy as more deserving of death."

For centuries, society has refused to execute the insane based on an "intuition that the execution simply offends humanity." As the Court explained in *Ford v. Wainwright* (1986),[30] retribution, "one of the death penalty's critical justifications," can only be "satisfied" if "the defendant perceives the connection between his crime and his punishment." Mentally retarded persons who meet the law's requirements for criminal responsibility should be tried and punished when they commit crimes. "Because of their disabilities in areas of reasoning, judgment, and control of their impulses, however, they do not act with the level of moral culpability that characterizes the most serious adult criminal conduct." Although ultimately the Court's own judgment led them to categorically exempt the mentally retarded from the death penalty in *Atkins v. Virginia* (2002),[31] a "social and professional consensus," the teaching of "religious communities," and views of the "world community"—especially the European Union—buttressed their conclusion.

The "overwhelming weight of international opinion" also rejected a juvenile death penalty. Murderers under 18 could not "reliably be classified" as the "worst offenders deserving of death," the Court held in *Roper v. Simmons* (2005).[32] "Their "underdeveloped sense of responsibility," vulnerability and susceptibility to "peer pressure," and immaturity meant that even their most heinous crimes would not necessarily indicate an "irretrievably depraved character." Thus, "whether viewed as an attempt to express the community's moral outrage or as an attempt to right the balance for the wrong to the victim, the case for retribution is not as strong with a minor as with an adult."

The Court not only limited the categories of killings and killers a state may single out for death, it also wrestled extensively with the decision-making process for inflicting death as punishment. Judges violate the Sixth Amendment right to an impartial jury trial by automatically excluding all those who express conscientious objections to capital punishment, the Court held in *Witherspoon v. Illinois* (1968).[33] But a state may exclude from capital juries all those whose views would "prevent or substantially impair" them from following instructions. Thus, a judge may excuse for "cause" all potential jurors who will *always* or *never* vote death for convicted murderers (*Wainwright v. Witt*, 1985; *Morgan v. Illinois*, 1992).[34] Either side may use "peremptory challenges" to strike from the jury anybody they choose, except prosecutors violate "equal protection" when they discriminate and "systematically exclude blacks" to keep the jury all-white (*Batson v. Kentucky*, 1986).[35]

Although some justices now believe that "retribution provides the main justification for capital punishment" and that a jury "more attuned to the community's moral sensibility" can better "express the conscience of the community on the ultimate question of life or death," nevertheless, as the court held in *Spaziano v. Florida* (1984),[36] a state may still choose to have a judge decide whether a convicted murderer gets sentenced to death. But a jury and not a judge must find the aggravating facts on which that death sentence is based (*Ring v. Arizona*, 2002).[37]

In *Booth v. Maryland* (1987),[38] the Court prohibited a capital sentencing jury from considering the impact of the murder on the victim's family or close friends because focusing on the harm might "divert the jury's attention" from the defendant's "personal responsibility and moral blameworthiness." But four years later, the Court reversed itself. To fully assess a "defendant's moral culpability and blameworthiness," it held in *Payne v. Tennessee* (1991)[39] a jury may be allowed "a quick glimpse of the life a defendant chose to extinguish" and see "the loss to the victim's family and to society." "Just as the murderer should be considered as an individual, so too, the victim is an individual whose death represents a unique loss.... Justice, though due to the accused, is due to the accuser also." Victim impact statements help "keep the balance true."

In summary, the Court seemed to require consistency in its *Furman* line, mandating a jury and judge's guided discretion during sentencing according to criteria specified in advance. At the same time, a majority seems to require "fairness" in the form of individualized nonmandatory capital sentencing (*Lockett* and *Eddings*), allowing the defendant to introduce all types of mitigating circumstances. "Our jurisprudence and logic have long since parted ways," Justice Scalia bemoaned in *Walton*, condemning the "simultaneous pursuit of contradictory objectives" while upholding the constitutionality of capital punishment itself. Some Justices, such as Blackmun, supported Scalia's claimed contradiction, famously announcing that he would "no longer tinker with the machinery of death" (*Callins v. Collins*, 1994).[40]

Despite its jurisprudential ebbs and flows, however, the death penalty so far constitutionally lives on.

The Court even seems willing to export its capital jurisprudence, striking down life without parole for juveniles in non-homicide offenses (*Graham v. Florida*, 2010),[41] and striking down *mandatory* life without parole for any juvenile, whatever the offense (*Miller v. Alabama*, 2012).[42]

SINE QUA NON
Acknowledgments

THE PEOPLE CLOSEST TO ME NOT ONLY SHARED AND SHAPED ME, but showed me the joys of life, amplifying the horror of unnecessarily losing it. My parents, Sophie and Arthur, and sister Susan indulged my childhood, keeping me steadily if erratically on my own course. My long suffering wife and life's love Marcia, lived and co-created every chapter with me, and then critiqued them all. Her brother Allan cheerfully solved so many of life's little problems, allowing me to focus on the insoluble. The preciousness of my only child, Betsy, kept me fully detesting Daryl Holton's evil. The love and innocence of our four little darlings, Isabella, Chloe, William, and James, drives home the full viciousness of child killers and the tragedy of survivors. The extreme views—he would call them reasonable—of my cousin Howard helped me feel moderate. My son-in-law Charles, a former homicide prosecutor, kept me feeling informed. My nephew Greg, a professional videographer, vainly attempted to turn me into one. My dear friend Andrew O'Connell trekked with me to many public clashes and often buoyed me after I got pummeled.

Many people made this book possible. Prof. Phil Heymann sent me on my prison journey. Lisa Leshne who began as this memoir's literary agent—opposing its perspective while maximizing its prospects—became my friend, representing it with great skill and tenacity, and by the end, much sympathy. Emily Carleton and Karen Wolny at Palgrave Macmillan embraced this genre from the start and although sometimes disagreeing with it, respected the perspective's integrity throughout, never sacrificing substance for surface appeal, and yet imposing the discipline necessary to make this account much more readable. Bill Frucht proved a valuable mentor throughout; Dave Blum gave this memoir's opening sections valuable public exposure. Elizabeth D'Antonio slogged through every draft, providing much needed critiques. Robert Whitbeck, along with Elizabeth, constructed the bulk of the endnotes and provided dozens of very useful suggestions. Steve Cohen, another outstanding New York Law School student, ruthlessly suggested cuts, keeping me in touch with essentials.

Of course this crime and punishment memoir owes so much to abolitionists: Professor Deborah Denno from the start defended the value in presenting both sides. Richard Dieter, Director of the Death Penalty Information Center, often proved this leading institution worthy of its name. Professor David Dow, my sometime public adversary, gave me a model with his own moving memoir. Kevin Doyle, my friend and co-teacher, acted as a constant classroom sparring partner, making it much easier to face all others in the public arena. Marty McClain, my early co-teacher, demonstrated integrity with tenacity. David Kaczynski and James Liebman, sometime public opponents, sought and found some moral spots of common ground. James Acker, David Baldus, Susan Bandes, Hugo Bedau, Bob Bohm, Abe Bonowitz, Bill Earlbaum, Jeffrey Fagan, Norman Greene, Craig Haney, Robert Johnson, Jeffrey Kirchmeier, Charles Lanier, Martin Leahy, Samuel Levine, Charles Ogletree, Michael Perlin, Michael Radelet, Austin Sarat, Barry Scheck, Bill Schulz, Jordan Steiker, Victor Streib, and Ron Tabak—opponents yet colleagues—enriched my understanding.

Newspaper Journalists Bill Glaberson, Adam Liptak and Jeremy Peters of the *New York Times,* Kris Fischer of the *New York Law Journal,* Carolyn Lumsden and Peter Pach of the *Hartford Courant,* Robert Schwaneberg of the *Star Ledger,* Nancy Szokan of the *Washington Post,* and Richard Willing of *USA Today* subordinated their own abolitionism to give retributivism its public place. Nancy Grace, Kimberly Guilfoyle, Andrea Peyser and Gerry Wagschal, and Bob Ward, all sympathetic journalists, did what they could to amplify this perspective. Bruce Klein produced and financed the documentary. Chris Cuomo and Alex Witt lent their support, but kept their own views under wraps.

A small band of fellow sympathizers supported our common mission. Clatsop County prosecutor Josh Marquis acted as a frequent sounding board and co-combatant. Kent Scheidegger, Legal Director of the Criminal Justice Legal Foundation, provided consistent sober scholarly support as we faced off against the abolitionists together. Dudley Sharp tirelessly took on every opponent in sight, displaying endless energy and tenacity. Charles Putnam took on the abolitionists in New Hampshire. Psychiatrist Michael Welner used his depravity scale to give medical credibility to the notion of evil. Professors Paul Cassell and Barry Latzer added erudition to our common cause.

Prosecutors Ron Eisenberg along with Angela Backers, Sean Byrne, Susan Boleyn, Preston Draper, Alice Lustre, Tim Prichard, Carolyn Snurkowski and Tom Thurman helped me greatly. Their colleagues, a tireless band nationwide including Kirk Brown, Gena Bunn, Ward Campbell, Kent Cattani, John Connelly, Robert Dean, Robert Ellman, Dane Gillette, Bruce Hahn, Mike Hood, Gordon Ladner, Christine Landers, Kevin Lyons, Stephen Maher, Sylvia Mandel, Paul McMurdie, Bernard Murray, Patricia Nigro, Stephen Plazibat, James Reams, Fredericka Sargent, Connie Vietz, Linda Woloshin, Steven Yarbrough and Donald Zelenka also battled for justice against the odds, increasing the incentive to argue our collective case.

And finally of course, to those murdered victims in graves across the world, who would not want us to forgive or forget.

NOTES

CHAPTER 1: KILLING THE WRONG PEOPLE

1. "Slain Youth's Body Seen by Thousands," *New York Times*, September 4, 1955.
2. "Frank Indicted in Phagan Case," *The Atlanta Constitution*, May 1913.
3. "Grim Tragedy in the Woods," *New York Times*, August 19, 1915.
4. Elaine Marie Alphin, *An Unspeakable Crime: The Prosecution and Persecution of Leo Frank* (Minneapolis: Carolrhoda Books, 2010), 123.
5. Carl Sandburg, *Lincoln: The Prairie Years and the War Years* (New York: Sterling), 1954.
6. *New International Version,* Deuteronomy 7:1–2; 20:16.
7. Leviticus 20:13 (NIV).
8. Exodus 20:10 (NIV).
9. Exodus 20:12 (NIV).
10. "President's Assassin Shot to Death in Jail Corridor by a Dallas Citizen," *New York Times*, November 25, 1963.
11. Dwight D. Eisenhower, *Mandate for Change, 1953* (Garden City, NY: Doubleday & Company, Inc. 1963), 372.
12. *The People v. Speck,* 41 Ill.2d 177, 242 N.E.2d 208, Supreme Court of Illinois (1968).
13. *Miranda v. Arizona,* 384 U.S. 436 (1966).
14. Nick King, "The Fight Over Death Penalty Not Yet Ended," *Boston Globe,* November 3, 1982.
15. Plato, *Theaetetus* (New York: Penguin Books, 1987), 152a.
16. Aristotle, *Nicomachean Ethics* (Oxford: W. Baxter Press, 1826), 174.
17. Jeremy Bentham, *The Principles of Morals and Legislation,* Ch. 14, Of the Proportion between Punishments and Offenses, XVI, XVII, XVIII, XIX, XX; Cesare Beccaria, *An Essay on Crimes and Punishments* (Boston: International Pocket Library, 1983), 51.
18. Pope John Paul II, *Evangelium Vitae (The Gospel of Life),* Paragraph 56, issued on March 25, 1995.
19. William MacDonald, *Documentary Source Book of American History* (New York: Burt Franklin, 1916), 189–190.
20. Thucydides, *The Peloponnesian War* (Baltimore: Penguin, 1954).
21. Plato (translated), in E. Hamilton and H. Cairns (Eds.), *The Collected Dialogues of Plato*. Princeton, NJ: Princeton University Press; Protagoras, 324a.
22. Plato, Laws A. E. Taylor (trans.), in *The Collected Dialogues of Plato,* edited by E. Hamilton and H. Cairns. Princeton, NJ: Princeton University Press, 862-d;

Gorgias, 525c, cf. M. Henberg, *Retribution: Evil for Evil in Ethics, Law and Literature* (Philadelphia: Temple University Press, 1997), 97.

23. Immanuel Kant, *Metaphysical Elements of Justice* (New York: Hackett Publishing Company, Inc., 1981), 138.
24. Ibid., 139.
25. Ibid., 140.

CHAPTER 2: PLAYING THE GAME

1. See *McGautha v. California,* 402 U.S.183 at 189, US Supreme Court (1971).
2. Aristotle, *Nicomachean Ethics* (Oxford: W. Baxter Press, 1826), 174.
3. Vincent Bugliosi and Curt Gentry, *Helter Skelter: The True Story of the Manson Murders* (London: Arrow Books, 1992), 596.
4. *McGautha v. California.*
5. Arthur Koestler, *Reflections on Hanging* (New York: Macmillan, 1957), 17, 51-52.
6. Edwin R. Keedy, "History of the Pennsylvania Statute Creating Degrees of Murder," 97 *U. Pa. L. Rev.* 759 (1949).
7. Ibid.
8. *McGautha v. California.*
9. *McGautha v. California.*
10. Attributed to Heraclitus by Plato, *Cratylus* (Cambridge: Riverside Press, 1902), 402a.
11. *Witherspoon v. Illinois,* 391 U.S. 510 (1968).
12. Elliot Osborn, "Bobby's Next Move," *Newsweek,* July 31, 1972.
13. *McGautha v. California.*
14. Emile Durkheim, *The Division of Labor in Society* (New York: Macmillan, 1933).
15. *People v. Anderson,* 493 P.2d 880, 6 Cal.3d 628 at 656, Supreme Court of California (1972).
16. Ibid.
17. Ibid.
18. *Furman v. Georgia,* 408 U.S. 238, US Supreme Court (1972).

CHAPTER 3: TWO SIDES TO *EVERY* QUESTION?

1. H. DeLong, *A Profile of Mathematical Logic* (Redding, MA: Addison-Wesley, 1970), 10.
2. Robert Johnson Bonner, *Lawyers & Litigants in Ancient Athens* (Chicago: University of Chicago Press, 1927), 66–68.
3. American Bar Association Model Code of Professional Responsibility, Canon 7, EC 7-1 through EC 7-10.
4. "Slayer's 2 Lawyers Kept Secret of 2 More Killings," *New York Times,* June 20, 1974.
5. Bryce Nelson, "Ethical Dilemma: Should Lawyers Turn in Clients?" *Los Angeles Times,* July 2, 1974.
6. "Slayer's 2 Lawyers Kept Secret of 2 More Killings."
7. Ibid.
8. Anthony Farmer, "'78 Escape Ended in Killer's Death, Massive Manhunt Went on for 3 Days," *Poughkeepsie Journal,* June 16, 2003.
9. Geoffrey Hazard Jr., "Lawyer for the Situation," 39 U. Valpariso L. Rev. 2 (2004), 377.

10. American Bar Association Model Code of Professional Responsibility, DR 4-101(C4).
11. Genesis 19:17 (NIV).

CHAPTER 4: RICHER THAN THE RULES OF LAW

1. R. J. Bonner and Gertrude Smith, *The Administration of Justice from Homer to Aristotle* (Chicago: Chicago University Press, 1930), Vol. 1, 103_114; Vol. 2, 194_203.
2. Oliver Wendell Holmes, *The Common Law* (Boston: Little, Brown and Company, 1881), 33.
3. *Gregg v. Georgia, Proffitt v. Florida,* and *Jurek v. Texas,* 428 U.S.153, US Supreme Court (1976).
4. *Gregg v. Georgia,* 428 U.S.153 at 183, US Supreme Court (1976).
5. *Gregg v. Georgia,* 428 U.S.153 at 184, US Supreme Court (1976).
6. *Proffitt v. Florida.*
7. Nelson Goodman, *Ways of Worldmaking* (Indianapolis: Hackett Publishing, 1978), 94.
8. Kurt Godel, *On Formally Undecidable Propositions in Principia Mathematica and Related Systems* (Mineola: Dover Publications, 1962), Theorum VI, XI.
9. Ernest Nagel and James Newman, *Godel's Proof.* New York: New York University Press, 2001.
10. John Locke, *Second Treatise on Civil Government* (London: R. Butler, 1821), chapter XIV.
11. Aristotle, *Nicomachean Ethics* (Oxford: W. Baxter Press, 1826), 174.
12. John Rawls, *A Theory of Justice* (Cambridge: Belknap Press of Harvard University Press, 1971), 58, 136.
13. Cf. J. Rawls "Two Concepts of Rules" in *Collected Papers,* edited by Samuel Freeman (Cambridge, MA: Harvard University Press, 1999), 20.
14. Cesare Beccaria, *An Essay on Crimes and Punishments* (Boston: International Pocket Library, 1983), 51.
15. Adam Smith, *The Theory of Moral Sentiments* (London, 1759), 113, 116, 117.
16. Smith, *The Theory of Moral Sentiments,* 113, 129, 152.
17. Roger Manvell and Heinrich Fraenkel, *Hess: A Biography* (London: Granada Press, 1971), available at http://avalon.law.yale.edu/imt/08-31-46.asp.
18. *New York Times,* March 6, 1977; *New York Times,* March 27, 1977; Saxon and Wolfgang, "Spandau Prison, Hess's Lonely Dungeon," *New York Times,* August 18, 1987; *Sydney Morning Herald,* March 7, 1977; "How Nixon Showed Pity for 'The World's Loneliest Man,'" *The Guardian,* September 28, 2007; "Russia Blocked UK Plans to Free Rudolf Hess," September 28, 2007.
19. *Coker v. Georgia,* 433 U.S. 584 at 597-598, US Supreme Court (1977).
20. Adam Smith, *The Theory of Moral Sentiments* (London, 1759), 113.
21. Ibid., 112.
22. Robert Johnson Bonner, *Lawyers & Litigants in Ancient Athens* (Chicago: University of Chicago Press, 1927), 60.

CHAPTER 5: ONE RAGGEDY LAWYER

1. *Enmund v. Florida,* 458 U.S.782 at 784, 800, US Supreme Court (1982).
2. *Enmund v. Florida,* 458 U.S.782 at 800-801, US Supreme Court (1982).
3. *Enmund v. Florida,* 458 U.S.782 at 801, US Supreme Court (1982).

4. Adam Smith, *The Theory of Moral Sentiments* (London, 1759), 123.
5. Heraclitus, *Fragments: The Collected Wisdom of Heraclitus,* translated by Brooks Haxton (New York: Penguin Classics, 2003), 69.
6. John Allen, *Assault with a Deadly Weapon: The Autobiography of a Street Criminal* (New York: Pantheon Books, 1977).

CHAPTER 6: BETWEEN RIGHT AND WRONG

1. I have changed this name along with several others.
2. Adam Smith, *The Theory of Moral Sentiments* (London, 1759), 164.
3. Smith, *The Theory of Moral Sentiments,* 140.
4. Ibid.
5. Exodus 21:29 (NIV).
6. Johan Thorsten Sellin, *The Death Penalty: A Report for the Model Penal Code Project of the American Law Institute* (Philadelphia: American Law Institute, 1959), 68.
7. Ibid.
8. *Enmund v. Florida,* 458 U.S.782 at 788, US Supreme Court (1982).
9. *Tison v. Arizona,* 481 U.S.137 at 138, US Supreme Court (1987).
10. Ibid.
11. *Tison v. Arizona,* 481 U.S.137 at 172, 149, 157, 158, US Supreme Court (1987).
12. *Enmund v. Florida,* 458 U.S.782 at 785, US Supreme Court (1982).

CHAPTER 8: UNDER THE INFLUENCE

1. Immanuel Kant, *Metaphysical Elements of Justice* (New York: Hackett Publishing Company, Inc., 1981), 37.

CHAPTER 9: PLATE SIN WITH GOLD

1. George Bernard Shaw, *The Crime of Imprisonment* (New York: The Philosophical Library, 1946), 69.
2. Thomas Hobbes, *The Leviathan* (1651), 107.
3. John Locke, *Second Treatise of Civil Government* (1690), chapter XVI.
4. William Shakespeare, *King Lear,* Act IV, Scene VI.
5. *People v. Kibbe,* 35 N.Y.2d 407, 321 N.E.2d 773 (1974).
6. *People v. Warner-Lambert Co.,* 51 N.Y.2d 295, New York Court of Appeals (1980).
7. *Grimshaw v. Ford Motor Co.,* 1 19 Cal.App.3d 757, California Court of Appeal, Fourth Appellate Division Two (1981).
8. Cf *Godfrey v. Goergia,* 446 US 420 (1980).
9. Walt Kelly, "Pogo," *New York Star,* October 4, 1948.

CHAPTER 10: THEIR CRIME/OUR PUNISHMENT

1. Robert Blecker, "Haven or Hell?" *Stanford Law Review* 42, no. 5 (May 1990).
2. Robert Blecker, "Among Killers: Searching for the Worst of the Worst," *Washington Post,* December 3, 2000.

CHAPTER 11: BEHIND THE GLASS

1. Demps v. State, 395 So.2d 501 at 503, Supreme Court of Florida (1981).

2. Cesare Beccaria, *An Essay on Crimes and Punishments* (Boston: International Pocket Library, 1983), 68.
3. James Knudsen, "A Killer on Campus," *People Magazine,* September 17, 1990.
4. Danny Rolling and Sondra London, *The Making of a Serial Killer: The Real Story of the Gainesville Murders in the Killer's Own Words* (Portland, OR: Feral House Books, 1996).
5. Jim Leusner, "Rolling Indicted in Gainesville," *Orlando Sentinel Tribune,* October 16, 1991, A1.
6. Brad Gray, "Letters," *St. Petersburg Times,* April 6, 1994, 15a.
7. David Cox, "Inmates Wives, Mothers Protest Ban on Touching," *South Florida Sun Sentinel,* April 13, 2000.
8. Rick Bragg, "Living With a Grief That Will Never Die, After the Murders of 2 Loved Ones," *New York Times,* March 22, 1999.

CHAPTER 12: ONE STEP REMOVED

1. *Demps v. State,* 395 So.2d 501, Supreme Court of Florida (1981).
2. *Proffitt v. Florida,* 428 U.S.153 (1976).
3. *Demps v. Dugger,* 874 F.2d 1385, Eleventh Circuit Court of Appeals (1989).
4. *Demps v. State,* 395 So.2d 501 at 506, Supreme Court of Florida (1981).
5. M. Greenberg, "Some Postulates of Biblical and Criminal Law," in *The Jewish Expression,* edited by J. Goldin (New York: Bantam Press, 1970), 26–27.
6. Robert Johnson Bonner, *Lawyers & Litigants in Ancient Athens* (Chicago: University of Chicago Press, 1927), 60.
7. Numbers 35:31 (NIV).
8. *Booth v. Maryland,* 482 U.S.496 at 504, 505, 517, US Supreme Court (1987).
9. *Payne v. Tennessee,* 501 U.S.808 at 825, 808, 828, 830, US Supreme Court (1991).
10. Adam Smith, *The Theory of Moral Sentiments* (London, 1759), 117.
11. Exodus 21:13 (NIV).
12. Cf. R. J. Bonner and Gertrude Smith, *The Administration of Justice from Homer to Aristotle* (Chicago: Chicago University Press, 1930).

CHAPTER 13: CURTAIN TIME

1. The Associated Press. "Hours from Execution, Inmate Says 'I'm Innocent,'" *Sarasota Herald-Tribune,* June 7, 2000.
2. Rich Tucker, "Convicted Murderer Due to Die Today: He Says Death Sentence Punishes for Earlier Crime," *The Florida Times Union,* June 7, 2000.
3. Rich Tucker, "Demps Execution Troubled," *Florida Times Union,* June 8, 2000. Statement of Debra Buchanan, Department of Corrections spokesperson, June 7, 2000.

CHAPTER 14: THE PRIVILEGED AND THE DAMNED

1. Council of the City of Philadelphia, Resolution No. 000068, Adopted February 10, 2000.
2. "Maryland's Governor Issues Death Penalty Moratorium," CNN, May 14, 2002.
3. Jeffery M. Jones, "Vast Majority of Americans Think McVeigh Should Be Executed," Gallup News Service, May 2, 2001.
4. "Ashcroft Announces McVeigh Execution Plans," *ABC News,* January 7, 2006.
5. Model Penal Code Tentative Draft No. 9, May 1959, Section 201.6.

6. Richard Willing, "Death Penalty Gains Unlikely Defenders," *USA Today,* January 6, 2003.
7. Robert Blecker and James Liebman, "Common Ground," *Houston Chronicle,* May 23, 2003.
8. *Ring v. Arizona,* 536 U.S.584 (2002).

CHAPTER 15: FLIP A SWITCH

1. Bluestone and McGahee, "Reaction to Extreme Stress: Impending Death By Execution," *American Journal of Psychiatry* 393 (1962): 119.

CHAPTER 16: BUT GOD SPARED CAIN

1. *State v. Holton,* 126 S.W.3d 845, Supreme Court of Tennessee (2004), Exhibit 28, Holton Police Interview transcript, November 30, 1997, Shelbyville Police Department.
2. Dan Barry, "Death in the Chair, Step by Remorseless Step," *New York Times,* September 16, 2007.
3. *State v. Holton.*
4. *Miranda v. Arizona,* 384 U.S.436.
5. Exodus 21:12 (NIV).
6. Exodus 21:13 (NIV).
7. Ibid.
8. James Fitzjames Stephen, *A History of the Criminal Law of England* (London: Macmillan, 1883), 94.
9. Royal Commission on Capital Punishment, 1949–1953, September 1953, Section 499.
10. *Woodson v. North Carolina,* 428 U.S.291 at 291 (1976).
11. Genesis 4:8 (NIV).
12. Genesis 4:9 (NIV).
13. Genesis 4:15 (NIV).
14. Genesis 4:15 (NIV).
15. Genesis 4:8, 9, 15 (NIV).
16. Genesis 4:5–8 (NIV).
17. *State v. Holton,* 126 S.W.3d 845 at 858.
18. *State v. Holton,* 126 S.W.3d 845, Exhibit 85, Holton Second Police Interview transcript, December 3, 1997, Bedford County Jail.

CHAPTER 17: THE MAN NEEDS TO DIE

1. Timothy Roche, "Andrea Yates: More to the Story," *Time Magazine,* March 18, 2002.
2. Rick Bragg, "Arguments Begin in Susan Smith Trial," *New York Times,* July 19, 1995.
3. *Skipper v. South Carolina,* 476 U.S.1, US Supreme Court (1986).

CHAPTER 18: THE NICEST THING

1. *Callins v. Collins,* 510 U.S.1141 at 1145, US Supreme Court (1994).
2. *Callins v. Collins,* 510 U.S.1141 at 1141-1143, US Supreme Court (1994).

3. Numbers 35:33 (NIV); R. J. Bonner and Gertrude Smith, *The Administration of Justice from Homer to Aristotle* (Chicago: Chicago University Press, 1930), Vol. 1, 50_54; Vol. 2, 200–201.
4. Emile Durkheim, *The Division of Labor in Society* (New York: Macmillan, 1933).

CHAPTER 19: A ONE-MAN CHAIR

1. *Holton v. State,* 201 S.W.3d, 626, Supreme Court of Tennessee (2006).

CHAPTER 20: DEAD RIGHT

1. Transcript of Competency Hearing, Daryl Holton, Testimony of Dr. Bruce G. Seidner, September 5, 2006, p. 11.
2. Affidavit of Kelly Gleason, Daryl Holton, Testimony of Dr. Bruce G. Seidner, September 5, 2006.
3. Transcript of Competency Hearing, Daryl Holton, Testimony of Dr. Bruce G. Seidner, September 5, 2006, p. 12.
4. Transcript of Competency Hearing, Daryl Holton, Testimony of Dr. Bruce G. Seidner, September 5, 2006, pp. 12–14.
5. Transcript of Competency Hearing, Daryl Holton, Testimony of Dr. Bruce G. Seidner, September 5, 2006, p. 15.
6. Transcript of Competency Hearing, Daryl Holton, Testimony of Dr. Bruce G. Seidner, September 5, 2006, p. 48.
7. Transcript of Competency Hearing, Daryl Holton, September 5, 2006, pp. 70–71.

CHAPTER 21: WHOSE VOICE?

1. *Holton v. State,* 201 S.W.3d, 626, Supreme Court of Tennessee (2006).
2. 161 Eur. Ct. H.R., European Court of Human Rights (1989).
3. Craig Haney, "Hiding From the Death Penalty," *Huffington Post,* July 26, 2010.

CHAPTER 22: WHY AREN'T YOU DEAD?

1. *In re Winship,* 397 US. 358, US Supreme Court (1970).

CHAPTER 23: TURNING GREY

1. Public Hearing Before the N.J. Death Penalty Study Commission, 55 [hereinafter Pub. Hearing, October 11, 2006] (testimony of Robert Blecker). Retrieved October 11, 2006, from http://www.njleg.state.nj.us/legislativepub/pubhear/DPSC101106.pdf.
2. N.J. Death Penalty Study Comm'n Report (2007) [hereinafter Comm'n Report] (introductory letter from Chairman Rev. M. William Howard, Jr.). Available at http://www.njleg.state.nj.us/committees/dpsc_final.pdf, p. 67.
3. *Witherspoon v. Illinois.* 391 U.S.510, US Supreme Court (1968).
4. Ashok Selvarn, "Verdict Brings Closure to Palatine Police Officers," *Daily Herald,* September 29, 2009. Retrieved March 6, 2013, from http://classifieds.daily herald.com/story/?id=325254.

5. GH Ryan, Report Governor's Commission on Capital Punishment, April 15, 2002. Available at http://illinoismurderindictments.law.northwestern.edu/docs /Illinois_Moratorium_Commission_complete-report.pdf.

CHAPTER 24: SIX FEET OVER

1. Adam Liptak, "Positive He's a Killer; Less Sure He Should Die," *New York Times*, May 21, 2007.

CHAPTER 25: DEATH WATCH

1. Ashley Fantz, "Executed Man's Last Request Honored—Pizza for Homeless," *CNN*, Mary 10, 2007. Retrieved April 5, 2013, from http://www.cnn.com/2007/ US/05/09/execution.pizza/
2. See generally Johan Huizinga, *Homo Ludens* (London: Routledge and Kegan Paul Ltd., 1949).
3. Immanuel Kant, The Metaphysical Elements of Justice II, E1, "The Public Law: The Right to Punish."
4. See generally Robert Johnson, *Death Work: A Study of the Modern Execution Process* (Los Angeles: Wadsworth Publishing Co., 2005).
5. Robert Johnson, *Death Work: A Study of the Modern Execution Process* (Los Angeles: Wadsworth Publishing Co., 2005), 89.

CHAPTER 26: KILLING THEM SOFTLY

1. Michel Foucault, *Discipline and Punish: The Birth of the Prison* (Paris: Gallimard, 1975), 11.
2. Stuart Banner, *The Death Penalty: An American History* (Cambridge: Harvard University Press, 2002), 74.
3. Stuart Banner, *The Death Penalty: An American History* (Cambridge: Harvard University Press, 2002), 120.
4. Michel Foucault, *Discipline and Punish: The Birth of the Prison* (Paris: Gallimard, 1975), 9.
5. *In re Kemmler,* 136 US. 436, US Supreme Court (1890).
6. *Baze v. Rees,* 553 US. 35, US Supreme Court (2008).
7. *People v. Morales,* 770 P.2d 244, 249-50 (Cal. 1989).
8. Cesare Beccaria, *An Essay on Crimes and Punishments 51-52* (1788), 20.
9. James Fitzjames Stephen, *A History of the Criminal Law of England* (London: Macmillan & Co., 1983), 81.
10. Beccaria, *An Essay on Crimes and Punishments 51-52,* 55.
11. Adam Smith, *The Theory of Moral Sentiments,* edited by Knud Haakonssen (Cambridge: Cambridge University Press, 1759), Section II, Chapter III.
12. Brief for American Association of Jewish Lawyers and Jurists (AAJLJ) as Amicus Curiae Supporting Petitioners, *Baze v. Rees,* No. 07-5439, 2008 WL 1733259 (US, April 16, 2008).
13. Tom Geoghegan, "The Search for a 'Humane' Execution," *BBC: News Magazine,* January 14, 2008.
14. David Belcher, "Portillo and the Ultimate Punishment," *Herald Scotland,* January 16, 2008.
15. Beccaria, *An Essay on Crimes and Punishments,* 51–52, 66.

16. Ibid., 51.
17. See generally Jeremy Bentham, *The Works of Jeremy Bentham: Principles of Penal Law*, Part II, Book I, Chapter V, edited by William Tait (1843). Available at http://oll.libertyfund.org/title/2009/139816.

CHAPTER 27: BEARING WITNESS

1. *Dawson v State*, 554 S.E.2d 137, Supreme Court of Georgia (2001).
2. Ibid.; quoting *In re Kemmler*, 10S. Ct.930, US Supreme Court (1890).
3. *In re Daryl Holton*, Judicial Order No. M2000-SC-DDT-DD, Filed September 11, 2007, Supreme Court of Tennessee at Nashville.
4. David Raybin, "Daryl Holton's Electric Chair Execution Should Be the State's Last," *The Coalition for Truth and Justice*. Retrieved March 9, 2013, from http://cftj.org/electric-chair/.
5. Dan Barry, "Death in the Chair, Step by Remorseless Step," *The New York Times*, September 16, 2007.
6. Barry, "Death in the Chair."
7. Raybin, "Daryl Holton's Electric Chair Execution."
8. Barry, "Death in the Chair."
9. Ibid.; Raybin, "Daryl Holton's Electric Chair Execution."

CHAPTER 28: THE 13TH JUROR

1. Hugo Bedau, *The Death Penalty in America: Current Controversies* (New York: Oxford University Press, 1997), 232.
2. Marvin Henberg, *Retribution: Evil for Evil in Ethics, Law and Literature* (Philadelphia: Temple University Press, 1990), 96–97.
3. Robert Johnson, *Death Work: A Study of the Modern Execution Process* (Los Angeles: Wadsworth Publishing Co., 2005), 233.

CHAPTER 29: NO WORD FOR IT

1. *State v. Ross*, 230 Conn. 183, 286, 646 A.2d 1318 (1994), cert. denied, 513 U.S. 1165, 115 S. Ct. 1133, 130 L. Ed. 2d 1095 (1995).
2. Telephone conference before Hon. Robert N. Chatigny, Chief U.S.D.J., Hartford, Ct., January 28, 2005; Matthew Kauffman, "Federal Judge Berates, Pleads with Ross Lawyer," *Hartford Courant*, January 29, 2005, A12.
3. "DSM_IV_TR Diagnostic Criteria Sexual Sadism," in *Diagnostic and Statistical Manual of Mental Disorders*, Fourth Edition, Text Revision (Arlington, VA: American Psychiatric Association).
4. Telephone conference before Hon. Robert N. Chatigny; Kauffman, "Federal Judge Berates, Pleads with Ross Lawyer," A12.
5. Robert Blecker, "God Love Him," *Hartford Courant*, February 6, 2005.
6. Ashby Jones, "Why Wasn't Robert Chatigny Re-Nominated?" *Wall Street Journal: Law Blog*, January 6, 2011. Retrieved March 6, 2013, from http://blogs.wsj.com/law/2011/01/06/why-wasnt-robert-chatigny-re-nominated/.
7. Robert Blecker, "The Road to Consider: A Statement by Professor Robert Blecker to the Judiciary Committee," The Connecticut General Assembly. Retrieved March 6, 2013, from http://www.cga.ct.gov/2011/JUDdata/Tmy/2011SB-01035-R000307-Professor%20Robert%20Blecker-TMY.PDF.

8. State of Connecticut Department of Correction, "Administrative Directive 1.1, Mission Statement." Retrieved March 6, 2013, from http://www.ct.gov/DOC /lib/doc/pdf/ad/ad0101.pdf.
9. Public Hearing Before NJ Death Penalty Commission, July 19, 2006, New Jersey, at p. 57.
10. Blecker, "The Road to Consider."

CHAPTER 30: THE HERSHEY BAR

1. Connecticut Legislature, JUD Committee Hearing Transcript for 03/07/2011 (http://www.cga.ct.gov/2011/JUDdata/chr/2011JUD00307-R001130-CHR .htm).
2. Connecticut Legislature, JUD Committee Hearing Transcript for 03/07/2011 (http://www.cga.ct.gov/2011/JUDdata/chr/2011JUD00307-R001130-CHR .htm).
3. Connecticut Legislature, JUD Committee Hearing Transcript for 03/07/2011 (http://www.cga.ct.gov/2011/JUDdata/chr/2011JUD00307-R001130-CHR .htm).
4. *Furman v. Georgia,* 408 U.S.238, US Supreme Court (1972) (Blackmun, H., dissenting).
5. Robert Blecker, "Letters: Learning from the Madoff Case," *New York Times,* June 30, 2009.
6. Diana Henriques, "Madoff Is Sentenced to 150 Years for Ponzi Scheme," *New York Times,* June 29, 2009.
7. Joseph Rhee and Shana Druckerman, "Like a Mafia Don: Bernie Madoff's Boastful Letter to Angry Daughter-in-Law," *ABC News,* October 20, 2011. Retrieved November 12, 2012, from http://abcnews.go.com/US/mafia-don -bernie-madoffs-boastful-letter-angry-daughter/story?id=14777562.

CHAPTER 31: IN A PERFECT KINGDOM

1. *Witherspoon v. Illinois,* 381 U.S.510, US Supreme Court (1968).
2. *Wainwright v. Witt,* 469 U.S.412, US Supreme Court (1985).
3. Fred Musante, "No Jurors Picked for Komisarjevsky Trial on First Day," *Cheshire Patch.* Retrieved March 17, 2011, from http://cheshire.patch.com/groups /editors-picks/p/no-jurors-picked-for-komisarjevsky-trial-on-first-day.
4. Maureen Dowd, "Killing Doesn't Make Us Evil," *New York Times,* May 7, 2011.
5. Available at http://newyork.cbslocal.com/2011/05/12/ct-home-invasion-defen dant-joshua-komisarjevsky-seeks-trial-delay/.

CHAPTER 32: EVERYWHERE ELSEWHERE

1. *Caldwell v. Mississippi,* 472 U.S.320, US Supreme Court (1985).
2. R. D. Laing, *The Politics of Experience* (London: Penguin, 1967), 56.
3. *Simmons v. South Carolina,* 512 U.S.154, US Supreme Court (1994).
4. Alaine Griffin, "Komisarjevsky Defense: 'Doomed From Birth,'" *Hartford Courant,* October 25, 2011.
5. Robert Blecker, "Why Komisarjevsky Must Die," *Hartford Courant,* October 25, 2011.
6. William Glaberson, "Death Penalty for 2nd Man in Connecticut Triple-Murder Case," *New York Times,* December 9, 2011.

CHAPTER 33: I CAN LOOK YOU IN THE EYES

1. *In Re Troy Anthony Davis Order,* Hon. William T. Moore U.S.D.J. Savannah, GA. August 24, 2010. Retrieved March 10, 2013, from http://multimedia .savannahnow.com/media/pdfs/DavisRuling082410.pdf.
2. Ibid.
3. Ibid., 117.
4. Ibid., at 120, fn 44.
5. NAACP Legal Defense Fund statistics, as constituted, confirmed by Death Penalty Information Center, Richard Dieter e-mail, July 25, 2013.
6. See *McClesky v. Kemp,* 481 U.S.279, US Supreme Court (1987).
7. Pulaski David Baldus and George Woodworth, "Arbitrariness and Discrimination in the Administration of the Death Penalty: A Challenge to State Supreme Courts," *Stetson Law Review* (1986).
8. Jennifer L. Eberhardt, *Research Report: Looking Deathworthy, Psychological Science* (2006). Available at http://www.psychologicalscience.org/pdf/ps/deathworthy .pdf.
9. Robert Blecker, "The Pack That Cried Wolf," *The Daily Report,* December 16, 2011. Retrieved March 10, 2013, from http://www.dailyreportonline.com /PubArticleDRO.jsp?id=1202551126827&The_pack_that_cried_wolf.

CHAPTER 34: NONSENSE ON STILTS

1. *Gafgen v. Germany,* Grand Chamber- European Court of Human Rights, June 1, 2010. Retrieved March 10, 2013, from http://hudoc.echr.coe.int/sites/eng /pages/search.aspx?i=001-99015.
2. John Locke, Second Treatise of Civil Government, Chapter XIV: "Of Prerogative."
3. *Gafgen v. Germany.*
4. Ibid.
5. Ibid.
6. Ibid.
7. Ibid.
8. Ibid.
9. Jeremy Bentham, Principles of Legislation, Chapter XIII.
10. Richard Connor, "Child Murderer Wins Damages Over Police Torture Threat," *Deutsche Welle,* April 8, 2011. Retrieved March 10, 2013, from http://www.dw.de /child-murderer-wins-damages-over-police-torture-threat/a-15295473-1.

CHAPTER 35: THE CHANCE TO SOMEDAY

1. *Atkins v. Virginia,* 536 U.S.304, US Supreme Court (2002); *Roper v. Simmons,* 543 U.S.551, US Supreme Court (2005).
2. *Roper v. Simmons,* 543 U.S.552, US Supreme Court (2005) (W. Rehnquist, A. Scalia, C. Thomas, dissenting).
3. Ibid.
4. *Roper v. Simmons,* 543 US 551, 622, 623.
5. James Q. Whitman, *Harsh Justice: Criminal Punishment and the Widening Divide between America and Europe* (New York: Oxford University Press, 2003), 97–108.
6. Ibid., 100.
7. Andrew Hammel, *Ending the Death Penalty: The European Experience in Global Perspective* (New York: Palgrave Macmillan, 2010), 63.

8. German Criminal Code (Strafgesetzbuch [StGB]), Section 46: Principles for Determining Punishment, Subsection 2; German Criminal Code, Section 57a: Suspension of the Remainder of a Punishment of Imprisonment for Life; cf. Liora Lazarus, *Contrasting Prisoners' Rights: A Comparative Examination of Germany and England* (London: Oxford University Press, 2004), 50–71.

9. *Life Imprisonment Case,* 45 BVerfGE 187 (1977), excerpted in Donald P. Kommers and Russell A. Miller, eds, *The Constitutional Jurisprudence of the Federal Republic of Germany,* 3rd ed. (2012), 363–368.

10. James Q. Whitman, *Harsh Justice: Criminal Punishment and the Widening Divide between America and Europe* (New York: Oxford University Press, 2003), 87; Lazarus, *Contrasting Prisoners' Rights,* 84–86.

11. Basic Law for the Federal Republic of Germany, Article 2, Section 1.

12. Cf. Liora Lazarus, *Contrasting Prisoners' Rights: A Comparative Examination of Germany and England* (London: Oxford University Press, 2004), 87–90.

13. *War Criminal Case* 72 BVerfGE 105 (1986); Kommers and Miller, 369; *Life Imprisonment Case,* 45 BVerfGE 187, 363–368.

14. Joshua Kleinfeld, "The Concept of Evil in American and German Criminal Punishment," *Northwestern Public Law Research Paper No. 12–42.*

CHAPTER 36: A TRAMP ABROAD

1. V. A. Musetto, "Robert Blecker Wants Me Dead," *New York Post,* February 27, 2009.

2. William Lee Adams, "Sentenced to Serving the Good Life in Norway," *Time,* July 12, 2010.

3. Ibid.

CHAPTER 37: RIGHT BODY, WRONG PERSON

1. Barbara Kirwin, *A & E Biography: The Manson Women.* Available at http://www.biography.com/tv/biography/episodes/the-manson-women.

2. Jennifer Kahn, "Can You Call a 9-Year-Old a Psychopath?" *New York Times,* May 11, 2012.

3. Houten, *A & E Biography.*

4. *Tucker v. Johnson,* 115 F3d 216, US Court of Appeals, Fifth Circuit (1997).

5. William Shakespeare, *Measure for Measure,* Act III, Scene 1.

CHAPTER 38: THE UGLY MIRROR

1. US Holocaust Memorial Museum, Washington, DC, web site Encyclopedia. Last updated June 10, 2013.

2. Viktor E. Frankl, *Man's Search for Meaning* (New York: Simon and Schuster, 1985), 25–26.

3. Ibid., 36.

4. Ibid.

5. James Fitzjames Stephen, *A History of the Criminal Law of England 82* (New York: Palgrave Macmillan, 1883).

APPENDIX A: COUNTERING THE ABOLITIONISTS

1. Royal Commission on Capital Punishment 1949–1953, Section 59.

2. Ibid., 57, citing James Fitzjames Stephen, "Capital Punishments," *Fraser's Magazine*, June 1864.
3. Ibid., 59.
4. Shakespeare, *Measure for Measure*, Act III, Scene 1.

APPENDIX D: US SUPREME COURT HIGHLIGHTS

1. 99 US.130.
2. 144 US.323.
3. 136 US.436
4. 217 US.349.
5. 356 US.86.
6. 337 US.241.
7. 402 US.183.
8. 408 US.238.
9. 428 US.153.
10. 428 US.242.
11. 428 US.28.
12. 428 US.325.
13. 438 US.586.
14. 455 US.104.
15. 476 US.1.
16. 498 US.308.
17. 544 US.133.
18. 462 US.862.
19. 479 US.538
20. 497 US.639.
21. 548 US.163.
22. 433 US.584.
23. 554 US.407.
24. 458 US.782.
25. 481 US.137.
26. 446 US.420.
27. 486 US.356.
28. 497 US.639.
29. 507 US.463.
30. 477 US.399.
31. 536 US.304.
32. 543 US.551.
33. 391 US.510.
34. 469 US.412; 504 US.719.
35. 476 US.79.
36. 468 US.447.
37. 536 US.584.
38. 482 US.496.
39. 501 US.808.
40. 510 US.1141.
41. 560 US.48.
42. 132 S.Ct.2455.

INDEX